Teen Media

TEEN MEDIA

Hollywood and the Youth Market in the Digital Age

Valerie Wee

McFarland & Company, Inc., Publishers
Jefferson, North Carolina, and London

Portions of Chapter Five have appeared in two previously published articles: "The *Scream* Trilogy: 'Hyper'-Postmodernism and the late '90s Teen Slasher Film" (*Journal of Film and Video*, 57.3 [2005]: 44–61, copyright 2005 by the Board of Trustees of the University of Illinois; used with permission of the University of Illinois Press); and "Resurrecting and Updating the Teen Slasher—The Case of *Scream*" (*Journal of Popular Film and Television*, 34.2 [2006]: 50–61, reprinted with permission of the Helen Dwight Reid Educational Foundation; published by Heldref Publications, Washington, D.C., copyright © 2006).

Portions of Chapter Six appeared as "Teen Television and the WB Television Network" in *Teen Television: Essays on Programming and Fandom* (ed. Sharon Marie Ross and Louisa Ellen Stein, Jefferson, N.C.: McFarland, 2008, 43–60).

Library of Congress Cataloguing-in-Publication Data

Wee, Valerie, 1968–
    Teen media : Hollywood and the youth market in the
digital age / Valerie Wee.
        p.   cm.
    Includes bibliographical references and index.

    ISBN 978-0-7864-4269-0
    softcover : 50# alkaline paper

    1. Mass media and teenagers—United States.   2. Internet
and teenagers—United States.   3. Digital media—Economic
aspects—United States.   4. Teenage consumers—United States.
5. Mass media—United States—Marketing.   6. Mass media
and culture—United States.   I. Title.
P94.5.Y722U74   2010
302.230835'0973—dc22   2009051293

British Library cataloguing data are available

Cover images ©2010 Shutterstock

Manufactured in the United States of America

McFarland & Company, Inc., Publishers
    Box 611, Jefferson, North Carolina 28640
    www.mcfarlandpub.com

For my family

Acknowledgments

I owe a significant debt of gratitude to a group of colleagues that I am also fortunate enough to call friends, Sunita Abraham, Susan Ang, Robin Loon, Tomasina Oh and Lionel Wee. They provide immeasurable support and encouragement on a daily basis. Both directly and indirectly, each of them has helped in the successful completion of this project.

This book originated from doctoral research undertaken in the Radio-Television-Film Department of the University of Texas at Austin. I would like to thank Thomas Schatz, Horace Newcomb, Charles Ramirez-Berg, Mary Kearney and Katherine Arens. These faculty members contributed valuable comments and criticism to early versions of this project.

Finally, none of this would have been possible without my family.

Table of Contents

Preface

In the final years of the twentieth century, the teen/youth market, largely neglected by Hollywood in the early '90s, began receiving increased attention from the American media industries. Teen-oriented films began flooding the movie theatres and dominating the box-office. Teen television moved from daytime slots to prime time, boosted by the launch of a new teen-focused television network and the support of advertisers willing to pay high advertising rates in order to reach teenagers. Teen music, long associated with boy bands and teenage female pop stars, began dominating music charts and sales.

Teen Media focuses on the resurgence of the teen/youth market from the late 1990s to the 2000s. It pays particular attention to Hollywood's systematic attempts to exploit the millennial teen market across a range of media platforms, and considers how this has shaped the development, production, marketing, and content of teen-oriented texts. Specifically, this project examines the impact of contemporary social, institutional, and technological changes such as the emergence of a significant teen demographic, increased media conglomeration, and the rise of digital technologies on the aesthetic traits of contemporary teen-oriented entertainment texts. By investigating the distinctive qualities that characterize this new millennial teen cycle, *Teen Media* tracks the evolution of Hollywood's attempts to target and service the entertainment and consumer demands of this volatile youth demographic.

Teen Media also emphasizes the importance of exploring the largely ignored interaction between the media industries and their products. It examines how an increasingly converging multi-media industry has reshaped the nature of teen entertainment in terms of the creation, promotion and circulation of these texts. In short, *Teen Media* combines industry analysis with textual analysis to elucidate the ways in which the media industries' commitment to the teen market has shaped the content and style of contemporary teen media. In doing so, *Teen Media* bridges the divide between teen culture studies and industry studies focused on the entertainment/media industry.

To date, studies focusing on teen culture are severely limited in that interest in teen texts tend either to focus on issues of representation or to adopt an ethnographic or anthropological perspective on teenagers and the media they consume.[1] Industry studies, on the other hand, tend to adopt the political economy approach in which larger industrial and economic considerations are

1

examined while the textual products generated by the media industries are ignored.[2] Few studies attempt to integrate the textual and industrial approaches, exploring the decisions and practices of the media industries as they intersect with teen entertainment texts.

One notable book that adopts this framework is Thomas Doherty's *Teenagers and Teenpics: The Juvenilization of American Movies in the 1950s*, which discusses the intersection between teen culture and the larger context of its production.[3] As highlighted in the title, however, the study is restricted to teen culture of the 1950s. Jack Banks's *Monopoly Television: MTV's Quest to Control the Music* offers valuable insight into the commercial and industrial considerations that shape the production, distribution and exhibition of music videos on the youth-focused MTV.[4] However, Banks's focus is restricted to a single entertainment platform, MTV, and to a particular era, 1981–1995. More recently, Glyn Davis and Kay Dickinson's anthology, *Teen TV: Genre, Consumption and Identity*, considers the role of just one medium — television — in representing teens, in encouraging youth consumption and in producing teen identities.[5] Given that most of the existing work on teen media restrict their attention to a single entertainment medium, specifically film, television or music, there is little sustained discussion of how each medium connects or interacts with other forms of media entertainment. Furthermore, most studies focus on teen culture before the late 1990s.

Millennial teen culture has not received the scholarly attention it deserves, considering that teen cultural texts have evolved in response to social and cultural changes as well as shifts in the media industries. *Teen Media* is a focused study of the ways in which the development of the media industries leading into the twenty-first century and the evolving nature of the market have changed the face of teen media. A key characteristic of commercial millennial teen media is the tendency towards simultaneous, interconnected, multi-media, product launches. Whereas earlier teen media cycles embraced a hierarchical approach to repackaging activities — a hit teen film would generate a television show whose success would lead to merchandising deals in a linear, chronological process — millennial teen media texts are, from their initial conception, devised as a range of multi-media entities. To fully appreciate this particular teen media cycle, we must recognize that it consists of multi-media products that do not recognize medium-specific limits or boundaries. Instead, contemporary teen texts intentionally and strategically blend together stylistic and aesthetic formats of traditional and new media, resulting in a range of disparate texts with increasingly similar visual and aesthetic qualities. This development has resulted in an aesthetic evolution that deserves closer scrutiny.

Teen Media explores an area and an era that has yet to receive sustained critical scrutiny, namely, the intersection between teen culture and the multimedia industries that characterized the period between the late 1990s and 2000s, a situation that must be addressed if we wish to understand how contemporary teen media culture is created, promoted and circulated, and how it has responded to new technologies, changing social conditions and cultural behaviors. In particular, *Teen Media* emphasizes the need to examine each newly emerging cycle of teen culture, recognizing that contemporary youth and teen cultures, like contemporary social and cultural conditions, may bear little resemblance to past eras.

To that end, *Teen Media*'s focus begins with the emergence of the late 1990s teen cycle, most often linked with the arrival of the teenage cohort born between 1980 and 2000, and goes on to examine how the teen cycle evolved into the new millennium as the later half of this teen demographic came of age. This project's historical perspective offers vital insight into how teen entertainment texts have evolved in the volatile period beginning in 1995 and extending into the first decade of the twenty-first century. Within the United States, this period was marked by significant developments technologically (with the rise of new digital entertainment platforms), industrially (as evidenced by Hollywood's expansion into these new media technologies as well as into the global market), and culturally (with the emergence of new, social networking sites, for instance). All of these developments have had a tremendous impact on how youth engage with, consume, and experience the media, and also on the nature, organization and creation of media texts themselves.

In a nutshell, *Teen Media* seeks to:

- highlight the increasingly multi-media nature of contemporary commercial teen entertainment, unlike existing studies that continue to restrict their examinations to a single medium;
- acknowledge the distinctive industrial, technological and social events that have motivated a significant intensification of market practices intent on exploiting a specific demographic;
- bridge the gap between macro studies of the entertainment industry and more text-oriented analysis of media products, an approach seldom attempted in existing scholarly work, and
- point to larger trends and practices that characterize Hollywood's activities in the digital age, as a result of the developments highlighted in the study.

Unlike other books on teen entertainment that focus on a single entertainment medium, whether teen films, television or music, *Teen Media* traces the complex multi-media matrix characterizing contemporary teen texts, and highlights the increasing stylistic and aesthetic convergence across various media formats. *Teen Media* explores how these developments can be linked to a range of social, industrial and technological developments that emerged in the final decades of the twentieth century, and that continued to evolve into the next millennium.

Introduction: Commercial Teen Culture, 1995 to 2009

In December 1996, *Scream*, a teen slasher film about a group of high-school students menaced by a knife-wielding serial killer, opened in American theaters. A clever, ironic treatment of the genre, *Scream* drew teenagers to movie theaters in droves. Grossing over $100 million domestically, *Scream*'s success resurrected the dormant teen slasher genre, and marked the resurgence of popular teen culture, decisively ending Hollywood's almost decade-long neglect of the teen market. Teen culture's return to the forefront of public attention gained momentum when *Scream*'s sequel, released in December 1997, went on to match the original film's box-office earnings. Five months later, the increasingly teen-oriented WB television network broadcast an episode of the popular teen drama *Dawson's Creek* (1998–2003) titled "The Scare" that paid homage to *Scream* and its sequel. In "The Scare," the show's characters replicated scenes from the film even as they engaged in lengthy, self-conscious, discussions highlighting the similarities between the incidents in the show and the events in the films. The intertextual relationships between the film and television texts were enhanced by the fact that several actors in the *Dawson's Creek* episode had roles in *Scream 2* and its forthcoming sequel, *Scream 3* (2000). It is also worth pointing out that Kevin Williamson, who scripted the *Scream* franchise, created *Dawson's Creek*.

In September 1999, an episode of the teen television sit-com *Sabrina the Teenage Witch* (1996–2003) featured teen pop star Britney Spears in a guest appearance. Titled "There's No Place Like Home," the episode revolved, in part, around Sabrina's (Melissa Joan Hart) great wish to attend the singer's concert. Spears' appearance included a performance of her single "(You Drive Me) Crazy," which had been released just days before the *Sabrina* episode aired. The release of the single and the broadcast of "There's No Place Like Home" also coincided with the opening of *Drive Me Crazy* (1999) in American movie theaters, a teen romance starring *Sabrina* star, Melissa Joan Hart. Trailers promoting the film appeared during the sit-com's advertising breaks. This particular instance of cross-promotional synergy culminated with the episode's end credits screened against Spears' *Drive Me Crazy* music video, which featured the pop songstress cavorting with Melissa Joan Hart. This music video was simultaneously enjoying conspicuous exposure on MTV, the cable channel catering primarily to the teen demographic — the very same demographic vital to the commercial success of Spears, Hart, *Sabrina*, and both the song and the movie, *Drive Me Crazy*.

In June 2008, Disney targeted the teen and tween demographic with *Camp Rock*, a musical telemovie that was conceptualized from the outset as a multiplatform release. Within a single week, the show was broadcast on the ABC television network, cablecast on multiple Disney-owned cable channels including ABC Family and the Disney Channel, streamed online on Disney.com, and simultaneously "audiocast" on Radio Disney. The show also included a multimedia promotional and advertising blitz that featured the show's main stars, the Jonas Brothers, teenage actor-musicians who were signed on with the Disney Company.[1] Screenings of *Camp Rock* were preceded by music videos for the Jonas Brothers' single, "Burning Up," which was featured on their album *A Little Bit Longer*, slated for release in August 2008. The show also promoted the Brothers' up-coming tour, which was the subject of a 3-D feature film, *Jonas Brothers: The 3D Concert Experience*, released in 2009.[2] A few months later, the cable television series, *Jonas* (2009) debuted on the Disney Channel.

The events described above highlight Hollywood's intense, multi-media activities aimed at catering to the teen market in the years leading out of twentieth century and into the twenty-first. Prior to the events mentioned above, the teen market had been largely marginalized and neglected by the media industries since the late 1980s. This situation changed dramatically in the late 1990s when Hollywood began recognizing the commercial potential of a newly emerging youth/teen demographic. In 1996, film studios began to produce an increasing number of "teenpics"—films directly and specifically aimed at the teen movie-going audience. At the same time, the newly launched WB broadcast television network began targeting the narrow teen/youth demographic as a new generation of boy bands and teenage female pop stars began scaling and dominating the Billboard charts. Teenagers were back on Hollywood's radar. A new millennial teen cycle had arrived.

Hollywood's vigorous response to this previously neglected market and the resulting explosion of teen-oriented media texts provoke a range of questions: What specific factors triggered Hollywood's renewed interest in the teen demographic? How did contemporary institutional, marketplace and technological forces shape Hollywood's efforts to capitalize on the teen market? What strategies did Hollywood use to marshal this teen cohort's profit potential? How does the contemporary cycle of teen entertainment media compare to previous cycles? Do millennial teen media texts share any specific textual markers? What conditions instigated these textual qualities?

Teen Media examines the state of the entertainment industries at the end of the 1990s and into the new century, assessing how capitalist interests and technological advances helped shape popular commercial teen texts in the digital age.

Changes in Hollywood's industrial structure, the development of new technologies, as well as the emergence of a new teen market have had a significant impact on the latest cycle of commercial teen media. This study emphasizes the need to examine each newly emerging cycle of teen culture and acknowledge how each cycle borrows from past eras, even as it discovers new, more efficient strategies for exploiting an increasingly profitable market.

The work undertaken here is founded on the belief that any attempt to explore and understand millennial teen culture requires a framework that acknowledges the vital role that commercial, technological, and industrial exigencies play in constructing, shaping and manipulating the cultural. In adopting such a perspective, this book investigates how the increasingly complex media terrain that existed during the late twentieth and early twenty-first centuries affected decisions of production, distribution and exhibition/consumption of popular millennial teen media texts. I also interrogate how these decisions helped shape content, style and aesthetics at the textual level. The primary focus is on the interaction between industrial context and media text. In highlighting the relationship between text and context, *Teen Media* makes manifest the social, industrial and technological factors that act upon and (re)shape the nature, form and content of the highly visible, popular and accessible entertainment texts that represent millennial teen media. Fundamentally, this investigation identifies and examines what Gomery and Allen term the "generative mechanisms" that have led to both the resurgence of the teen market and the specific articulations of the teen text.[3]

How did the contemporary situation evolve? In the following chapters, I argue that larger industrial, structural, technological and cultural forces paved the way for these developments. The subsequent chapters illustrate the complex negotiations and tensions between context and text, proceeding from the supposition that any attempt to examine and understand the contemporary cycle of popular teen media must acknowledge the extensive history of teen entertainment if we are to accurately position this latest millennial teen cycle within the evolving history of commercial teen culture. Attention to how macro social, industrial and technological forces shape commercial teen texts has been relatively limited. The work here is thus aimed at contributing to a larger understanding of teen (media) culture, an area that, while actively studied, still tends to cluster around three popular approaches, as outlined below.

Studying Teens and Teen Culture

For as long as teenagers and the entertainment industries have interacted over the decades, media scholars and social scientists have examined and speculated on the complicated nature of that connection. The relationship between teenagers and teen media culture has a complex history that has been studied from a variety of perspectives that can be categorized broadly as (1) Effects/Reception Studies, (2) Youth Culture as Subculture and (3) Youth/Teen Representations.

Teenagers and Teen Media: Effects/Reception Studies

Effects studies are possibly the most popular approach to examining the relationship between teenagers and teen media culture. Social workers and social scientists have long expressed their concern about the impact of popular culture on youth. Many scholars within this area privilege the "culture industry" model that sees youth as "the product of mass media manipulation, coercion, and market strategy."[4] In such arguments, the media industries are credited with possessing the power to shape teenage identity and create and exploit youth-oriented culture via the texts and products they create and distribute. Some of the earliest studies arguing the highly negative impact of mass media on a young, vulnerable and impressionable audience include William Healy's *The Individual Delinquent*, William Short's *A Generation of Motion Pictures*, and William Marston Seabury's *The Public and the Motion Picture Industry* and *Motion Picture Problems*.[5] This perspective received further support from the Payne Fund Studies conducted in the early 1930s to understand the impact of the mass media on children and youth. This particular view of the media industries' overwhelming ability to shape and influence generations of passive, helpless teenagers encouraged advocates to adopt a protectionist view that continues to hold sway in on-going contemporary debates regarding the media industries' dangerous influence over children and youth.

Other studies investigating the effects of media culture on teen and youth audiences have adopted a more descriptive approach with an emphasis on how actual audiences respond to teen texts. Susan J. Douglas' *Where the Girls Are: Growing Up Female with the Mass Media* considers the varied ways in which media messages and representations exerted pressures on female identity, behavior and values over four decades from the 1950s to the early 1990s.[6] E. Graham McKinley's *Beverly Hills 90210: Television, Gender and Identity* is another example of a reception study that offers a more narrowly focused analysis of how young women consumed and read the early 1990s teen television series *Beverly Hills, 90210* (1990–2000), highlighting the ways in which the series' representations, principles and content influenced the largely female audiences' notions of gender and self-identity.[7] While Douglas's and McKinley's examinations are more nuanced in their acknowledgment that the media can have occasionally positive and empowering effects on young women, both scholars continue to adhere to the effects studies' primary concern, that the media have a direct and powerful influence over its audience. While this traditional view of youth as largely passive victims of an all-powerful, manipulative culture industry continues to have currency, other scholars prefer to accord youth a greater measure of independence and agency with regard to their interactions with the media.

Teenagers and Teen Media: Examining Youth Subcultures

Stuart Hall and Paddy Whannel, Dick Hebdidge, Simon Frith, and Sarah Thornton have all acknowledged a more complex relationship between the media and youth.[8] These scholars reject the simplistic cause and effect relationship advocated by proponents of the effects model. Instead, Hall and Whannel, Hebdidge, Frith and others argue for the recognition of "youth's autonomy within and despite the marketplace."[9] As Hall and Whannel point out, mass culture is "a contradictory mixture of the authentic and manufactured — an area of self-expression for the young and lush grazing ground for the commercial producers."[10] Far from being passive, manipulated consumers or victims of the culture industries, Hall and Whannel see young people as enjoying some autonomy and engaging in a bilateral interaction with the culture industries to create and evolve their own culture. This optimistic and progressive account is shared by scholars such as Hebdidge and Thornton, both of whom assert that youth actively use (and produce) popular culture to stage their own unique rituals of resistance. Subscribing to the Birmingham School that conceptualizes youth culture as separate and distinct from commercial media activities, these scholars define youth culture in terms of local cultures that are produced *by* youth themselves for their own enjoyment. In arguing against the notion that youth are passive victims of the omnipotent culture industries, Hebdidge, Thornton and other British youth subculture scholars often evacuate the world of commerce, and thus mainstream teen culture, from their analysis of youth subcultures.

Teenagers and Teen Media: Representing Teens

The third dominant perspective on teenagers and teen culture focuses on issues of representation. In America, teen entertainment culture largely consists of textual commodities created by the media industries for the entertainment, use and consumption of teenagers. Media scholars began to wonder just how teenagers were being represented by and in the media and what these depictions revealed about actual teenagers and how larger social and industrial institutions perceived them. Most of these studies generally engage in textual analysis centering on the representation of teenagers and discussions of the themes and messages of specific youth-oriented cultural texts. David Considine's *The Cinema of Adolescence*, Jon Lewis' *From Romance to Ruin* and more recently, Timothy Shary's *Generation Multiplex* are three such studies that examine the representation of teenagers in teen-oriented films.[11]

The Cinema of Adolescence by David Considine is a wide-ranging study of how teenagers have been portrayed on screen. His primary aim is to evaluate the accuracy of these representations. In his extensive chronological study of Hollywood's representation of teenagers in teen films released between the 1930s and the early 1980s, Considine concludes that there is a significant disjunction between actual teenagers and their counterparts depicted in Hollywood movies. Jon Lewis' *The Road to Romance and Ruin* concentrates on identifying and examining the key themes that characterize representations of youth and teenagers in teen films of the 1950s to the late 1980s. Lewis's interest lies in examining "how youth culture and the films that represent it speak to the central issues of post–World War II society."[12] While Lewis claims to be interested in examining how teenagers have been represented in American teen films, his analysis tends to be limited by his primary interest in arguing that teen films reflect a largely nihilistic, selfish and delinquent response to mainstream authority. Timothy Shary's *Generation Multiplex* adds to the on-going interest in teen representations by examining the image of youth in American films in the 1980s and 1990s. Shary's particular focus is on identifying and analyzing the distinctive subgenres that are most often associated with the larger notion of the teen film. His interest, like Considine's, is in asking how these various subgenres reflect the teenage experience while also tracking the ways in which these representations have evolved in response to social change.

As a category, existing work on teen culture attends to issues of representation, the construction of ideologies and values, and the identification of key motifs and patterns that run across teen-oriented texts so as to uncover their social and cultural power. But, while these studies make important and revealing contributions to the larger understanding of teen-oriented popular media culture, their focus is restricted to exploring cultural stereotypes or considering the social and/or psychological impact of media culture on actual teenagers and youth.

Unlike effects studies, *Teen Media* does not focus on critiquing the influence of media texts on actual teen behavior, values or beliefs. Neither does this project seek to evaluate how teenagers negotiate with the culture industries in their attempts to create their own culture. While issues of representation are addressed, my aim is to understand how these images reflect Hollywood's attempts to capture the target teen audience, rather than to interrogate the validity, accuracy or ideological implications of these portrayals. Instead, this work is motivated by an interest in understanding how the larger inter-linked practices of production, promotion and consumption have shaped the nature of the contemporary teen text, i.e. how the state of the media industries leading into the twenty-first century and the evolving nature of the market have changed the face of teen media.

In focusing on millennial teen media, this investigation also deviates from the common tendency to adopt a single, medium-specific focus. Most of the previously discussed studies restrict their attention to a single entertainment medium. However, commercial millennial teen media is characterized by the tendency towards simultaneous, interconnected, multi-media products that no longer recognize medium-specific limits or boundaries. Instead, they strategically blend together the stylistic and aesthetic formats of different media resulting in a range of disparate texts with increasingly similar visual and aesthetic qualities. Any attempt to understand these developments must enlarge the medium-specific approach often used to study teen culture to include a wider, multi-media perspective. For the record, this study does not identify or describe the teen culture and identity created by actual teenagers themselves. I am not engaged in a social critique on the effects of media culture on teenagers, nor do I provide ethnographic or anthropological insights into how actual teenagers engage with, use, or process media culture. While issues such as gender, race and class certainly have an impact on the nature of teen culture, these considerations fall outside the scope of this work and are not addressed in detail, except where they directly relate to specific moments within the millennial teen culture context.

Instead, this work presents a preliminary exploration of the nature, content and form of teen media culture in terms of the industrial and commercial contexts that surrounded their conception and creation within a distinct phase of their evolution in the final years of the 1990s and into the first decade of the new millennium. My investigation is structured around two key considerations: (1) What are the characteristics of millennial teen culture? And (2) how did industrial, marketplace and social factors shape these qualities? In other words, I interrogate how economic and institutional changes—including the multi-media conglomeration of the entertainment industry, the rise of new media technologies, the emergence of new marketing methods, and changing production and distribution strategies—extended and modified significant traits of the teen-oriented text.

Teen Media: Contextual and Textual Examinations

In so far as this project addresses the decisions and practices of the media industries, specifically how these industries go about catering to the entertainment interests and demands of the teen market between 1995 and 2009, it belongs within an existing tradition of work that interrogates the negotiations that occur between teen entertainment texts and developments in society, the industry, the marketplace, and technology. The most developed and sustained of these investigations to date is Thomas Doherty's *Teenagers and Teenpics: The Juvenilization of American Movies in the 1950s*, which provides a comprehensive examination of how industrial, technological and marketplace conditions led to the rise of the teen film in the 1950s.[13] In particular, Doherty provides valuable insights into a series of post-war factors that resulted in the emergence of the teenpic. According to Doherty, the increasing significance of the youth demographic, the impact of the Paramount decree, the emergence of new modes of exhibition, and the growing recognition that television was beginning to supplant film as the primary form of mass entertainment, forced the film industry to shift its focus from a mass, urban audience to a much younger, suburban one. This in turn forced the film industry to revise its production practices and develop new, more niche-oriented films.

One of the strengths of Doherty's study is his decision to move beyond a discussion of production, distribution and exhibition to explore how changes in these practices (re)shaped the textual elements of 1950s teenpics. For instance, Doherty demonstrates the relationship between an increasing degree of narrative repetition and redundancy in teenpics and the highly distracting environment of the drive-ins in which these teenpics were consumed. Doherty also relates the teenpics' strongly repetitive plots and over-reliance on gimmicks best represented by "classics" such as *The Day the World Ended* (1956), *I Was a Teenage Werewolf* (1957), and *Beach Blanket Bingo* (1965), to the independent studio's mode of production which emphasized budgetary frugality, a minimum of pre-production preparation and short production schedules. In bridging the gap between industry, society, and text, Doherty's work offers a broader, more comprehensive engagement with a complex and highly sophisticated situation that arose during a volatile period in Hollywood's history. *Teenagers and Teenpics* serves as a useful starting point for exploring the relationship between external industrial and social forces and commercial teen-oriented entertainment culture.

While not specifically focused on teens, Justin Wyatt's *High Concept: Movies and Marketing in Hollywood*, which considers 1980s Hollywood's shift to big-budget, blockbuster films, also offers relevant perspective.[14] While delving into an entirely different era of Hollywood's development, *High Concept*, like *Teenagers and Teenpics*, adopts the view that industry and text are inextricably intertwined, and focuses on exploring the bilateral negotiations that occur between industrial and market conditions and the nature and substance of the commercial entertainment text. According to Wyatt, the industrial structure of Hollywood in the 1980s affected the form and style of '80s films as well as how they were marketed. He argues that the rise of the commercial blockbuster and the high concept film in the 1980s can be traced to Hollywood's shift towards conglomeration. As economic interests began obscuring all other considerations, the form and style of 1980s Hollywood movies evolved in ways that would best aid marketing and promotional activities. Wyatt highlights how textual aspects such as the casting of established stars, the use of popular music, the growing importance of merchandizing, and the tendency towards familiar themes and narratives were all tied to the entertainment industry's structure and business interests. Wyatt thus provides valuable insights into the relationship between text and industry and how each shaped, constrained and affected the other. While Wyatt's work serves to further illuminate a series of events vital to a historical understanding of Hollywood's evolution, it focuses primarily upon entertainment texts directed at a large, mass market in the 1980s. This project aims to expand upon the invaluable foundation provided by the works highlighted above by adapting and building upon the arguments and approaches expressed in these studies as it examines how the media become mass and niche in new ways.

Millennial Teen Media: Contexts and Texts

In exploring the teen products created, distributed and marketed by Hollywood, I am particularly concerned with illustrating how ownership patterns, regulatory practices, economic policies, technological developments and market trends ultimately affect the developmental, creative and aesthetic decisions that the media industry make in relation to the products they finally release. Examining the interactions between the larger contexts of production and how they shape the nature, form and content of the text requires the merging of an industry analysis approach with an in-depth textual analysis of the media texts themselves. Though these two approaches are not often combined, adopting this less conventional perspective will, I believe, help illuminate the complex interactions that occur between the creation of a commercial cultural text and its larger context. The aim is to trace the ways in which developments taking place at the level of ownership, corporate policies, new technologies as well as evolving marketing and promotional techniques, translate into distinctive textual traits.

Millennial Contexts: The (New) New Hollywood

Over the decades, teen entertainment media have evolved as a result of changes taking place within the larger entertainment environment that is Hollywood. Where "Old" Hollywood was associated with vertically integrated studios engaged in the production and distribution of motion pictures, New Hollywood is a different animal altogether. Since then, the original motion picture studios have been absorbed into larger multi-media conglomerates in which the film business is only one part of a larger range of entertainment interests that include television, music, publishing, and forays into new (digital) media platforms—developments that are discussed in greater detail in Chapter Two. Consequently, the term "Hollywood" has taken on a wider, multimedia association and definition.[15] Furthermore, Hollywood has effectively expanded its entertainment-related activities beyond its geographical limits, evolving into transnational conglomerates with a complex network of holdings and interests extending across the globe.[16]

These evolving industrial structures and business practices have long received sustained interest from a range of media scholars. Political economists in particular, have investigated the media industries and tracked the various developments in ownership trends, technological advances and capitalist pressures, with an eye to revealing the wider implications that these shifts may have on media content and ideological perspectives. As media scholars and critics such as Ben Bagdikian, Robert McChesney, Edward S. Herman and Noam Chomsky point out, conglomeration, the turn to global markets, and the development of digital technology, heralded distinct shifts in the media marketplace and the ways in which production, distribution and exhibition could be conducted in the last decade of the twentieth century.[17] Most political economists tend to agree that shifts towards larger, multi-media conglomerates, many of which operate on a global stage, do not bode well for ideological freedom and individual dissent, since corporations ultimately disseminate media messages aimed at maintaining their own power and dominance. This may well be the case. However, these assertions are often made in broad, generalized terms, often without any discussion of the actual texts created by these media conglomerates, or any attempt to illustrate how these texts function socially and culturally to limit freedom, discussion and ideological critique. In other words, while the political economy approach is valuable because it highlights and interrogates the developments taking place on the larger economic and industrial level, it fails to consider the actual products generated by these media industries. While a strict political economy approach offers valuable insights into the key trends and developments characteristic of the culture industries, it does not illuminate the detailed processes of cultural production or the form and content of the cultural products themselves.

Commercial Millennial Teen Texts

As mentioned above, the analysis of the media industries in general and the political economy approach in particular tend to ignore textual details. At the other end of the spectrum, pure textual analysis has a tendency to limit its focus to reading and analyzing textual specifics, often without considering the complex contexts surrounding the creation of that text. Furthermore, textual analysis has tended to restrict its attention to exposing the ideological messages contained in the text or to examining the process of representation. In most textual analysis, there is little sustained discussion of the degree to which forces and decisions that have taken place at a higher, macro level, shape the textual elements.

As media corporations respond to new regulatory and legislative decisions, as new corporate structures supplant earlier ones, and new technologies replace older ones, each event reshapes the production, distribution, consumption, and content of the entertainment text/product. My aim is to investigate how these developments have affected the nature, content and aesthetics of millennial teen media. This project, therefore, is motivated by an attempt to synthesize historical/industry analysis and textual analysis to better illustrate how larger institutional forces set limits and bring specific pressures to bear on the entertainment text itself. Studying the recent trends and developments that have characterized Hollywood in the digital age provide the historical and industrial backdrop for the complex activities and decisions taken during the production, distribution and exhibition of teen media products. The textual analysis of specific teen media texts is in turn directed at understanding how textual elements are shaped to reflect the needs and interests of the industry as well as acknowledge the perceived needs and interests of the target market.

To fulfill this objective, I define teen media in terms of the commodities created by Hollywood for a niche teen market, focusing attention on a range of commercially produced, mainstream, popular, distinctly teen-oriented, media texts that emerged out of the complex negotiations that took place between industrial imperatives, technological advancements and economic considerations beginning around 1995 and extending into the first decade of the twenty-first century. Media in the form of teen-oriented art-house/"indie" films, underground music acts popular with youth, and cultural texts produced by actual teenagers outside mainstream Hollywood's commercial structure, though richly deserving of attention, fall outside the limits of this study.

Even within these stated parameters, the range of relevant teen media products remains impractically broad as it would include teen-oriented publications such as serialized novels (*Sweet Valley High* and *Roswell High* are two examples), graphic novels, teen magazines (*Teen, Teen People, Seventeen, Teen Style*, etc.), and corporate media's attempts at co-opting extreme sports, in addition to the more common teen media products like films, television shows, music, and music videos. It is certainly beyond the scope of this project, to address such a wide and complex range of products. Consequently, this interrogation of millennial teen media focuses primarily on film, television, music and digital new media (although, where relevant, there is some discussion of the broader range of related cultural texts). In the area of film and television, attention is restricted to those popular, commercial texts that feature teen characters in dominant roles, and that are primarily concentrated on exploring teen issues. Texts that feature teenage characters tangentially or address teen concerns as part of a more adult-oriented situation, fall outside the parameters of this study. Similarly, although the music industry is largely youth-oriented, this project concentrates mainly on teen performers and teen-associated acts such as boy bands, rather than on performers with a broader appeal that includes the youth market. The primary focus is on tracing and examining how these particular media converge and interact in the new millennium.

Teen Media proceeds from the basic position that each new cycle of teen culture is marked by defining qualities that have been shaped by specific social, cultural and industrial conditions. I am not, however, proposing that this latest cycle marks the emergence of an entirely new or unique media phenomenon. For the most part, millennial teen media, while a new phase in the evolutionary cycle, continues to embrace a range of conventional industrial practices and retains characteristics of teen media that are familiar and stable. Many of these traditional strategies remain fundamental to contemporary teen media, but some of these strategies have had to adjust and respond to new media policies, industry changes, and technologies, developments that have distinct consequences for this latest cycle of teen texts.

In light of the relatively contemporary nature of this study, this examination of how media industries function and how they shape culture was conducted, in part, by an in-depth analysis of news, trade journals and media reports, since these publications generally provide the most up-to-date information available, being particularly efficient at noticing and tracking the rise of cultural trends, the directions these trends take, and the forces that shape their evolution. In addition, mainstream media and trade magazines are some of the most effective vehicles for tracing the ways in which media practitioners, advertisers, cultural producers and consumers conceptualize and shape American society.

In tracking Hollywood's resurging interest in the teen market, I collated and examined all the articles relating to teen media that appeared in *Variety*, *Broadcasting & Cable*, *AdWeek* and *Billboard* between 1990 and 2009. I selected these four publications because they represent the key trade journals for the film, television, advertising and music industries respectively. Collectively, they report and comment upon the key media industries central to this study, providing insight into the practices, interests, activities and cultural products focused on in this volume. I began by confirming that there was little media industry interest in the teen market or teen culture documented in these trade journals between 1990 and 1995. It is only from 1995 onwards, that these publications report the rise, escalation and peaking of teen culture, providing invaluable insight into the nature and evolution of the phenomenon. These reports, thus, provide the industrial and cultural insight central to my research. The core information gathered from these four trade publications is augmented by secondary material derived from more mainstream news publications like the *New York Times* and the *Los Angeles Times*.

While trade and mainstream publications can reveal significant insights into the industrial response to the teen market's renaissance, they offer little information in terms of the content, form and nature of the texts and products created by the media industries. This is where textual analysis, of the sort generally conducted in film, television and media studies, comes into play, as I consider how the form, style and aesthetics of specific media texts have been shaped by significant industrial, cultural, political and technological developments in the years leading up to and following the millennium. The first three chapters of this volume examine the rise of the millennial teen market, the contemporary state of Hollywood, and the key characteristics of millennial media content respectively, while Chapters Four through Eight focus upon a specific site of intense teen-oriented media activity and track the key media events that shaped and characterized this distinct cycle of millennial teen culture. One such event is the complex interaction between *Scream* and *Dawson's Creek* described at the beginning of this chapter.

In terms of the dynamic that I explore in detail in the following chapters, each site of intense teen media activity is characterized by a complicated play of forces: script elements are borrowed and replicated across media texts; certain conventions of narrative and casting are co-opted and adopted by alternative media; creative personnel cross between media platforms and corporate institutions; marketing and advertising practices are embedded in traditional content; and, very specific niche markets are brought into contact for specific outcomes. In turn, these acts, managed by the institutions and individuals involved, are commented upon, enacted, contracted, and planned within a certain horizon of expectations that ultimately creates a distinctive "dialect" of the general youth culture that becomes the new "branding" for specific media institutions intent on becoming prime sites of teen cultural activity.

In all these instances, the industrial structure and the economic imperatives of the institutions involved become wedded to certain individual (and commercial) goals in order to produce a particular and recognizable body of texts, identities, practices, and rationales/ideologies that use the political economy of the media in a particularly distinctive way. These activities are not unique to the *Scream/Dawson's Creek* incident, but became a familiar mode of practice within the area of millennial teen media entertainment, as evidenced by the Melissa Joan Hart/*Sabrina*/Britney Spears/*Drive Me Crazy* instance, and Disney's multi-platform, multi-media *Camp Rock* event, described earlier in this chapter, demonstrate. The body of evidence for such activities is necessarily an ensemble of sites, texts, acts, statements, and interpretations. Each event that I focus on is, first and foremost, situated within a particular site of teen culture, since that culture seems to be the most aggressive locus for the mutation of media industry practices in the millennial years, and is the place where much of the most original and surprising (or aggressive) crossover statements (culminating in refreshed genres, new social forms, novel marketing and advertising gimmicks) have arisen.

The case studies in this book begin by identifying a significant teen media event, which emerges in response to a particular moment in the media institution amidst specific social and industrial conditions and which ultimately produces an acknowledged (and usually very popular) series of texts—a series of media performances and commodities (some combination of films, TV series or episodes, concerts, CDs, videos, advertisements in specific media, websites, and consumer goods) designed to link to each other and to attract the youth market. Each investigation considers the aspects in these artifacts that are part of the linked phenomenon, as well as the stylistic, content, and financial features that unite what might initially seem to be a disparate set of items. As highlighted earlier, millennial teen entertainment distinctively refuses to respect textual boundaries at the level of both content and style. Chapters Four to Eight examine the archive of style, content, audience, and institutional factors that define this particular media moment's construction of these "interlocking" teen media texts.

Essentially, this book represents the search for a way to study this latest phase of teen media culture. With the increasing degree of multi-media convergence on both the textual and industrial front, this work represents a specific approach to studying an evolving media phenomenon. It also expands beyond the specific event to consider how it is representative of the larger industry-wide response to teen culture, the better to understand how these practices and strategies illustrate how media culture at large functions. I also consider the implications of these developments in terms of our greater understanding of popular and commercial culture and teen entertainment media's role in the development of larger cultural trends, the modification of consumer and social identity and the changing structure and nature of the culture industries.

Chapter One, "Targeting Teens," begins by charting the renaissance of the teen market and teen culture that began in the mid 1990s. The factors that led to its resurgence, and the culture industries' perceptions and constructions of this contemporary teen market are examined. In discussing the (re-)emerging teen market, I detail the specific qualities, characteristics and behaviors associated with this new demographic that made it particularly attractive to Hollywood and American retailers and advertisers. In trying to understand commercial teen culture, I locate its development within a nexus of far-reaching and complex developments within Hollywood and amidst greater economic, social and cultural changes.

Where Chapter One examines the larger economic, social and demographic conditions that resulted in the resurrection of the teen market, Chapter Two, "Hollywood and Teen Media—A Historical Overview," traces Hollywood's evolving industrial developments and considers how these shifts shaped the production of teen media texts over the decades, before focusing on the distinctive characteristics of the media industries and the consumer marketplace that witnessed the resurgence of the millennial teen market. In examining the contemporary state of the American media industries, I emphasize the industrial, regulatory, technological and political events affecting Hollywood in the last decades of the twentieth century and into the millennium.

Chapter Three, "The Millennial Teen Media Text," considers how the industrial developments discussed in the preceding chapter affected the content, structure and aesthetics of millennial teen media. This chapter identifies the key features of millennial teen texts and links their emergence to a range of social, industrial, and technological developments that took place in the late 1980s and 1990s. In critiquing the interaction between production and product, this chapter sets the groundwork for the case studies that follow in Chapters Four through Eight.

Chapter Four, "Beyond Music Television," examines MTV's contemporary incarnation as a global, multi-media youth culture site. By the late 1990s, the name "Music Television" was a misnomer as the cable channel had expanded beyond music videos and youth television programs to include other entertainment formats including film and digital media. This case study considers how the cultural shift in musical interests, pressures on the recording industry and MTV, as well as the rise of a newly powerful "teen" market instigated a series of specific media practices, resulting in the development of a range of MTV-linked, teen-oriented multi-media texts and products. Specifically, I examine how changes within MTV's industrial structure and the marketplace at large as well as the emergence of related entertainment institutions (such as Jive Records) affected MTV's programming mandate and more specifically, a range of MTV-linked teen-oriented texts. In examining these issues, examples and analyses focused on the varied and numerous texts surrounding teen musical phenomenon Britney Spears feature prominently in this investigation. I also consider how this entertainment brand has responded to the rise of new digital technologies, exploring the ways in which MTV has leveraged its various multi-media activities into digital and mobile domains.

Chapter Five, "A New Dimension to Teen Media" begins with the resurgence of the slasher teenpic, and its multiple links to other teen-oriented media texts, tracing how larger industrial, commercial and social factors contributed to the emergence and evolution of yet another multi-media teen entertainment site, in this case, the interrelated matrix formed by Dimension Films, Kevin Williamson and the *Scream* franchise. This discussion focuses on Dimension's teen-oriented films, specifically the *Scream* trilogy, detailing how the studio updated an exhausted genre for a new teen generation and then exploited the films' success across a range of media and marketing activities that brought together television, music, video, and retail. This chapter also looks at how the *Scream* films reshaped the wider range of 1990s teen media texts in terms of content, media aesthetics and style. I argue that the trilogy stands as a "blueprint" for later teen films that adopted similar stylistic, aesthetic, promotional and marketing strategies in the effort to replicate *Scream*'s success.

Chapter Six outlines developments in the mid–1990s television industry, with an emphasis on the events and rationalizations that led to the launch of a new broadcast television network focused on the teen market — Time Warner's launch of the WB television network. In particular, I explore how the WB's commitment to servicing advertisers' interest in the "teen" and youth demographic impacted the style, format, nature and content of the media artifacts it created. In tracing the intricate matrix within which the network (and its conglomerate parent's television, film, music, and digital/online interests) shaped the development, nature and content of its teen-targeted media products, I discuss how the network's teen television shows, including *Buffy the Vampire Slayer* (WB, 1997–2001; UPN 2001–2003), *Dawson's Creek*, and *Roswell* (WB, 1999–2001; UPN, 2001–2002), interacted with and were (re)shaped by other teen media artifacts including film, music, digital media, advertising and retail. The final section examines the factors that led to the WB merging with its rival UPN to form a new teen-focused network, The CW. I focus on how the new network refined the teen-oriented strategies adopted by the WB to better reach its target, how the emergence of new digital and mobile media technologies were integrated into The CW's varied on-air content, and how these new media opportunities affected its broadcasting, marketing and promotional activities.

From the CW, Chapter Seven turns to another significant t(w)een media site that was particularly successful in targeting and exploiting the emerging millennial t(w)eens: Disney. Whereas previous chapters focus largely on Hollywood's attempts to cater to older teens within the millennial cohort (those born between 1980 and 1987), Chapter Seven, "Disney and the Youth Market — It's a T(w)een World After All," shifts attention to the younger segment of Generation Y (born between 1987 and 1995), with an eye to understanding how the strategies adopted in the late 1990s influenced and shaped the media activities directed at those still in their tweens or about to enter their teen years in 2000. The teen market has always been characterized by the short lifespan of the teen demographic, a problem alleviated by its self-replenishing nature (as one group ages into the demographic even as another ages out of it). This constant progression has led to numerous challenges in tracking the (sometimes subtle) differences between each cohort so as to better serve their needs. This chapter examines several of Disney's most successful multi-media tween entertainment franchises, including the *High School Musical* series (2006, 2007, 2008), *Hannah Montana* (2006–) and *Camp Rock*. It highlights how the activities discussed in the earlier case studies (Chapters Four to Six), such as the heightened commitment to multi-media synergy, the exploitation of new media delivery platforms and technologies, and the blurring boundaries between disparate media formats, gained further momentum and intensified within a few, short, years. The discussion of these developments acknowledges how Disney's industrial structure and holdings have aided in its increasingly complex, multi-media activities.

Any consideration of commercial millennial teen media cannot ignore the vital relationship between the youth demographic and digital technology. Although the rise of new media technologies is discussed in preceding chapters, a number of key developments dating from 2000 deserve attention, particularly in terms of their (potentially) significant, if still unresolved, impact on the media industries. Chapter Eight, "Bridging the Digital Divide" examines the emergence of new digital technologies that have been especially popular with youth and teens. These include social networking sites (such as Facebook, and MySpace), the launch of new media sites aimed at providing entertainment content via online platforms (for example, YouTube and Hulu.com), and mobile media service providers. "Bridging the Digital Divide" considers how Hollywood has responded to these new technologies, examining the strategies it has adopted to exploit the marketing, distribution and profit potential of these diverse new media, and its attempts to adapt and refine its traditional content to accommodate these new media platforms. The fact remains that these newly emerging media platforms pose a challenge for Hollywood because the potential of, and the means of profiting from, these technologies, still remain unclear and unresolved at this point. While Hollywood has become extremely efficient in exploiting the established and familiar forms of traditional media, the practices and structures that the media industries have adopted in response to new media have met with varying degrees of success. This chapter identifies and evaluates the different, and in some cases, emerging strategies that Hollywood has embraced to better exploit the new digital opportunities. Particular attention is paid to how these approaches have affected, and perhaps even reshaped, the nature, form, and content of the teen-oriented multi-text.

Teen Media asserts that the cultivation of the teen market in the late 1990s was fundamental in laying the foundation for new entertainment platforms such as digital media and innovative online distribution technologies that have continued to evolve, presenting even more opportunities for entertainment texts to expand into other media. At the same time, as actual teenagers within the demographic have aged out of the category, they take with them the kinds of cross-media entertainment demands, expectations and behaviors that they developed as teens. This has distinct implications for how the media industries will have to evolve and accommodate these new consumption activities. In its closing chapter, *Teen Media* points forward to changes to come by highlighting how teen culture in turn is shaping the larger media landscape. Just as Hollywood has had to evolve and respond to the arrival of these latest cycles of the teen market, current practices and strategies will have to keep pace with the market as it ages up into adulthood, even as many of the strategies are applied to ensuing teen cycles. The specific qualities and practices of this latest cycle of teen entertainment culture will have a significant impact on how entertainment in general will develop.

In addition, American teen media has a significant impact globally — a situation brought about by the American media conglomerates' continuing expansion internationally (MTV and Disney are two obvious examples), amidst the rise of new media technologies that offer individuals, particularly teens, easy access to all forms of American media texts and culture. These developments have given rise to an increasingly global teen market. As a result, millennial teenagers worldwide may have more in common with one another in terms of the media they consume, the technology they use, and the ideas/ideologies they are exposed to, than previous groups of teenagers before them. The extent to which Hollywood is aware of, and consciously cultivating this emerging global teen market, and the strategies adopted to do so, is discussed in the concluding chapter. How have the events covered in the book paved the way for new developments in media entertainment? To what extent does this study redefine our understanding of the relationship between popular culture and economics; between text and industrial structure; and between industrial structure and market[place]? How does this study offer an alternative, or evolving, framework through which teen texts and teen culture in general can be understood? And what does this imply for our greater understanding of popular and commercial culture, in particular, teen entertainment media's role with regard to the development of larger cultural trends, the modification of consumer and social identity and the changing structure and nature of the culture industries? *Teen Media* hopes to answer these questions while raising further questions for future research.

ONE

Targeting Teens — The Return of a Vital Demographic Market

In December 1996, the teen slasher film, *Scream*, earned over $100 million at the U.S. box-office domestically.[1] In January 1997, an issue of *Billboard* magazine focused on the music industry's neglect of teen pop music and the teen market, warning against such a strategy.[2] In June 1997, the two-year-old WB television network, described as "a struggling, almost pathetic sixth-placer in the prime-time wars,"[3] announced its decision to target youth and teen audiences.[4] By August 1997, teen-oriented boy bands Hanson, The Backstreet Boys, and 98° were climbing the pop music charts.[5] *Billboard*'s 1997 year-end review noted, "pop music made by teens for teens [had come] roaring back."[6] Nine months later, in May 1998, a feature article in the advertising trade journal *Adweek* triumphantly declared teenagers "the United States' hottest demo of the moment."[7] And, by August 1998, advertising rates on the still low-rated, increasingly teen-oriented WB television network had risen from $35,000 to between $150,000 and $285,000 for 30-second ads on the network's prime time drama *Dawson's Creek,* a show that ranked number one with teenage viewers, even though it languished at number 132 in overall household ratings.[8]

Taken separately, each of these events showcases the significance of the teen market and its potential value to specific media and culture industries within North America in the final years of the twentieth century. Taken together, they demonstrate the resurgence of a teen demographic market, and hint at the impact that the phenomenon was having on American culture and society at the time. While these events are noteworthy in themselves, they are particularly remarkable when viewed against the fact that the institutions profiting from the teen market in the later half of the 1990s had been ignoring that niche market only a few years earlier.

In fact, during much of the 1980s and early 1990s, Hollywood's major film studios were principally focused on developing and producing either big-budget, popular films aimed at mass audiences, or smaller more targeted films aimed at adults.[9] Companies such as Coca-Cola, McDonalds, adidas, Dr. Pepper/7-up, Revlon, Columbia Pictures and Converse reportedly did not consider teenagers an important target market in the 1980s.[10] Reflecting advertisers' lack of interest in the youth market, the three major television networks, ABC, CBS and NBC, largely ignored teens and focused on the quality adult demographic; FOX television, the sole network actively catering to a younger, youth audience in the 1980s, had begun aging up and targeting a broader mass audience by the 1990s.[11] Even in the music industry, where teenagers tended to be viewed as a reliable and loyal market, teen music or "bubblegum pop" had peaked in the late 1980s, when the then-teenaged Debbie Gibson and Tiffany, and boy bands such as New Kids on the Block, had found success. By the early '90s, teen pop music was largely dismissed as too marginal and insignificant to warrant the music industry's attention, which had shifted towards more adult grunge and alterna-rock genres.

The youth market's marginalization was corroborated by the complete indifference to any and all things youth-related on the part of the relevant trade and mainstream publications. The little attention that *was* paid to the teen market tended to echo a news report stating that the teen market "[had] dwindled markedly since the '70s–'80s," quoting a film industry analyst who maintained that "[c]hildren in their midteens ... comprise the smallest part of our population."[12] Reflecting this belief, retailers largely ignored the niche youth market, prompting David Bianculli, the television critic for *The New York Daily News* to state that "For a long time, [the teen market] was the bottom of desirability" for advertisers.[13] The scant attention paid to teenagers tended to dismiss them as an insignificant market, arguing that as a cohort, they lacked the numbers that would make them a group worth marketing and catering to.[14] Also, with the United States experiencing a recession in the late 1980s and early 1990s, it was a generally held belief that the teenage demographic lacked the financial clout and purchasing power necessary to entice the media and consumer industries to cater to their specific needs and interests.[15] However, a series of events in the mid 1990s instigated a fundamental shift in the media industries' view of the teen market.

An early sign of the teen market's potential value appeared with the release of *Clueless* in 1995. This high-school romantic comedy earned in excess of $56 million at the box-office, suggesting that there was an untapped and underserved teen market. A year later, *Scream*, topped the American box-office and doubled *Clueless*' gross. The teen market's immense impact on the Hollywood box-office was reconfirmed in 1997, when teenagers were credited with making *Titanic* the highest grossing film in history.[16] These were the same teenagers that were driving teen popular music up the charts and emerging as "a red-hot advertising market."[17] These events were portentous enough to convincingly herald the onset of a new, noteworthy youth market and convince the larger media and culture industries to reconsider their neglect of the teen market. Teenagers and the teen market, dismissed as "the bottom of desirability" in the mid–1990s, had become "the United States' hottest demo of the moment" by 1998.

Hollywood's subsequent response to this newly emerging demographic was significant enough that teen-oriented entertainment culture, long existing on the margins of popular culture in decades past, began to encroach upon and even dominate mainstream media, entertainment and lifestyle domains. Beginning in the late 1990s, newspapers, trade journals, and other popular publications began to discuss and describe the emerging teen movement, even as commercial brands and retailers joined Hollywood in turning their attention to promoting and selling teen-oriented products and lifestyles.

Any attempt to understand how Hollywood decided to cater to the millennial teen demographic, and how advertisers determined to reach them, must begin by first addressing several obvious questions: Why were teenagers viewed as such a vital and important demographic segment after years of dismissal and marginalization? What factors prompted the degree of intense media and market interest that began surfacing in the late 1990s? Who were these teenagers that were quickly becoming so vital to both Hollywood and Madison Avenue? Answering these questions paves the way towards a clearer understanding of the complex strategies adopted by the media to attract and profit from this market.

The Resurgence of the Teen Market: Historical Comparisons

The millennial teen cycle, though significant in impact and magnitude, can be better understood against the historical backdrop of previous teen cycles. In many ways, the current teen market possesses many of the characteristics that made earlier teen cycles popular with the media and culture industries. In fact, comparing this contemporary incident to the events witnessed during the emergence of the last great teen cycle, baby boomers in the 1950s and '60s, is particularly revealing, not least because the teenagers coming of age in this millennium are the offspring of the baby boomers.

Scholars who have examined the rise of popular, commercial, teen culture, including Thomas Doherty, Susan Douglas, and Kelly Schrum may disagree about when the original teen market emerged, but they do concur on the combination of factors that initially led to the birth of commercial teen culture.[18] In fact, they agree that the same factors have been responsible for the re-emergence of each subsequent teen cycle through the decades since the "teens" were first acknowledged as a separate life stage distinct from childhood and adulthood, and teenagers were first targeted by the media and culture industries as a viable and lucrative consumer market. Since the 1940s, the teenage market had waxed and waned in response to shifting social and cultural events, and by the late 1990s, economic and demographic developments had again coincided to usher in a new ascendant teen cycle.

Historically, the rise of the teen market was, and continues to be, inextricably tied to raw demographic numbers. Beginning in the mid–1990s, significant numbers of children began entering their teenage years. America was witnessing a demographic shift unseen since the first baby boomers attained their teen years. And, just as the sizable post-war demographic quickly earned itself an identifying label: "baby boomers," over half a century later, the demographers, marketing analysts and consultants, advertisers and media buyers studying and describing the contemporary situation began coining various labels to identify this newly emerging teen cohort. As they were the children of the original baby boomers, some chose to label them the "echo boom." Because they are the generation following Generation X, they were also referred to as Generation Y. And, since many of them would come of age around, or during the millennium, yet others designated them Millennials.

Regardless of the label, this demographic's most notable characteristic was its size. In the later half of the 1990s, there were reportedly "76 million American echo kids [who were] the offspring of 79 million American boomers."[19] Indeed, the size of the millennial teen demographic was expected to eventually exceed that of their baby boomer parents—the demographic group responsible for the last, great youth explosion. In the United States during the post-war years between 1946 and 1951, 22 million children were born "forming the first bulge of that demographic goiter in the population known as the baby boom."[20] Though Thomas Doherty is commenting on the original baby boom when he notes that, "[i]n density alone, the massive teenage presence was something of a statistical anomaly," the sentiment also accurately describes the millennial situation.[21]

Just as the baby boomers evolved into a significant force when they aged into their teenage years, so too did their Generation Y offspring. David K. Foot predicted and explained Generation Y's emerging influence in 1998, noting that "[a]s the millennium approaches, most of the echo is in its teen years with the oldest entering young adulthood.... The predictable result is that, at the approach of the millennium, the echo is becoming a more important social and economic force than it was until just recently."[22] This teen population's growing significance was enhanced by the observation that the cohort's numbers would continue expanding well into 2010 as more and more children of the baby boomers aged into the 12- to 19-year-old range.[23] Like the "statistical anomaly" represented by the original baby boom, this echo was poised to shape and direct American society and culture in the final years of the twentieth century and well into the twenty-first. In the millennium, based on sheer numbers alone, teenagers, their needs, interests and behaviors, were becoming impossible to ignore again.

Yet in any era, sheer demographic numbers alone are insufficient to generate the intense media and marketplace attention without the coincidence of an intense period of protracted economic growth. In the 1950s, baby boomers were coming of age during one of the most significant economic boom periods in American history, a development that resulted in "the triumphal enthronement of American consumer culture."[24] 1940s and '50s American society fully embraced the culture of mass production and consumption in the wake of this strong economic growth. This in turn saw a corresponding growth in consumer goods and advertising budgets, ultimately resulting in an expanding marketplace that encouraged heightened consumer purchasing.[25] This increased spending was not restricted to adults but included teenagers who enjoyed the monetary rewards of part-time and full-time jobs.[26]

In the millennium, echo teens, like their parents before them, enjoyed a period of unprecedented affluence. After experiencing a recession in the 1980s, the economic recovery began in the early 1990s and extended into 2000. This growing prosperity translated into intense consumer expenditure, with tremendous increases in teenage spending in particular. By 1998, the $10 billion dollar teen market from 1959 had evolved into a $122 billion market.[27] The echo boom, like the baby boom generation before them, was marked by a similar confluence of events that include an increase in teen demographic numbers and a strong economy, which inevitably led to the teen market's increased spending power.

With the optimum combination of economic power and demographic figures, teenagers emerged as one of the most significant segments ripe for economic, market and media attention. Before this exploitation could occur, however, teenagers needed to be identified and isolated as a specific, separate cohort, with interests and a culture all their own. This was certainly true of the earlier cycles of teen culture, when "teenage" as a concept, and notions of teen culture as a category separate and distinct from mainstream, mass, popular culture, were still relatively new. As Thomas Doherty observes, "[While d]ollars and demographics are two necessary measures of the original teenagers' originality, ... the decisive element is generational cohesion, an acute sense of themselves as a special, like-minded community bound together by age and rank."[28] In the 1940s and '50s, a series of social developments helped to encourage and eventually cement this "generational cohesion." According to Kelly Schrum, rising high-school attendance after the 1940s "increased the potential for a distinct, age-specific identity dependent on peers" even as it encouraged the teenagers' separation from the adult sphere.[29] Lucy Rollin in turn cites the increased independence and freedom from parental supervision that resulted from the war years. Other factors include the growing number of teenagers entering the workforce and the car culture explosion after the war that allowed teenagers the means of accessing and "colonizing" spaces for themselves outside the home. As Rollin notes, all of these events contributed to the rise and increasing visibility of teen culture in the 1940s and after.[30]

Even as teenagers were finding increasing cohesion as a distinct cohort, society at large was beginning to define youth and adolescence as a discrete life stage distinct from childhood and adulthood. This was expressed in a number of publications and studies that emerged in the post war years that specifically focused upon youth. According to Leslie Johnson, "in the USA, studies and writings about youth became a major industry after the Second World War."[31] Citing *The Lonely Crowd* by David Reisman and Paul Goodman's *Growing Up Absurd* as examples, Johnson argues that "in focusing on youth, these writers contributed to the construction of youth as a separate category of person ... with particular needs and with shared concerns."[32] This increasing social recognition was matched by institutional attention. Thomas Doherty points out that "[w]hat lent ... teenagers a sense of group identity ... was that their generational status, their social position *as teenagers*, was carefully nurtured and vigorously reinforced by the adult institutions around them."[33] And some of the adult institutions most interested in shaping the group's shared interests were the media and culture industries.

Throughout the war years, and extending into the decades after World War II, the optimal convergence of economic growth with the emergence of a distinct, significantly large social cohort quickly came to the attention of American marketers, advertisers and the mass media. In fact, all three worked in increasingly collaborative ways to nurture and develop the teenage-identity, motivated by the phenomenally profitable market that this group and its subculture represented. Jon Lewis notes that "[j]ust as sociologists and cultural historians began talking about the phenomenon of youth culture, the advertising, recording, television, and movie industries took aim at this new target market."[34] The situation was repeated at the turn of the millennium as Hollywood and the wider culture industries again turned their attention to a teen market that was already displaying early indications of its sizable numbers, economic clout, and its adoption of media and entertainment-friendly behavior.

Given the focus of this work — examining the range of mainstream, commercial Hollywood texts and products that were created for the millennial teen market and understanding how the complex social, industrial, and technological forces of the period shaped the creation, form and content of these texts — a preliminary understanding of how this teen market was defined and conceptualized as a distinct audience and consumer is essential. It is these considerations and conceptualizations that would ultimately pave the way for Hollywood to profit from the dual activities of directly serving this increasingly significant teen market, and servicing the many marketers and advertisers who were also intent on doing the same.

The Millennial Teen Market: Perceptions and Constructions

Even since teenagers emerged as a separate demographic cohort with access to a disposable income, marketers, advertisers, and the media have attempted to construct the teenager as audience, as consumer, and as a marketing concept. Teenagers obviously consume products and entertainment. But, the notion of a teen consumer or the concept of a teen audience is not a naturally occurring or readily existing one. Instead, these categories have to be consciously shaped and crafted into existence. The American commercial and entertainment industries have consistently had a vested interest in transforming the teenage "subject-as-citizen" into the teenage "subject-as-consumer."[35] Julie D'Acci has referred to television as a "consumer-producing industry"— a term that could be applied to the practices of the larger entertainment industry and the consumer marketplace.[36] Over the decades, the descriptions and definitions of the contemporary teen market, and teens as consumers and audiences, have continually undergone revision and contestation as different institutions have imposed their own interests on these terms. Often, these constructions have significantly less to do with the behaviors and interests of actual teenagers, and more to do with the hopes, desires and specific interests of the institutions intent upon forging these teenagers into an identifiable, and subsequently exploitable and profitable, market.

In analyzing and critiquing Hollywood's strategies for targeting and exploiting the millennial teen demographic, it is vital to begin our investigation with an understanding of how Hollywood and the closely intertwined marketing, advertising and consumer industries conceptualized the millennial teen market. Since these institutions create their products based on a constructed notion of their target market, the qualities, characteristics, behaviors and identities assigned that market are a fundamental starting point to specifically understanding the key factors and events that shaped the production, content and aesthetics of mainstream teen-oriented entertainment texts. As the teen demographic again became increasingly important to Hollywood and Madison Avenue, numerous discussions centered on categorizing the millennial teen as a crucial market segment deserving of its own products, advertising campaigns and entertainment.

Recognizing the rising significance of the emerging teen cohort, advertising and media trade journals, mainstream newspapers, and marketing research agencies quickly resumed the previously neglected activity of transforming teenagers into a definable and exploitable market of distinct and identifiable consumers—a practice that had not been at the forefront of advertiser or marketer activities for some time, but which had reversed by the late 1990s as numerous articles and reports began trumpeting the growing importance of the teen market. The rising numbers of media reports detailing the entertainment and consumer industries' efforts to cater to this increasingly critical demographic offer some of the earliest indications of the millennial teen market's growing dominance. Trade journals ranging from *Advertising Age, AdWeek, Variety, Billboard* to *Broadcasting and Cable* as well as mainstream publications such as *USA Today,* the *New York Times* and the *Los Angeles Times* began weighing in on the surging significance of the teen market in the late 1990s.[37]

The ways in which the millennial teen cycle was being described in popular and scholarly discourses—in terms of the concerted efforts to distinguish the cohort from the adult market, alongside the intense attempts to describe their demographic numbers, their spending power, their behaviors, interests and preferences—recall existing discourses and perspectives expressed about the earlier baby boomers. Hollywood and marketers concentrated on producing constructions of a teen market and audience that would suit their specific agendas. These (occasionally competing) discourses became active sites in which the millennial teen was ultimately established as a distinct and unique demographic cohort, a specific consumer, as well as a valued commodity that various media institutions could package and deliver to advertisers and marketers.

Many of these reports echo the inflated rhetoric characteristic of the claims made by marketing consultants and market researchers extolling the value of the teen market. Between 1995 and 2000, various books offering advice on how to target and exploit the teen market were published, among them, Peter Zollo's *Wise Up to Teens: Insights into Marketing and Advertising to Teenagers*, which focused on promoting the commercial value of the American teen market, and Elissa Moses' *The $100 Billion Allowance: Accessing the Global Teen Market*. In the former, Peter Zollo, a founder of market-research firm Teenage Research Unlimited (TRU), declared teenage echo boomers "a consumer segment too powerful and a marketing opportunity too profitable to ignore."[38] Elissa Moses describes the teen market in even more hyperbolic terms, declaring, "What I know with certainty is that we are at the starting gate of the biggest teen sales and marketing opportunity in world history."[39]

While these media reports provide little insight into actual teenagers, they do reveal the vested interests of the institutions engaged in constructing a description of the teen market and the teen consumer. Responding to the foremost concerns of retailers and advertisers, the many descriptions of the teen market begin by emphasizing the cohort's spending power. Robert Williams, executive director at the Rand Youth Poll, an institution that had been tracking teenagers since the 1950s, labeled millennial teens "the most prosperous group we've ever seen."[40] In describing millennial teens as a valuable market, many articles also actively characterized the group as ideal consumers. A 1998 *New York Times*/CBS News poll of teenagers asserted that 49 percent of respondents claimed to have a part-time job, reinforcing the general perception that teenagers possessed the financial means to become good consumers. Reports of teen consumer spending supported these observations. In 1998, the teen market had a reported value of $122 billion.[41] By 2003, teenagers had evolved into a $175 billion dollar market.[42]

With teenagers again emerging as an intensely attractive market, the entertainment and consumer industries began to turn their attention to investigating and identifying the material and entertainment desires of this demographic. A process that involved first understanding the behaviors, values and preferences of this particular teen cohort. Although media reports acknowledged that Generation Y was ultimately a highly fragmented and often unpredictable demographic, this did not prevent media, advertising and marketplace trade publications from revealing findings and observations that made the cohort particularly attractive to the media and culture industries. The consistent assertion expressed in these profiles depicted Generation Y an avid audience for, and consumers of, Hollywood entertainment and commercial products.

In examining Hollywood's relationship with teens, it is worth noting that a distinction can be made between the branches of Hollywood that function as advertiser-supported enterprises and Hollywood as the producer of teen-oriented products. As the former, Hollywood functions as a "middle-man," serving advertiser needs by delivering the increasingly valuable teen consumer to interested advertisers, while as the latter, Hollywood is itself the producer of teen products aimed at teen consumers/audiences. While the activities and practices it adopts in each capacity may not be conspicuously different, the content, aesthetics and structure of the teen media text are shaped (sometimes subtly) by the specific nature of the interaction.

Hollywood and the Millennial Teen Audience

By the late 1990s, Hollywood's recognition of the millennial teen market's value had gained focus and momentum. The impact that teen audiences had on the box-office grosses of *Clueless*, *Scream* and *Titanic* "spurred new considerations of the teen audience, a segment [that had] largely been ignored by the majors for the past five years."[43] Many of these circulating discourses identified the millennial teen as Hollywood's most important audience and consumer.

After 1997, a number of surveys and polls of movie audiences focused on distinguishing significant trends in the behaviors and attitudes of different audience segments towards movie-going and other forms of entertainment. The survey's findings pointed to just how valuable the teen demographic was to both the immediate and long-term future of the film business, further convincing the studios that teens were a valuable target worthy of special and specific attention. According to the Motion Picture Association of America, huge box-office numbers were reported for 1998, a year in which 1.48 billion tickets were sold.[44] Moviegoers aged 12 to 24 accounted for 37.4 percent of that total, while audiences aged 25 to 39 accounted for 27.4 percent and those over forty, 35.3 percent. While these statistics might initially suggest that the over–40 audience might have rivaled teens in their movie-going attendance, the MPAA's year-to-year findings suggested that since 1996, adult theatrical attendance numbers were actually decreasing, while teen film-going numbers were rising, thus reinforcing the importance of the teen market.

This was confirmed a year later in 1999, when the MPAA declared that teenagers formed the largest movie-going audiences in the nation. According to the Association, the under-25s accounted for almost 40 percent of movie audiences in 1998; the same demographic had expanded to half the film-going audience just a year later. Furthermore, these younger audiences represented half the film patrons classified as "avid," which meant that they habitually watched three or four films a month. The MPAA report also indicated that 48 percent of teenagers between the ages of 12 to 17 claimed that they went to a movie at least once a month compared to just 26 percent of people 18 and older. A survey by the Los Angeles–based Artists Rights Foundation and Boston's Institute for Civil Society revealed that 92 percent of teenagers maintained that watching films was their number one pastime.[45] When we consider that younger people's movie-going dominance extends to the world of videos as well, as a *Los Angeles Times* Poll showed, the Hollywood studios' growing commitment to the teen audience in the late 1990s seems inevitable. According to the *L A Times*, a substantial 36 percent of people ages 18 to 29 said that they had rented five or more videos in the last month.[46] Once the teen movie-goer's impact at the box-office was confirmed, the studios rushed to cater to this newly revitalized market segment, releasing more than 60 teen-oriented films between 1995 and 2000.

The studios' growing recognition of the resurgent power of the teen audience in general was accompanied by a growing perception that the teen girl audience was cultivating a unique set of interests and behaviors that marked them as an even more important market for Hollywood. Peter Zollo, who carried out extensive surveys and studies of the teen film-going demographic, reports that a higher percentage of teen girls than boys were going to the movies in the late 1990s.[47] This hypothesis was borne out by the *Titanic* phenomenon, generally considered the watershed event that proved the market power of teenagers in general, and teen girls in particular. According to media analysts, teenage girls flocked to see the film multiple times. They were also the most avid purchasers of the film's CD and licensed merchandise, contributing significantly to the film's final multi-billion dollar box office.[48]

The millennial teen market's burgeoning importance was not restricted to its impact on the Hollywood studios. Even as the film industry was waking up to the increasing need to respond to the entertainment interests of this particular demographic, they were joined by marketers and advertisers who had also awoken to the teen demo's economic and commercial potential. The perceived value of this niche market would have significant consequences far beyond the film industry, encompassing a wider swathe of Hollywood and American culture and society at large. Like their baby boomer parents before them, echo teens had became "an immediate boon to the nation's ... consumer based economy."[49]

The Millennial Teen Consumer

Trade publications began examining and constructing profiles of the 1990s teenager and their consumer behaviors via surveys, interviews and market observations. These tended to share a common consensus, declaring millennial teens "the most enthusiastic group of young consumers ever."[50] *AdWeek* trumpeted that "this demographic embraces [consumerism] passionately," citing a *Fortune* magazine report that claimed that teenagers visited malls 40 percent more often than other shoppers in the late 1990s. In particular, almost 90 percent of teenage girls (demographically defined as 13- to 17-year-olds) were visiting malls "in record numbers."[51] Characterized as "America's most free-spending [consumers],"[52] numerous articles in the mainstream and trade presses were quick to reference an increasing amount of statistical information detailing teen spending, reporting that "10- to 19-year-olds spent $91.5 billion," an amount "57.8 percent higher than the discretionary spending of their predecessors ten years ago."[53] In addition to its spending power, this teenage generation's shopping and entertainment habits made the cohort particularly attractive to marketers, advertisers and the media industries. The Rand Youth poll revealed that teenagers were spending their earnings on both traditional purchases such as movies, recorded music, clothes and snacks as well as much higher ticket items including computers, television sets, audio equipment, personal telephone lines and even cars.[54]

Media reports further enhanced the attractiveness of the millennial market by highlighting the cohort's apparent ability to influence the family's purchasing decisions, noting that teens are "asserting unprecedented impact on their families' purchasing preferences."[55] Since "teens are ... responsible for more of the family shopping," in 1997, they controlled a $48.8 billion family grocery shopping budget.[56] Consequently, this encouraged consumer brands previously uninterested in teenagers to reconsider their relationship with this cohort.[57] In addition, that same year, teenagers were credited with influencing parental spending on electronic equipment and adult apparel to the tune of $246.1 billion.[58]

In identifying and describing the millennial teenager, many marketing analyses also focused on highlighting the qualities that separated this current cohort from its predecessors. Descriptions of Generation Y often portrayed them as the antithesis of their anti-consumerist Generation X predecessors— for one thing, millennial teenagers were perceived as a highly brand-conscious cohort. According to Robert Williams, executive director at the Rand Youth Poll, Generation Y is "exposed to so many different products on TV, in the mall and through their friends. It's a generation who grew up with excess as a norm."[59] Tom DeCabria, senior vice president of the New York–based Paul Schulman Co., an ad buyer for marketers including The Gap, notes that "[w]hen we were teenagers, we wore the same pair of frayed jeans and flannel shirt...."

[In contrast, t]his generation is very brand conscious and loves to shop."[60] Peter Ferraro, associate publisher of advertising for the hip-hop publication *The Source*, concurs, "This is a branded generation. These kids want people to know they're wearing Tommy [Hilfiger], Ralph [Lauren], Dolce & Gabbana or a Versace shirt.... They've got to have these brands and they'll spend whatever they have to for them."[61] According to market analysts, this generation of teenagers, like their baby-boomer parents before them, expected to be acknowledged and catered to. It is worth pointing out at this juncture that although these reports focused on offering a description of teens, their values, attitudes, and behaviors, these very articulations and pronouncements also served to actively *produce* and reinforce the very characteristics and qualities they were extolling. These depictions of teenagers as committed shoppers with a well-developed branded-mentality in control of a significant disposable income were extremely popular with marketers and advertisers, convincingly bolstering the perception of teens as "the hottest demo of the moment."

Even as these trade journals and market researchers were actively constructing teens as valuable and avid consumers with access to significant disposable income and a devotion to branded products, there were also many attempts to provide additional insights into the behaviors, values and attitudes of this particular generation that made it a challenging consumer and market to attract and exploit. The picture that emerged of the "typical" millennial teenager was of someone constantly on the lookout for new trends, whose attention was difficult to attract and retain, and whose propensity for distraction was nurtured by the heightened access to new technologies and multi-media platforms. *Adweek* declared that "these kids are developing their interests in a world of exploding technological opportunity, learning through computers, video and a bursting array of cable options. ... these early adopters rush into ever-changing technology."[62] The *New York Times* variously described Generation Y as "elusive, even fickle,"[63] and possessing "cutting-edge tastes."[64] *Billboard* echoed a popular sentiment regarding the multiple distractions fighting for the millennial generation's attention, "[Teenagers are] increasingly bombarded with other forms of entertainment."[65] According to Mike Ressolo, Walt Disney Records (U.S.) VP of marketing, "Today's kids are sophisticated and media-savvy, and they are all over the place in terms of taste."[66] These assertions essentially suggest that millennial teens are spoilt for choice where their consumer and entertainment preferences are concerned. As their media options expand alongside a growing number of technological means of accessing information and entertainment, the millennial teen's attention and interest has become increasingly difficult to target and retain.

Many of the discourses implied that while adult consumers could be successfully targeted via traditional media platforms such as mainstream broadcast television, such a strategy would be less effective for the teen demographic, whose attention was much more diversified across a range of entertainment media. The mounting array of entertainment distractions available to the millennial teen audience had led to rising and intensifying competition for the teen market's attention. The heightened advertiser interest in teens resulted in an exponential increase in the number of commercials and advertisements directed at the cohort across a range of platforms. As a consequence of this "media-[overload]," this teen generation that "has been bombarded with more advertising than any before it," has become progressively more immune to such messages, developing a growing degree of cynicism towards such messages, and a heightened ability to tune them out.[67] Of course, such a message essentially justifies the advertising agencies' and media buyers' *raison d'être.* In offering a scenario in which the explosion of new entertainment options, delivery platforms and technological advancements embraced by the teen demographic complicated any traditional attempts to construct an effective, targeted advertising campaign, these reports helped promote certain dominant notions about how to better reach the millennial teen consumer. Identifying (and helping construct) a "vital" market, while characterizing that market as increasingly difficult to target, helps the agencies involved to justify their existence, their activities, and their high rates of remuneration.

Whether this picture of the millennial teenage consumer accurately describes actual North American teenagers is less important here than the ways in which these particular conceptions of the teen market shaped the strategies adopted by marketers, media buyers and Hollywood to best attract and target this demographic. While the nature of these discourses is, in large part, a reflection of the media's attempts at self-interested promotion and the need to enhance the importance of their views and findings, their claims cannot be entirely discounted as they do offer some insight into the increasing importance of the teenage demographic as well as hinting at the effort made to understand how this demographic behaves, what their interests are, and where their concerns lie. The fact remains that these constructions of the teen market and consumer cannot and do not accurately portray the complexities and differences within the cohort. In describing the millennial teen demographic, the perspectives offered are intentionally strictly restricted to specific vested concerns of the parties involved. Market analysts and advertising agencies seek to identify the most promising group of consumers and help cultivate the behaviors and values that would best serve the welfare and needs of their clients, the creators of consumer products. Advertisers and marketers want insight into the market segments they are targeting, and information on the most efficient ways to reach and capture that consumer. At the same time, Hollywood, particularly the branches that serve the needs of advertisers and marketers, clearly benefit from discourses that depict the target market as special, particularly valuable, and distinctively hard to reach, as any media outlet able to effectively target this demographic can then "sell" them to interested marketers/advertisers at premium rates.

Keeping in mind these overlapping and interlocking interests that direct the activities of the various parties involved, it is not unusual that the mainstream, commercial media discourses on the teen market make little attempt to look beyond the commercial, economic and consumerist aspects of the teen market. For the commercial and institutional parties involved, the prime focus lies in cultivating those aspects of the target market that directly benefit commerce and profit. Since Madison Avenue's interest ultimately plays a significant role in motivating the development of media channels and vehicles to deliver this invaluable audience, it provides some explanation for the surge in teen-oriented media texts encompassing a wide range of television shows, teen films, teen publications and teen personalities that could deliver that coveted group of consumers to interested advertisers.

Hollywood: Courting Advertisers and the Millennial Teen Audience/Consumer

As outlined above, marketers and advertisers' mounting interest in the teen market resulted in an escalating pursuit for entertainment platforms that could effectively and efficiently attract and deliver these heavily sought after consumers. In 1995, there were few media outlets that could be relied upon to meet these specific advertiser needs. These were limited to MTV, the teen-focused cable network, and sporadic daytime broadcast slots that had been set aside for "youth programming," which tended to be a very broad term often encompassing children and teens. The only mainstream broadcast television network targeting teens was FOX. By the mid 1990s, however, it was in the process of shifting its attention to a more adult demographic.[68] The re-emergence of the teen market in the late 1990s would have far-reaching impact on the nature and structure of the advertiser-supported entertainment industries in the second half of the 1990s and into the 2000s.

Recognizing the intense degree of advertiser interest in the teen market, and the growing importance of the teen audience, the teen-focused cable network MTV began to court these advertisers, even as it expanded its creative activities beyond music and television to include film production. The traditional television broadcast network model founded on attracting and delivering the coveted adult 18 to 49 audience to advertisers also began to evolve as advertisers were encouraged to view the long dismissed and neglected teenage consumer as an increasingly valuable target.[69] Between 1996 and 2006, a newly launched broadcast network, the WB, was able to succeed on the strength of its popularity with teens. How MTV responded to the rise of the millennial teen market is discussed in Chapter Four, while the events related to the WB television network are discussed in Chapter Six.

The discussion of the teen market thus far has focused on the factors leading to the reemergence of the millennial teen market, and on tracing the teenage demographic's escalating appeal to marketers, advertisers and Hollywood. In these discussions, the term "teen" has unambiguously referred to actual teenagers. However, such a straight-forward definition fails to acknowledge a series of social and cultural developments that had taken place in the previous decades, developments that complicate the notion of "teen," and that have far-reaching consequences for the many institutions trying to target this demographic market as well as for this study. In the late 1990s, when American social, cultural and media attention honed in on the teen market, the term "teen" could no longer be limited to a specific and identifiable age group.

From Teenage to "Teen"

During the 1940s and '50s, "teenage" was conceptualized as a distinct life stage defined by biological age. In the intervening decades, however, the notions of teenage and the teenage identity have evolved, having less to do with biological age and increasingly more to do with lifestyle and shared cultural tastes and interests. Over the decades, the concept of "age" has been removed from the idea of "teenage," leaving us with a "teen" culture that is lifestyle- rather than age-specific. This shift can be traced to various factors. Since the emergence of teen culture, the idea(1) of youth has gained increasing social and cultural value. As a result, "youth" and "teenage" in the late twentieth century have achieved a much broader appeal and have come to represent a range of idealized qualities such as vitality, excitement, vigor, promise and cutting-edge interests. These qualities may be associated with youth but are increasingly being embraced by all of society regardless of age. In the youth-obsessed culture of American society in the twentieth century, it is no longer how young you are, but how young you think you are, or choose to be, that matters.

This particular shift in mindset began in earnest in the 1980s and intensified in the '90s and was strongly incited by the media and the marketplace. Throughout the 1980s, the definition of youth had been reshaped by the media who were successfully re-constructing notions of "youth" (and its related products) as a commodity to be sold to both a teen and a non-teen audience. In the 1980s, Hollywood was producing media texts that were apparently aimed at "mass" audiences, yet the prevailing notion of this "mass" audience was distinctly youthful.[70] Consequently, Hollywood played a vital role in transforming broader audiences into "youthful consumers." In fact, the media and consumer industries were actively engaged in encouraging America's obsession with youth and the belief that it can be maintained past the chronological stage. By the 1990s, "adolescence [was] not a biological stage but a lifestyle choice" and this shift was due in part to media texts with a vested interest in "making youth culture available to all viewers" and in doing so, these media texts "denat-

uralize[d] the teen-age years."[71] As a result, the teen market in the 1990s consisted of consumers aged 13 to 19, but also included consumers both above and
below that age group.

In the final decades of the twentieth century, the trends and attitudes associated with youth began to have a pervasive effect on American society. While
teenagers and young adults generally made up only a proportion of the American population, they began to exert tremendous influence on an even larger
"youth-oriented" or "youth-conscious" adult market. By the end of the twentieth century, even younger demographics were beginning to embrace teen attitudes. In October 1999, an NBC news report mentioned the emerging concept
of "consumer maturity" and described the "'teen-ing' of childhood" in which
the market industries were looking at "millennial kids," aged four to twelve,
as the next group of emerging big consumers who had adopted a teenage consumer identity.

These developments suggested that the "teen" market in the 1990s was
even more significant than it had ever been, extending far beyond actual
teenagers to include a large segment of people outside their teenage years who
embraced the "teenage" lifestyle and identity. In response, the advertising, marketing and media industries began constructing a youth/teen demographic
market that ignored the traditional boundaries of the actual teenage years.

Thus, while teenagers were a vital target of the media, advertisers and
marketplace in the late 1990s and 2000s, these industries recognized that the
actual "teen" market was no longer restricted to those in the narrow 13 to 19
age demographic. This was especially true for an increasingly youth-obsessed
American society at the turn of the millennium. By industrially defined, demographic standards, the teen market in the '90s included both teenagers and anyone who chose to adopt a teen-oriented lifestyle or identity. Responding to this
development, the media industries created target teen-oriented demographic
markets that extended beyond the teenage-defined "13 to 19" segment to include
the "12 to 24" and even the "12 to 34" demographic targets. Interestingly
enough, all of these industry-defined demographics were used to delineate a
"teen" or "youth"-identified market.

While it is clear that the culture and retail industries were targeting the
teen market as their audience/consumer, they were also engaged in a complex
exercise of constructing and selling a teen lifestyle/identity to audiences and
consumers both within and outside the 13 to 19 age demographic. This teen
lifestyle became increasingly popular over the years owing to teenage identities that were equated with particularly valuable and positive qualities or features. In fact, the word "teen" gradually became a sort of brand, indicative of
particular, idealized qualities associated with youth and, within a commercial
or media context, with specific products and media artifacts that one purchased
and consumed as part of the teen lifestyle.

Often, these teen identity constructions (many of which eventually evolved into specific teen brands) existed separate from actual teenagers and often did not even originate from them. Rather, in the United States in particular, teen culture and constructions and codifications of teenagers or a teen identity were often inextricably intertwined with the media and culture industries.[72] These industrially-motivated ideological conceptions of "teenagers" branded "youth" or "teenage" with idealized notions of vigor, vitality, excitement, promise, fun and attractiveness as well as particular cultural and consumer goods available to teenage and "teen"-identifying consumers. The television and advertising industries' definition of the teen demographic in relatively broad age ranges ("12 to 24" or "12 to 34") is an indication of how little "real age" factors into the equation. As America became increasingly youth-obsessed, the advertising and media industries became more committed to the belief that older consumers were likely to follow the lead of younger, trendier consumers.

Distinguishing Between Teenagers, the Teen Demographic Market and Teen Identity Constructions

By the 1980s, the term "teen" had transformed into a multi-layered, polymorphous term that could be used to reference actual teenagers, distinct and different teen demographic markets, and even teen identity constructions. Since all of these concepts are central to the concerns of this study, it is vital that they be distinguished for clarity and coherence. I begin with the most obvious and easily defined concept, actual teenagers. These are the individuals between the ages of 13 and 19 who were becoming a vital and significant economic power and demographic segment in the mid–1990s and beyond. I denote them by the default, unmarked term "teenagers." I use the phrases "teen market" and "teen demographics" in turn to refer to the group of consumers who, regardless of actual age, have chosen to embrace a teen lifestyle or identity. Finally, the terms "teen brand" and "teen identity" are used to denote those cultural constructions identified with the teen label, but that tend to avoid any age definitions.

By the late 1990s, Hollywood and advertisers had begun to believe that attracting teens was an increasingly crucial imperative. Hollywood film studios began developing a growing number of teen-oriented films. MTV and the WB were actively targeting teens and the advertisers who valued them. These included an increasing number of American businesses that had turned their attention to the reemerging teen market. Make-up brands including Cover Girl, Maybelline and Neutrogena launched new product lines that served the specific needs of teenagers. In malls nationwide, stores such as The Gap, Abercrombie and Fitch, J.Crew and Tommy Hilfiger began constructing and cultivating a particularly desirable teen brand image, part of their strategy to attract the increasingly significant teen market consumer. These stores found great success offering products tailored to a youthful, teen-identified lifestyle and mindset. The cultural zeitgeist became increasingly marked by an almost obsessive focus on the lifestyle, mindset and consumer preferences of youth in general and teenagers in particular.

However, the desirability of that demographic was matched by its perceived elusiveness. Teens were popularly characterized as a distracted group with multiple media options competing for their time and attention. Where earlier cycles of teens could reliably be reached via specific media such as music or teen films, millennial teens were the product of a cultural environment that had fragmented into a wide range of entertainment possibilities. As Hollywood exploited an ever-growing range of technologies while evolving into increasingly complex multi-media conglomerates and expanding its entertainment practices into new forms, it reshaped the teen relationship to and consumption of entertainment. As the primary aim of this study is to interrogate the decisions, practices, and strategies Hollywood adopted in the creation of teen-oriented commercial media in the millennium, we must now turn our attention to this particular site of commercial, cultural production. Only by recognizing the distinctive qualities of Hollywood in the millennium can we gain greater insight into the forces that shaped the millennial teen text. Hollywood in the late 1990s was a very different industry from that in previous decades. Changes in the industrial structure, in technology and organization had a significant impact on the commercial Hollywood teen text, as discussed in the next chapter.

Two

Hollywood and Teen Media — A Historical Overview

Teen Media posits that any attempt to examine millennial teen commercial culture must consider how larger developments in the media industry, including structural shifts, dominant business practices, and technological developments, shaped the production, content, form and structure of contemporary teen texts. Chapter One addressed the specific set of economic, social and demographic conditions that led to the resurrection of the millennial teen market. This chapter considers the distinctive characteristics of the media industries and the consumer marketplace during the same period.

In stressing the need to adopt a historical approach to each (newly emerging) cycle of teen media, this study also highlights the evolution of the industrial and technological contexts against which these events have occurred. While numerous aspects of teen culture may remain familiar, with many of the contemporary practices adapted from long-established strategies, the state of the industries and the evolving nature of the market have led to changes in terms of how these strategies are worked out. The main focus of this chapter lies in examining how Hollywood's attempts to effectively target, attract and exploit the teen market in the decade leading up to 2000 and the decade after, were shaped by larger industrial shifts, technological developments and Hollywood's adoption of strategic creative and commercial practices. By investigating the distinctive regulatory, industrial and technological environment in which commercial teen texts were conceptualized, created and marketed, we can gain greater insight into the ways in which the business interests and forces existing during the period shaped the contemporary teen media products.

The dominant events that characterized Hollywood at the turn of the twenty-first century and that would have a direct and powerful impact on commercial millennial teen media involve

1. the intensifying shift towards multi-media conglomeration, a movement that originated in the late 1960s and that had been evolving and building since then;
2. the increasing fragmentation of media platforms and products amidst the heightened corporate consolidation;
3. the emergence of new media technologies with the potential

to reshape the nature, form and experience of traditional
entertainment;
4. Hollywood's enhanced global reach and influence.

Any discussion of millennial Hollywood must acknowledge that these dominant characteristics have evolved from activities practiced in previous decades.
Scholars focusing upon the media industries in the 1990s have commented
upon the developments mentioned above, tracing the earlier industrial conditions behind them, as well as tracking the extensive changes to the entertainment business as a consequence.[1] Conglomeration, the development of digital
technology, and the turn to global markets all heralded distinct shifts in the
media marketplace and the ways in which production, distribution and exhibition were conducted in the last decade of the twentieth century.

These developments have also had a significant impact on how teen/youth
media was conceptualized, packaged and marketed in the millennium. Arising
out of these specific conditions, a typical commercial teen entertainment product is characteristically multi-media in nature, often consisting of simultaneously released components across various platforms including film, television,
music and online. In the millennium, Hollywood's transnational holdings have
also resulted in the development of much more efficient ways to distribute this
expanding range of linked teen media products to a global market.

At first glance, the preceding description of millennial teen media may not
appear that different from previous cycles of commercial teen media culture.
With the exception of the digital dimension, which is a new technological development, earlier teen media also straddled multiple media. Since the 1930s, successful teen texts had been repackaged across a range of media that include
print, radio, television, and film. Over the decades, many of these texts also
successfully crossed national and cultural boundaries, appealing to an international audience. This seeming immutability has resulted in a tendency, within
scholarly discourse, to "talk about 'youth' [and youth/teen culture] as a tran-
shistorical and timeless entity,"[2] when the reality is that contemporary youth
and teen cultures, like contemporary social and cultural conditions, may bear
limited resemblance to past eras. The close scrutiny of previous teen cycles,
alongside their contemporary regulatory, industrial and technological contexts
in this chapter reveals some noteworthy differences. Multi-media conglomeration, the development of digital technologies and the globalization of the marketplace have all had a distinct impact upon millennial teen culture. Certainly,
these industrial, marketplace and technological changes demand a rethinking
and reevaluation of the "rules" defining teen culture and teen texts, as well as
the strategies adopted in studying this increasingly complex situation.

Before exploring Hollywood's response to the millennial teen market, however, we need to look back at how the relationship between Hollywood and
teenagers has evolved. Just as many of the characteristics of millennial teen

media are built on previous cycles, the Hollywood media landscape at the end of the twentieth century is predicated on a range of political, legislative, industrial and market contexts from earlier periods. The following pages explore in greater detail the regulatory events, industrial developments and technological advances that have affected the evolution of teen media culture through the decades.

Hollywood and Teen Culture: A (Very) Brief Look Back

The term "teenager" has a history reaching back to the 1920s. However, it was only in the 1930s that teenagers and teen culture began receiving cultural attention. Grace Palladino notes in *Teenagers, an American History*, that the pre-war Depression years in the 1930s forced teenagers out of the workplace and into high-schools, motivating the emergence of a new, separate, "teenage" generation, one that was associated with the high-school experience and community.[3]

As teenagers became identified as a separate sub-group, they also gained recognition as a distinct demographic market, one that the media industries of the time began targeting with entertainment products. It is impossible to fully explore the complex and wide-ranging events that mark the many cycles of teen culture, or provide a comprehensive perspective on the intricate forces that shaped the development of the various entertainment media industries within Hollywood in a single book, let alone a chapter. So, I will not attempt to do so here. What follows is an admittedly brief overview of a select number of noteworthy events that show how the development of teen culture in previous decades was directly shaped by larger legislative, industrial and technological shifts. In selecting the events to address, I am guided by an interest in identifying the key developments that would offer the necessary background and insight into the characteristics associated with millennial Hollywood that I highlighted earlier.

Hollywood and the Teen Market in the Classical Hollywood Era: 1920–1965

In the 1920s and '30s, teen media culture was largely associated with radio, in the form of music by Benny Goodman, Duke Ellington and Count Basie, and publishing — as evidenced by the emergence of teen-oriented novels such as the Nancy Drew mystery series and magazines like *American Boy* and *Boys' Life* aimed at teenage boys, and *American Girl* and *Everygirl*, directed at teenage girls.[4] During and after the Second World War, the film industry joined these more established media in catering to the teen demographic. Mickey Rooney appeared as the popular teenager Andy Hardy in a series of successful MGM films released between 1937 and 1947, and the teenaged Deanna Durbin was one of the biggest box-office draws of the era, credited with "single-handedly saving Universal Studios from bankruptcy."[5] On the radio, popular programs such as *The Aldrich Family* (1939–1953), featured teenagers as main characters and addressed teen concerns. Even at this early point in teen culture history, many teen media texts were not confined to a single medium. *The Aldrich Family* had its origins as a Broadway play, *What a Life* (1938), before becoming a long-running radio series (1939–1953), and later a television series (1949–1953).[6]

At this early stage in broadcasting history, radio and television programs were created and owned by the shows sponsors who then bought broadcast time on a radio or television network for the programs. Consequently, the broadcast networks had little interest in, or control over, the programming and served primarily as providers of a nation-wide distribution system for the advertisers' shows. Even as sponsors were approaching *What a Life* playwright Clifford Goldsmith to create a radio program featuring characters from his play, Paramount Pictures was simultaneously acquiring the rights to the Broadway play and planning to remake it as a film.[7] At this point, there were no corporate links between any of the parties involved in these negotiations. Although similar content was translated across a range of media platforms, the companies involved in the creation of these different media texts were largely separate and unrelated and there were no collaborative arrangements between the companies in this instance. This is not to suggest that Paramount, or any of the other major movie studios, was oblivious or indifferent to the potential benefits a studio could reap if it could gain entry to broadcasting.

It would be naive to think that this period was entirely free of the collusive inclinations associated with the tightly diversified multi-media conglomerates characteristic of post–1980s "New" Hollywood. Between the 1920s and 1940s, the major motion picture studios were actively engaged in the quest for diversification into the emerging realm of broadcasting. Warner Bros. was the first to enter broadcasting when it purchased a radio station in Los Angeles in 1925. In 1929, Paramount Studios acquired a 49 percent stake in the Columbia Broadcasting System (CBS). Broadcasters, similarly, were actively staking a claim in the movie business. The Radio Corporation of America (RCA), which owned NBC, formed the major film studio RKO (Radio-Keith-Opheum) when it merged with the Keith-Albee-Orpheum theatre chain to enter the film production and distribution business.[8] Despite these early attempts however, legislative decisions would play a key role in thwarting these initial multi-media ambitions.[9]

Through the 1930s and '40s, a series of regulations and legislative rulings imposed by congress and the FCC contained the various media industries' attempts at expansion into related media. Most of the rulings ostensibly focused on maintaining existing boundaries between potentially related media industries with the goal of promoting competition and inhibiting monopolistic activities within Hollywood. An early attempt at enforcing anti-trust regulations in the mass media industry resulted in the Paramount Decree of 1948, when the Supreme Court ruled against the Hollywood studio system, arguing that the vertically integrated Hollywood Majors (Fox, Loew's Paramount, RKO and Warner Bros.) that controlled the production, distribution and exhibition of movies, were guilty of anti-trust activities. To avoid further prosecution, the studios were forced to sell off their theatre holdings as part of an effort to reduce the majors' oligopolistic control over the movie industry.[10] Yet, throughout the 1940s, even as the major studios were embroiled in their struggle with the Supreme Court, they were actively attempting to establish a controlling interest in the nascent television industry by buying broadcast stations and applying for broadcast licenses with the FCC. However, the FCC continually stymied these efforts by stalling on approving these licenses.

When the Supreme Court passed the Paramount Decree in 1948, there were concerns that legitimizing the major studios' entry into television would result in a television system mirroring the recently outlawed vertically-integrated studio system, in which a small number of studios would be able to control the production, distribution and exhibition of television programs and thereby dominate the television market the way they had previously controlled the film market. This led the FCC to begin investigations into the studios' requests for station ownership while declaring a freeze on television station licensing that lasted from 1948–1952.[11] Although the FCC never actually passed a ruling against the studios, the investigation, along with the licensing freeze and awareness that the 1934 Communications Act authorized the FCC to refuse station licenses to any individual or organization convicted of monopolistic practice, convinced the studios to reconsider their strategic response towards broadcasting.[12] As a consequence, the major film studios shifted their focus from acquiring broadcast stations and licenses to producing and supplying the existing networks with programming. These decisions would have far-reaching consequences on the film and television industries' complex relationship for several decades, establishing them as both competitors and allies within a media context in which each industry would benefit from potential collaborative arrangements in some areas, even as they remained competitors in others. More importantly, the movie industries' gradual emergence as producers and suppliers of programming to the television networks would eventually culminate in the multi-media integration of the media industries witnessed in the millennium.[13] The trend toward diversification and the eventual triumph of multi-media conglomeration did not, however, proceed without additional obstacles.

The relationship between the film and television industries through the 1950s and '60s is well-documented.[14] Television's increasing presence in the suburban home and its offer of "free" entertainment made it an alluring alternative to film entertainment. It did not take television long to supplant film as the newest and most popular form of mass entertainment, forcing film to redefine itself for narrower, niche markets in an effort to survive. However, as I noted earlier, the relationship between the film and television industries is marked by a much more complex history than straightforward competition. While television certainly posed a threat to film exhibitors who saw their audiences dwindle in the wake of television's ascendance, this was matched by a growing recognition that film producers and the television industry were poised to enjoy a degree of mutually beneficial partnership. Television, as the growing medium, was desperately in need of programming, and the production arm of the film industry soon realized that they were in the ideal position to meet this demand.[15] Producing for television allowed the studios to profit from their competitors. As Nina Leibman points out, "[u]ltimately, ... the film industry fought the television threat by becoming its heaviest supplier and a consistent advertiser, and by using it as a testing ground for genres, screenplays and personnel."[16] The arrangement had the effect of forcing both industries to engage in paradoxical activities of helping maintain each other's success while simultaneously limiting each industry's influence and control over the larger media marketplace.

Two successful collaborations between the film and television industries in the 1950s, involving arrangements between ABC and Disney, on the one hand, and ABC and Warner Bros., on the other, marked the origins of what would become a complete integration of movie and television production in Hollywood that would significantly shape the film-television relationship and directly impact youth entertainment culture of the period. These initial arrangements are particularly relevant here as they are linked to the network's interest in targeting the youth/baby boomer generation that was coming of age in the 1950s and '60s. ABC's interest in aligning with the movie studios and acquiring studio products for broadcast was based on the realization that as the weakest of the three existing television networks, it needed to find a way to distinguish itself from its stronger, better financed, network rivals. Since ABC did not have the resources to create its own programming, it turned to the studios which were beginning to explore television as a means of promotion and as a possible consumer of studio-created products. Consequently, ABC signed a deal with Disney and Warner Bros., in 1953 and 1955 respectively, agreeing to swop network broadcast time for lower licensing fees to exclusive, studio-produced programming.[17]

In keeping with ABC's attempt to lure youthful families, in particular, the new baby boomers, Disney and Warner Bros. programs joined a growing schedule of shows that were specifically targeted at youthful audiences. Following the increasingly popular *Disneyland* (1954–1958), which packaged its cartoons and documentaries within an educational discourse aimed at young viewers, ABC's later youth and teen-focused schedule included *The Patty Duke Show*

(1963–1966), about the adventures of teenage cousins Patty and Cathy Lane, and *Gidget* (1965–1966). Like the previous instances of teen texts appearing in multiple media, the teenage Gidget began as the main character in a 1957 novel, then appeared in a series of teen-oriented films (1959, 1961, 1963) from Columbia Pictures before making the transition to television in 1965, when *Gidget*, the television series, produced by Columbia Pictures' television arm Screen Gems, was broadcast over ABC.

By the end of the 1950s, the networks and studios were already engaged in a closely collaborative relationship. These cross-media links are early examples of what would eventually emerge as highly complex, interconnected associations across a wide and varied range of media in the multi-media conglomerates that dominate millennial Hollywood. Perhaps the most significant precursor of the giant multi-media conglomerate of the period was Disney. Its initial agreement with ABC was directly motivated by the Disney brothers' interest in acquiring financial support to build the Disneyland theme park. The early seeds for a multi-media conglomerate with control over diversified entertainment content and product lines were already being planted as Disneyland paved the way for a string of media-related merchandizing, all of which would help promote the television shows, the rides in the theme park, the movies in theatres, and vice versa. These related activities were effecting the rise of an increasingly integrated leisure market.[18]

Amidst the growing collaborations between the film and television industries between the 1940s and '60s, several regulatory decisions aimed at containing the potential size and marketplace dominance of the emerging networks were imposed to maintain diversity and competition in the national broadcast arena. This was achieved by policies restricting the number of television stations that any company or network could own at the national level. In 1941, the FCC capped the number of stations that a single company could own within the national market at three stations.[19] To further contain the growth of broadcast companies at the local level, between 1941 and 1943, the FCC also instituted the Duopoly rule, which prohibited any corporation from owning more than one television, FM, and AM radio, broadcast station in any market.[20] These activities went some way towards limiting the size and influence of the various broadcast companies while also upholding some of the boundaries between different media.

But, despite the various legislative constraints, attempts at media integration continued to advance. In addition to the growing relationship between the film and television industries, alignments between the film and music industries were also developing. Decca Records acquired Universal Pictures in 1952,[21] allowing for greater integration between the two media. As the music industry catered to teenagers in the '50s with rock 'n' roll, the music found its way into numerous teen films. The film industry's B-grade exploitation movies such as *Teenage Devil Dolls* (1952) and *Teenage Crime Wave* (1955), as well as the 1955 classics *Rebel Without a Cause* and *Blackboard Jungle* featured soundtracks that included the popular music of the period. As teen culture continued to evolve, '50s exploitation pics made way for the beach movies of the 1960s, with some of the most popular ones starring Annette Funicello and Frankie Avalon, both of whom contributed songs to the films' soundtracks. Not one to ignore the teen audience's partiality for popular music, ABC television network began targeting teens with daily doses of Dick Clark and *American Bandstand* (1957–1963), bolstering the already strong relationship between teenagers and popular music. The activities described above, including the collaboration between the film and television industries and these early mergings of music, film and television, would eventually evolve into the mega multi-media mergers that would characterize millennial Hollywood, but this shift would only evolve over several decades and after taking several detours.

Hollywood and Teen Media in the Era of Loose Conglomeration: 1965–1984

The initial steps towards multi-media integration took place in the 1960s when non-entertainment-based corporations began purchasing Hollywood studios primarily to exploit the studios' valuable film libraries and television production operations. These buyouts represented a strategy of loose conglomeration, in which corporations engaged in expansionist moves into unrelated businesses as part of an attempt to spread the risks and benefits across a range of disparate industries and markets. Consequently, in 1966, Gulf & Western, a company with business interests in a range of manufacturing sectors including cigar and paper factories, auto finance, and sugar refineries, bought Paramount Pictures for $130 million.[22] In 1967, Transamerica, a company with interests in the airline industry, car rentals, insurance, and business services, purchased United Artists.[23] Two years later, in 1969, Kinney National Services acquired Warner Bros. for $400 million. The studio was added to Kinney's vast and varied list of holdings, including real estate, construction, car rentals, parking lots and funeral services.[24] That same year, financier Kirk Kerkorian acquired a 50 percent interest in MGM.[25]

Due to the largely unrelated nature of the parent companies and their media acquisitions, and the fact that these companies did not go about vertically integrating their media holdings, the barriers that previously existed across the different forms of media remained largely intact. For one thing, owing to the varied and vast holdings of these parent companies, of which media interests consisted only a small segment, these trans-industrial corporations did not appear to fully recognize the potential benefits of media consolidation. Consequently, the synergistic activities discussed later in this chapter did not emerge as a key strategy until the 1980s. To some extent, the media-oriented mergers and acquisitions of this period were also constrained by newly introduced federal regulations.

In the 1970s, Federal legislators imposed further regulations as part of on-going attempts to ensure competition, protect against monopolistic inclinations and retain the preexisting media boundaries. In 1970, the FCC instituted the Financial Interest and Syndication Rules (Fin/Syn), prohibiting the corporate owners of television networks from engaging in the production and ownership of the programs broadcast on their networks. Since the three existing television networks (ABC, CBS and NBC) already controlled distribution on a national scale, and had interests in exhibition via the television stations that they owned and operated (often in the largest television markets), allowing them to produce and own their programming would be tantamount to replicating the vertically-integrated structures of the movie industry under the studio system that had been declared illegal by the Supreme Court in 1948. In addition, since the major studios at the time were the primary producers of television programming for the networks, this rule was a significant obstacle to any studio interested in establishing an ownership or financial interest in a television network. In 1975, the FCC enacted the Newspaper/Television Cross-Ownership Prohibition Rule, in effect outlawing a form of horizontal integration that would have brought two separate but related media industries under a single corporate umbrella.

All of these regulatory decisions helped impede the rising tendency towards media consolidation and integration that was beginning to gain momentum in the 1970s. However, changes within the government, in technology and in corporate America, eventually led to the elimination of all of these obstacles, paving the way for the shift towards multi-media conglomeration in the 1980s. This tactical shift to tight conglomeration was motivated by the growing realization that the perceived profit potential of loose conglomeration never materialized. Recognizing the ineffectual outcomes of these mergers, many of these conglomerates set off another wave of buying and selling in the 1980s when they began to divest themselves of non-entertainment related divisions and focus on expanding their entertainment holdings.

Any discussion of Hollywood's strategic shifts from the diverse and loosely related conglomerates in the '60s and early '70s to the strictly media-focused conglomerates of the '80s cannot ignore the vital role played by technological developments. Technological advances in the field of entertainment have often had a significant impact on Hollywood. Examples of evolving technologies that reshaped Hollywood's response to the business of entertainment and the entertainment product in the 1970s and '80s include home video, cable and satellite technologies. These technologies led to the development of new delivery systems that would ultimately redefine the nature and experience of popular entertainment while also motivating the fragmentation of the media experience and media market.

Video and cable encouraged the growth of the diversified media marketplace and the expansion of the media product line. The videocassette recorder spawned a new market for film and television content that could now be sold directly to consumers to be enjoyed in the privacy of their homes at their leisure.[26] Similarly, cable technology led to the rise of pay television, yet another market by which entertainment texts could be delivered to interested consumers, and cable television, which allowed for an almost limitless number of available television channels and services.[27] Cable technology's potential was augmented with the launch of the first commercial cable satellite, SATCOM I, in 1975, which ushered in the era of commercialized satellite cable transmissions.[28]

These events would set the stage for cable's growth and the subsequent reconsiderations of traditional definitions of television, developments that would eventually have far-reaching consequences for the media industries.[29] The traditional perspective of broadcasting was founded on the belief that since broadcast stations used the public airwaves, the medium was required to serve the public interest. Furthermore, the scarcity doctrine, which argued that only a limited number of broadcast stations could exist in any single market due to spectrum scarcity, justified the need for congressional and FCC oversight, and the imposition of regulations intended to uphold the public interest, and that often led to restrictions on corporate activities and on programming content.[30]

The advent of cable and satellite technology, while still under the purview of the FCC, negated scarcity concerns, offering the possibility of unlimited channels.[31] This would have significant consequences for the media industry, particularly in the realm of broadcasting and television. Cable and satellite technology ushered in an era of media deregulation with its offer of increased competition. With the potential of virtually unlimited television channels, the age-old scarcity doctrine was appearing increasingly irrelevant. The belief was that in the cable age, the previous limitations on competition, on alternative viewpoints and perspectives would be removed. These developments allowed for a revision of how broadcasting, television in particular, could and should be defined. Television, traditionally conceptualized as a medium serving the public interest, could now be freed from this limited and limiting definition. This development allowed the Reagan Administration, which staunchly advocated deregulation, to begin dismantling many of the existing rules that constrained the business activities of the major media companies, ultimately opening the door for increased multi-media conglomeration.

The consequences of cable's rise went far beyond the shift to deregulation. It also changed the ways in which television defined and conceptualized the viewing audience. Cable networks, unlike their broadcast counterparts, were not interested in catering to a mass, undifferentiated audience. Instead, as part of a strategy to distinguish themselves from the established national broadcast networks and an ever-increasing number of cable competitors, each cable network decided to carve out its own specialized niche by narrowcasting to a select audience.[32] Since the earliest adopters of cable technology and paid programming tended to be middle- or upper-class, white, affluent suburban house-holds who could afford, and were willing to pay for entertainment to be deliv-ered directly to the home, cable presented the opportunity to carve the mainstream audience into smaller niches that could not only be more efficiently targeted with specialized programs, but also be sold to advertisers for a pre-mium. These conditions paved the way for the launch of MTV in 1981.

MTV, the first strictly teen-focused network, owed its existence to cable's emergence as a viable delivery platform, the growing importance of niche mar-kets, the rise of multi-media conglomeration, the music-television-film con-vergence and the corporate exploitation of synergistic opportunities. From its inception, MTV was perceived and exalted as a unique platform aimed at pro-moting and marketing music on television. Borrowing from the *American Band-stand* template, the founders of MTV believed that "visual radio" would be an effective way to market popular music to teenagers.[33] This strategy allowed MTV to serve the promotional interests of the music industry and advertisers, establishing the cable network's dominant commercial and promotional man-date. From this initial idea, MTV would eventually emerge as a favorite net-work of teenagers, built on a commitment to marketing film, television and music, thereby evolving into a "one-stop" entertainment channel aimed solely at teenagers, offering them a variety of ways to experience and access teen-oriented entertainment drawn form music, television and film. (The details of MTV's emergence and its evolutionary phases will be discussed in greater detail in Chapter Four.)

The rise of niche-oriented cable networks signaled a new phase in televi-sion and the ways in which television audiences were conceptualized. As a con-sequence, Hollywood's attempts at targeting teens shifted from mainstream, network-based activities (last witnessed when ABC established itself by target-ing the baby boomer teen audience as part of a broader, mainstream interest in young families) to narrower, more marginalized efforts centered on the launch of new cable networks. Amidst these industrial developments and tech-nological innovations, as the traditional network broadcast television system adjusted to the rise of cable, the more traditional forms of teen media enter-tainment, particularly the film industry, continued to service youth and teen audiences in the 1970s and early 1980s. The period witnessed the rising popu-larity of film sub-genres such as teen slasher films and the high-school roman-tic comedies most often associated with director John Hughes.

Hollywood and Teen Media in the Age of Multi-Media Conglomeration: 1985–1995

Hollywood in the 1980s was characterized by a turn towards heightened multi-media conglomeration motivated by a growing deregulatory environ-ment in the United States. This shift, alongside the rapid growth of cable tech-

nology, paved the way for the emergence of another new youth-oriented entertainment platform, the FOX television network, and the continuing growth of
the MTV cable network, media sites that became synonymous with commercial youth/teen culture in the late 1980s and the early '90s.

The 1980s wave of mergers and acquisitions is significant because it marked
the industry's shift away from loose diversification (in which the major film
studios were absorbed into corporations largely engaged in a range of non-
media related corporate activities) towards a strategy of tight diversification,
in which these same conglomerates began divesting themselves of their non-
media holdings while expanding their interests in strictly media, entertainment and information-oriented industries. The period was marked by a series
of high-profile mergers between communications and entertainment behemoths intent upon expanding their interests across multiple media outlets and
in so doing, increasing their share of the media marketplace. Much of this activity was motivated by the wave of deregulation under the Reagan administration. Newly relaxed media ownership rules and legislation began eroding many
of the pre-existing legal constraints that prohibited media corporations from
expanding both vertically and horizontally. News Corp.'s multi-media expansion in 1985 is representative of these larger trends and activities within Hollywood during the 1980s and '90s.

Rupert Murdoch's News Corp., which began as an Australian-based
publishing conglomerate, initiated the shift towards heightened multi-media
conglomeration when it purchased 20th Century–Fox in 1985 and launched
the FOX television network a year later as part of a plan for a multimedia,
global, entertainment conglomerate. Murdoch's purchase of 20th Century–
Fox and subsequent launch of the FOX network would have been in breach
of existing legislative and FCC rules. However, Murdoch circumvented
the problem by arguing that FOX should be exempt, since it programmed
less than fifteen hours a week and thus could not be considered a full-fledged
television network. Furthermore, Murdoch also argued that since FOX was
not a mature television network, it should not be subject to the Fin/
Syn regulations that prohibited network owners to own the shows they broadcast.[34]

Murdoch's success with these arguments reflect the climate of increasing
deregulation at the time, a product of a White House administration sympathetic to the interests of big business. Consequently, although News Corp.'s
ownership of 20th Century–Fox Studios, which produced television programs
that it then distributed via its FOX television network, and exhibited on its
owned and operated television stations, was clearly a vertically-integrated company, it was able to circumvent all the existing anti-trust regulations. The FCC
even waived the Newspaper/Television Cross-Ownership Prohibition Rule in
Murdoch's favor.[35] By the time Murdoch launched FOX, he was even able to
take advantage of the FCC's revised ruling that allowed broadcasting compa-

nies to increase its station ownership to twelve,[36] thereby reaping even greater profits from the enterprise,[37] all the while eluding the constraints that were placed on its other network competitors. These events eased the way for Murdoch to create "the world's first global television, publishing and entertainment operation."[38]

The launch of the FOX network had a direct impact on teen culture of the period. Having successfully navigated past FCC regulations and gotten on the air, FOX was faced with the challenge of finding an audience. Postulating that the major broadcast networks were underserving younger audiences, FOX, not unlike ABC before it, decided to target the youth demographic. FOX's commitment to a narrower, niche audience was in keeping with the marketplace's increasing interest in more specialized demographic subgroups. Interestingly, while FOX decided to skew young, it did not focus primarily on the high-school set, targeting instead, the slightly older college-age viewer. FOX's senior vice president of research and marketing, Andrew Fessel, called college students "the opinion leader audience. They're the first to explore the dial."[39]

FOX's interest in youth demographics led to the debut of the 20th Century–Fox produced, youth-focused, *21 Jump Street* (1987–1991), a series about youthful police officers who worked undercover at high schools and colleges. The animated cartoon *The Simpsons* (1990–) and the teen-oriented *Beverly Hills, 90210* also appeared on the FOX schedule. While *The Simpsons* presented a distinctly irreverent youth perspective, portraying the adventures of a dysfunctional family and focusing on the main character, Bart, a hyperactive, anti-authoritarian young boy, *Beverly Hills, 90210* was aimed more specifically at the high-school contingent (at least in the series' early years). Exploring teenage twins Brenda and Brandon Walsh's experiences after moving to Beverly Hills from Minnesota, the show was patterned after primetime dramatic soap operas, but with a distinctly teenage spin. Although FOX was replicating ABC's strategy of targeting youth audiences, one significant difference between the two lies in the fact that in the 1950s, ABC was prohibited from producing or owning the shows it broadcast. In the mid–1980s, the shows broadcast on the FOX television network were produced and owned by 20th Century–Fox.

News Corp.'s success in harnessing the synergistic and profit potential of a tightly diversified, horizontally and vertically integrated media enterprise prompted other companies to engage in a rising wave of mergers and acquisitions in the 1980s and '90s. Warner Communications' changing industrial activities provide a prime example of this shift in corporate practice. Before the 1980s, Warner Communications was a loosely diversified trans-industrial conglomerate with diverse holdings in a range of "leisure-oriented" industries including entertainment, cosmetics, sports teams, toys, restaurants and other non-media firms. In 1982, the corporation decided to restructure and consolidate its interests in entertainment-oriented media. Consequently, Warner sold off its interests in Atari, Warner Cosmetics, the Franklin Mint, Panavision, and the New York Cosmos soccer team. This allowed Warner Communications to focus its interests in the production and distribution of film and television programming, recorded music and publishing.[40] In 1986, Warner Communications, with its film, television and music holdings, expanded its multi-media interests by merging with publishing giant, Time Inc. Other media corporations also engaged in a series of mergers and acquisitions. In 1989, Sony expanded into film, television and music when it purchased Columbia and CBS Records, while Viacom, whose ownership interests included radio, cable, and television services, acquired Paramount Studios in 1994.

These industrial, technological and cultural developments resulted in the marginalization of youth and their culture/entertainment. Both Thomas Schatz and Justin Wyatt have examined how these industrial changes in the '70s and '80s led to the rise of a "New," post-classical Hollywood studio system.[41] As both Schatz and Wyatt point out, the rising multi-media interests of the post-classical Hollywood studio directly impacted the nature of the film texts as well as the ancillary products associated with these films. The entertainment content generated by this "New Hollywood" was characterized by a turn towards big-budget, high-concept films targeted at mass audiences, and an increasing focus on the marketing and promotion of these films.

Furthermore, as entertainment corporations expanded their interests into other entertainment media, they discovered new ancillary product lines, and new markets to exploit. The New Hollywood of the late 1980s and early 1990s, in which popular entertainment texts began to integrate the styles and content characteristic of other media formats in the interests of enhancing marketing and promotional opportunities, represent the commencement of specific industrial, aesthetic, and textual practices that would gain increased momentum and heightened effectiveness in succeeding decades. These particular practices would evolve and be adopted and adapted to target the increasingly significant niche/teen audiences in the millennium.

Throughout the 1980s and early 1990s, MTV and News Corp.'s youth-oriented FOX network continued Hollywood's relationship with teenagers, even as teen culture was increasingly relegated to the margins of popular culture. This marginalization coincided with the decline in the numbers of teenagers during this period. According to demographer David K. Foot, the American birthrate experienced a distinct decline between 1967 and 1979, which translated into reduced numbers of teenagers in the 1980s and early 1990s.[42] Lacking the figures to constitute any sizable critical mass, Hollywood's interest in youth was largely limited to the young adult set, while the teen market was generally ignored during this period. It would take a few years before the numbers of children aging into their teenage years would become significant enough to attract the attention of marketers, advertisers and the media industry.

Hollywood and Teen Media in the Millennium

As noted earlier, the dominant industrial traits that typify Hollywood in the millennium, namely, multi-media media convergence, market fragmentation, the increasing significance of new media technologies, and global expansion, had their roots and origins in earlier decades. However, by the turn of the twenty-first century, Hollywood's commitment to these ideals and practices had escalated in terms of both scope and activity, as explored in the following pages.

Corporate Consolidation (or Multi-Media Conglomeration) and Multi-Media Fragmentation

In the last five years of the twentieth century, the wave of media mergers and acquisitions surged. This period witnessed three of the largest media mergers in history. The first "mega-merger" took place in 1995 when Disney bought Capital Cities/ABC for, at that time, an unprecedented $19 billion. This amount, and the size of the merger, was eclipsed in 1999 when Viacom merged with CBS in a deal that amounted to $38 billion. This merger was itself dwarfed by the AOL merger with Time Warner in 2000, in a $166 billion deal that led to the creation of one of the largest media companies in the world.

These instances of corporate conglomeration are inextricably linked to deregulation and media fragmentation. In the 1990s and 2000s, legislators began another round of deregulations raising the opportunity for the media industries to finally expand without restrictions.[43] At the same time, technological developments resulted in an increasing line of media products and platforms offering opportunities for further expansions of the media marketplace. Media corporations, fearing competition, began to expand into any and every (potentially) related form of entertainment media available. One key consequence of this escalating media consolidation was the emergence of a handful of multi-media giants that controlled a steadily increasing range of media outlets and products. Ben Bagdikian's *The Media Monopoly* highlights the heightened degree of corporate media consolidation that took place within the culture industries in the later half of the twentieth century and the resulting concentration of media control under a small number of corporations. The trend towards media consolidation made it increasingly difficult to identify the dominant firms in each separate medium. After the 1980s, a steadily decreasing number of corporations began to dominate and control an expanding range of media forms including newspapers, magazines, books, radio, television, films, and even retail. By 2004, six multi-media conglomerates dominated the global media market and ranked among the largest corporations in the world.[44] These shifts reshaped the industries' conceptualization of the commodity-text and how economic interests impacted the strategies of promoting the text itself.

An intriguing consequence of the intensifying conglomeration of the media industries was the increasing fragmentation of the market and the multiplication of media texts and products through the 1980s and beyond. As multi-media conglomerates continued to expand further into new entertainment media and technology, they became more active and efficient in parsing out and exploiting the existing media/entertainment markets. Media scholars including Ben Bagdikian, Eileen Meehan, and Thomas Schatz have noted that as the number of media corporations shrink with each announced merger/buyout/consolidation, the number of media platforms and product lines on the market have been expanding.[45]

The motivation for the diversification of the multi-media product line is simple: the wider the range of media platforms a conglomerate owns, the greater the opportunities for leveraging a single concept across this range of media via the practices of multi-purposing, repackaging, and cross-promoting. Theoretically, this means that a multi-media conglomerate could exploit, and profit from, a single entertainment concept/show across multiple outlets including a broadcast network, several cable networks, sold as videos/DVDs, streamed online, etc.[46] Expanding multi-media corporations such as News Corp., Disney, Time Warner and Viacom became better poised to manipulate and profit from the continual expansion of the product line, and adapted new ways to promote and sell them. The term most commonly employed to describe these particular activities is "synergy."

Synergy

Synergy is a concept predicated on diversification. In the business of media entertainment, it occurs when a corporation recognizes the potential of owning a wide range of related media holdings and platforms that can then be further leveraged by having each holding co-promote and extend the increasingly linked media products in an expanding line. It basically refers to the process of exploiting the profit-potential "brought about by the cross-marketing of a commodity or related commodities in multiple media."[47] This practice of spinning out an entertainment product across multiple media outlets, the better to exploit the numerous branches of a multi-media corporation, highlights another key characteristic of the American culture industries in the late twentieth century. Multimedia conglomeration encouraged the culture industries to turn towards increasingly sophisticated practices of synergy to better exploit the promotional and marketing opportunities that accrued from blurring the boundaries of media texts rather than maintaining the integrity of a media figure as a commodity in a single medium.

The turn towards diversification, even as the media industries continued to merge, was accompanied by changing perceptions of what constituted the commodity media text. As Thomas Schatz observes, the increasing degree of deregulation that ushered in the age of multi-media conglomeration, led to a significant reconceptualization of the entertainment text,

> The ideal [entertainment product/text] today is ... [a] promotion for a multimedia product line, designed with the structure of both the parent company and the diversified media marketplace in mind. ... the New Hollywood has been driven (and shaped) by multipurpose entertainment machines which breed movie sequels and TV series, music videos and sound track albums, video games and theme park rides, graphic novels and comic books, and an endless array of licensed tie-ins and brand-name consumer products.[48]

The combined impulse towards conglomeration and product diversification in turn resulted in the dominance of "the franchise" which

> ... comprises a profitable product line and a cultural commodity whose form directly reflects the structure of the media industry at large. It indicates, too, that the industry can scarcely be treated in terms of movies and video games and theme-park rides as separate entities or isolated media texts. Rather, they are related aspects, or "iterations" of entertainment supertexts, multimedia narrative forms which can be expanded and exploited almost ad infinitum, given the size and diversity of today's globalized, diversified entertainment industry.[49]

As these corporations expanded their interests into numerous forms of entertainment media including film, television, music, publishing, and retail, they became better poised to profit from the continual expansion of the product line.

There are significant benefits from spinning a single entertainment concept into a wide range of related media texts that can be accessed and experienced in multiple ways. One obvious and increasingly important benefit is impact. As the media environment gets progressively more complex and fragmented, and attracting and retaining audience attention becomes increasingly more difficult, launching a single product across multiple platforms is one effective way of cutting through the media clutter.

Within youth culture, this resulted in an ever-expanding list of linked products in a variety of media, all of which originate from a single hit concept. Certainly, millennial teen media's practice of exploiting multi-media opportunities is hardly original. Teen entertainment culture has a long tradition of extending a popular concept across different mediums, and exploiting the potential benefits gained from transplanting a popular product across multiple delivery platforms. The traditional practice was to simply translate a hit entertainment concept from one format to another. For instance, as mentioned earlier, in the 1950s and '60s, *Gidget* evolved from a novel into a series of successful films and then a television series.

In these earlier cases, the repackaging of a concept followed a hierarchical approach — a popular novel would become a hit teen film, which would generate a television show, whose success would lead to merchandizing deals in a linear, chronological process that would often occur over a significant period of time. Restrained by the media regulations of the period, these repackaging activities often entailed separate arrangements between the different media entities involved. Where synergistic opportunities emerged, these tended to be of a relatively limited scope. The radio and television versions of *The Aldrich Family*, for instance, were created by sponsors who acquired the broadcast services of NBC. But, no corporate links existed between the program sponsors, NBC, or the theater producers who staged the Broadway show. Columbia Pictures reaped the profits from *Gidget*'s popularity across both film and television, since the movie studios had settled into the approved role as producers and suppliers of television programs to the networks. In this case, the television series was licensed to ABC and the production studio had to await syndication before it could profit from producing the show.

In the 1990s and after, Hollywood clearly continued the practice of repackaging content across different media platforms. However, the industrial changes wrought by multi-media conglomeration led to distinctly new and vastly heightened synergistic strategies. Within the increasingly tightly integrated multimedia conglomerates of the 1990s and 2000s, synergistic activities ceased to occur in a linear, chronological manner, evolving into a tightly synchronized scheme in which a single entertainment concept was immediately and simultaneously developed to launch on multiple media platforms. In the millennium, many teen texts were concurrently devised as teen films with the potential to spawn film sequels, television series with the possibility for spin-offs, soundtracks and music videos, even extending into merchandise including clothing, books and magazines.

Many millennial teen texts were simultaneous launches that functioned in very different ways than the media roll-outs of teen films in the 1960s, television shows in the 1970s or music videos in the 1980s, which had a clear hierarchy of intents and interests and explicitly positioned a single media text as the origin of the process.[50] In the millennium, the premiere of Disney-owned *Camp Rock*, in addition to being broadcast over multiple (Disney-owned) platforms, was linked to the simultaneous launch of a wider array of other related Disney-produced and owned teen texts that included music videos, *Camp Rock* soundtracks, concert tours and CDs featuring the show's stars, and other related merchandise.

What is interesting, however, is that Hollywood did not adopt this form of the simultaneous multi-product spin-off as its only or dominant technique to target and exploit the millennial teen market. In fact, many of the extremely popular teen films released between 1996 and 2009 were never remade as television shows in the tradition of *Gidget*. Instead, millennial teen media is also characterized by a "looser," if more complex, multi-media interaction across a wide range of often *unrelated* texts. The television episode of *Dawson's Creek* that consciously and overtly references the slasher film *Scream* is one example. The film and the television series are entirely separate entertainment entities insofar as they have no characters in common, belong to different genres, and appear in separate mediums. Despite these disparities, however, the film and the TV episode "The Scare" were deliberately linked by a range of intertextual references, shared aesthetic elements, as well as narrative shifts and interactions that function to draw these previously unrelated texts together, and insert them into a larger cultural phenomenon. Thus, one factor that distinguishes the millennial teen cycle from previous ones is the simultaneous emergence of a range of teen texts across a wide array of media that have obvious links with each other, even though they are not spin-offs in the traditional mode. This particular strategy is examined in greater detail in the next chapter.

In the late 1990s and early 2000s, new technological advances that were sweeping the media exacerbated the blurring of media boundaries alongside the collapse of media-specific aesthetic and stylistic qualities and communications landscape.

New Media/Digital Technologies and the Trend Towards Convergence

In January 2000, when AOL merged with Time Warner, it was announced as the largest "high-tech-meets-media-merger" in American corporate history.[51] Discourses describing the event hailed it as the timely marriage between traditional twentieth century media, represented by Time Warner's established position as the producer and distributor of traditional media, and the increasingly significant new media technologies of the twenty-first century, epitomized by AOL's interests in digital technologies as a new communication system.[52] This marriage of "old" and new media was expected to catapult both companies into a new arena that merged the two increasingly related businesses of media and communications, a maneuver that would offer AOL Time Warner significant new opportunities for greater synergies across its new holdings. Industry and media watchers predicted that this would have serious consequences for the ways in which information and entertainment would be produced, distributed and consumed.[53] At the heart of these lies the significant potential for multi-media convergence offered by new digital technologies that have the ability to promote convergence by erasing key differences in the ways entertainment texts and products are created, distributed, accessed and experienced.

Up until the 1970s, despite the increasing turn towards multi-media convergence and integration embraced by the industry, some medium-specific boundaries still existed that distinguished certain forms of entertainment from others. Film was predominantly enjoyed in the movie theatres where images captured on celluloid were projected on a big screen. Television was still the dominant mode of entertainment in the home, where television shows (and live events) were broadcast over the airwaves. Recorded music could be purchased and played back on magnetic audiotape. Although music was heard on both film and television shows, and motion pictures were available on television, there were still distinctive markers (in terms of delivery format, mode of consumption/experience, and in some cases, content and aesthetics) that identified and differentiated one entertainment medium from another. The rise of the digital age removed many of these defining characteristics.

Format Convergence: The Importance of Software

Digital technology is distinguished by the reliance on binary codes to store any and all forms of information. Digital technology reduces data in any format, whether it is an image, text or sound, into a series of 1s or 0s. Storing and transmitting any and all information in this binary format effectively erases any differences between diverse media forms. A digital file makes no distinctions between the kind/type of information, the content, or the medium. Whether the information takes textual, visual or aural form, consisted of still or moving images, all information is stored as a running series of "1"s or "0"s. Thus, the pre-existing boundaries between traditionally separate forms of media (film vs. video, still vs. moving image, visual vs. aural, broadcast vs. cable) are completely irrelevant in the digital age when any media text can (and increasingly does) exist as a string of binary codes recorded as a digital file. These advances in digital technology have made Internet movies, interactive television and downloadable music a reality. This instance of format convergence has led to the rise of new entertainment platforms that have changed how audiences/consumers access, consume and experience their popular entertainment.

The Internet Age: Getting Caught in the World Wide Web

In existence since the 1960s, the Internet is basically a global network of computers. This increasingly complex system of interconnected computers emerged as a particularly efficient means of transferring and delivering packets of digital data across these connections. The public's appreciation of the Internet's true potential is largely a result of the emergence of the World Wide Web (www), which consists of information sites that exist in cyberspace, accessed via the Internet. The first websites went online in 1991 and the subsequent development of browsers that allowed the public to search for what they wanted from the vast number of websites effectively changed the way people accessed and received their information.

In the early 1990s, "surfing the web" was largely restricted to the quest for information, which tended to be presented primarily in a textual format, due to limitations in the bandwidth. At the time, technological limits on available bandwidth meant that delivery speeds were dependent on the size of the digital file. While smaller files could be delivered quickly and efficiently, large files would severely retard delivery speed. It was not until the development of broadband as a global distribution technology that the Internet's potential and power as an information and entertainment network surfaced.

The Internet and the World Wide Web in the millennium benefited from the potential of democratized packaging and the ubiquity of the distribution network.[54] Democratized packaging refers to digital files that reduce all information, regardless of the original form or format, into binary codes. These files could then be distributed across the Internet and then decoded into its original format when it was received. The development of broadband, with its significantly enhanced delivery speed, has removed the initial limitations on the size of the digital file that can be efficiently delivered. In the broadband age, huge digital files (such as films and other entertainment texts) are increasingly available and accessible. This development, alongside the global growth of the Internet itself has meant that national delivery systems such as television and radio, with its geographic limitations, are now limited in ways that the Internet is not. Democratized packaging, an ubiquitous distribution system, and superior delivery speeds has had the effect of transforming any digital media device, almost anywhere in the world, into a multi-media entertainment and information hub.

The Age of the Multi-Media Device

Before the arrival of the digital age, distinct forms of entertainment media were experienced on different platforms and accessed through different devices, but in the millennium, with the potential for format convergence offered by digital technology, the age of the digital multi-media device had arrived. Entertainment content, whether it was a film, a television show, an audio recording, a computer game, or a printed page, was being accessed increasingly via the personal computer and on personal, often mobile, digital devices such as cellular phones, MP4 players and PDAs (Personal Digital Assistants). The ability to convert all information to a digital format and then distribute that digital file across computer networks led to the personal computer's evolution into a multi-media entertainment hub. In the millennium, the computer became a device that allowed users/audiences/consumers virtually unlimited access to multiple forms of media entertainment including movies, television shows, music, computer games, and online versions of traditional print media. This single device had the potential to make traditional home-media appliances obsolete, but the personal computer is not the only multi-media device changing how entertainment is accessed and consumed in the millennium.

As technology has evolved, entertainment has become increasingly portable and mobile. Hand-held devices, such as iPods, cell-phones and other mobile entertainment devices have gained popularity, giving users a growing number of ways to experience and consume various forms of media entertainment in virtually unlimited locations.[55] In light of these developments, any attempt at tracing how an increasingly multi-media integrated Hollywood has adapted its creative activities with regard to traditional media, such as film, television and music, must also focus on the strategies the industry has adopted to exploit a growing range of new media, including digital video streaming, online social networking sites and mobile media platforms.

According to *Advertising Age*, in 2007, only 23 percent of younger adults prefer to watch videos on television. 36 percent of those aged 18 to 24, have reported "that the [personal computer] is competing with the television for their entertainment time" with "almost a quarter of online Americans [believing] that the Internet is the future of video viewing, with younger adults expressing more confidence in that prediction."[56] According to the Online Publishers Association's analysis of Internet activity, the amount of time Internet users spent with online content rose from 34 percent in 2003, to 47 percent in 2007.[57] A 2007 *Los Angeles Times* report highlighted that for the first time, "nearly half of all teenagers bought no compact discs," and as a consequence, "the number of CDs sold in the US fell 19% in 2007 from the previous year, while sales of digital songs jumped 45%" according to Nielsen SoundScan.[58]

These statistics suggest that audiences in general, and youth and teenagers in particular, are shifting away from traditional means of accessing and consuming media, and embracing the new possibilities offered by digital technologies. As a consequence of these new technological developments, and the innovations they offer, youth are increasingly developing a different relationship with entertainment in terms of how they access their content and how they experience it. For instance, television, with its regularly scheduled programming is no longer the form of delivery that teens prefer. Instead, with digital technologies and the Internet, teens/youth appear to prefer a more fluid, less structured way of consuming, accessing and defining their entertainment. This suggests that the media conglomerates interested in targeting the teen/youth demographic, must discover ways to expand into and experiment with the newly emerging delivery platforms.

As the distribution platforms for media texts have expanded in line with the growth of these new technologies, the ability to experience and consume a single media text in myriad ways, in multiple forms and at various geographical locations, has become a reality. As access to entertainment and information, and the range of products and platforms have multiplied, the need to create enough impact to make a product stand out has intensified. Increasingly, only the huge multimedia conglomerates appear to possess the capital, the media holdings and the global access to achieve the critical mass necessary. Yet, despite the significant holdings amassed by the multi-media Hollywood conglomerates, the drive towards greater industrial convergence continues.

Industrial Convergence

The development of digital technologies has brought the fields of media, computing and telecommunications into close proximity and interaction. The profit potential of dominating a digital world is tremendous, and has sent corporations in all these related areas scrambling for increased market share, seeking out potential means of expanding into areas in which they do not yet have a significant influence. This is certainly the case with the multi-media conglomerates that are expanding their holdings into any and every emerging technology and platform potentially compatible with and supportive of their entertainment interests, including the digital front. As a consequence, the boundaries between traditional media communications, computers and telecommunications are steadily collapsing. In the millennium, cable service providers (many of them owned by multi-media conglomerates, such as Time Warner Cable), are offering phone services and Internet access, while computer software firms are collaborating with cable companies to deliver cable-based media and communications access.[59]

Globalization

A final key characteristic of millennial Hollywood is the growing world dominance of the largest media conglomerates, including News Corp., Time Warner, Disney and Viacom. According to Robert McChesney, the "most striking development in the 1990s has been the emergence of a *global* commercial media market, utilizing new technologies and the global trend towards deregulation."[60] While Hollywood has always appreciated the value of accessing a global audience, a number of developments in the 1990s and after have made the practice particularly lucrative and increasingly significant to the corporate bottom line.

Over the decades, a series of technological advances have helped spur Hollywood's increasing global influence. In the 1970s, the launch of communication satellites and the development of cable television paved the way for the export of popular Hollywood product. MTV, one of the most established teen brands in the world, began as a cable network launched in the United States in 1981. As cable and satellite technology penetrated into overseas markets, MTV began its global expansion in 1987 when it launched MTV Europe. By 2007, MTV Networks International (the global arm of MTV) operated over 130 channels cablecast in 25 languages that attracted a global viewership of over one billion.[61] The Disney Corporation, another company with a vested interest in the youth and young adult market has also expanded its global interests. In the early 1990s, Disney's international interests were largely restricted to English-language markets such as Britain and Australia, but in 1995, it launched a Chinese language Disney Channel headquartered in Taiwan.[62] Subsequent international expansions have continued into non–English markets. Between January and June of 2005, the Disney Channel launched new services in Asia, including Cambodia, Palau, Thailand and Vietnam.[63] More recently, the rise of commercial broadband and digital technologies has continued to expand the reach and influence of the American multi-media conglomerates.

Hollywood's growing interest in global markets has also been motivated by the saturation of domestic markets, a situation that has encouraged media companies to look overseas in their ongoing attempts at sustaining corporate and market growth. In addition, the vast holdings and financial resources of these huge media conglomerates make them especially well-equipped to take on smaller, less well-financed local media companies in other markets. While overseas local media producers are often hampered by the limited nature of their markets, a condition that severely limits the revenues and subsequent production budgets of these local companies, the American conglomerates have access to the largest (American) media market in the world, the profits from which help finance the production of content that is far superior to much of the entertainment content that is produced locally in other countries. The fact that revenue from international markets can be gained at very little additional expense to these media conglomerates (since the costs of content production is largely incurred in upfront activities[64]), makes these international markets particularly attractive.[65]

As American media conglomerates expand their operations and holdings into more and more overseas markets, they are able to increase their influence and power by benefitting from the significant revenues from these markets, while also influencing the perceptions, behaviors and attitudes of audiences in these markets. Douglas Kellner has argued that popular media culture, such as television, has become a dominant means for "integrating individuals into the social order, celebrating social values," by offering "models of thought, behavior, and gender for imitation."[66] As media corporations export an increasing range of popular media products abroad, the values, identities and behaviors advocated by these media texts are likely to have a significant influence on teen audiences potentially susceptible to the ideological messages and identities depicted in these commercial media texts. Just what these messages are, how they are expressed and portrayed, and how they are influenced and shaped by the complex entity that is Hollywood in the millennium is the focus of the next chapter.

The re-emergence of the teen demographic in the millennium coincided with a series of industrial, technological and cultural shifts that would have a deep impact on how this increasingly significant demographic market would be targeted, serviced and entertained. In millennial Hollywood, conglomeration has resulted in increasing multi-media convergence at the same time as new technologies have emerged, leading to the development of new media outlets and media products. Consequently, a shrinking number of steadily expanding multi-media corporations produce, own and control an expanding majority of media products. The commitment to synergy and leveraging on the cross-promotional opportunities offered by these multi-media holdings are dissolving the traditional boundaries between distinct and separate media industries, resulting in the emergence of more integrated multi-media texts.

These qualities have a direct impact on the discussions of teen media addressed in the following chapters. What are the defining characteristics of the millennial teen media text? How have they been shaped by the changing structure and organization of the Hollywood conglomerates? How have the emergence of new media technologies and delivery platforms affected media content and aesthetics? These are the key questions addressed in the next chapter.

THREE

The Millennial Teen Media Text

During the 2000–2001 television season, the teen-branded WB television network premiered *Popstars*, a reality series tracking the creation of a pop group called Eden's Crush. The series, produced in association with music producer/songwriter David Foster, featured a week by week exploration of the group's formation, from the multiple rounds of auditions to the selection of the final members, the rehearsals for their musical performances, the recording of their first single and the filming of the group's music video. The WB further promoted the group by having them appear and perform on other WB teen television series such as *Sabrina the Teenage Witch*.

This enterprise is a representative case study in how corporate and multimedia synergies were exploited to effectively target the teen demographic. While the Time Warner–owned WB network broadcast the reality series tracing the group's creation and provided sustained on-air promotion for the album and single, Warner Music Group's WEA/London-Sire Records, a division of Time Warner, produced and released the group's album. Aided by this intense promotional commitment, Eden's Crush's first single, "Get Over Yourself," went to number one on the American music charts. The song's video also went into heavy rotation on MTV, and the group appeared on the cable network to further promote their single, gaining Eden's Crush, *Popstars* and the WB additional exposure with the cable network's teen audience. *Popstars* is an example of the quintessential millennial teen media event. No longer restricted to a single, isolated media product, commercial teen media in the millennium is a simultaneously launched multi-media, multi-platform, multiple product line, very often owned by a single media conglomerate intent on exploiting its varied media holdings to better target and profit from a valuable consumer demographic, yet also participating in a range of collaborative promotional opportunities involving other teen media sites and companies.

To fully appreciate the increasingly complex nature, form and content of the millennial teen media texts, we must acknowledge the equally complicated structures and features of the entertainment industries that created these texts. The "echo boom" teen market emerged amidst a specific set of social, industrial and technological conditions that directly shaped both the business activities adopted to cater to this demographic, and the media products aimed at the teen market. As highlighted in Chapter Two, another cycle of mergers and acquisitions had gained momentum in the mid–1990s, marking another stark expansion phase for the existing multimedia conglomerates. In the final decade of the twentieth century, already powerful entertainment conglomerates continued to expand their holdings in film studios, television production, television stations, cable systems, book/magazine/comics publishing and recorded music, amongst others. This increased industrial convergence allowed a shrinking number of multimedia giants to diversify into and dominate sectors of the growing entertainment and communications market. This heightened frequency of mergers and acquisitions equipped these increasingly diversified conglomerates with the financial base from which to expand their activities globally.[1] The 1990s and 2000s were also characterized by developments in digital, satellite and computer communications technologies, technological developments that directly supported global expansion by offering efficient and effective ways of traversing geographical distances and crossing national borders. How exactly did these developments affect millennial teen media texts? The following discussion of the dominant characteristics of millennial teen media illustrates the intricate ways in which these industrial, technological and cultural shifts shaped the millennial teen texts across a wide range of media and contexts.

Niche Markets and Targeted Formats: Catering to Teens

Joseph Turow's *Breaking Up America: Advertisers and the New Media World* notes that advertisers and the media industries began shifting their attention away from mass markets towards more focused, niche markets in the late 1970s, motivated by a complex range of social, technological and media and market industry-oriented factors occurring in the 1960s and 1970s.[2] The emerging civil rights and feminist movements that coincided with the rise of the psychedelic era of the 1960s, and the subsequent events of the Vietnam War in the 1970s, steadily undermined the dominant perception of the United States as a homogenous society united in a common purpose that had prevailed into the 1950s. These shifts resulted in a growing sense of social and cultural fragmentation in the wake of a growing range of alternative ideologies and lifestyles during the period. A key feature of these alternative perspectives was a fundamental swing from a commitment to ideas of larger, collective interests, towards a preference for individualism. Growing affluence also led to an emerging propensity for self-indulgence that reinforced the turn towards individualism and the growing belief that social and lifestyle differences should be recognized and acknowledged, not least by the dominant players in the culture industries.[3]

In the wake of these social and cultural changes, a series of technological and structural developments were taking place within the media, advertising, and marketing industries. Through the 1970s and '80s, audience and consumer research companies, including A. C. Nielsen, were instituting more sophisti-

cated ways of measuring and parsing out audience and consumer demographics.[4] This was also the period when debates were circulating about the compar-
ative value of targeting a mass, undifferentiated audience, and adopting a more
focused approach that could isolate the "quality" audience/consumer that was
likely to have a greater disposable income and more efficient access to
consumer goods.[5] This conceptual shift coincided with the rise of cable networks that chose to distinguish themselves from their broadcast counterparts,
who traditionally catered to a mass, undifferentiated audience, by focusing
on narrowcasting to a select, niche audience instead. By the 1980s, marketers
and advertisers' were convinced of the value of serving narrower demographics.

Turow describes the increasing complicity between advertisers and the
mainstream media to fragment and segment the American consumer market
as part of their pursuit of greater profits and more efficient methods of advertising and selling. This growing interest in niche markets encouraged the media,
particularly those segments dependent on advertiser support, to engage in
strategic attempts at attracting the distinct demographic segments that most
appealed to advertisers. Turow argues that the turn towards niche audiences
and targeted markets forced competing media to focus upon increasingly specialized formats that would project the ideal identity that would attract "the
right audience" and consumers, while simultaneously "urging the people who
do not fit the desired lifestyle profile *not* to be part of the audience."[6] Successful formats would make "the community more pure and thereby more efficient
for advertisers" and consumers.[7] In tracing the situation, Turow highlights how
the interests in niche markets "guide the way [advertisers and the media] create formats and content for the media systems" and how the relationship
between market interests and media content was particularly significant within
this specific context.[8] Turow goes on to argue that "the desire to label people
so that they may be separated into primary media communities is transforming the way television is programmed, the way newspapers are 'zoned,' the way
magazines are printed, and the way cultural events are produced and promoted."[9] These developments are directly relevant to teen culture in the millennium.

As discussed in Chapter One, the emergence of a significant teen demographic in the midst of an economic boom in the United States caused networks and advertisers to focus their attention on the long neglected teen
demographic and to view teenagers and youth as a valuable demographic market deserving of focused media and marketplace attention. Interest in niche
audiences had a distinct impact on the style and format of the commercial teen
media text. To more efficiently attract and profit from this growing demographic market, Hollywood needed to create entertainment products with the distinct content, style and form that would appeal to a new generation of teenagers.

Media producers keen on servicing Generation Y's entertainment interests needed to recognize the range of qualities, values, and behaviors this generation embraced. One noteworthy quality is the millennial teen audience's relationship with media and technology. This was the first generation to come of age in a world of cable, VCRs, computers and digital technology, all of which offered them the greatest degree of access to all forms of media. With this increased access, millennial teenagers had surpassed previous generations in their awareness of, and exposure to, both past and contemporary media texts. This easy access to classic films and television shows on cable and video, and classic pop radio stations, has helped encourage Generation Y's familiarity with film, television and music history. Given their heightened access and exposure to media information and entertainment, and the central role that entertainment texts and the media play in the teen lifestyle, echo boomers and millennial teens possessed a heightened media-oriented consciousness. As such, the millennial teen audience was more likely to respond to texts that acknowledged their specific perspectives and catered to their needs. Their exposure to and familiarity with media entertainment would have a profound impact upon the ways in which the culture industries proceeded to attract and cater to the echo boom's entertainment preferences and interests.

In the late 1990s, advertisers' and networks' interest in teen niche audiences had a distinct impact on the content, style and format of the Hollywood entertainment text. In attempting to appeal to this new generation of teenagers, Hollywood adopted a series of narrative, stylistic and aesthetic decisions across the range of entertainment media that were directly aimed at attracting the increasingly valuable teen audience.

Millennial Teen Media: An Overview

A cursory survey of millennial teen media culture reveals several noteworthy characteristics,

1. the intensive exploitation of multimedia synergies in the wake of the heightened media conglomeration of the 1990s;
2. the increasing importance of branding as a promotional activity, resulting in the emergence of the branded teen text;
3. the evolution of the multi-media teen-branded personality who easily and consistently "crossed-over" between different media;
4. the intensification of stylistic and aesthetic convergence across the range of multi-media, marked by the collapsing boundaries between film, television, music and music-video texts; and,
5. the turn towards postmodern "hyper-"intertextuality, indicated by a notable degree of interaction and cross-referencing across multiple teen media texts.

Some of these characteristics can be traced back to earlier attempts to attract and cater to previous cycles of teenagers. Yet in almost every instance, these practices have either intensified or evolved further in response to changes in the media industry, the arrival of new technologies, or social and cultural developments, all of which have had a manifest impact on the form and content of millennial teen entertainment texts. Any attempt to understand the contemporary teen phenomenon requires an examination of how Hollywood has marshaled its increasingly intricate corporate structures, navigated the terrain of newly emerging technologies, and recognized the specific interests and behaviors of the millennial teen consumer, to re-shape the teen entertainment text in its attempt to target the profitable teen market.

The Synergistic, Multi-Media
Teen Entertainment Product

The first striking characteristic of the millennial teen entertainment experience, one borne out by the *Popstars* event that opened this chapter, is the synchronized extension of a single entertainment concept into multiple media streams. In the millennium, a typical teen-oriented media text was seldom restricted to a single media artifact. Rather, it consisted of a complex product line that included a mix of various interlinked components across a range of media formats. This particular development can be traced to the surge in multimedia conglomeration in the 1980s and 1990s that allowed corporations to expand their holdings and interests into film, television, music, publishing, retail and the Internet. This led the media industries towards an increasing commitment to exploit the promotional and marketing opportunities that accrued from repackaging a single media concept across as wide a range of media products and platforms as possible. In the millennium, any teen entertainment concept could, and often would, simultaneously exist as an interconnected web of entertainment products that included a film or television series with links to a range of other multi-media spin-offs that often included soundtrack releases, comic books or novelizations, a related online website, a computer game, and other merchandise, a corporate practice referred to as synergy.

One example of a successful, synergistic, multi-media teen franchise was 20th Century Fox's *Buffy the Vampire Slayer*. *Buffy* was originally a moderately successful teen film released in 1992. At the time, the teen market was still in dormancy and, with the exception of a soundtrack, the 1992 film did not generate any other related media texts. In 1996, however, Hollywood began turning its attention to a newly emerging teen market, and *Buffy* was resurrected as a television show. This time, the television show generated a television soundtrack, and was quickly repackaged into an assorted and extended range of related media/commodity products. The nature of the entertainment-commodity text became increasingly complex as it continued to mutate into infinitely varied forms. The list of related merchandise included videos and DVDs of the film and television show,[10] *Buffy* novels, magazines and comics based on the show, a *Buffy*-inspired clothing line, dolls, posters, and a computer game, among many others. Reflecting the growing trend in millennial teen culture, every product in the line helped to promote and market the other products. A teen-oriented television series, such as *Buffy*, functioned as the advertisement that promoted not only the original film on which the series was based, but also the videos and DVDs of the television show, the show's soundtrack, as well as all the other music featured on the series.

Admittedly, the practice of merchandizing and repackaging is not original. There has always been a measure of media cross-over where teen entertainment is concerned — since the 1950s, rock 'n' roll acts have appeared on television and contributed to film soundtracks, teen characters have appeared on film, and television, cut records and been marketed in a range of consumer products. Teenage fans of Patty Duke and Gidget were encouraged to express their devotion by purchasing the shows' licensed merchandise that included lunch-boxes, jewelry and make-up. *The Monkees* (1966–1968), a television show about the antics and adventures of a constructed boy band, was another popular teen text representative of cross-promotional activities. This fictional television band released records, and appeared on merchandise including lunchboxes, binders and folders. These examples highlight the long-established nature of the culture industries' symbiotic activities with regards to teen-oriented entertainment culture.

Once the film, television and music industries recognized the mutual benefits, they willingly engaged in collaborative strategies that catered to the then emerging teen market. From the beginning, teen culture was built upon the collaboration between the film and music industries. The combination of "Rock Around the Clock" and *Blackboard Jungle*, one of the earliest films to find success with the teen audience, established the recipe for most of the teen-pics to follow. The film industry had discovered the promotional benefits that a soundtrack played over the radio could provide. As *Billboard* pointed out in 1956, "never before in the history of the film business has the disc jockey and the value of recorded music been so graphically evident or so vitally important."[11] Recognizing the teenager's love of rock and pop music and noting the success that the film industry had achieved marrying image to music, it was not long before television began exploiting music's potential for attracting teenagers.

In August 1957, ABC, the television network most interested in youth audiences at the time, launched Dick Clark's *American Bandstand* on sixty-seven of the network's affiliate stations.[12] The show offered teen audiences rock 'n' roll in a visual medium. "In a matter of months, most of the names familiar to Top 40 listeners would be seen on *Bandstand*.... With a lock on the after school market, *American Bandstand* became a prime 'exposure' venue...."[13]

From that point on, having recognized the mutual opportunities and substantial profits that the teen and youth market offered, the different media industries were motivated to engage in a limited degree of cooperation. However, while rock 'n' roll acts appeared on television and contributed to film soundtracks, and while teen personalities appeared on film and television, and cut records, these collaborative practices in the 1950s and 1960s were taking place between industries that were largely separate and independent entities with their own goals, interests and activities.

These attempts at collaboration were often fraught with obstacles and problems, many of which grew out of the different industries' mutual competitiveness and distrust, since these activities involved partnerships between different companies that were understandably focused on protecting their own interests against the requirements of their competitor-partners. Early instances of cross-promotional synergy in the 1950s through to the 1970s were largely restricted to the marriage of music and either a film release or television broadcast. Negotiations between the film studio or television network and the music labels could be acrimonious, particularly when the involved parties could not agree on mutually beneficial release dates for their interlinked products.

Such conflicts of interests were resolved in the era of the multi-media conglomerate. Conglomeration brought an expanding range of media, distribution platforms, and product lines under a single parent corporation with clearly linked interests. This allowed for a heightened efficiency in collaborative cross-promotional practices, particularly since all the activities would serve the interests of the conglomerate. The shift to multi-media conglomeration that began in the 1980s encouraged the culture industries to develop an increasing commitment to exploiting the promotional and marketing opportunities across the growing range of their corporate holdings.

Unlike previous cycles of teen media, the cross-media marketing and promotional activities of millennial teen-oriented culture was marked by an unprecedented degree of intersection across multiple forms of media and distribution outlets born of the media corporations' expanded holdings across film, television, music, publishing, retail and digital media. Soundtracks, music videos, trailers, fashion, magazine features, television appearances and other promotional opportunities expanded the many textually linked components that were in circulation, functioning as both related and competing intertexts, all of which functioned to promote and publicize the other elements within this complex media web. As Wyatt notes, these promotional aspects tended to "multiply the meanings from the texts in order to increase the audience base," a strategy that has been successful for several decades.[14] In many cases, it was hard to distinguish between the text and the commercial for the texts since most of the articulations functioned in both capacities. Hence, a teen text seldom existed in isolation within a single medium, but became a part of a steadily expanding series of media products.

In addition to the increasingly simultaneous multi-media, multi-product spin-off, millennial teen media also displayed a heightened propensity for cross-references between unrelated teen texts. While synergy is usually used to describe the collaborative activities within a single corporate entity aimed at leveraging and exploiting its various linked holdings to enhance profits and benefit economically, in the case of millennial teen entertainment, collusive practices were not restricted to the range of multi-media spin-off products created within the various branches of a single company. Instead, a looser form of mutually beneficial, cross-corporate, and cross-media promotional activities emerged in which disparate media texts and products were assembled and employed to promote and market a range of competing teen texts.

When Melissa Joan Hart's feature film *Drive Me Crazy* was released, the 20th Century Fox–produced film was promoted on the actress' Viacom-produced television series *Sabrina the Teenage Witch,* that was initially broadcast on the ABC television network, by integrating Britney Spears' performance of the film's title song, which was released on the Jive record label. The inclusion of the song and Spears' performance effectively promoted both the film and Spears' about to be released album on which the song appears. In this complex cross-promotional event, the television series *Sabrina* and the teen film *Drive Me Crazy* had no direct link in terms of content. The only element in common is the actress, Melissa Joan Hart, who stars in both vehicles. Britney Spears' album, ... *Baby One More Time* (1999), which includes the song "(You Drive Me) Crazy," is a separate entity from the television show and the film. Furthermore, the various components of this web were produced by different production companies, removing the traditional synergistic justification for such a complicated, collusive activity. In spite of this, all these texts and performers were brought into contact with the primary goal of promoting and marketing one another, providing a series of loose links between products that are solely focused on targeting the teen demographic. Here, a hugely popular teen pop star (Spears) who did not have an established acting presence on television outside of her music video appearances that were primarily restricted to MTV, crossed over into network television. This incident illustrates some noteworthy qualities about late twentieth century/early twenty-first century teen culture. First and foremost, it points to the highly intertwined nature of the film, television and music industries' focus on attracting and harnessing the teen market. It also showcases Hollywood's focused attempts at carefully identifying and branding a wide range of teen products as part of its sustained efforts at targeting this niche demographic.

These cross-over activities resembled the ties that bind the *Scream* film series to the *Dawson's Creek* episode in which the TV show's characters discuss the slasher film and even re-enact sequences from the film. This allowed the film franchise to benefit from the promotional exposure on a hit teen television show, even as the television show itself actively set out to attract the very teenagers who were responsible for the success and popularity of the film franchise. These cross-promotional activities were supported, despite the fact that Dimension Films, a subsidiary of The Disney Company, owned *Scream*, while *Dawson's Creek* was produced by Columbia-Tristar, which was owned by Sony, and broadcast over the Warner Bros.–owned WB television network.

In these instances, the primary goal revolved around product interaction, a process whereby unrelated media texts (i.e. texts that were not traditional spin-offs) were deliberately brought into contact and interacted with each other as part of an attempt to reinforce their teen brands and attract a similar target audience. They were simultaneous launches, blendings of disparate texts that functioned in very different ways than the media roll-outs in the 1970s or the 1980s, which had a clear hierarchy of intents and interests, and where a single media product is explicitly positioned as the origin of the process.[15] Millennial teen media culture is, thus, characterized by products that refuse to confine themselves to a single medium, but which instead intentionally and strategically cross over into other media forms, establishing ties and connections between disparate texts, resulting in an explosion of multi-media related products from their initial conception.

The Fine Art of Multi-Media Branding

The growing importance and heightened commitment to cultivating brand names was another significant characteristic of the millennial teen phenomenon. As the product line for teen entertainment texts expanded in response to evolving delivery systems, and as the media industries pursued niche markets and audiences, media producers began to recognize the increasing importance of forging distinct, recognizable brand names. Within the media environment, "branding" involved "the relentless marketing of the studio's name, its corporate logo, and its trademark stars and media figures."[16] The brand was used to direct the media product at a specific target audience, one that, by the 1990s, was becoming more and more select and distinct.

The discussion thus far has emphasized Hollywood's interest in teen audiences and consumers, without acknowledging its attempts at further fragmenting this audience into narrower, niche segments. Long recognizing that teenagers are not a homogenous group, Hollywood actively parsed out the valuable teen market into more focused and carefully defined segments, aware that this would pave the way for more efficient ways of creating specialized products that would be better positioned to target the narrower segments. Building an established brand identity, which involves the construction of particular associations and "meanings" that are explicitly linked to a brand name, would allow greater differentiation and distinction between products in a market cluttered by a steadily rising number of entertainment options across a growing number of platforms. Media producers could cut through the clutter more effectively if they had a distinctive brand identity to attract a target market, raising that consumer group's awareness and interest in the diverse but related entertainment texts within the identifiable brand, while simultaneously profiting from selling that market to interested advertisers. Joseph Turow suggests that the media industries' interest in branding was informed by attempts to create effective "branded formats."

> A media format comprises the layout and general approach to content (including advertising) that a specific vehicle — a TV network, magazine, newspaper — takes to its material. It is the format that creates what people think of as the "personality" of a network, magazine, newspaper. When a company touts the distinctive identity of its format, that identity is known as a "brand."
>
> Creating a "branded format," then, means arranging materials — songs, articles, programs — into a package that people in a target audience would see as reflecting their identity.[17]

Granted, notions of "format" and "branding" did not originate in the 1990s. However, as Turow remarks, these practices intensified as the media industries and the marketplace shifted their concentration towards increasingly narrowly defined audiences and market segments. As Turow points out, a successful branded format would effectively appeal to and attract the ideal niche target, and an established brand would ultimately serve a valuable promotional and marketing purpose, attracting the target niche audience on little more than the implied promise of relevant and potentially appealing programming.

In the decade leading into the millennium, a number of media institutions were motivated to cultivate a teen-focused format and brand identity as part of a publicity and promotional strategy aimed at attracting that particular demographic. Of these, the MTV cable network, WB television network, and Dimension Films enjoyed a significant measure of success in the late 1990s, and were joined by Disney, which emerged as one of the most significant sites of t(w)een media culture in the 2000s. In attempting to attract the teen demographic, these media sites emphasized content that was primarily teen or youth oriented. The signature texts associated with MTV, Dimension Films, WB and Disney revolved around teenagers or teenage characters and adopted a definite teenage attitude and outlook.[18] However, each site offered a distinctly different interpretation and definition of its ideal teen identity, which was then articulated in very specific ways to establish their teen brands around certain signature elements that tended to involve particular types of music, programs, content, as well as personalities. Every element was carefully selected to create a distinct brand identity that would attract a particular ideal teen audience.

Although focused on the teenage perspective, these media institutions made conscious attempts to emphasize their differences. MTV adopted a cutting-edge, urban, avant-garde, rebellious teenage attitude and sensibility. In contrast, the WB teen personality was more conservative, suburban, self-aware and reflective. Dimension Films branded itself by committing to specific horror film genres with a special teenage appeal, specifically, the slasher film and the sci-fi, alien invasion film. Disney, in keeping with its mainstream, wholesome brand, and its primary focus on the younger teen and tween set, tended towards a younger teen identity that was fun, innocent, idealistic and optimistic. Therefore, while each entertainment entity embraced the teen perspective, they also made a conscious effort to cultivate a carefully differentiated, teen-identified brand, one that each could then use for identification and promotional purposes. The case studies in Chapters Four through Seven underscore how these media sites established their distinct personalities. What strategies, content, aesthetic styles and formats did each media site adopt? How did these elements help construct their distinct brand identities? Were there any similarities and/or differences in their branding efforts? These are key considerations in the next four chapters.

The dedication to cultivating a teen brand also led to an increasing interest in teen-oriented talent, who themselves emerged as significant teen brands in their own right. The cultivation of a star as a teen brand is distinct from the more familiar and general notions of stardom, which is defined in terms of pubic recognition, audience identification and fame, and that is largely applied to individuals. In equating these teen stars to branded entities, I am intentionally defining them as commercial products and cultural commodities, rather than identifying them as individuals and personalities. Reflecting the multimedia nature of millennial Hollywood, these teen-branded personalities were particularly successfully in establishing themselves across a range of media.

The Cross-Over[19] Trend and the Resurgence of the Teen-Branded Celebrity

In the millennium, teen media entertainment was dominated by a number of brand names that were associated with a range of different media simultaneously. Commercial teen culture during this period was founded, marketed and appeared to revolve around a rather finite set of teen-branded stars and personalities,[20] who consolidated their teen-oriented status by consistently and simultaneously appearing across a variety of teen entertainment media. The growing popularity of teen personalities such as Jennifer Love Hewitt, Brandy, Usher, and Britney Spears in the late 1990s and early 2000s, and Miley Cyrus, the Jonas Brothers, and the stars of Disney's *High School Musical* in the mid-to-late 2000s, was not restricted to their dominance of any single entertainment medium. Instead, these teen-branded stars, managed to straddle the wide range of industries by appearing on record labels, magazine covers, in retail advertising campaigns, in films and on television, effectively tapping the attention of the teen demographic and weaving together the various strands of an increasingly vast entertainment tapestry.

Crossing-over was by no means new or unique to teen culture. Annette Funicello, the star of numerous beach films began on *The Mickey Mouse Club* (1955–1959) on television, released records and then moved into films. Pat Boone, Elvis Presley, and The Beatles began in music, performed on television, and quickly shifted into making films. But the activity became particularly prevalent in specific ways in the 1990s and after, arising out of the heightened integration of multiple forms of media in the wake of the industries' increased multi-media conglomeration. As media corporations expanded horizontally across other forms of media, there arose greater opportunities to promote and market their products and stars across various media formats, often simultaneously.

Britney Spears, for instance, made guest appearances on television's *Sabrina the Teenage Witch*, sang and promoted her CDs on MTV and headlined the film *Crossroads* at the movie theatres. Jennifer Love Hewitt starred on television in *Party of Five* (1994–2000) and its spin-off *Time of Your Life* (1999–2000) while also enjoying box-office success in teen films such as *I Know What You Did Last Summer* (1997) and *Can't Hardly Wait* (1998), in addition, she sang on the soundtracks of both films. Melissa Joan Hart starred in the teen television series *Sabrina the Teenage Witch* and the feature films *Can't Hardly Wait* and *Drive Me Crazy*. Sarah Michelle Gellar was Buffy on television's *Buffy the Vampire Slayer* while also appearing in theatres in *I Know What You Did Last Summer*, *Scream 2*, *Cruel Intentions* (1999), and *Scooby-Doo* (2002). Scott Foley starred in television's *Felicity* (1998–2002) and *Scream 3*. Joshua Jackson, from television's *Dawson's Creek,* appeared in *Scream 2*, *Urban Legend* (1998), and *Cruel Intentions*.

In almost every instance, these stars established their teen following in one media form and immediately began leveraging that popularity across a range of other entertainment media. Their increasing popularity and rising profile with teenagers marked them as teen stars and allowed them to cultivate their own teen-oriented brand. These stars then further reinforced their brand by appearing in other teen entertainment texts. The ability to shift between these media had a definite impact upon the nature of the teen text, particularly at the level of plot and characterization. Teen stars Jennifer Love Hewitt and Brandy both starred in television series, had recording contracts and film careers. Both women's television shows acknowledged and exploited their singing talents by constructing plots that allowed them the opportunities for musical performances. These musical sequences helped to promote their singing careers and sell their CDs. According to producer Neal Moritz, "The recognizability of these actors makes them valuable ... they have a built-in awareness [with the teenage audience], and [their work on television indicates that] they're a proven commodity."[21]

The interaction between these teen actors and their film, television, and even music, projects provide further insight into how synergy and teen branding functioned. In casting an established teen television star in films, the film and television texts attempted to exploit the star's teen-oriented following, hoping that the star would draw his/her teenage fan base to the new project. At the same time, the star also benefited by further consolidating his/her teen brand by cultivating yet another association with a teen text. Hewitt, Gellar and Jackson, like many of their peers, successfully transferred their television success onto the big screen, appearing in many of the most popular teen films of the 1990s. In the late 1990s, teen-oriented "multimedia world ... celebrities and brand names cross over easily to the big screen from sophisticated, highly marketed small-screen programming — and they bring their audience with them."[22]

Stars were not the only personalities cultivating and exploiting a teen-affiliated brand. Even creative personnel managed to cultivate a cult teen-oriented brand. Arguably the most popular brand name with teenagers in the late 1990s, was not an actor, but screenwriter and director, Kevin Williamson, who scripted the popular and very successful teen slasher film, *Scream*. That success prompted the entertainment industry to transform the Williamson name into a brand signifying smart, hip, popular teen entertainment. When Miramax marketed *The Faculty* (1998), a teen sci-fi/horror film co-scripted by Williamson, none of the film's advertising mentioned the film's stars. Rather, it was publicized as a film "from the screenwriter of *Scream* and *Scream 2*," with numerous television ads touting the tag: "written by Kevin Williamson." Mark Gill, president of Miramax/Los Angeles declared, "When you have the opportunity to say your movie is from Kevin Williamson, it's an awfully potent marketing tool. Among under-25 moviegoers, the billing 'the writer of *Scream*' is a valuable calling card."[23] The WB network also exploited this calling card when it acquired the Williamson-created television series, *Dawson's Creek*. The television series featured then unknown actors and was therefore advertised and promoted as Williamson's creation. The power and appeal of Williamson's brand name with the targeted teen demographic helped the television series became one of the most successful teen television shows on the WB in its first season.

As the Williamson case shows, the practice of cross-over was not restricted to on-screen talent but extended to creative personnel as well. In fact, teen culture's propensity for synergy and cross-over contributed towards an increasingly blurred line between the film and television media themselves. While filmmakers' involvement in television was not necessarily a new or unique development, it evolved into a late 1990s teen television trend, one that particularly characterized the teen-identified WB television network's relationship with feature filmmakers. The WB was especially aggressive in luring filmmakers to television based on the belief that if teenagers were the most avid filmgoers at the time, they could also evolve into devoted television watchers. And, what better way to lure them to both mediums than to ensure that teenagers had access to the very same brand names both at home and in the movie theater? In fact, there was a significant surge in the number of film writers who were engaged in creating series for television. Speaking to *Variety*, Jordan Levin, president of programming at the WB noted,

> We've been very fortunate to have very fresh talent from the feature business interested in expressing their unique voices to our audience, which demands a cinematic styling. Our audience speaks to [the filmmakers'] sensibility because the 12- to 34-year-olds are moviegoers, and film writers don't have to adjust their voices [at the WB] to succeed.[24]

Attracting "fresh talent from the feature business" made good sense if the network hoped to distinguish itself as specifically teen-oriented and sell itself to that audience.[25] Hence, many of the creators, producers and scriptwriters most clearly associated with commercial teen culture were people who comfortably, and successfully, shifted between television and film. Both Kevin Williamson, who went from scripting the film *Scream* to creating *Dawson's Creek* for television, and Joss Whedon, who began in music videos and then worked on films including *Speed* (1994), *Toy Story* (1995) and *Alien Resurrection* (1997) and who was responsible for *Buffy the Vampire Slayer*, were early WB successes. Subsequently, the WB entered into a series of development deals with creative personnel from feature backgrounds including scriptwriters, directors, and production designers.

As filmmakers were lured to television, the movie studios that were also recognizing the value of integrating televisual elements into their creative considerations also increasingly valued the shift. In 1991, Timothy Corrigan commented on the growing connection between separate media when he noticed that big-budget films were attempting to recuperate their large budgets by ensuring the product's viability across ancillary markets particularly on television, whether on video, pay-per-view, or for eventual network broadcast. "This accounts," Corrigan notes, "for the common, easy mobility of actors and directors between television and film (usually bringing television styles with them)."[26]

While stars and creative individuals such as Williamson and Whedon were being cultivated as brand names that were effectively exploited across a wide range of media, it bears explicit mention that these individuals successfully escaped being identified with a particular entertainment medium, genre, style or singular talent. Instead, these individuals crossed back and forth between film, television and music. In an industry in which "the manic rush of media giants toward market dominance has made the thousands of outlets increasingly imitative and narrow, [with] a sameness that flows from huge bureaucracies with identical goals and strategies," branding provides distinction, differentiation and the benefits of a recognizable, marketable, identity.[27] That this identity was effective across a range of media made them even more valuable.

Millennial entertainment benefited from and encouraged the active mobility of creative talent, a trend that accelerated through the '90s and led to a
growing convergence in style and aesthetics across teen-oriented films, television and music videos. In fact, one of the key qualities of teen-oriented texts
in the late 1990s was the degree of stylistic and narrative consistency that flowed
across different texts and different media. In the past, fairly obvious distinctions existed between, for instance, film and television that marked each as a
separate medium. By the 1990s, however, these boundaries disintegrated, as
many teen television shows were shot on film in a single-camera filmic format
offering the rich, organic visuals characteristic of the filmic, rather than televisual, image. Further stylistic mixing occurred on the level of thematic content, and narrative structure.

Stylistic and Aesthetic Convergence Across Media

Millennial teen-oriented texts were characterized by a heightened degree
of stylistic and narrative consistency that flowed across different texts and different media. In addition to expanding across these media formats, many of
the related texts also began borrowing and incorporating the aesthetic and stylistic qualities of these different media platforms within the expanding range
of products. *Popstars* was, simultaneously, a reality show, a talent contest, and
a musical program. It incorporated a curious mix of the musical showcase, the
"behind-the-scenes" show and a "making of" promotional text. Stylistically
and aesthetically, the series offered a curious blend of various diverse textual
conventions. A single episode could, and often would, shift from the seemingly
unedited camera work and unscripted events associated with the reality series,
to the type of camerawork and staging associated with the broadcast of a staged
musical performance, to the much more stylized, "packaged" artifice associated with the popular music video tradition. The fact that the group, Eden's
Crush, would appear on *Popstars* practicing their performances and making
their videos, and then proceed to then perform on other platforms such as
MTV, which would also feature their music videos, further blurred the boundaries of the *Popstars* text. As these activities became increasingly common in
the millennium, it became more and more difficult to identify and recognize
the limits of the millennial teen product at the level of the medium, or the text.

Admittedly, this was not a recent development. It has always been difficult
to draw distinct boundaries between film, television and music when so much
of teen culture has historically been characterized by the blending of all three
media since the 1950s. Even in earlier decades, teen culture was characterized
by a high degree of media-mixing. The teen beach movies of the 1960s blended
music and film image and often featured teen stars that moved from television
to films and the recording studio. The teenage Gidget was the main character
in a series of films before making the transition to television with a series named

after the character. *The Patty Duke Show* and *Gidget* on television often blended musical elements in their narratives and showcased stars that also shifted from television to film appearances.

In the past, however, fairly obvious narrative and aesthetic distinctions existed between, for instance, film and television that marked each as separate media. Until the 1980s, the film industry, which produced both film and television shows, had a vested interest in differentiating the two media so as to maintain film's artistic and cultural value over the commercially-oriented, and thus culturally less exalted television tradition. This translated into a series of specific differences. Aesthetically, the vast differences in production budgets—feature films consistently had significantly higher budgets than television series—had a significant impact on the visual aesthetics of the respective texts. Narratively and thematically, feature films tended to embrace a more epic scope, while television shows tended to focus on the ordinary and the domestic.

Differences in technology and format also helped distinguish the cinematic and television text. The traditional size of the film screen followed an aspect ratio of 1.33:1, often referred to as the Academy Standard.[28] After the arrival of television, the broadcast industry decided to embrace the Academy standard, adopting a similar 1.33:1 aspect ratio.[29] The Hollywood studios' response to this decision by what it then perceived as its competitor, was to embrace widescreen as a means of differentiation. So in the 1950s, the film image was expanded to a 16:9 aspect ratio, making it noticeably wider than the television screen.[30] These format differences in turn had significant consequences for the stylistic and aesthetic elements of each medium. For instance, the wider cinematic screen was ideal for wide shots that could be used to emphasize scale and scope, while the more moderate size of the television image corresponded to a more intimate setting.[31]

By the 1980s, however, the distinctions became increasingly blurred, as the need for differentiation diminished in response to industry, technology and social changes. With multi-media conglomeration, the historical competition between the film and television industries was removed and replaced by a more collaborative relationship, even as the turn to conglomeration ushered in a new era of intense competition created by the exponentially increasing range of media and entertainment options. As media corporations developed new product lines to accommodate their expanded multimedia interests, a different process of creating and marketing the entertainment text arose in the 1980s. This resulted in what Justin Wyatt describes as "the necessity of film 'playing' across a wide range of media, and the move toward more commercially 'safe' product, with inherent marketing hooks which would ensure a return on investment."[32]

The need for greater media convergence was aided by technological developments. Television technologies had been advancing in ways that were diminishing any disparities between the two media. Home entertainment systems with surround sound, and high definition screens that embraced the cinematic widescreen aspect ratio of 16:9 were increasingly available, allowing viewers to enjoy the cinematic experience at home. With these developments, newer generations of audiences and consumers were embracing a more fluid sense of how media can be accessed, experienced and consumed. In response to these industrial, technological, and audience shifts, the very nature, style and content of films, television and music changed. Cross-media mobility accelerated through the '90s and led to a growing convergence in style and aesthetics across film, television and even music videos. This practice of cross-over was not restricted to actors and creative talent but also encompassed media styles and visuals, and occurred on a variety of fronts including: thematic content, visual style, and narrative structure.

Justin Wyatt's *High Concept* provides an insightful study of how the industrial and commercial shifts of the 1970 and '80s affected the content, creation and marketing of big-budget, mainstream entertainment texts, and helped shape a commercial, "high concept" form of product development in both the film and television industries. The high concept film is an entertainment product that is distinguished in two key ways: "though an emphasis on style within the films, and through an integration with marketing and merchandizing."[33] Since marketability is the primary consideration of high concept, the most notable elements of an entertainment text, including the narrative, star power, and subject matter are all constrained by marketing considerations.[34]

In short, high concept privileges commercial considerations above those of the creative and innovative.[35] Ideally, narratives have a simple, preferably single-sentence, concept that can be used as an ad line in the marketing/publicity campaign. High concept texts tend to feature stars with a distinct image and persona, who can aid in the marketing of the film/television show. The subject matter is necessarily trendy and fashionable, the better to enhance its relevance and promotability. In addition, big budget, high-concept films of the 1980s tended to espouse a youth-oriented perspective, the better to attract the audience demographic most committed to theatrical film consumption. Wyatt provides a comprehensive list of qualities characteristic of the high-concept, "post" classical Hollywood films of the 1980s, many of which would actually become even more pronounced in the 1990s, especially in teen culture.

According to Wyatt, the decision to privilege marketing concerns directly affected the aesthetics, content and style of films. One consequence was the adoption of advertising style in high-concept filmmaking. Since the key consideration was the creation of a film that would aid in its own marketing, what better than a film that mimicked an advertisement in style and image? As advertising style tended to revolve around striking visuals, the physical perfection of the image and the selling of a glamorized lifestyle, many high concept films of the 1980s also began reflecting similar qualities. Wyatt observes, "These qualities of the advertising image — the physical perfection, the attempt to sell both a product and a lifestyle — parallel the style of the high concept films."[36] The assimilation of advertising style created instances in which narrative and plot development were often neglected, or even suspended, in favor of accentuating the film's formal composition. Consequently, high concept films began encouraging the appreciation of style and aesthetics over that of plot and narrative, a development that Wyatt labels "excess":

> Certainly the physical design or "the look" of the film can be viewed as excess which can easily be replicated in the high-tech trailers or television commercials. Similarly, the high concept films are perfect for the publicist: the physical design matched with the characters as models and adherence to genre allow for publicity stills which, on the one hand are aesthetically striking and, on the other hand, accurately represent the film.[37]

Interestingly, this stylistic and visual "excess" that Wyatt noted in 1980s films, was also increasingly evident in 1980s television, as noted by another media scholar, John Thornton Caldwell. Caldwell argues that the visual excess dominating television (and other media) in the 1980s and 1990s "was a function of audience," and that the "the cultural abilities of audiences had ... changed.... Many viewers expected and watched programs that made additional aesthetic and conceptual demands not evident in earlier programming."[38] Although Wyatt and Caldwell's examinations focus on conditions in the 1980s, their comments remain relevant in the millennium. Cable television, videocassettes, and more recently, digital recording and computers, have cultivated a youth audience with a finely-tuned media awareness, who are increasingly accustomed to a mounting degree of visual excess in its media texts. Generation Y was thus well-positioned to appreciate the cross-media, cross-era references characteristic of the emerging visual excess that would escalate through the 1990s and 2000s.

Evolving levels of media literacy and audience preferences were not the only significant factors reshaping popular teen entertainment. Hollywood's changing structures were another factor in the escalation of visual excess. Due to increasing multimedia conglomeration, the lines separating the different media have blurred considerably, leading to heightened stylistic and aesthetic integration across media. In addition, evolving new technologies continued to add to the already surplus media texts already in circulation. According to Doherty, the chief characteristics of 1980s Hollywood cinema include "the breakdown of traditional boundaries, [and] the promiscuous cross-pollination among once autonomous breeds ... [so that] ... [t]he elements in the generic mix become progressively dizzying."[39] Doherty suggests that this is born of the televisual experience, and credits the post–1970s audiences' "tolerance for generic mix-and-match and the shift in generic brand loyalty ... [to] the influence of television-trained spectatorship," arguing that "[t]elevision spawned a generation of genre-wise (and genre-surfeited) spectators, trained experts in the tropes, conventions, and twists of formula programming."[40] Certainly, Doherty's description of the spectator who has "logged thousands of video hours in front of the small screen before adolescent passage into R-rated theatrical cinema, schooled in the lexicon of genre, zapping between narrative realms," aptly describes a generation of increasingly media-savvy echo boomers whose formative years were spent in the company of the 100-channel television universe and who have emerged supremely equipped to "readily digest several genre menus at one sitting."[41]

Unlike previous cycles of teen media, then, the current millennium is characterized by the increasing convergence of stylistic, aesthetic, and often narrative elements that extend across the multiple media texts. Through the *Aldrich* and *Gidget* era, the format and style of the different media experiences were largely distinct. It would be impossible to confuse the radio show with the film or television versions. Millennial teen entertainment, in contrast, distinctively refuses to respect medium-specific or textual boundaries at the level of content and style, despite being entirely separate products. This is evident, for example, in the *Dawson's Creek* episode "The Scare," which is stylistically and visually similar to the cinematic *Scream*, replicating, in large part, the conventions, characters and aesthetics of that teen-oriented horror film.

The convergence at the stylistic and aesthetic levels was matched by an increasing confluence at the narrative level as well. Millennial teen media is also characterized by the rising dominance of the serialized narrative format that, while typical of the television series, had not been commonly adopted by the cinematic medium in decades. While serialized films had once been popular from the silent era well into the 1950s, they had fallen out of favor since.[42] Even the rise of the blockbuster franchise in the 1970s did not bring them back. Leibman notes that through the 1950s and '60s, it was conventionally accepted that

> one of the most significant ... differences between film and television texts is that a film operates as a distinct entity, while a television episode is part of an ongoing series.... [This difference] in narrative closure significantly influenced the way each medium's [narratives] solved their various crises.[43]

As Leibman points out, film narratives were generally characterized by decisive closure. There was a finality to the end of a film that was inherently absent in the experience of the television serial/series. The key distinction here was that television adopted a serial format in which single episodes may end but the narrative continues, whereas a film characteristically had a final and conclusive ending. Through the 1970s and 1980s, film franchises dominated the box-office, but tended to offer familiar characters in self-contained narratives, rather than having on-going narratives that stretched across several films.[44] In the millennium, however, the serial form became particularly characteristic of teen culture in general. The popular *Scream* film series was just one of the many teen films that adopted a continuing, serialized narrative structure, a point I consider in greater detail in Chapter Five. These films were not constrained by the limited scope of a finite film text. Embracing a serialized structure allowed these films the liberty of an evolving, sustained narrative, and offering complex characters that grow and change across films. This adoption of narrative strategies more commonly associated with the television medium was yet another instance of the growing convergence between what was once considered separate media.

As Hollywood and media and entertainment producers begin to respond to the digital age, and the developing opportunities posed by technologies that are making entertainment and information available and accessible on mobile digital devices, the need for media/entertainment texts to play across multiple platforms will have to address the challenges posed by these gadgets that sport very small screens. While this current digital trend is in its developmental stages, a few partnerships between Hollywood studios and new media companies have begun to experiment with multi-media series conceptualized to play across television, online and over mobile interfaces. These series are at the forefront of contemporary attempts to initiate an even greater degree of stylistic and narrative convergence across a wider range of platforms. Hollywood's ongoing attempts to explore the profitabilities of the new digital media, its experiments in amortizing digital entertainment, will have considerable implications for the nature, format and content of these texts, as examined in Chapter Eight.

Postmodern "Hyper-" Intertextuality

The stylistic and aesthetic coincidence across media, the intense and increasingly seamless degree of media mixing, the intertextual links, the collapsing boundaries between different texts and media formats, all point to the next characteristic of the millennial teen text, one that occurs across the range of entertainment media: the tendency towards postmodern "hyper-" intertextuality. No longer a new or unique theoretical perspective by the 1990s, postmodernism and its impact on contemporary media texts has received significant scholarly attention since the 1980s.[45] Postmodernism is characterized by a distinct set of qualities including the gravitation towards the visual and the simulacrum, a heightened emphasis on the artificiality and constructedness of a text, often with an accompanying tendency for intertextual referencing, and the breakdown of traditional boundaries between high and low forms of art, between genres, between historical periods, and between distinct texts.

Justin Wyatt argues that since the 1980s, media texts have been characterized by their collective reliance on "a vast network of references to other films, television shows and forms of mass media" as a structuring device.[46] Since then, many teen-oriented media texts have displayed the intertextuality, pastiche, and multiple and collaged presentational forms that are the properties of postmodernism. Millennial teen texts are often structured and defined by their incessant intertextual citations. In millennial teen culture, self-reflexive, intertextual references occur across multiple media and between numerous and varied popular, often teen-oriented, texts. If we look back at previous teen media, we notice that the practice has a historical tradition. Many teen texts, including the exploitation films of the 1950s and 1970s, have engaged in the activity. In those earlier cases, however, the references tended to be either opportunistically derivative or tongue-in-cheek moments of sub-text that often amounted to often obscure inside-jokes.

In contrast, the millennial situation is distinctive because the referencing is not restricted to the occasional passing allusion. Rather, in millennial teen media, the referencing exists as a vital part of the textual content. Entire episodes of teen television shows and films engage in self-conscious, highly self-reflexive discussions and commentaries on the nature and conventions of (teen) media texts. These intertextual elements often occur as dialogue, as narrative content, and as aesthetic and stylistic features. Specific instances of these intertextual references and self-reflexive characteristics are examined in greater detail in Chapters Four to Seven. Meanwhile, the current discussion explores the historical origins, tracing the interrelated set of technological, industrial and cultural preconditions that prompted this trend.

A primary precondition involved "the proliferation of signs and their endless circulation" in the 1980s and after, a situation "generated by the technological developments associated with the information explosion (cable television, VCRs, digital recording, computers, etcetera)."[47] The development of new technologies played a significant role in reshaping youth's experience of and relationship with media entertainment. The rise of the internet and digital technologies that allow easy and quick access to information and entertainment from almost any era, have joined earlier technologies such as television and cable in enhancing our increasingly sophisticated experience of media entertainment. In the decades since the 1970s, a growing range of technological developments have allowed the media industries to extend the shelf life of media products indefinitely. Consequently, texts from past classical eras continue to be available and accessible to audiences along with more recently released material. This has resulted in a condition where what Umberto Eco calls the "already said," continues to circulate, even as newer texts began to cite and rephrase the "already said."[48]

Another central feature of postmodernism involves the refusal to distinguish between older and more contemporary media texts, expressed in a tendency to reduce every citation "to a series of perpetual presents."[49] "What is postmodern in all of this is the simultaneity of these competing forms of rearticulation — the 'already said' is being constantly rearticulated, but from very different perspectives ranging from nostalgic reverence to vehement attack or a mixture of these strategies."[50] As Collins points out, these adoptions and rearticulations acquire entirely different cultural meanings that are separate from their initial significance within their original texts and context.[51] Thus, as new texts join older ones, all of which remain indefinitely accessible, they offer numerous and competing messages and signs which often referenced and re-circulated signs from older media texts. This has resulted in an explosion of texts, all of which offer numerous and competing messages and signs which "must constantly be defined over and against rival forms of expression."[52] Also significant is what Collins identifies as "the *hyperconsciousness* of postmodern popular culture" which refers to the trend in which post–1980s media texts displayed a heightened awareness of "its cultural status, function, and history, as well as of the conditions of its circulation and reception."[53]

Continuing this trend, millennial teen media, whether referring to a teen film, television show, music video, or online website, displayed an accelerated shift towards self-reflexivity, and visual and semiotic excess that was reflected in the appropriation and absorption of other popular entertainment texts through the re-circulation of iconic or familiar images, multiple references to popular texts and/or the adoption of generic plot lines. These often self-conscious and overt visual and aural references and citations further intensified the teen media text's propensity for visual and stylistic excess already mentioned in the previous section. According to Caldwell, '80s and '90s television's growing tendency towards a form of visual excess he termed "televisuality" reflected the medium's increasing turn towards intertexuality and the interest in the visual image over narrative.[54]

Caldwell argues that '80s and '90s television "moved from a framework that approached broadcasting primarily as a form of word-based rhetoric and transmission, with all the issues that such terms suggest, to a visually based mythology, framework and aesthetic based on an extreme self-consciousness of style."[55] During the period, television's mode of production embraced a generalized commitment to constantly reinventing and updating the visual style in its programming. This shift developed in conjunction with the trend towards "a structural inversion" which led to the ascension of image and style over narrative and content.[56] Changes within the industry, which included technological advancements (such as the evolution of production tools including digital video, and video-assist) and personnel "upgrades," which introduced new production personnel trained in creating new visual effects, also supported the rise of the kind of stylistic excess that would intensify and come to characterize the millennial teen media text.

This intensification of postmodernist intertextual elements within 1990s and 2000s popular teen culture relates to issues of marketing, promotion, commodification, and consumption. According to Jean Baudrillard, the postmodern era is inextricably linked to the emergence of a particularly problematic form of consumerism. He argues that in a cultural zeitgeist in which knowledge, meaning, and identity are constructions, where simulations direct our experiences and behaviors, human beings are increasingly led to believe that their needs can only be met through the act of consumption.[57] It is via consumption that one asserts one's identity, ambitions and goals.[58] However, con-

sumerism in the postmodern age is largely constrained by the carefully constructed behaviors and boundaries advocated by the media, the advertisers, and
those dominating the marketplace.[59] It is noteworthy that beginning in the
1980s, and intensifying into the millennium, teen entertainment texts were
functioning increasingly as cross-promotional advertising for a range of other
linked media. The *Popstars* media event, the *Scream/Dawson's Creek* incident,
and the *Sabrina*/Melissa Joan Hart/*Drive Me Crazy*/Britney Spears episode, are
characterized by a defining commitment to marketing, and an increasing tendency to adopt advertising's aesthetics and visual styles which made them
resemble commercials, for "commercials get us accustomed to thinking of our-
selves and behaving as a market rather than a public."[60]

By the millennium, industrial, technological and economic developments
had motivated changes in popular teen entertainment texts that made it more
and more difficult to rely upon narrative, stylistic and aesthetic factors to distinguish between a film, a television, a music video, or an advertisement text.
At that point, teen culture had evolved into an almost amorphous entity blending television, film, music, the internet, magazines, and mall culture, with each
media arm collaborating with the others to promote, market and sell each others' products. Most of the distinctive qualities of millennial teen culture are
inextricably linked to the significant industrial and marketplace changes that
characterize the contemporary media landscape. The following chapters are
organized around the principle that this latest wave of teen culture is structured and constrained by industrial, technological and marketplace developments characteristic of the period as I have sketched them briefly above.

The media industries' shift to multi-media conglomeration and horizontal integration as well as the accompanying commitment to exploiting all available media forms have directly shaped the nature, form and content of the
millennial teen media text, encouraging the stylistic and aesthetic integration
of previously distinct media forms. Evolving new technologies, particularly the
new digital and mobile technologies, continue to add to the media texts already
in circulation, while also aiding the media industries' dominance over an
increasingly global marketplace have also had a distinct impact upon millennial teen culture. With increased access to media and technology, millennial
teenagers surpassed previous generations in their capacity for media-oriented
hyperconsciousness—emerging as the most culturally literate and media-
saturated cohort ever encountered. These developments presented a cultural
environment that encouraged the emergence of several noteworthy characteristics in millennial teen texts. These industrial, marketplace and technological
changes demand a rethinking and reevaluation of the "rules" defining teen culture and teen texts, as well as the strategies adopted in studying this increasingly complex situation.

This overview of millennial teen media trends highlights the difficulties
in separating the film, television and music industries' efforts at harnessing the

teen market. However, there is little doubt that the media and entertainment industries are actively involved in exploiting the market. Within these industries, certain specific corporate entities have emerged as sites of intense teen-identified media activity. MTV and Jive records, Dimension films, the WB television network, and Disney represent the key corporate entities most directly associated with the resurgence of teen culture. These corporate entities serve as sites of specific activities that directly shaped the production of millennial teen culture. The following chapters investigate these specific activities, tracking their evolution and progress against a background of these corporations' industrial, commercial and economic interests, with the final intention of elucidating how these factors have impacted the teen-oriented media artifact.

FOUR

Beyond Music Television

MTV celebrated its twentieth anniversary in 2001. In the two decades that the cable network had been on the air, it successfully consolidated its position as one of the most successful internationally recognized youth-oriented brand names. During that time, MTV underwent significant evolution in its programming, its entertainment mandate and the way it capitalized on the continually evolving cycles of youth/teen culture. As a quintessential teen culture brand, MTV represents one of the key sites in which multimedia conglomeration, globalization, and a highly synergistic marketplace have combined to create a new conceptualization of the millennial teen market.

This chapter investigates MTV's distinct evolutionary phases, tracing its development from a popular music-oriented cable network into a multi-media, global brand, paying special attention to the period between the late 1990s and late 2000s. This latest millennial cycle must be understood in terms of both MTV's larger historical context and contemporary developments. In the 1990s and 2000s, MTV's industrial structure, the marketplace at large, as well as the emergence of teen related entertainment institutions have all affected MTV's programming mandate, and more specifically, MTV's teen-oriented texts. In keeping with the assumption that media sites, texts and practices evolve in response to larger industrial, economic, and social changes, I examine specific examples of MTV's programming strategies in the decade between 1997 and 2007 and interrogate how the network's content, style and aesthetics evolved in response to these larger, macro forces.

MTV's development can be divided into three distinct phases: (1) 1981 to 1985, characterized by its adoption of 24-hour music video programming (2) 1986 to 1996, which witnessed the shift to more conventional cable network programming, and the adoption of diversification and globalization activities, and finally, (3) a phase which began in 1996 and extends into the new millennium that saw MTV evolve into a multi-media, multi-platform, teen entertainment hub. In line with this project's interest in millennial teen media, the following examination of MTV focuses primarily on the latest phase. The discussions of the earlier two phases will be brief, in part because these historical events have already received fairly extensive discussion and coverage.[1]

1981–1985: MTV Origins — The Birth of the 24-Hour Music Video Channel

MTV was launched on August 21, 1981, after John A. Lack, Warner Cable's executive vice president of programming and marketing, and Robert Pittman, a radio program executive hired as director of Warner-Amex's pay–TV division, recognized that there was a distinct gap in cable networks directed specifically at teenagers and youth.[2] Owned and operated by Warner Communications and American Express at its inception,[3] MTV represented an attempt to exploit the emerging cable technology while also servicing the recording industries' needs for a promotional and marketing platform to replace the declining radio format.

At the time, MTV was directed at the middle- or upper-class, suburban, white, young adult male, who was deemed to have the best access to cable and who would be the most likely viewer of video music programs, just as they were the early purchasers of music products.[4] According to Marshall Cohen, vice president of programming at MTV in 1981, the network-commissioned audience surveys convinced MTV that its most likely viewer would be "the twenty-three, twenty-four-year-old educated, affluent, suburban viewer" which subsequently became "the [essential] profile of MTV."[5] Warner executives reasoned that music would be the most effective means by which to attract this youth demographic since music was considered one of the central elements of a youth-oriented lifestyle and culture.

Steered by its initial commitment to a white, male, youth audience, Warner executives turned their attention towards developing a distinct format, style and identity for MTV that would most appeal to its target demographic. As part of a move to distinguish the cable network from other available network and cable services, MTV rejected the established programming strategies of broadcast television networks and embraced a unique, 24-hour music video programming format instead.[6] Consequently, MTV eschewed conventionally structured programming blocks of discrete shows in favor of a fluid, amorphous format that consisted of an endless stream of music video clips introduced by a group of "vee-jays"/"VJs" (i.e. video jockeys, a play on the established term disk jockeys). Robert Pittman declared that MTV would be "a channel with no programs, no beginning, no middle, no end."[7] While music videos were not exclusive to MTV, the network's privileging of music videos and their distinct aesthetic style in its programming schedule contributed to the overall style of the network in the 1980s.

Early discussions of MTV have tended to discuss this era in postmodern terms based on the network's distinctive programming strategies and content. Music videos are generally constructed of a seamless flow of images, and the cable network's programming strategy mirrored this seamlessness as one video followed another, often with little interruption. Pat Aufderheide, John Fiske,

E. Ann Kaplan, David Tetzlaff and Peter Wollen all utilized the postmodern paradigm in studying music videos and MTV in the 1980s.[8] Tetzlaff equates MTV with the postmodern, which he describes as "fragmentation, segmentation, superficiality, stylistic jumbling, the blurring of mediation and reality, the collapse of past and future into the moment of the present."[9] Most of these studies have concentrated on examining how viewers process the postmodern aspects characteristic of both MTV and music videos, which are structured by an obsession with visual spectacle, and an excessive focus on style and image, often at the expense of narrative coherence and simulation.

In "Music Video and the Spectator: Television, Ideology and Dream," Marsha Kinder describes music video as a complex blend of performance and visually fragmented images that consistently disrupt any sense of temporal and/or spatial unity,[10] qualities that could also be ascribed to the cable channel itself. Many of MTV's most popular videos featured fragmented images "borrowed" from already existing images often associated with other media. For instance, Madonna's "Material Girl" video (1984) was structured around a visual simulation of Marilyn Monroe's iconic performance of "Diamonds Are a Girl's Best Friend" from the movie *Gentlemen Prefer Blondes* (1953). Paula Abdul's video of her hit single "Rush, Rush" (1991) in turn recreated key scenes lifted directly from *Rebel Without a Cause*, and cast actor Keanu Reeves—most famous at the time for playing the teenage Ted in the popular teen hit film, *Bill and Ted's Excellent Adventure* (1989)—in the James Dean role. For her 1986 "Don't Get Me Wrong" video, singer Chrissie Hynde appears as a leather-clad sex symbol—part of an homage to the Emma Peel character from the '60s British television series *The Avengers* (1965–1968). This "borrowing" has led Jack Banks to argue that,

> The channel subverts any aesthetic sense of history by indiscriminately mixing together material from film genres, and art forms from various historical periods. MTV also repudiates linear conceptions of history, rejecting conventional distinctions between past, present and future, instead placing itself in a timeless present.[11]

MTV's postmodern attitude, its uniqueness, and unconventionality, attracted a youthful audience who appreciated the network's distinct and very different content and format. The medium's emphasis on provocative visual images blended with pulsating music, punctuated by frenetic, kinetic editing, and its tendency towards intertextual visual and aural references, eventually came to personify the "MTV style."

MTV, Postmodernism and Consumerism

As previously discussed in Chapter Three, considerations of postmodernism's ascension within popular culture have often highlighted links to the subsequent rise of consumerism. Collins, Featherstone, Aufderheide and Morse are just some of the scholars who have noted the vital relationship between postmodernism and consumption.[12] Echoing Jameson, and Baudrillard, these scholars have equated the rise of postmodernism in 1980s popular culture with an accompanying shift towards consumerist values. MTV and its propensity for the postmodern played a notable role in breaking down the boundaries separating television programming and the commercially advertised product. From its inception, the cable network and the music videos it programmed were actively engaged in transcending the traditional lines separating the television text from advertising. With the advent of MTV, the programming became the product to be bought and consumed.[13] Margeret Morse highlights that, even as music videos' primary aim is to promote and sell compact disks and tapes, they also serve a broader, more complex function since they also promote

> (b) video tapes of itself, (c) the image of a rock star, (d) box-office and video tape sales of movies as well as soundtrack albums, and (e) products and services related not just to the music performers, but also to the lifestyles and world-view depicted in the visuals of the rock video.[14]

MTV played a key role in encouraging its viewers to adopt consumerism as the cornerstone of their lifestyles by reshaping the youthful consumer's relationship with the media and his/her definition of consumption, recasting the act of consumption as an assertion of identity, thereby stimulating the consumer's demand for an increasing range of commercial products. According to Virginia Fry and Donald Fry, MTV advocated consumerism by depicting and glamorizing an MTV lifestyle and identity explicitly associated with products featured on, and "endorsed" by, the cable network, thus seducing, or inducing viewers into purchasing those products.[15]

While MTV, as its name implied, began by forging a link between the television and music industries and pioneering a product that integrated the two aesthetic forms, it is also worth noting that MTV did not serve solely as a link between television and the music industry but was also nurturing a vital relationship with the film industry at a time when poplar music was being increasingly integrated into film soundtracks. Certainly, the relationship between music and films has a long history leading back to the first sound film. However, as Justin Wyatt observes, while these earlier films used music to serve a dramatic purpose, in the 1980s, music was more often included to serve marketing and promotional interests.[16] Alexander Doty in turn points out that "Hollywood's growing awareness of a large and monied 'youth market' finally led industry publicists to fully recognize the potential for music-and-movie exploitation implicit in the conglomerate entertainment networks."[17] Many mid–'80s teen romantic comedies were greatly influenced by MTV, which motivated the movie industry's increasingly significant employment of popular music on film soundtracks, and on promotional music videos as part of a strategy to attract young audiences. Rob Owen remarks how "Before MTV, if people wanted to hear music from a popular movie, they had to listen to the radio or buy the soundtrack album. Now, they can watch MTV and see a video from the movie, see an interview with the star of the movie, and see the star host videos."[18]

MTV's decision to build their programming around music videos and its integration of the music and film industries in the service of the network's interests have had a tremendous and far-reaching impact upon both entertainment and consumer culture. Indeed, MTV and music videos have been credited with redefining the very relationship that exists between television, film, advertising and consumption by drawing these diverse products and their activities into a much closer interaction. A noted feature associated with media texts of the 1980s in general is their collective reliance on "a vast network of references to other films, television shows and forms of mass media" as a structuring device,[19] a development that MTV helped encourage.

By 1985, MTV's distinctive 24-hour music video format had successfully established the MTV brand and the cable network was steadily attracting its targeted niche audience. Despite these developments, American Express decided to extricate itself from the cable business to focus on its financial services.[20] In the same year, Warner Communications and American Express sold MTV to Viacom International, thereby precipitating the next phase of MTV's evolution.[21]

1986–1996: MTV in Transition — Diversification and Globalization

At the time of the purchase, Viacom was a communications conglomerate with ownership interests in cable systems, pay-movie services, television production and syndication as well as radio and television stations.[22] Viacom's MTV purchase was an attempt to acquire a greater interest in specialized cable program services. Viacom's purchase was characteristic of an entertainment industry engaging in an intense degree of mergers and acquisitions, all with an eye towards tight diversification. These activities gained momentum in the 1980s as corporations began acquiring businesses that offered access to related entertainment content and outlets in order to extend their market reach and increase profit margins. Such activities allowed these corporate entities to evolve into increasingly powerful multimedia conglomerates whose control over the entertainment industries grew exponentially.

Sumner Redstone, who acquired Viacom in 1987, was one of the prime directors of Viacom's multimedia corporate growth. Prior to taking over Viacom, Redstone owned a chain of movie theatres in both the U.S. and the United Kingdom.[23] Redstone's Viacom purchase was only his first step towards conglomeration and multimedia diversification. In 1994, Viacom merged with another media conglomerate, Paramount Communications. Paramount's holdings included the Paramount film studio, Paramount Books as well as publishing company Simon & Schuster.[24] According to Banks, "the merger made Viacom the second largest media conglomerate in the United States after Time Warner."[25] Redstone was particularly committed to encouraging synergy and cross-medialization between Viacom's different media enterprises. In the wake of the Paramount merger, Viacom planned to fully exploit the newly acquired media holdings by mandating

> more cooperation among its own divisions and the various subsidiaries of Paramount through joint ventures and cross-media promotions. Viacom [had] plans to take advantage of its newly diverse interests in film, publishing, cable television and broadcasting to produce more coordinated campaigns to market a concept, artist, or program affiliated with the company's subsidiaries.[26]

Expansion and Diversification

As corporations diversified into other related media, they began to integrate the activities of these initially distinct and separate media industries, all in the interests of exploiting the potential for increased revenues that could accrue from repackaging a single entertainment text into multiple commercial products. According to Meehan,

> the interpenetration of the music, film, print and video industries does not arise in response to demand from movie goers, record buyers, or comics subscribers. Rather, this interpenetration is orchestrated by the conglomerate in its search for more profitable and cost-efficient ways to manufacture culture.[27]

As Viacom diversified into multiple media formats, it began to reconceptualize MTV's media activities as well as the cable network's role within the greater corporate system. According to Banks, "after the Paramount takeover, Viacom executives were anxious for MTV to develop films for Paramount's studio and books for Simon & Schuster that would appeal to the channel's young audience."[28] In short, Viacom planned to diversify the MTV brand into television and film production, a music label, as well as publishing. The decision to expand the MTV brand beyond a cable network broadcasting music videos motivated the cable network's shift into a more traditional programming format.

By 1986, it was apparent that MTV's original 24-hour music video concept was forcing the cable channel to remain reliant on the music industry for content, preventing it from expanding into other forms of programming, or from producing, owning, and thereby, profiting from creating its own shows. Furthermore, while 24-hour music videos were distinctive, the format encouraged a "grazing" attitude in its viewers. As there were no specific shows to commit to, MTV's audience tended to tune in and sample some videos before moving on to other channels, behavior detrimental to MTV's audience numbers and ratings. MTV responded to the problem by shifting away from music videos and introducing distinct programming blocks as well as discrete shows in which music videos took a marginal role. From 1986 onwards, MTV expanded its schedule to include syndicated comedies such as *Monty Python's Flying Circus* (1969–1974) and *The Monkees*, and began producing its own original shows such as the game show *Remote Control* (1987–1990) and the *MTV Half-Hour Comedy Hour* (1988–1993). While music videos still appeared on the network, they no longer constituted the bulk of MTV programming but were instead interspersed with more conventional television series.

Changes in programming were also motivated by MTV's evolving target youth demographic. Through the 1980s, national cable access had expanded beyond the suburban areas to achieve a higher degree of national penetration into the large, urban cities, including New York, Los Angeles and Detroit. Consequently, an urban, multi-ethnic, multi-racial, younger teen demographic emerged as a potential audience. During this period, MTV shifted its focus from the young adult demographic to attend to the 12 to 24 range, with more attention to teens in particular. Realizing that the white, suburban rock that MTV initially offered did not appeal to this new demographic, MTV responded by skewing its programming towards a younger demographic and reconfigured what remained of its music mandate to include music-video-oriented shows that revolved around different musical genres. This included *MTV Top 20 Video Countdown* (1984–1997), aimed at mainstream pop and contemporary music fans, *Club MTV* (1985–1992), which featured dance music, *Yo! MTV Raps* (1988–1995), targeted at rap fans, and *Headbangers' Ball* (1987–1995), which catered to heavy metal fans.

A number of shows were also developed to exploit Viacom's multimedia holdings at the time. These included *MTV Unplugged* (1989–1997), a concert series in which musicians offered acoustic renditions of their work, and *MTV The Real World* (1992–), which focused on the "real" life experiences of a group of young adults (generally in their early twenties) who were selected by MTV and invited to live together for a year while MTV filmed their daily experiences. The animated *Beavis and Butt-head* (1993–1997), was another popular series on the cable network. The show revolved around its two title characters whose principal activity was watching excerpts of music videos and indulging in rude, mocking commentary about what they saw. Each of these series allowed Viacom to engage in a range of synergistic practices. In addition to the profits that accrued from owning and syndicating these shows, performances from *Unplugged* were repackaged into a series of CDs, episodes of *The Real World* were retailed on video, and *Beavis and Butt-head* generated videos and video games. All of these products were distributed and retailed through Viacom-owned Blockbuster stores. Furthermore, MTV Books, launched in 1995 in association with Viacom owner Simon & Schuster's Pocket Books, also published numerous books that were tie-ins with these programs. *Beavis and Butt-head* in particular played a significant role when Viacom expanded MTV's brand into film production.

MTV's move into film production and distribution in 1996 represented a further attempt to expand the MTV brand beyond the cable medium into another component of the highly diversified conglomerate. At this point, MTV's initial forays into film production were opportunistic one-off events in which MTV Productions aligned with a major studio to produce and distribute individual films. *Joe's Apartment* (1996), a feature film built around a short MTV segment first cablecast on MTV, was a co-production between MTV Networks and Warner Bros. Pictures. While *Joe's Apartment* failed at the box office, MTV's other film release *Beavis and Butt-head Do America* (1996), was a significant box-office success.[29]

Unlike *Joe's Apartment, Beavis and Butt-head Do America*, adhered to a textbook formula of how a highly diversified corporate entity could exploit the synergistic potential of its media holdings and their established content. These were the considerations that prompted MTV to capitalize on its youth-brand cachet and hedge its bets by producing a film based on the cable channel's already established, and highly popular, Beavis and Butt-head characters. *Beavis and Butt-head Do America* was released as a co-production between MTV Films and Paramount, which were both owned by Viacom. Patterned after the highly successful live action film, *Dumb and Dumber* (1994), *Beavis and Butt-head Do America* traced the duo's adventures as they trekked across America in pursuit of their stolen television set. The film consisted of little more than random, bizarre plot developments that arose out of Beavis and Butt-head's encounters with a series of strange characters. Containing familiar doses of vulgar irreverence, a propensity for crude jokes and dialogue, as well as the obnoxious personas of the title characters, *Beavis and Butt-head Do America* was a major box-office hit. The film possessed all the earmarks of a high-concept film, as evidenced by the pre-sold nature of the film's content, the cross-over of the MTV signature style and aesthetics to a film context, and the full force of the cable network's promotional backing.[30] The film's adoption of these qualities was evidence that the high-concept mode of production that Wyatt associated with the blockbuster films of the 1980s had developed beyond the blockbuster genre and been absorbed in the production of a niche-oriented teenpic by the mid 1990s. Much of *Beavis and Butt-head do America*'s success must be attributed to the film subject's already established popularity with its target youth audience, as well as the intense promotional backing that the film enjoyed on MTV's cable channel. Produced for less than $20 million, the film grossed $63.1 million domestically, "making it the highest grossing, non–Disney animated feature at that time."[31]

MTV and Globalization

In addition to Viacom and MTV's increasing success at exploiting the synergistic potential of their highly diversified media holdings, MTV was also simultaneously expanding its global media influence. Through the 1980s and after, Viacom and MTV actively worked to develop the latter's high-profile teen-oriented brand from a national entity into an international enterprise. Taking MTV international was a conscious attempt at developing ancillary markets that would eventually represent the most promising forms of future growth for the company. As Tom McGrath explains, "with the cable frontier in America largely tamed, any further spread of MTV in the States was likely to be slow. As a result, if ... the channel [was] to have significant growth, the smartest strategy was to take MTV around the planet."[32] This made particular financial sense since the network could further the profit potential of the entertainment products that MTV created for its domestic market and earn additional profits from products whose costs had already been incurred. Of course, the globalization of MTV's interests could never have occurred without advances in cable, and satellite technology, not to mention the international communities' adoption of these technologies. As Barker notes, these technologies

> enable media organizations to operate on a global scale by assisting in the process of international organizational communication and in allowing media products to be distributed across the world. Both functions of new technology are intimately bound up with the globalization of media in general.[33]

With these considerations and motivations in play, MTV Australia was launched on April 1987, and MTV Europe began broadcasting in August of the same year. In 1990, MTV expanded into Eastern Europe, and in 1991, MTV Asia was born. MTV's expansion into these markets placed it in an ideal position to service advertisers interested in reaching a global youth audience. MTV was also able to help market and promote cultural texts, be they musical acts, films or television shows on a global scale. According to Banks,

> MTV exemplifies the growing globalization of popular culture and moreover is a key agent fostering this trend. Large cultural producers of various media (theatrical film, television and recorded music) seek global audiences for their offerings. MTV's worldwide network of services encourages the emergence of this global market both through its program content and advertising. In terms of programming, music video clips presented on MTV are a hybrid of film, television, and music so that the clips themselves can promote these cultural products globally.[34]

By the early 1990s, MTV had grown from a music-defined, youth-targeted cable network into a very profitable component of Viacom, a highly diversified, multi-media conglomerate with worldwide interests and access. In addition, MTV itself had evolved beyond the cable television medium, expanding its interests into television and film production, publishing, and a music label. What had started as a single cable channel telecasting an uninterrupted stream of music videos from relatively unknown artists had emerged as a globally identifiable corporate brand.

This evolution brought with it both positive and negative consequences. MTV's multi-media interests allowed MTV to attract an audience that extended beyond that segment of youth solely interested in music. By the early 1990s, MTV was also reaching the larger youth market via MTV Films, MTV Books, and MTV's own recording label. As a result, MTV's cable network became only one aspect of the steadily expanding MTV entertainment empire. These changes ensured that the cable network was less dependent on the music industry for its content and, therefore, no longer as vulnerable to the shifts of a single entertainment industry, or as completely reliant on any particular music corporation. Furthermore, MTV had progressed towards producing much of its own media content, which it could then market on a global basis via their worldwide cable interests, thus expanding the profitability of the programming. In making these evolutions, MTV, in the mid–'90s, represented "Music Television" in name only. It could no longer make any real claims to its original identity as a purely *music*, or *television* entity.[35]

These changes did create a dilemma for MTV's cable network, which was witnessing a steady dilution of its ideal, core teen demographic audience, the 12- to 24-year-old music fans that the network had identified as its most valuable target, and who were inextricably associated with MTV's initial, music-oriented, brand identity. The cable division was in a quandary: "Did it risk alienating the core demographic of music fans aged 12–24 on whose shoulders it had built a billion-dollar brand, or did it run for the new found audience winners instead?"[35] The answer to this particular dilemma would be found in a series of larger social and industrial events that took place in the late 1990s.

1997–2000s: MTV in the Millennium — A Multi-Platform, Multi-Media Teen Entertainment Hub

In the late 1990s, MTV underwent a further evolution, this time brought about by the rise of a new, significant teen demographic, an increasingly integrated entertainment industry structure, the continuing importance of the global market, the development of digital technology, a distinct shift in musical trends and the success of Jive Records. As detailed in Chapter Two, the mid-nineties witnessed the beginnings of a notable demographic change in America when teenagers reemerged as a vital, valuable and important market segment — one that would replace MTV's previous target, Generation X. By 1996, Generation X (those born between the early 1960s and 1976) were steadily aging out of MTV's 12 to 24 target demographic. In contrast, the oldest wave of Generation Y, that demographic segment born between 1977 and 1995, were entering their teens at the time. Generation Y's significant numbers meant that it would have tremendous influence over American culture, society, and industry, as marketers began acknowledging their presence.

Unlike their Gen X predecessors, who rejected commercialism and exces-sive consumption, Gen Y embraced consumerist behavior and was character-ized as extremely brand-conscious. As marketers began responding to this demographic, flooding the market with products aimed specifically at teenagers, advertisers began seeking ways to reach that audience. MTV found itself in an enviable position. Having built its identity as *the* primary youth-oriented net-work, MTV was well placed to service the needs of these advertisers. By then, MTV could also offer access to the increasingly significant *global* youth mar-ket. According to Moses, there were "560 million teens between 15 and 19 world-wide in 2000 ... and their spending [totaled] more than $100 billion a year."[36] In addition, youth under 25 were the largest population segments in develop-ing nations including China, India and Brazil at the end of the twentieth cen-tury.[37] The global teen market was a definite consumer force worth targeting, and with MTV's established success in expanding into the global media mar-ketplace, it was a market that MTV was well-positioned to both service and exploit.

As Hollywood turned its attention to the burgeoning millennial teen mar-ket, different outlets and media organizations, some of which were in direct competition with each other, began identifying and constructing different teen identities to target and cater to. As was true of the artificially constructed notion of the teen market itself, these attempts at segmenting and differentiating the teen market were themselves self-conscious and contrived. Since its inception, MTV had engaged in defining its target market, an ongoing and evolving prac-tice that was subject to social and industrial considerations. At MTV's launch, its primary target was young, adult, suburban males, the demographic segment that was most likely to have access to the then newly-emerging cable technol-ogy. After cable achieved greater penetration into urban markets, MTV's tar-get evolved accordingly, shifting towards a more multi-racial, urban, young adult segment. With the rise of the millennial teen market, MTV again revised their demographic focus, embracing programming and adjusting their brand to attract a younger, teenage audience. The MTV Teen was a variation on MTV's already established multi-racial, urban audience and possessed the familiar qualities associated with the MTV brand, qualities that included a degree of edgy irreverence, a preference for the new and cutting-edge, and the adoption of a healthy anti-establishment attitude. MTV's commitment to this particu-lar teen construction can be traced to the media content it developed during this particular millennial phase.

Even as Generation Y began to influence popular media, a large propor-tion of MTV's cable programming itself was not necessarily tailored to this lat-est teen cycle. Through the mid-1990s, MTV was primarily focused on rap, hip-hop, grunge and alternative music — the music embraced by Gen X. By 1995, MTV was behind the curve as these musical genres began to decline, even as Gen Y was quickly resurrecting teen pop music.[38] This resurgence of teen pop was aided by the economic recovery of the mid '90s, when the disillusionment associated with economic decline, recession and the accompanying atmosphere of insecurity in the late 1980s and early 1990s was replaced by a growing optimism ushered in by economic recovery and resumed consumer confidence in the second half of the decade. Beginning in the mid–1990s, the Spice Girls and Hanson both found phenomenal global success with their bouncy, cheery, pop dance tunes which were embraced by Gen Y, which was still in its pre-teen or "early" teen years at the time. Despite these successes, teen pop was still far from the phenomenal mainstream cultural event it eventually would become. Ultimately, Hanson and the Spice Girls were only the early rumblings of a phenomenon that would grow into a mainstream music movement in American culture in the late '90s. While the Spice Girls and Hanson did find significant success in America, they were perceived as specific, isolated phenomena, rather than part of a full-scale teen-oriented musical trend. It would take a few years for Gen Y to age out of their pre-teens into their teen years and evolve into the vital teen market with significant purchasing power.

Jive Records: Teen Pop and the Global Music Market

The ascension of the teen pop music phenomenon itself could be directly attributed to a single corporate entity in the recording industry, Jive Records, which cleverly read the social, industrial and marketplace shifts and capitalized on a unique moment of opportunity. While the larger music industry was apparently slow in recognizing and responding to the situation, Jive Records was ahead of the curve, almost single-handedly resurrecting the teen pop music genre. Media journalists examining the return of teen pop in the late 1990s all credited Jive Records with spearheading the trend.[39] David Thigpen asserts, "The beginning of the new century unquestionably belongs to Jive Records, the colossally successful independent label that has almost single-handedly brought the teen-pop revolution ... into homes across North America, Europe and Asia."[40] Studying the industrial structure and business activities of the record label, we find the same conditions that characterized the culture industries in the 1990s: Jive was part of a global enterprise with a diversified portfolio that allowed the label to exploit and profit from its numerous integrated business interests.

Jive Records was a component of one of the world's leading independent music operations, the Zomba Music Group. Zomba's global reach consisted of companies in Canada, Australia and France; operations in Germany, Switzerland, Austria and Benelux; a regional Asia-Pacific hub based in Singapore as well as a London-based international records division.[41] Furthermore, Zomba was a highly diversified enterprise that included various record labels, music publishing interests, music production libraries, record/software distribution and export, film/television music, and recording studios and equipment rental.[42] These holdings enabled Zomba to practice the synergistic activities that led to the corporation's growth. Zomba's global structure and its diversified portfolio played a significant role in Jive's ability to direct and exploit the international teen pop market in the late 1990s.

Jive's strategy in nurturing teen talent and guiding their music took highly regulated routes. Realizing that the U.S. market was not ready for the return of teen-oriented pop in the early 1990s, yet recognizing the popularity of the musical form in Europe, Jive exploited its international operations and sent its teen performers overseas. The most popular and successful acts of the late 1990s, including boy-bands The Backstreet Boys and 'N Sync, and teen pop star Britney Spears, all recorded their albums in Europe, in the Zomba-owned Stockholm studios of songwriter-producers Max Martin and the late Denis Pop, who between them were responsible for virtually every major hit by these pop stars.[43] Jive's next step was to utilize its global network to launch these acts in markets throughout the world. So, in addition to working with European creative talent, both Backstreet Boys and 'N Sync got their start in Europe, where their brand of European-produced pop was particularly popular. Years before finding success in the American market, these boy bands were already established stars in overseas markets including Europe and Asia. Thus, one of the key characteristics of late 1990s teen pop is its distinctly global nature, a characteristic that is directly related to Jive's globally based corporate structure. According to Jive president Barry Weiss, "Jive controls its own destiny on a world-wide basis. In many territories, we control our own marketing, promotion, and distribution. We're always making sure that our left and right hands are working in synchronicity."[44] Jive, like MTV and other major entertainment conglomerates, enjoyed the benefits of a globalized, diversified and vertically integrated business operation.

Jive's ability to identify, nurture and create teen-friendly pop acts and music was matched by the label's focus on marketing and promoting its artists. This commitment motivated the label to adopt a series of strategies aimed directly at targeting teen demographic consumers. Jive's plans to launch its teen-oriented acts in the U.S. involved a carefully conducted campaign to publicize the acts through a range of advertisements, contests and features in high-profile teen magazines.[45] In addition to these efforts, Jive also engaged in a particularly symbiotic relationship with MTV in the late '90s. Realizing that MTV was another vital means by which to exploit its teen artists, Jive produced videos to accompany each of their teen artists' released singles and made these stars especially available to the cable network. Jive and MTV's close collaboration in promoting and nurturing teen pop music directly shaped the nature of teen culture for the late 1990s teen market — and it defined the new generation of teen culture that would brand MTV for its next phase.

MTV and Jive Records: Repackaging Teen Culture for the Millennium

By 1996, the phenomenal success of Jive's teen-oriented pop acts had re-energized the teen music market, a market that MTV once ruled before it marginalized its music programming in favor of non-music television series. MTV recognized that it needed to regain its initial identity as a teen-oriented music television channel if it hoped to profit from the resurrection of teen pop music in the millennium. Consequently, the network began instituting a series of changes to its programming and content, while reevaluating its musical and entertainment direction. These changes did not go unnoticed by the entertainment trade papers, all of which provide accounts of the shifts and decisions that characterized MTV's latest evolution — one that, in part, involved a return to the network's music roots.

In the late 1990s, the network recognized the need to cater to a newer, younger, teenage market that had very definite and distinct entertainment preferences. MTV also realized that it needed to renew its relationship with the music industry, particularly Jive Records, which was enjoying tremendous growth in the teen music market at the time. To do so, MTV needed to reestablish its commitment to servicing the music industry's teen-oriented marketing and promotional needs.[46] However, the general trend towards multimedia conglomeration and tight diversification also meant that teen-oriented texts were no longer media specific but increasingly media integrated, with an intense degree of cross-media blending between film, television and music. MTV therefore needed to create programming that would not only attract a teen audience and reinstate music-oriented programming to its schedule, but also serve as a promotional platform for the increasingly integrated multi-media teen-oriented texts of the late 1990s. The shows that allowed MTV to fulfill these requirements: *Total Request Live* (1998–2008), *Fashionably Loud* (1996–) and *MTVdotcom* (1998), all premiered in the late 1990s. The following discussion highlights how these shows functioned as key teen media sites that helped to consolidate MTV's teen brand, while serving as launch-pads for a widening range of teen-focused multi-media content and products.

Total Request Live: *MTV's Teen-Oriented, Promotional Platform*

In response to MTV's redefined mandate, MTV launched *Total Request Live* (or *TRL*) in 1998, a video request show aimed specifically at the teen audience. This show, in particular, played a significant role in helping MTV regain its "young, cool, hip, and trendy" brand identity. *TRL* successfully re-established MTV's credibility with its core teen target audience while functioning as a new promotional platform to service the entertainment industries intent on targeting the teen market. Ostensibly a show dedicated to screening videos requested by its viewers, *TRL* was scheduled to run every weekday between the hours of three and five in the afternoon, coinciding with the time when teenagers were likely to return home from school. The show was broadcast live from MTV's studios in New York's Times Square, a location that emphasized the show's urban, hip, cosmopolitan attitude. To attract its target audience, *TRL* took steps to brand itself in explicitly teen-oriented terms.

One key strategy involved inviting a live audience to participate in the *TRL* broadcast (gesturing back towards the historical *American Bandstand*). From the outset, *TRL* filled its studio solely with teenagers and encouraged them to express their interests, views, and entertainment preferences on the air. Teenagers nationwide were also invited to submit their video requests via telephone, e-mail and on-air appearances.[47] *TRL*'s teen-oriented mandate also meant that the show's musical and video content were disproportionately skewed towards teen pop music — or at least what the music industry and MTV identified as teen pop. When Spears released her single, "Oops! ... I Did It Again" (2000), in anticipation of the impending release of her CD of the same name, the song's video was "exclusively previewed" on *TRL*. Spears made a guest appearance on *TRL* to introduce her video and promote her new CD. In the weeks approaching the CD's release, Spears was again invited to appear on *TRL*, this time to participate in an exclusive question-and-answer session with her teenage fans who could interact with the star as part of a select studio audience, or by phoning in their comments and questions. That particular segment on *TRL* was yet another promotional exercise that interwove the question-and-answer session with musical breaks during which segments of her songs from the new album were played for *TRL*'s audience. MTV actively promoted the event as yet another network "exclusive," since the CD was not available in stores for some weeks yet.

TRL's style and format continued MTV's characteristic postmodern attitude by embracing the stylistic and visual conventions associated with commercial advertising. Caldwell has traced Madison Avenue and commercial advertising's growing influence over American television's increasingly postmodern visual style, arguing that the trend emerged in the 1980s:

> Commercial spots continue to be the most dynamic sites for visual experimentation on television. Packed into tiny temporal slugs of thirty and sixty seconds, advertising spots were probably the first type of programming to exploit the discursive and emotive power of hyperactive and excessive visual style.... Visual style became visually excessive and temporally hyperactive on network television, one might argue, because ads must fight for the attention of distracted viewers during breaks from the program.[48]

Given *TRL*'s primary status as an advertising and promotional platform, the show's propensity for excessive visual style, fragmentation and its rejection of narrative coherence can be understood as the cable network's adoption of the highly successful advertising style and format.

TRL's visual and stylistic excess was not restricted to blending film, television and music videos, or borrowing from advertising style. Its format was also an attempt to replicate that of its greatest challenger: the Internet, with its offer of infinite choice without the need for coherence. In addition to showing only portions of music videos, films, television shows and short celebrity interviews, the *TRL* format further rejected the integrity of any image by superimposing additional visual and aural texts over the primary visual image. For instance, while a requested video played, mini "windows" would appear around the margins of the screen showing teenage fans screaming their appreciation of the video. At these points, the visual image and aural soundtrack of the music video blended with the visual image and aural soundtrack of the teenage viewers articulating their requests, all of which combined into a barely comprehensible whole. In other instances, the broadcast video would be interrupted by scrolling text that appeared on the bottom half of the screen, simulating the "crawl" that appeared on Internet websites (and which subsequently appeared on cable news broadcasts). In *TRL*'s case, these texts were transcriptions of the e-mail requests that MTV's teenage viewers had sent to *TRL*'s website. This strategy ignored any established boundaries between television and the Internet, and instead merged the look and style of both media. This blurring of distinct media formats highlighted MTV's ability to integrate its cable content with its online ventures. This visual and stylistic cross-over allowed both branches of the multi-media corporation to function synergistically and promote each other.

With *TRL*'s fragmented format, the program evolved and changed at a hyperactive pace. The blending of film and television trailers, music videos, celebrity appearances and interviews, as well as access to an interactive website, also exposed the viewer to the entire range of entertainment distractions listed above. *TRL*'s goal was to become a one-stop entertainment outlet for media-obsessed teens. As such, the show offered a viewing experience in which the text constantly moved on to the next thing before its audience could get bored. The tendency towards fragmentation, and visual and stylistic blending was a function of trying to keep the material interesting, active, and changing, rather than slow, static and predictable. The quick turnover in content also encouraged its audience to tune in and pay attention since the very short shelf life of the media products on show meant that if the teen audience aimed to stay current, it could not afford to neglect the show for fear of being left behind.

In addition to expanding the music programming on MTV, the increasingly multi-media, multi-platform brand was also consolidating its film interests. While MTV's early film releases were co-productions with established studios, in 1998, Viacom and MTV officially announced the launch of MTV Films, a co-partnership with Viacom-owned Paramount Studios. With the teen market's resurgence, it made particular business sense to exploit MTV's growing brand popularity with the youth demographic. Benefiting from "the most recognizable brand name in the teen universe," MTV Films was deemed to have immediate access to an established and increasingly valuable niche market from the outset.[49] In addition, MTV Films would also benefit from unlimited access to the highly efficient and influential marketing and promotional abilities of MTV's cable network.

These obvious synergistic advantages were clearly and effectively exploited in January 1999, when MTV Films released its football drama *Varsity Blues*. Set in high school and tracing the coming-of-age experiences of a teenage boy torn between football and more esoteric pursuits, and exploring the typical romantic entanglements characteristic of high-school life, *Varsity Blues* was a film that spoke directly to Generation Y's concerns. The film also had another important draw: it featured an attractive group of up-and-coming actors, including James Van Der Beek, who had already garnered a huge (female) teenage following as the star of the WB's teen-oriented television drama *Dawson's Creek*. Interestingly, Paramount initially had acquired the project, but the studio handed it over to MTV Films, which produced *Varsity Blues* for well under $20 million.

The film was the first true test of the channel's ability to market a product that was not based on a road-tested MTV property such as *Beavis and Butt-Head*.[50] The network went about building interest and "buzz" around the film weeks in advance of the opening. MTV's first promotional activities involved airing interstitial spots to introduce the film's teenage characters, in scenes compatible with the MTV style. One spot featured Van Der Beek doing push-ups while a thought bubble above his head posed the question "Do I care more about football or Kurt Vonnegut?" The advertising spots emphasized the film's combination of sexual content, sports, and teen angst. The film was also accompanied by a soundtrack and music video promotion on the cable network. While the film's trailers flooded MTV's commercial airtime, the film's stars also appeared on *TRL*, which also featured scenes from the film as part of MTV's promotional blitz. The combination of Van Der Beek, sex, high-school football, cheerleaders in whipped cream bikinis and MTV's brand name proved irresistible to teenagers. The film succeeded at the box-office, grossing $53 million in North America.

In the late 1990s, *TRL* emerged as a significant cultural/promotional site and helped MTV regain its credibility with the teen market. In the first quarter of 1999, MTV witnessed a 66 percent increase in 12- to 34 year-olds in *TRL*'s 3:30 to 4:30 timeslot; the show also helped MTV's three P.M. to seven P.M. block increase its 12 to 34 demo by 40 percent.[51] In addition to developing a teen-branded series that brought the music industry "closer" to its target audience, *TRL* allowed MTV to increase the proportion of music videos featured on the network, without actually returning to its early twenty-four-hour video-laden format. More importantly, *TRL* did so within a program framework that enabled the network to service the promotional needs of an increasingly integrated media industry in which music videos were often only a single aspect of a greater multi-media enterprise that often included film, television, music, celebrity and even fashion interests.

Fashionably Loud: *MTV, Glamour and Designer High-fashion*

MTV's focus on the consumer-oriented, brand conscious Gen Y teen audience, its interest in servicing the marketing and promotional needs of the culture industries, and its commitment to consumerism have also directly shaped the network's programming and aesthetics in another way: the interaction between music, celebrity and fashion. This interactive situation is not new.

One of MTV's defining characteristics is an obsession with style and image. Certainly, MTV's image, style and aesthetics have always reflected the fashion and trends of its time — often with the most popular musicians reflecting the look and style of their moment.[52] Over the years, MTV has had a significant role to play in consolidating the relationship between music, celebrity and style.

Through the 1980s and early '90s, MTV was a site where fashion trends began. It popularized punk fashion, thrift-store clothing (Madonna and Cyndi Lauper in the mid–80s), iconographic style statements (Michael Jackson's single, sequined glove) and grunge, to name just a few. MTV then mined the margins of culture (the punk movement, the New York dance-club scene, the Seattle grunge sub-culture) and popularized their unique styles, which then gained popularity and eventually were co-opted by mainstream fashion designers.

While MTV continues to integrate fashion, celebrity and entertainment, the dynamic took an interesting turn in the late 1990s. This was an era characterized by a powerful economic recovery, and the rise of a highly brand-conscious teen market. Furthermore, the fashion industry was increasingly intent upon cultivating a relationship with the entertainment industry and exploiting the promotional opportunities associated with the cult of celebrity. In response to these developments, MTV's style, image and aesthetics shifted towards youth, glamour, and an increasing obsession with designer fashion.

Never before in MTV's history had considerations of celebrity style been so completely and directly associated with brand name designers as opposed to cutting-edge trends associated with marginal sub-cultures. By the late 1990s, MTV had shifted from its earlier role in breaking new fashion trends towards merely showcasing and promoting new designer fashions. MTV became just another cultural site marketing and publicizing fashion designers and clothing brands. This shift was evidenced by MTV's *Fashionably Loud*, which overtly blended glitzy brand-name fashions with pop music by showcasing teenage models walking the runway in high-priced, designer outfits supplied by Guess, Tommy Hilfiger, Earl Jeans, DKNY and Moschino, among others, while different pop groups and musicians provided live accompaniment.

The synergy between MTV, celebrities, music and brand-name designer fashion could also explain the trend towards excessive glamour and glitz seen in the contemporary music videos on MTV. This development was particularly clear in the teen pop videos that dominated the network's schedule. Britney Spears and other teen pop stars like Mandy Moore and Jessica Simpson were packaged as fashion-conscious celebrities who wore designer items in their videos and in their numerous other appearances on MTV. Their videos were high-budget, slick productions that consciously attempted to replicate the kinds of images represented in high fashion and beauty magazines. In these videos, fashion, style and image supplanted the story-telling strategies of earlier videos (for instance, Michael Jackson's 1983 "Thriller" video).[53] In fact, Spears' popular "Don't Let Me Be the Last to Know" (2001) music video, which showed the skimpily dressed, drenched singer cavorting on a beach with a young male model, was directed by Herb Ritts, a high-fashion photographer famous for his *Vogue* and *Harper's Bazaar* covers and his celebrity shots. The aesthetics of these high-fashion photographs were transposed onto the visuals for Spears' video.

This synergy between music, television and fashion was further reinforced by fashion magazines such as *Seventeen* and *InStyle*, which ran regular features identifying the fashions, styles and "looks" found in popular music videos. These magazine spreads named the fashion designers (including Tom Ford for Yves St. Laurent Rive Gauche, Chanel, Moschino, and Earl Jeans) and beauty products (by Calvin Klein, MAC, and ARTec among others) used in the videos and taught their readers to replicate the clothing and the makeup. This development supports Caldwell's argument that "television creates images that consume images, the importation of stylistic motifs and contexts from other art forms is a crucial issue in the study of television ... the new television seems infatuated with other *visual* art forms (photography, film, modeling, performance art)."[54]

Shows such as *TRL* and *Fashionably Loud* displayed an increasing stylistic and aesthetic cross-media convergence. In addition, each show functioned as a central site within a complex multimedia matrix with links to numerous other shows, films, celebrities, music and consumer products. The style, content and format of these shows were shaped by a combination of factors including the emergence of a new, media-saturated, culture-obsessed and technologically advanced teen demographic, MTV's own multimedia interests as well as the larger culture industries' synergistic interests across multiple media. Between 1997 and 2001, MTV reigned as the number-one cable channel in the 12 to 24 audience demographic; the period also saw MTV's ratings grow by 50 percent.[55] By 2002, MTV was ready to advance even further along the path to synergy, joining with Jive/Zomba's newly launched film division to further exploit the cross-media potential of teen star Britney Spears.

Crossroads: *The Intensification of Cross-Corporate Synergy*

In 2002, the interest in media diversification, synergy and teen culture media integration reached a new level with MTV's collaboration with Filmco Enterprises, a newly-launched film division under Zomba/Jive Records. The arrangement involved both conglomerates in the production and distribution of a new film, *Crossroads* (2002), starring Britney Spears. Spears' film debut was tied directly to Zomba/Jive Records' decision to diversify beyond the music business and expand into film production the better to fully exploit its teen star across a variety of media texts. *Crossroads* was, therefore, one of the most overdetermined media exercises imaginable. The teen film's release schedule was set to coincide with the launch of Spears' next album, which featured songs from the film. The film was produced by Ann Carli, a former member of the artist development unit at Jive Records, and financed by Clive Calder, the owner of Jive records, and distributed by Paramount Pictures in association with its marketing partner, MTV Films.[56]

The film's pedigree revealed the complex relationships that result when powerful conglomerations come together to generate product. Considering Filmco/Jive's multi-media interests, the film was part of a huge multi-media entertainment "event," which included the release of Spears' third, eponymously titled album that featured songs from the film. Zomba/Jive's ownership interests allowed the conglomerate a high degree of control over the film, its content, production, packaging, marketing and release date, as well as the related Spears album, its content, production, marketing and release date. *Crossroads* represents a particularly conscious attempt at controlling and steering the multi-media aspects of an artist's career. Instead of losing control of a talent and missing out on the profits that can accrue when that star moved from one entertainment medium to another (as often has been the norm), Jive effectively consolidated its ownership by expanding into filmmaking. To further ensure the film's potential success, Jive partnered with MTV Films to distribute the film. This partnership effectively ensured that Spears, her movie and her album would receive intense, interlocked promotional support, with coverage and publicity via the teen-oriented MTV cable network, and on MTV's online web site, effectively reaching the very audience that had already embraced Spears and her work.

The Paramount/MTV-Filmco/Zomba arrangement is one more instance of a media conglomerate joint venture — another feature of the highly oligopolistic nature of the media markets in the second half of the twentieth century. According to McChesney, these "joint ventures are attractive because they reduce the capital requirements and risk on individual firms and permit the firms to spread their resources more widely."[57] *Crossroads* is an example of a media product created by "conglomerates eager to maximize the marketability of every media product. [It is] a film with marketing assets sewn into its aesthetic construction [which] lowers the inherent financial risk of commercial filmmaking."[58]

The film revolves around the coming-of-age experiences of an over-achieving teenage girl (Spears) who travels cross-country seeking a reunion with her mother who had deserted her. During the journey, she participates in, and wins, a singing contest. As director Carli acknowledged with regard to production demands, "There were certain things that we had to do—songs from her new album that she wanted to sing in the movie."[59] In many ways, *Crossroads* is a millennial teenpic version of the '80s high-concept film. The film has a "pre-sold element" with which to "increase the audience's identification with the material"—in this case, Britney Spears as the film's star.[60] Furthermore, Spears' CD functions as the film's soundtrack, since she performs a number of tracks off the CD in the movie. Thus, the publicity for both the movie and the CD serve a dual purpose by promoting each other. Finally, the marketing campaign conforms to Wyatt's description of high-concept advertising campaigns which privileged "the close match between content and marketing, the emphasis on style, the reducibility to a single image—[all of which] are repeated in the visual marketing forms: trailers and television commercials."[61] *Crossroad*'s advertising revolved around Spears' star persona, with Spears' music video for the film, and the film's trailers highlighting her musical performances, playing during teen-oriented television shows on MTV and the teen-oriented WB television network.

The Jive/MTV/Britney Spears synergistic promotional activities began with the November release of Spears' CD. Between November 3rd and 6th, 2001, MTV ran multiple telecasts of its special, *Total Britney Live*. A special edition of *Total Request Live*, the two-hour publicity/promotional blitz was hosted by Carson Daly with Spears herself in attendance. Part promotional event, part *This Is Your Life*, the show featured Spears performing both old hits and new songs, and samples of the other tracks from the new, soon-to-be-released album intermingled with "documentary"-like home video footage of the singer growing up in her hometown in Louisiana, video clips of her friends and family, and a look back on the star's entertainment career. Other segments include a showcase of Britney's "trendsetting style," with both a fashion show highlighting the different outfits the singer wore in her various music videos, as well as a "shop for Britney" contest in which actual teenage fans were challenged to shop and put together an outfit for their idol. MTV also promoted *Crossroads*, offering fans a preview of the film's trailer, accentuated by the singer's own comments on the experience. The need to market and promote multiple products accounts for *Total Britney Live*'s highly fragmented and disjointed nature. Each segment existed to advertise a different text/product, be it Britney's latest CD, her upcoming film, the star's celebrity persona, or her fashion choices.

Considering MTV's vested interest in the film's success, it is unremarkable that the cable network exploited every opportunity to publicize the film.

In addition to *Total Britney Live*, MTV made multiple attempts to showcase Spears' music video for the song "I'm not a girl..." (2001) that was featured in the film. MTV featured the filming of the video in its *Making the Video* series. The video itself, which received heavy airplay in the weeks leading up to the film's release, actively promoted the film by intercutting scenes from the film with scenes of Spears performing the song. As Wyatt notes, "part of this 'raiding of the text' involves the fictional world of the high-concept film expanding beyond the film and into the promotional music video. This type of cross-referencing ... [maximizes] the audience's point of contact with the film" which functions as a particularly effective form of publicity.[62] But in the late 1990s, these promotional activities were much more complex and sophisticated. In the '80s, music videos were largely confined to promoting both the film text and the soundtrack. By the 1990s, MTV and its programming was only a small part of larger marketing activities that promoted activities that ranged beyond Britney, her CD and film to an expanded range of products that included the Britney doll, her magazine, and her preferred fashion and beauty brands. The publicity that MTV generated in connection with the star, her CD and her film continued through to the February 15th, 2002 release of *Crossroads*. MTV's online website MTV.com featured news coverage on the star and her film, interviews, the opportunity to download the film's trailer as well as video and audio access to Spears' music. Spears also made a promotional appearance on *TRL* the day of the film's premiere, and took part in an interview session that included another retrospective of her music videos.

With *Total Britney Live*, and the other promotional activities, MTV took the marketing of entertainment culture a step further than any media conglomerate to that point. Teen culture after the late 1990s could no longer be isolated to a single media, or a single event. Rather, it consisted of an expanding series of (inter-)related media events and activities that blur any existing boundary between entertainment, promotion, information and product. *Total Britney Live* represented the further integration and hybridization of television genres—the show was in turns part documentary, music video, film trailer, fashion show, and celebrity interview. As the show segued through multiple formats, styles and functions, it highlighted the near impossible task of distinguishing the originary, primary product from the ancillary tie-ins. Was the film, *Crossroads*, the album, *Britney*, the television special, *Total Britney Live*, or the star, Britney Spears, the point of origin for this highly integrated cultural activity? There appeared to be an equal, symbiotic relationship between the film, the album, the television show and the star herself. The MTV/Jive Records/Britney Spears project was an indication of the increasing media convergence that characterized the entertainment industries in the late 1990s and beyond as well as the kind of stylistic and content synergies that were forced into existence as a result.

MTVdotcom: *Embracing the Digital Generation*

MTV's role in maintaining a teen culture that increasingly integrated film, television, music, fashion and celebrity into a single entertainment-based experience gained further influence and exposure via MTV's digital advancements. Coming of age in the era of e-mail, the Internet, Instant Messaging, Napster, and web-casting, teenagers in the '90s were extremely technologically savvy and forged their own conceptions regarding the relationship between digital technology and entertainment. While previous generations turned to books, films, radio, television and cable for their entertainment, Generation Y had access to all those, as well as their computers. This rise in digital technology led to a generation of teens with an unprecedented degree of global access and global interaction.

MTV realized that to remain relevant to this generation of teenagers, they would have to stake an early claim on the Internet and its relevant technologies. MTV also realized that expanding its presence online was an ideal means of reaching and servicing its national and global audience communities. By encouraging a world-wide MTV audience to access and log-on to a single website, and experience and embrace a single source of content and popular entertainment culture, MTV online could foster and promote an MTV identity that had an international scope, one that went beyond the limits of nation-specific cable systems. The advent of digital technology provided further means by which MTV could access a global teen audience.[63]

MTV's foray into digital technology began in July 1995, when Viacom's Paramount Television Group launched Paramount Digital Entertainment as part of the conglomerate's continuing efforts to keep pace with both media technology and the youth generation's increasing interest and skill with the emerging digital advances. Paramount Digital Entertainment was slated to develop online, Internet programming which, Viacom realized, would become yet another avenue through which MTV could promote and market its consumer products and product-oriented lifestyles and identities. The decision to embrace digital, interactive entertainment offered the opportunity to tie the network's programming directly to its online content. This process had an impact on both the website and the programming content in distinctive ways.

In 1996, MTV launched MTV Prime Time Online, cablecasting four prime-time programs on its online AOL website offering content that was directly tied to its television shows. Considering the state of the technology at the time, MTV confined its online interactive programming to the rather more restrictive game and talk show formats. *Butt Heads with Kennedy* was a cablecast talk show built around online discussions; *Singled Out Online*, based on MTV's dating game *Singled Out*, allowed people to "meet" online; *The Love Doc* was a relationship advice forum in which MTV's online participants could seek relationship advice from host Dr. Gilda Carle and a musical guest.[64] At the time, video-streaming capabilities, digital cameras and real audio were not particularly advanced, which restricted network and audience interaction to written exchanges. These regularly scheduled interactive programs allowed MTV's computer literate audience to log on to its AOL website and interact with the shows' hosts, converse with them in real time and participate in on-air discussions as well as introduce issues or concerns—formats that paralleled MTV's on-air content. The online content on MTV's Internet website, MTV.com, was also, initially, similarly limited. Primarily restricted to information dissemination, MTV's early web pages offered a user-friendly home page with links to MTV news and information, transcripts of particular MTV shows, as well as information on new music and video releases. As the technology improved, however, MTV began offering audio samples of new music as well as new video programming available online, in order to attract and cater to Generation Y's computer-literate demographic.

By 1998, technological progress allowed MTV to create television programming with a much more sophisticated relationship with the network's online website. While *TRL* loosely "borrowed" the visual format associated with the Internet, *MTVdotcom* cablecast on MTV, was a television series whose format was directly linked to the network's online content. *MTVdotcom* offered music videos, celebrity interviews and entertainment information, all of which were presented via an entirely web-based visual format. The television screen took the form of a computer desktop. The show's content, including all celebrity interviews, music videos, as well as the host's contributions, would appear as pull-down windows. The show even replicated the less sophisticated visuals characteristic of video-streaming, transferring the jerky jumps and low-definition image quality associated with the online interactive experience to the television screen intact. Further amplifying the computer-based experience, a cursor arrow randomly appeared on the screen and clicked on "hypertext" that scrolled across the lower portion of the desktop window. This action produced another pop-up window providing further relevant information. At any time during the show, two or more "windows" would be open offering different, but related, information. For instance, one window would screen a music video, while simultaneously, another onscreen window would feature an interview with the performer. At the same time, text would continue to scroll across the bottom of the screen offering other information about the video, the musician or the show. Throughout, and after the broadcast, viewers were encouraged to log-on to MTV.com for additional, or further information and content. The entire experience replicated the fragmented, barely coherent programming style characteristic of MTV in the late '90s, not to mention the highly disjointed experience associated with surfing the web.

One of the great challenges posed by digital technology is the advanced pace at which developments and changes occur. After the launch of MTV.com, MTV was consistently forced to keep pace with the quickly evolving nature of the Internet and other digital developments. In 2001, MTV launched MTV360, a campaign that coordinated programming between the website and the cable's television content on MTV and MTV2.[65] In this latest development, viewers who watched an artist perform live on MTV could then turn to MTV2 to catch the artist's body of videos, and subsequently access the website for further information including interviews, music information, concert dates and the like. The strategy aimed to provide a multi-dimensional entertainment service for the current generation of teenagers.

MTV's multi-media, multi-platform, multi-format commitment reached another milestone in 2006 when advances in broadband technology led to the launch of MTV Overdrive, an internet-based, video-on-demand service available through MTV.com. Overdrive's most innovative content was a real-time link to MTV's live shows, including *Total Request Live* and *MTV's Music Video Awards*. Viewers of these shows were able to access additional behind-the-scenes content that was cybercast live, alongside the cablecast show. In addition, Overdrive offered live interactive opportunities. Viewers who were logged on to the cybercast had the opportunity to participate in real-time surveys and discussions that could then be picked up and addressed during the television show's broadcast. This integration of the television and online experience was an attempt to acknowledge Generation Y's increasing facility and tendency to multi-task across a range of media.

Other attempts to integrate MTV's television and online content included forays into virtual reality. Based on the concept of virtual communities that were increasingly popular on social networking sites, Virtual Laguna Beach was brought into existence in 2006. Built around MTV's hit reality series *Laguna Beach* (2004–2007), Virtual Laguna Beach, again accessed via MTV.com, allowed fans of the cable show to create avatars of themselves that could then inhabit the virtual settings that simulated the existing real world locations, and interact with other fans/avatars. Even in these virtual environments, MTV's commitment to marketing and promoting its own and its clients' media products remained strong. MTV was quick to proclaim that advertising existed even in its virtual world. Advertisers who signed on to participate in Virtual Laguna Beach could ensure their visibility and even attract the focused attention of the shows fans via a system that "paid" avatars that were willing to engage with the advertising. This online currency could then be spent on virtual goods available in this virtual world.[66]

In MTV's multi-media, multi-platform, multi-format phase, it became increasingly difficult to identify the boundaries separating different forms of media. MTV, post–1996, was focused on fully exploiting its multi-media conglomerate holdings and further expanding its brand into other media outlets including film, videos, video games, books, and the internet. During that period, MTV's discourse on "youth" adopted a decidedly teen-oriented, and teen-defined stance, one characterized by teenage pop stars, high glamour, and the accommodation of new teen-embraced media and teen interests. All these efforts influenced the nature, format and shape of the cable network's most recent, teen-oriented, pop culture phase.

The history of MTV is inexorably tied to youth. From the outset, the cable network was conceived as a commercial, youth-oriented cable channel. Over the years, the network evolved to keep pace with the ever changing nature of that youth audience, as well as shifting social, industrial and technological trends. MTV's first, 24-hour music video phase responded to the network's need to establish a distinct brand identity and cater to a narrowly defined niche audience and lasted between 1981 and 1985. Changing audiences, evolving corporate demands, and the interest in a global market ushered in MTV's second distinct phase (1985–1996) in which the network moved away from its initial music mandate and embraced a traditional programming schedule and conventional series programming. Beginning in 1996, a new wave of multi-media conglomeration and the phenomenal expansion of media corporations, the rise of digital technology, and the arrival of a distinct and significant teen demographic (Gen Y) all combined to bring about MTV's third phase, characterized by a noticeable shift towards teen pop music, a heightened degree of cross-media stylistic and aesthetic convergence and the recycling of postmodern fragmentation and televisuality last witnessed (in a less intense form) in the early 1980s (MTV's first phase).

MTV's programming, particularly in the late 1990s, had evolved in response to macro changes that characterized both MTV and the larger culture industries in general. Shows such as *TRL, Fashionably Loud, MTVdotcom* and specials like *Total Britney Live* highlighted the intense degree of media integration that was taking place within the culture industries as a whole, much of it in response to the surging multimedia conglomeration that characterized the 1990s. In addition to these entertainment conglomerates' diversification into related areas, the era also witnessed the increasing turn towards globalization, a shift aided by the advent of digital communication technology. As a result, stars and media products were no longer confined to a single market, but instead had access to an international one. Under these circumstances, a multi-media, global corporation such as MTV was particularly poised to benefit both from providing products aimed at a global teen audience, but also offering advertisers in the global marketplace access to that audience via its multi-national system of distribution platforms.

By 2001, MTV had expanded into a $20 billion, multi-media franchise with offices in thirty-five countries and access to a potential viewing audience of one billion people in 140 countries.[67] It was a globally recognized brand that has managed to remain significant and relevant to youth for over twenty years. The question is whether MTV will be able to sustain its teen/youth-oriented brand, especially as it ages. In the coming years, will new generations of teens and youth continue to flock to the network that their parents use to embrace in their youth?

MTV was not the only notable teen-oriented media site in the late 1990s. Other entertainment entities were turning their attention to the teen market in the period. MTV Films, for instance, was not alone in targeting the teen film audience. Dimension Films, a division of Miramax Films was another studio that recognized the teen demographic's significance and acted accordingly. Dimension's impact on the teen film market and the late '90s teenpic is addressed in the next chapter.

FIVE

A New Dimension to Teen Media

Throughout the late 1980s and early 1990s, the teen film lay quiescent, largely marginalized and dismissed as a barely profitable sub-genre that held little box-office appeal. In 1989, expectations of the teen market had declined to the point that *Heathers*, a high-school teen comedy that earned a mere $1 million at the box-office, was considered a hit. *Entertainment Weekly* declared that "by the end of the '80s," "those heady days of teen steam began to sputter out."[1] Then, in December 1996, Dimension Films released *Scream*, a teen slasher film that actively played with the established conventions of the familiar genre. *Scream* went on to resurrect the dormant teen slasher genre, help revive Hollywood's interest in the teen market, and revise both the slasher genre and teen media for a new generation of teenagers.[2] In keeping with the primary concerns of this book, I show that in spearheading these developments, Dimension's activities and decisions were shaped by the larger industrial, technological, social and marketplace trends of the period.

In this chapter, I trace how the nature, structure and content of the teen slasher franchise was reshaped by the emergence of a new generation of teenagers, the impact of evolving media technologies, the dominance of multimedia conglomerates committed to synergistic activities, and the growing cooperation between media and retail organizations. I show how these factors motivated the emergence of a range of distinct textual characteristics, notably the shift to a heightened form of postmodern intertextuality expressed at the level of narrative content and in the larger proliferation of inter-linked multimedia texts marked by convergences in content, style and aesthetics, and the adoption of narrative, stylistic and aesthetic revisions intended to directly appeal to a new teen generation. This examination also addresses how two of the key narrative elements central to the slasher film genre, specifically the monster-villain and the final female survivor, have been revised in distinctive and significant ways to acknowledge the contemporary issues and concerns relevant to the teen generation that came of age in the final years of the twentieth century. At the same time, these revisions also reflected Hollywood's growing interest in the teen girl audience. This chapter concludes with a discussion of how the practices and qualities associated with the *Scream* trilogy were absorbed and integrated into popular millennial teen media in general.

Teen Films' Origins

To fully grasp the contemporary state of the teen film and the ways in which the '90s versions represent a departure from its predecessors, we must first address the historical precedents set in the genre's earlier cycles. According to Thomas Doherty, teen and youth audiences were largely ignored by mainstream Hollywood well into the mid 1950s. As late as 1956, the major Hollywood studios remained committed to the broad, mass, "family" audience that it had successfully targeted since the industry's early days.[3] Where the majors were deliberately ignoring the growing numbers of teens and youth, independent producers and distributors were waking up to the potential value of this niche audience.

During the 1950s and '60s, the teen film was the product of studios on the margins of the film industry. Producers and directors including Sam Katzman and Roger Corman, and independent distributors such as American Independent Pictures (AIP) were key players in the rise of the teenpic. The films associated with this original cycle of teen films were characterized by a tendency towards mildly controversial content that often addressed timely issues. Early films such as *Teenage Crime Wave* and *Rock Around the Clock* (1956) revolved around the suspect rock music genre and juvenile delinquency. These films were specifically pitched at teenagers, were relatively inexpensive to make (thus enhancing their profit potential), and tended to engage in collaborative tie-ins with teen-driven rock music.[4]

These characteristics have remained consistent markers of the teen film even as specific genres within the category have evolved in subsequent decades. Over the years, even as JD films (as films dealing with juvenile delinquency were labeled) and monster/horror teenpics declined, other genres emerged to take their places, including high-school films, teen romances, teen sex romps, and teen slasher films. In the millennium, it was the slasher film that helped resurrect the millennial teen film cycle and sparked the subsequent reemergence of other teen genre films.

The Teen Slasher Film: Emergence and Evolution

The horror-slasher film has a complex history stretching as far back as Hitchcock's *Psycho* (1960), the first film that featured a sexually attractive woman being stalked by a knife-wielding serial killer that included scenes of unexpected and shocking violence and brutality.[5] The genre has evolved through the subsequent decades. The late '70s marked the heyday of the teen slasher genre, when numerous slasher film franchises were launched.[6] Scholars generally agree that *The Texas Chainsaw Massacre* (1974, henceforth *Chainsaw*) and *Halloween* (1978) generated the cycle.[7] Both were pioneering films in a number of ways:

1. They featured a group of young teenagers as victims, marking the arrival of the teen-oriented slasher film.
2. They inaugurated the virtually indestructible, psychotic villains associated with the slasher film; and,
3. they originated the trend towards spin-offs, sequels and imitators, sparking off a rash of successful slasher film franchises.[8]

The success of *Chainsaw* and *Halloween* paved the way for other slasher film series, including *Friday the 13th*, and the *Nightmare on Elm Street* series.[9] With the release of each installment in the series, the conventions of the genre were repeated and consolidated. The growing popularity of these films was in fact tied to the increasing familiarity of these conventions. As Andrew Britton argues, film audiences were drawn to the very predictability of the plots, so that "the only occasion for disappointment would have been a modulation of the formula, not a repetition of it."[10]

By the mid–1980s, however, the slasher film appeared to reach a point of exhaustion. The formulaic nature of subsequent low budget, independently produced slashers, and the excessive repetition in the form of sequels, remakes and imitations, inevitably led to the audience's over-familiarity with the genre so that "by the end of the decade the form was largely drained."[11] By the late 1980s, the cycle of teen-oriented slasher films had played itself out. The teens that first embraced and nurtured the genre had aged out of the demographic and major studios turned their attention away from teens and youth. Consequently, the teen slasher genre fell largely into dormancy between the late 1980s and mid–'90s. In fact, as Leonard Klady noted in *Variety* in 1997,

> The teen audience ... [has] largely been ignored by the majors for the past five years. Major hits in recent memory aimed at 16- to 24-year-olds have been scarce.... Much more attention has been paid to creating event films meant to appeal to the full spectrum of filmgoers, or niche appeal family films and movies for thirtysomethings and older that had crossover potential.[12]

By the mid–1990s, however, the teen audiences that were largely ignored by the movie studios and the entertainment industries in general, were staging a demographic comeback. Population data showed "the North American teenage population rising to more than 55 million by 2005 — larger than the original baby boom at its peak."[13] Retailers, marketers and the other entertainment industries were noticing the arrival of a generation of teenagers that had few time constraints, large disposable incomes and a growing need to assert its independence. Dimension chief Bob Weinstein was one of the first to recognize the growing value of the Generation Y market. Weinstein's foresight and his interest in developing genre films allowed him to effectively exploit this newly emerging cohort. As head of Dimension Films, a genre-oriented production and distribution company, Weinstein's plan was to target this underserved audience with a genre film with proven teen appeal. He decided to revive the dormant teen slasher film, a decision would ultimately resurrect the teen film and mark a new phase in the commercial teen media cycle. These events are inextricably linked to the rise of Dimension films and the industrial conditions that precipitated that rise.

Dimension and the Resurrection of the Slasher Film

The launch and subsequent rise of Dimension Films, a subsidiary of the once-independent Miramax Films, is inextricably tied to the larger industrial trends that characterized the 1980s and '90s. Multi-media conglomeration, media diversification, the rising interest in niche audiences that resulted in an increasingly fragmented film market and the growing need to access a global market combined to transform Miramax and Dimension from small, independent film labels into valuable sub-components of the highly diversified, multi-media Disney conglomerate. This large backdrop of industrial shifts set the stage for the teenpic's evolution from derided, marginalized, cult releases to mainstream, commercial, studio products.

In the 1980s, the Hollywood majors were primarily engaged in producing big-budget blockbuster films that allowed the studios to better exploit their interests in related ancillary markets. This was also a period when the movie-going market was becoming increasingly fragmented. With the mainstream Hollywood studios focusing primarily on the big-budget feature, there were unfilled niches in the film market for low-budget, independently produced films.[14] Brothers Harvey and Bob Weinstein recognized distinct niches they could exploit and launched Miramax in 1979, and Millimeter Films (an early incarnation of Dimension Films) in the mid–1980s. While Miramax's goal was to cater to more highbrow niches by offering foreign language movies, British period films, and independently produced, art-house American fare, Millimeter focused on campy genre acquisitions such as *Return of the Swamp Thing* (1989), and forgettable thrillers such as *Edge of Sanity* (1989), and *Stepfather 2* (1989). Of the two, Miramax was the first to attain commercial viability and emerge as a successful brand in quality entertainment.[15]

The commercial and critical success that characterized Miramax's independent film releases, the increasingly fragmented nature of the movie audience and the larger film industry's interest in expanding and diversifying into alternative niche markets ultimately triggered significant changes in the structure of the film industry itself. Miramax's continuing box-office success with "specialty" independent films showed the major studios that there were profitable niche markets worth exploiting. In the continuing spirit of tight diversification, the major film studios began expanding their interest beyond popular, mainstream cinema and into the quality, art-house film market heretofore dominated by the independent Miramax.

In fact, Miramax has been credited with paving the way for the emergence of competing art-house labels that belonged to multibillion-dollar entertainment conglomerates including Fox Searchlight (owned by media giant News Corp.), Gramercy (formed by media conglomerate Universal and Polygram) and Sony Classics.[16] Backed by media giants with access to larger budgets and the synergistic support of highly diversified parent corporations with established production and distribution systems, these newly formed art-house divisions placed Miramax at an immediate disadvantage as a struggling independent entity. The Weinsteins' attempts to remain viable and competitive depended on becoming part of a tightly diversified conglomerate with access to the financial, synergistic and industrial support that such an institution could provide. Consequently, in 1993, the Walt Disney Company acquired Miramax for a reported $75 million dollars, retaining the Weinstein brothers to head the company.[17]

By the 1990s, Disney was a significant multi-media entertainment giant,[18] seeking to expand beyond its family/children-oriented brand name by diversifying into other more adult-oriented entertainment ventures, while keeping them separate from its Disney-branded operations. The Miramax-Disney deal allowed Disney the opportunity to expand into the foreign/British film, and independent, art-house niche markets without diluting the parent company's family-oriented brand. Under the agreement, Disney would finance Miramax's future films and acquire the ancillary rights to those films, which included video, cable, television, and pay-per-view.[19] In exchange, Miramax and Millimeter Films would draw on Disney's financial strength, and global distribution and marketing operations.[20] Pre–Disney, Millimeter Films was handicapped by Miramax's cash-flow difficulties as well as the company's limited abilities to access a global mass market with a wide, heavily promoted release. Disney's acquisition provided Miramax with the ideal circumstances within which to re-launch a genre-focused film label. Since genre pictures generally tend to perform well both internationally and on video, the new genre division was perfectly positioned to use and exploit Disney's access to international markets, as well as its domestic and international pay TV and home video operations.

Consequently, the previously existing Millimeter Films was reborn as Dimension Films in 1993, the same year Disney bought Miramax Films. Run by Bob Weinstein, Dimension was marketed as the anti–Miramax, focusing on low budget genre movies—primarily horror, sci-fi and action films. While Dimension aimed to exploit its Disney connections, it was determined to retain its "independent" status and function as a separate division from both Disney and Miramax. In its arrangement with Disney, Dimension could independently greenlight films that cost less than $12.5 million per film.[21] Maintaining that budget meant that Miramax's new division would not have the resources to compete against the major studios in securing high-priced talent and creating costly special effects. Instead, Dimension would have to produce low-budget genre films that had box-office appeal. Historically, the slasher film was an independent film genre that succeeded at the box-office despite low-budgets, and the lack of big-name stars and expensive special effects. By the late 1980s and early 1990s, the slasher genre had been dormant for several years. The low-budget slasher was notably absent, creating a distinct gap in the market that Dimension could fill.

Bob Weinstein's interest in genre films was matched by his commitment to a niche audience that he believed had largely been ignored: "There were no movies being made for teenagers anymore. It had become an adult oriented business. I knew there was an audience that was not being satisfied."[22] This neglect of the teen audience was having a notable impact on the film industries at the time. In the early 1990s, the film industry noted a decline in the movie-going audience. While teenagers were still a vital movie-going segment, data collected by the Motion Picture Association of America indicated that the percentage of 12- to 17-year-olds who went to the movies at least once a month dropped from 47 percent in 1987 to 43 percent in 1995.[23] In the light of declining film audiences, increased interest in the video market, as well as film trends that were failing at the box-office, the idea of low-budget genre films with a built-in audience and a proven track record in home video format seemed perfect. Dimension recognized that it could establish its genre brand and target teens by revisiting the teen-oriented slasher film.

Reviving the tired and disreputable slasher genre for the millennial teen audience, however, posed a challenge. As a genre, the slasher film languished at the bottom of the horror heap, relegated to straight-to-video, B-grade releases with low production values and weak acting. If Dimension hoped to resurrect the slasher film, it needed to find a way to update the genre for a teen audience whose access to earlier films from the genre had made them over-familiar with the form's tired conventions, a condition linked to the industrial, technological and cultural changes that had taken place in the decades since the slasher film was last dominant.

The Impact of Multiple Delivery Platforms and New Media Technologies

Since the 1970s and early '80s, the turn to multimedia conglomeration and the increased integration between film, television, music and other culture/consumer industries had changed the business and economics of teen-focused media production and products. At the same time, the technological developments of the 1980s which enabled the emergence of a wide range of new distribution platforms including cable television, VCRs, computers, the rise of the internet and other digital technologies have changed how teens access and experience their media entertainment. In addition to presenting cross-media marketing opportunities that had not been available before, these technological developments allowed the media industries to extend the shelf-life of media products indefinitely. These technologies have also continued to add to an ever-expanding range of (teen) entertainment texts, contributing to the plethora of texts already circulating in the public domain.

As new texts joined older ones, all of which remain available and accessible, they offered numerous and competing messages and signs which often referenced and re-circulated signs from older media texts. These conditions contributed to an accelerated shift towards self-reflexivity and semiotic excess in media content that revolved around the appropriation and absorption of other popular entertainment texts through the re-circulation of iconic or familiar images, multiple references to popular texts and/or the mixing of generic plot lines. These technologies have definitely affected the relationship between text and audience, how audiences engage with entertainment, and, in turn, the nature and content of American teen culture in the late 1990s.

Generation Y and Media Hyperconsciousness

The late 1990s teen generation was a new and distinct demographic — media-obsessed and hence culturally literate, highly brand conscious, consumer-oriented and extremely self-aware and cynical — Gen Y exhibited traits and behaviors distinct from previous teen cohorts. With increased access to media and technology, American teenagers in the 1990s had surpassed previous generations in their exposure to and familiarity with media texts both past and contemporary. This was also the teen generation that was weaned on, and came of age with, MTV's particular brand of postmodern, commercial, multi-media excess (a condition I explored in Chapter Four). Not surprisingly, this group emerged as the most media-saturated generation ever encountered, with a heightened media-oriented hyperconsciousness. If Dimension hoped to resurrect the slasher film, it needed to find a way to maintain the integrity of the genre, which meant respecting many of its conventions, while simultaneously updating the material for a new teen generation that was probably already overly familiar with the established conventions of the slasher film. Dimension also had to contend with the fact that while the traditional target audience for slasher films was adolescent boys, in the 1990s, it was adolescent girls that were emerging as the more significant film-going demographic.

All these considerations would ultimately impact the nature, content and structure of the *Scream* films. How did the *Scream* films update the slasher genre for a new late 1990s teen audience? What identifying characteristics did these films possess? How did the contemporary films accommodate the specific commercial and institutional interests of the increasingly diversified, and mutually collaborative, multi-media organizations? And how did the *Scream* trilogy speak to its target demographics of teenagers in general and teen girls in particular? These questions are addressed in the next section.

Reinventing the Slasher Genre

Having decided to resurrect the teen slasher film, Dimension tasked established horror auteur Wes Craven and scriptwriter Kevin Williamson with the responsibility of reshaping and updating the genre. The creators decided to exploit the audiences' familiarity with the genre's conventions by creating films that commented on the highly formulaic nature of the slasher films while simultaneously playing off of the established traditions.

One of their most overt strategies involved the deconstruction of the genre's conventions and the insertion of tongue-in-cheek intertextual and self-referential comments highlighting the *Scream* trilogy's debt (and similarity) to earlier slasher film classics. At the same time, the films' attempts at reaching beyond its own textual boundaries were not limited to intertextual cinematic references, for the *Scream* texts also extended well-beyond the confines of the film medium to include related content that appeared on television, cable, in music, print, and online. Many of the *Scream* trilogy's elements, therefore, functioned to highlight the films' own artificiality by acknowledging their status as popular culture and highlighting their existence as a steadily expanding range of consumable media products. All these strategies intensify the distinctly postmodern nature of the millennial teen text.

The trilogy also reconfigured the genre's traditional, stereotypical treatment of the slasher villain and the female victim-hero, a move motivated in part by the need to update the genre's conventions, and also to address developments within the genre's core audience. The genre's conventions were revised in ways that offer interesting insights into a range of dominant social and cultural concerns of the period. Indeed, despite having roots in horror and occasionally featuring elements of the supernatural, slasher films have often reflected very real, contemporary concerns.[24] As a result, the final released products reflected an acknowledgement of the contemporary media environment, including the entertainment industry's escalating commitment to cross-media promotional and marketing practices, and the recognition that the new teen demographic in the United States was distinct from previous teen cycles.

From '80s Postmodernism to '90s Hyper-Postmodernism

Examining a number of popular genre films released in the early 1990s, Jim Collins remarks that

> what we have seen of postmodernism thus far is really a first phase, perhaps Early Postmodernism, the first tentative attempts at envisioning the impact of new technologies of mass communication and information processing on the structure of narrative.[25]

Although Collins makes no direct mention of the slasher film, his statement is vital to my discussion of the *Scream* films and their relationship to their cinematic predecessors.

Horror films of the 1980s have often been described as postmodern, with scholars listing a breakdown of boundaries, the decline of master narratives, a tendency for intertextual referencing, a propensity for ironic or parodic humor, the erosion of authority, as well as textual and generic mixing as key indicators. Isabel Pinedo defines "the postmodern [horror film] world" as

> an unstable one in which traditional (dichotomous) categories break down, boundaries blur, institutions fall into question, Enlightenment narratives collapse, the inevitability of progress crumbles, and the master status of the universal (read male, white, monied, heterosexual) subject deteriorates.[26]

Both Kim Newman and Isabel Pinedo consider the '80s slasher films' tendency towards generic hybridity, particularly the blending of disparate signs, codes and conventions associated with horror and comedy, a key postmodern characteristic,[27] while Tania Modleski identifies their open-ended narrative structures as postmodern.[28] The postmodern bent of the *Scream* films has already received some discussion, with scholars identifying *Scream*'s mix of horror and comedy and the serialized nature of the *Scream* narrative as recognizable postmodern characteristics whose origins can be traced to the earlier '80s slasher cycle.[29]

Despite these similarities, however, the *Scream* trilogy does not merely continue the postmodern, 1980s slasher cycle. Instead, the *Scream* franchise breaks from the '80s slasher cycle in representing a later stage in postmodernism's evolution, with a significant number of *Scream*'s postmodern elements signaling an *advanced* or *heightened* stage of postmodernism that I label "hyper-postmodernism."[30] In the *Scream* trilogy, hyper-postmodernism can be identified in two ways: (1) a heightened degree of intertextual referencing and self-reflexivity that ceases to function at the traditional level of tongue-in-cheek sub-text, and emerges instead as the actual *text* of the films, and (2) a propensity for ignoring film-specific boundaries by actively referencing, "borrowing" and influencing the styles and formats of *other* media forms, including television and music videos—strategies that have further blurred the boundaries that separated once discrete media formats. These developments are directly linked to the rise of the new millennial teen audience amidst very distinct cultural and technological contexts.

Intertextual Referencing: From Subtext to Text

One distinguishing aspect of the *Scream* trilogy involves its use of intertextual referencing. Certainly, instances of referencing are not unique to the *Scream* franchise. Many teen texts, including the exploitation films of the 1950s and 1970s, have engaged in the activity. *Halloween*, for instance, has a character named Dr. Loomis, which references *Psycho*'s Sam Loomis.[31] *Halloween 3* (1982) contains a self-reflexive scene in which a clip from the first *Halloween* film is seen playing on television while the film's hero, Dr. Daniel Challis, attempts to break free from the chair he is tied to. In these earlier cases, however, these references tend to be either opportunistically derivative or tongue-in-cheek moments of sub-text that often amount to little more than covert inside-jokes.

In contrast, the *Scream* trilogy is distinctive because the referencing is not restricted to the occasional passing allusion. Instead, a significant proportion of the intertextual referencing in the *Scream* films functions overtly *as text*. The films consist of multiple sequences in which characters engage in self-conscious, highly self-reflexive, sustained commentaries on the nature and conventions of the genre itself. The characters in all three films are individuals who are self-consciously conversant in the signs and codes of the classic slasher film, and who obsessively discuss other media texts, particularly teen slasher films. *Scream*'s[32] distinctive opening sequence revolves around a victim innocently discussing her favorite slasher films with her potential killer over the phone, setting the stage for numerous other scenes in which the film's characters engage in hyperconscious, self-reflexive, slasher movie-oriented observations, with characters comparing themselves to familiar figures from iconic slasher films. In *Scream*, two characters stand in a video store and comment that if the police watched more slasher films, they would be better equipped to deal with the killer. This conversation then continues with a detailed analysis of the various potential suspects and how each one conforms to familiar slasher film stereotypes. Later, a self-professed slasher film aficionado consciously enumerates the cinematic rules of survival, including the dangers of indulging in sex, drinking and drugs. In every instance, these articulations are arch confirmations of the viewing audience's own hyper-awareness of the genre and the ways in which these conventions traditionally play out.

This self-reflexivity is taken a step further in the sequel. *Scream 2*[33] transcends the original film's interest in discussing and critiquing other texts by actively discussing and critiquing itself. In other words, the intertextual referencing in *Scream 2* covers both other slasher films and numerous references to the original *Scream*. The movie opens in a theatre that is screening a movie called *Stab*, which is based on the "real" events depicted in *Scream*. The intertextual references to the original film occur at the level of *Stab*'s images, which are a recreation of the first murder in *Scream*. The sequel's commitment to self-reflexivity and self-critique is further sustained with many of the film's characters commenting on the repetitive nature of film sequels with extended conversations focusing on the problematic lack of originality in slasher sequels.

Scream 3[34] takes the intertextuality and self-consciousness even further. Much of *Scream 3* takes place on the set of *Stab 3*, which recreates the "real" setting of the first *Scream* film. Consequently, numerous scenes in the third installment directly echo those from the first, except that they are played out on a movie set. This has the effect of disturbing the boundaries distinguishing the events in the original film from the reenactment of those events in the film-within-the-film, while also heightening the self-reflexivity of every scene. An uncanny sense of déjà vu permeates a sequence in which Sidney, the series' female victim/hero, wanders onto the movie set and finds herself standing in a replica of her bedroom. As we hear dialogue from the first film play on the soundtrack, Sidney is attacked by the killer, which references an earlier attack that was first seen in the original *Scream*. As the sequence plays out, we see Sidney reenacting the same actions she performed in the original film, while trying to evade the killer yet again.[35] This sequence effectively collapses the spatial, temporal and textual boundaries separating *Scream* and *Scream 3*, leaving the audience momentarily confused and adrift.

In addition to referencing its own past and highlighting its filmic foundations, *Scream 3* also continues the tradition of directly commenting on and analyzing established movie conventions. A character self-consciously articulates the movie "rules" governing the concluding installment of a trilogy. These rules include warnings about the killer's seemingly-supernatural resilience, the possibility that even the hero will not survive the carnage, and the vital relevance of past events. Maintaining the film's heightened commitment to self-reflexivity, these rules point to events that ultimately take place in the course of *Scream 3*. Ultimately, *Scream* and its sequels are primarily films *about* slasher films. The *Scream* films, therefore, take the previously subtle and covert intertextual reference and transform it into an overt discursive act.

The *Scream* films are, thus, the products of filmmakers who recognize that the overwrought, intense nature of the traditional conventions can no longer be experienced "straight" by an American teen audience who has become overly familiar with and increasingly derisive of the horror genre's conventions. Consequently, these conventions are filtered through a much more cynical, knowing perspective that would allow the film's audience to engage and "interact" with equally hyper-aware, characters on the screen. These characteristics of hyper-postmodernism clearly articulate and help accentuate the central role that entertainment texts and the media play in the teen lifestyle. Discussions about films and other entertainment media dominate teen interests and concerns. Media texts and their consumption often function as the topics of teen conversation, exchange and even identity, a situation that is reflected and perhaps encouraged by the *Scream* films. These films, with their witty and humorous commentary on familiar horror-movie conventions, and the abundance of self-aware and self-referential statements, were specifically created for a generation steeped in pop culture. Many of the *Scream* trilogy's postmodern elements highlight the films' artificiality, acknowledging their status as popular cultural texts whose "circulation and reception are worked back into the 'text' itself."[36] These instances of overt self-reflexivity call attention to the artificiality of *all* the *Scream* films and by extension, all media products, highlighting their status as consumable cultural products.

Essentially, the films hold up a mirror to how teens actually converse and interact, while simultaneously encouraging them to adopt a media-oriented form of communication founded on the intense consumption of popular media text. The films reemphasize the vital role that media play in their lives. Within the *Scream* universe, knowledge of and familiarity with media texts is *literally* a matter of life and death. In keeping with that message, *Scream* and its sequels function to increase teen awareness of other media texts both past and present. The intense intertextual references help to introduce older slasher classics to new and younger audiences who may not have experienced them directly, encouraging a new teen generation/audience to seek out and consume these older texts by keeping these older texts relevant in terms of media literacy. Director Craven, screenwriter Williamson, and Dimension also exploited the demographic's devotion to multiple forms of media and entertainment by extending the *Scream* experience across a range of other contemporary media, ensuring that Scream remained foremost in teenagers' minds.

Intertextual Referencing: Crossing Media-Specific Boundaries

It is worth noting that the intertextual referencing and self-reflexivity that characterize the *Scream* trilogy is not restricted to explicit discussions of past slasher films or previous installments of the trilogy. Instead, the films' pop culture referencing crosses media-specific boundaries to include cheeky, self-aware nods to popular contemporary American teen television shows as well. The distinctive aspect of these instances of cross-referencing involves the extreme intersection and integration that occurs between different and distinct media texts on the levels of narrative, style and format.

One example of this intertextual referencing occurs between *Scream 2* and television's teen-oriented *Buffy the Vampire Slayer*, with *Buffy* star Sarah Michelle Gellar's appearance in the film. The film's target teen audience would have been aware of the ironies inherent in Gellar's appearance as a victim scrambling for her life, since every week on the television series, Gellar, as Buffy, subverts the "blonde-female-as-victim" convention directly associated with the slasher genre, playing a teenager who defends the world against an unending assortment of demons and monsters.[37] A majority of the teenagers in the *Scream 2* audience would have been familiar with Gellar's television alter ego, and have grasped the intertextual reference while watching her appear against type as a helpless female victim in the film.

Also significant are the ways in which the style and formal aesthetics of *Scream 2*, particularly Gellar's sequence, in which she is stalked and attacked, resemble those found in *Buffy the Vampire Slayer*, a television series that borrows many of its "monster stalking an unsuspecting female victim" visual techniques from earlier slasher films. The use of voyeuristic point-of-view shots of the female victims that are ascribed to the killer/monster, the lack of establishing shots to heighten spatial confusion, the cluttered mise-en-scene, and the reliance on low, dim lighting are characteristic of slasher films in general, the *Scream* films, as well as the television show, *Buffy the Vampire Slayer*. Consequently, it is almost impossible to distinguish between the feature film's style and aesthetics and the television show's style and aesthetics.

It is also worth noting that the intense, self-aware, hyper-intertextual referencing characteristic of the *Scream* films is not restricted to the films themselves. It was very quickly embraced and adopted by other teen-oriented texts. Consequently, while *Scream* may have started out referencing other slasher films as text, it quickly became the referent for other teen-oriented media texts. As first mentioned in my Introductory chapter, months after *Scream 2* was released, the popular teen television drama *Dawson's Creek* broadcast an episode titled "The Scare" that paid particular homage to *Scream* and its sequel with many of the *Dawson's Creek* characters engaging in lengthy, self-conscious, discussions deconstructing classic slasher films including *Scream*, *Halloween* and *Friday the 13th* in their conversations. The television episode also faithfully recreates the type of horror/slasher film aesthetics discussed in the previous paragraph. Although *Dawson's Creek* is a teen melodrama, it was able to seamlessly incorporate the style and aesthetics of a slasher film into its more conventional format. Entire sequences from the television show replicated scenes from the films, including *Scream*'s infamous opening sequence in which the killer makes his threatening phone call to his unsuspecting female victim. In a later scene, one of the show's characters appears in the same mask that the killers wear in the *Scream* films.

Besides the intertextual-referencing between the films and television programs such as *Buffy the Vampire Slayer* and *Dawson's Creek*, the hyper-postmodern *Scream* texts also extend well beyond the film medium to include soundtracks, magazine spreads, and television spots on youth-oriented networks such as MTV. This proliferation of texts has further weakened the boundaries that exist between distinct media texts, resulting in greater multi-media convergence.

Convergence and the Cross-Media Marketing Matrix

Scream exists within a complex interconnected multi-media matrix that was shaped by the exigencies of publicity, promotion and marketing. Since the 1970s, media companies have been evolving strategies to exploit the promotional opportunities offered by multiple media platforms including television, music videos and print. According to Justin Wyatt, this interest in capitalizing on multi-media promotional prospects has motivated an increasing convergence across the existing entertainment arena leading to the rise of high-concept films that have pioneered the strategy of "borrowing" or integrating stylistic elements from promotional media including advertising and music video visuals and aesthetic style as a new marketing method.[38] The adoption of this strategy has led to the creation of film texts that consist of "modular set pieces" built around different marketing components such as musical sequences that were then repackaged as promotional music videos, or stylistically sophisticated images that were then used in television trailers or print campaigns.[39] John Thornton Caldwell's contention that the rise of each new media technology, "not only influenced what was seen by viewers ... they also had a profound influence on how these images were constructed, altered, and displayed" was no less true in the '90s.[40] While Wyatt and Caldwell's comments were focused on the 1980s context, Dimension's marketing strategies for *Scream* and subsequent teen films evolved out of these earlier activities.

The *Scream* trilogy exhibits the same stylistic and aesthetic excess that Wyatt argues were directly shaped by marketing and promotional considerations, only in a heightened state. In marketing the trilogy, Dimension actively pursued a variety of promotional avenues including music soundtracks, music videos, print advertising and magazine features. In some instances, these promotional activities directly affected the nature, style and aesthetics of the *Scream* films themselves, as well as the teen audiences' experience and interaction with the text. The marketing campaign for the *Scream* films involved a range of media including radio, television and record store promotions, which resulted in an expanding range of related *Scream* media texts.

One of the cornerstones of Dimension's marketing campaign for the *Scream* trilogy involved the use of music, which was tied to the added publicity (and revenue) that could be derived from releasing the films' soundtracks. For instance, Capitol Dimension released the soundtrack to *Scream 2* on December 2, 1997. The soundtrack was targeted at the film's core "13 to 25" audience. The soundtrack's release increased the public's awareness of *Scream 2*, since the soundtrack was accompanied by an intense and focused marketing campaign that included "unavoidable" television, radio and record store retail campaigns designed to coincide with the release of the film on December 12, 1997.[41] These soundtracks were mined for their cross-promotional opportunities. The rock band Creed contributed a track, "What If?," to the *Scream 3* soundtrack (2000). The song was also featured on Creed's own CD, *Human Clay* (1999), which was released a few months before the soundtrack. Including the song on the movie soundtrack would help bring the *Human Clay* album to the attention of the target American teen market. The soundtrack component of the marketing strategy, and the even more vital accompanying music videos, were especially important in allowing Dimension to promote the films on MTV.

MTV, the quintessential teen/youth cable-channel, was a particularly effective way to target the *Scream* films' core teen and youth market. MTV aired an hour-long *Scream 2* special that featured interviews with *Scream 2*'s entire cast, clips both from the original *Scream* and the forthcoming sequel, and showcased music videos that integrated musical set pieces lifted directly from the films with music from the films' soundtracks. MTV was thus an active and vital participant in the creation of a complex and increasingly integrated matrix of (inter-)related media texts, all in the service of promotion and marketing. Creed's "What if?" music video, for instance, incorporated images of the band members being stalked by the masked killer from the film. One of the *Scream* trilogy's main characters, Officer Dewey (David Arquette) also appears in the video, effectively blurring the boundaries between the film text and the music video and heightening the degree of intertextuality between the texts, both of which serve to promote each other. The *Scream* trilogy's hyper-postmodern, intertextual elements are tied to a series of complex, cross-media promotional activities between the film industries and MTV.

In the same way, the distinctive intertextual referencing between *Scream* and *Dawson's Creek* mentioned earlier is yet another instance of contemporary multi-media, cross-corporate, promotional synergy. The intertextual references that crossed between *Dawson's Creek* and the *Scream* films allowed the film franchise to benefit from the promotional exposure on a hit teen television show, even as the television show actively set out to attract the teenagers responsible for the success and popularity of the film franchise. Not coincidentally, *Scream*'s scriptwriter, Kevin Williamson, is also the creator of *Dawson's Creek*.[42] The *Scream/Dawson's Creek* interaction was indicative of a growing trend in the 1990s when many of the creators, producers and scriptwriters most clearly associated with teen culture were individuals who comfortably, and successfully, shifted between television and film — a practice supported and advocated by an increasingly multi-media entertainment industry.[43]

This cross-media movement by teen stars and, more significantly, creative personnel associated with teen texts has led to a heightened stylistic and aesthetic convergence across previously distinct media, making it more and more difficult to rely upon stylistic and aesthetic factors to distinguish between the film, television and music video media where teen cultural texts are concerned. Williamson's decision to create texts for both film and television, for instance, paved the way for the *Dawson's Creek* episode "The Scare"'s replication of the narrative conventions, aesthetic style, and visual images from teen-oriented horror films including *Scream*. This stylistic and aesthetic convergence across media contributes greatly to the heightened postmodern intertextuality of the millennial teen text.

Dimension's quest to further publicize its slasher franchise escalated with the January 1998 issue of *Seventeen*, which actively promoted *Scream 2* with two stories. The first profiled *Scream 2* star Timothy Olyphant, while the second was a fashion piece to help its teenage readers dress like the film's female characters. The burgeoning cooperation between the entertainment industries and the fashion and beauty industries had advanced beyond MTV's *Fashionably Loud*. In fact, the role of fashion in teen films cannot be overemphasized. A few weeks after *Scream 2* premiered, the *Los Angeles Times* ran a profile detailing the fashion labels worn by the stars in the film, highlighting the key trends and providing full information on where to purchase the items and how to replicate the film's looks.[44] This was only the beginning of what would evolve into more explicit cross-promotional arrangements between the creators of teen texts and the producers of teen-oriented brand products.

Over the course of the *Scream* trilogy's releases, Dimension also realized the increasing importance of building an online presence to more effectively target its tech-savvy teen demographic. The trilogy's website offered a further opportunity to enhance the series' on-going commitment to blurring the "real" and "reel" boundaries. For instance, in anticipation of *Scream 3*'s release, the film's website (www.scream3.com) offered visitors links to Sunrise Studios, the fictional studio producing the slasher-film-within-the-film, *Stab 3*. The Sunrise site cheekily featured promotional information on the studio's other fictional hit genre releases such as *Amazombies*, *There's Something About Carrie*, and *Ice Scream Truck*.[45] Another link led to Gale Weathers' website (www.galeweathers.com). Featuring information on the character, it was patterned after actual celebrity websites. As promotional websites, these links effectively extended the films' dedication to humorous self-reflexivity and self-conscious intertextuality, and allowed its target teen audience the opportunity to extend their enjoyment of the films' seemingly irreverent approach to film production, the film industry, and the film text.

These complex interrelationships between progressively more convergent media industries have directly shaped the nature of the text and intensified its postmodern qualities. In many of these cases, it is increasingly difficult to distinguish between the text and the promotion of the text, since most of the articulations function in both capacities and tend to share, or at least blend, the visual styles associated with diverse media. Soundtracks, music videos, trailers, fashion, magazine features, and television appearances are just some of the many components circulating simultaneously and functioning as related and competing intertexts. These promotional aspects help to enhance the public awareness and profile of these linked text by extending their exposure to different audiences and communities, a strategy that exemplifies the relationship between postmodernism and consumerism noted by Frederic Jameson and Mike Featherstone, among others.[46]

Part of the intensification of postmodern intertextual elements associated with the *Scream* trilogy is inextricably tied to issues of technology, promotion and audience. The abovementioned intersections between the *Scream* trilogy and teen television shows as well as the increasing blending of narrative, stylistic and aesthetic elements across different media forms reflect a new level of the postmodern collapse of boundaries. These instances of intertextuality were motivated and driven by the overt technological, economic and synergistic imperatives that characterized the multi-media entertainment industry of the late 1990s.

Responding to a New Target Demographic

In addition to adapting to the industrial changes that had overtaken the film and media industries in the millennium, any attempt to successfully resurrect the slasher genre had to acknowledge the developments in the teen market that had taken place in the interim. During the genre's earlier phases, its prime audience consisted of teenage boys. In examining the audience for 1970s and early '80s slasher films, Clover notes that

> the majority audience, perhaps even more than the audience for horror in general, was largely young and largely male.... Young males are also ... the slasher film's implied audience, the object of its address.[47]

The films' obsession with the torture and brutal killing of nubile young women appeared to be a particular draw, especially for the genre's primary young, male audience. This situation changed dramatically in the millennium.

In the mid–1990s, adolescent girls were emerging as the more significant film-going demographic. In 1995, teenage girls were largely responsible for the $57 million box-office success of *Clueless*, a romantic comedy about a high-school girl's romantic misadventures. A year later, *William Shakespeare's Romeo and Juliet* (1996), also targeted at the teen girl demographic, grossed in excess of $46 million domestically.[48] While traditional wisdom argued that the slasher genre skewed towards adolescent male audiences, Dimension's Bob Weinstein, director Wes Craven and scriptwriter Kevin Williamson were keen to revive the genre with the conscious intent of making it more relevant to female audiences. They did so by rejecting the traditional slasher film portrayals of the slasher villain/monster and the final female survivor/hero by offering an original treatment of these iconic elements.

Reconsidering the Psychotic Serial Killer

In films such as *Psycho*, *Chainsaw*, through the *Halloween*, *Friday the 13th* and *Nightmare on Elm Street* series, the traditional slasher villains are almost consistently characterized as psychotic, virtually indestructible maniacs. Michael from the *Halloween* series survives across numerous installments, Jason, from the *Friday the 13th* films, returns in every sequel, as does Freddy Kruger from the *Nightmare on Elm Street* franchise. The convention of the undefeatable psychotic murderer/slasher has been reinforced historically across all these films. *Scream*, a film that positions itself securely within the genre, interestingly, adopts a novel reinterpretation of the convention.

In *Scream* (and its subsequent installments), the killers are not marginal-ized monsters in the tradition of Leatherface, or the supernatural Freddy Kruger, nor are they "seemingly invincible psychotics" in the tradition of Mike Myers and Jason.[49] While still psychologically disturbed maniacs, *Scream*'s villains are not misfits or outsiders, nor are they the uncharacterized monsters typical of earlier slasher films. Instead, the killers in *Scream* are seemingly normal, attrac-tive, popular individuals, often "insiders," boyfriends or friends who initially appear harmless until they go on a killing spree. Since slasher films tend to articulate the fears and concerns prevalent in their respective eras, the *Scream* trilogy's reinterpretation of the killers as the evil within, its portrayal of seem-ingly ordinary teenagers turned serial killers seems particularly contemporary and relevant in the light of the real-life incidents of teenage violence occurring in American high-schools at the end of the twentieth century. Like its slasher predecessors, the trilogy acknowledges and confronts the key anxieties of its era. As Trencansky observes,

> If the villains of popular late 1990s slashers are embraced by the adolescents today, perhaps it is because, in a culture of sudden random violence, exemplified in the school shootings that originate from one of their own, a villain that looks just like them makes sense.[50]

The *Scream* trilogy offers a world in which evil is closely aligned with the vic-tims. In these millennial slasher films, evil resides within the teenager's in-group. The trilogy's portrayal of seemingly ordinary teenagers turned serial killers is a direct commentary on the demons and terrors that impact actual Generation Y teenagers' lives in the light of real-life teenage violence in high schools across America, of which the tragic events in Pearl, Mississippi, Jones-boro, Arkansas, and Columbine are only the most publicized. The trilogy, there-fore, offers its teen viewers a form of cathartic release by exploring the terrors associated with high school, unexpected violence and the difficulty of know-ing or trusting one's peers. Indeed, the trilogy's representation of seemingly average, ordinary teenagers whose transformation into disgruntled, dysfunc-tional youth who slaughter their unsuspecting friends is particularly relevant to the films' millennial teen audience.

Reinterpreting the Final Girl

The slasher film's complicated relationship with gender was also updated and revised to better appeal to teen girls. *The Texas Chainsaw Massacre* and *Halloween* introduced the tough teenage girl who survives numerous violent attacks by the murderous, psychopathic villain. This girl's survival prompted Clover to dub her the "Final Girl," for she is commonly the last person left alive at the end of the film.[51] Although the slasher film's *raison d'être* is the torture and often brutal killing of nubile young women, as Clover observes, "the inde-pendent, low-budget [horror] film tradition has been central in the manufacture of the new 'tough girls' that have loomed so large in horror since the mid-seventies."[52]

In these early slasher films, female heroism was defined more in terms of the Final Girl's ability to survive and escape numerous attacks, than in her ability to triumph independently over her tormentor(s).[53] By the 1980s, these earlier conceptions of the Final Girl had given way to a more capable and active version who managed to survive numerous attacks and dispatch the killers by herself. According to Clover, these Final Girls are marked as exceptional females: while the typical female victim is sexually active, the Final Girl is not; where the former is naive and oblivious, the latter is "watchful to the point of paranoia. ... intelligent and resourceful in a pinch. ... the Final Girl is boyish, in a word."[54] While we can trace the evolution of the 1990s slasher film's tough girl to her predecessors who populated the genre in the 1970s and early '80s, the '90s incarnations of the Final Girl have undergone further developments to reflect more contemporary concerns.

Scream deviates from traditional genre conventions by offering two Final Girls: Sidney Prescott and Gale Weathers. One of the more interesting aspects in *Scream* involves the unconventional representations of these Final Girls. Unlike the Final Girls in classics such as *Halloween*, *Nightmare on Elm Street* (1984) and *Hellraiser* (1987), who are outsiders and rebels who reject mainstream social norms and behaviors,[55] Sidney is a popular high-school girl with a boyfriend and a group of close-knit good friends. Significantly, Sidney is not the outcast of the *Carrie* variety, nor is she the boyish virgin of *Halloween*. Gale Weathers, the television journalist, is an even greater deviation from the Final Girl norm. She is career-oriented, selfish, vain, ambitious and largely amoral, yet she emerges as the other Final Girl, allying herself with Sidney and facing down the killer. While these two women begin as adversaries, they overcome their differences and work together to defeat their tormentors. These final girls save themselves, and each other, without acquiring any monstrous connotations. More importantly, with the exception of Sidney's androgynous name, neither one is marked as particularly boyish, nor are they actively differentiated from the other women in the film. Sidney and Gale, therefore, do not conform to the traditional characterization of the Final Girl, who Clover describes as "compromised from the outset by her masculine interests, her inevitable sexual reluctance, her apartness from other girls."[56]

The fact that these Final Girls survive through all three installments and eventually transcend their terrifying experiences to emerge as independent, (relatively) well-adjusted, functional individuals is significant and represents a clear deviation from the traditional slasher movie convention of killing off the Final Girl in each subsequent sequel. The trilogy's revolutionary decision to break with the traditional slasher convention in which "the killers are normally the fixed elements and the victims the changeable ones in any given series of the 1970s and early '80s slasher films,"[57] was another acknowledgement of the distinctive concerns of the millennial teen demographic. The fact remains that the heroic female survivors of 1970s and '80s slasher films consistently fail to destroy and outlive their tormentors. One of the ironies of the conventional teen slasher film lies in the fact that while the Final Girl is strong, resourceful and powerful enough to seemingly defeat the monster, she almost never survives for long. In the *Nightmare* series for instance, the monstrous Freddy returns to torment and murder a new female hero in each subsequent film installment. As Williams, points out,

> A Final Woman may fight and sometimes defeat the monster. But her ultimate victory is undercut either by eventual death in a sequel (Adrienne King in *Friday the 13th, Part II* [1981]; Heather Langencamp in *A Nightmare on Elm Street III: Dream Warriors* [1987]) or insanity (the heroines in *The Texas Chainsaw Massacre I* and *II* [1986]; *Friday the 13th: Part II* and *III* [1982]; and *Hollowgate* [1988].)[58]

The Final Girls in the *Scream* trilogy subvert this trend, and reject this familiar narrative trajectory. Instead, the trilogy inverts the tradition, maintaining the longevity of the victim/survivors and introducing new villains with each sequel. The female survivors ultimately displace the killers as the recurring characters and inhabit the central narrative roles. This effectively allows the female characters to develop and evolve across the film's various installments. In the *Scream* trilogy, the (male) monsters are defeated and replaced, while the female characters continue to endure, evolve and grow, preserving the significance and importance of the female survivors over that of the (male) killers.

In re-conceptualizing the role of the Final Girl, *Scream* redefined the genre for the millennial teen and also successfully made the traditionally male-oriented genre relevant to the adolescent female moviegoer — a demographic and consumer market traditionally ignored by the genre. According to *Scream* director Wes Craven, writer Kevin Williamson intentionally oriented *Scream*'s narrative towards concerns particularly relevant to teenage girls. Williamson explains, "I try to write very smart women. ... [who have to] deal with issues of betrayal and trust."[59] One of the *Scream* trilogy's primary interests focuses upon the nature of boyfriends, who Williamson presents as "ordinary people ... capable of great deception."[60]

The films' plots essentially examine the issue of trust in romantic relationships, using the slasher film conventions as an allegory through which to explore the turmoil of female adolescence. In addition to confronting an unknown killer, Sidney and Gale must also deal with betrayals and lies in their personal friendships and romantic relationships. Craven in fact has remarked that the *Scream* series "has the emotional appeal of a soap opera, which he thinks plays better to woman than men. There are secret loves, haunting pasts, snobs, nerds and badly behaved boyfriends, twists that normally drive soaps."[61] That Sidney refuses to let these betrayals destroy her, that she learns self-reliance and independence and successfully overcomes the numerous events that threaten her, is a particularly empowering message for teenage girls.[62]

If young males were the target audience for the slasher genre in the past, the young female emerged as the ideal(ized) target audience at the box-office in the 1990s, even for a genre as conventionally male-oriented as the horror-slasher film. Much of *Scream*'s success came from appealing to an overlooked, increasingly influential, and powerful segment of the horror audience: girls and young women. Teen film producer Neal Moritz claims "all our research led us to believe that it's best to target young females. The guys who want to go on dates will follow."[63] CNN box-office analyst Martin Grove concurs: "[Teenage girls] tend to go to the movies in groups, which adds to the excitement of what's happening on screen."[64]

Scream's female-oriented perspective contributed significantly to its box-office success. The film became a cult classic for young women and girls. According to *USA Today*,

> Typically, only about 1 percent of moviegoers will pay to see a film more than once. With *Scream*, an estimated 16 percent of women age 25 and under who saw the film in theatres went more than once, according to polling by Miramax. By comparison, only 3 percent of young men who saw *Scream* returned for additional screenings.[65]

By broadening the slasher film's appeal beyond the young male demographic and actively appealing to young women, the three installments of the *Scream* series grossed $293.5 million, the highest combined box-office for a horror franchise,[66] far exceeding the combined box-office of other series such as *Halloween* and *Friday the 13th*, which had multiple sequels.

From Millennial Teen Films to Multi-Media Teen Entertainment

Scream and its two sequels deserve credit for breaking away from the traditional form of the slasher and updating several key conventions. In doing so, the films received both critical and box-office success and resurrected a largely dormant genre, making it relevant to a new generation of teenagers. *Scream*'s success in 1996 proved that teenagers could be lured back to the multiplex, and sparked off a new cycle of teen films in the millennium.

This noteworthy increase in teen/youth film attendance was, in many ways, a direct result of the increasing numbers of teen-oriented films that the studios were actively releasing in the late 1990s. In the decade following *Scream*'s release, numerous other teen horror and slasher films followed. The following list gives an indication of just how popular and widely imitated the slasher film was between 1996 and 2001.[67]

Date	Movie	Gross	Studio
Dec 16, 1996	Scream	$103 m	Dimension
Oct 17, 1997	I Know What You Did Last Summer	$72.2 m	Columbia
Dec 12, 1997	Scream 2	$101.3 m	Dimension
July 24, 1998	Disturbing Behavior	$17.5 m	MGM
Aug 5, 1998	Halloween: H20	$55 m	Dimension
Sep 25, 1998	Urban Legend	$38.1 m	Columbia
Nov 13, 1998	I Still Know What You Did Last Summer	$40 m	Columbia
Dec 25, 1998	The Faculty	$40.1 m	Dimension
Feb 4, 2000	Scream 3	$89.1 m	Dimension
Mar 17, 2000	Final Destination	$53.3 m	New Line
April 7, 2000	The Skulls	$35 m	Universal
July 7, 2000	Scary Movie	$157 m	Dimension
Sep 22, 2000	Urban Legends 2	$21.5 m	Columbia
July 4, 2001	Scary Movie 2	$71.3	Dimension

Dimension and *Scream* resurrected not only the teen slasher genre but also teen-oriented sub-genres such as the High School Teen Romance and the Teen Sex Farce. After 1996, teen audiences were not restricted to slasher-horror films for their entertainment. *Scream* also inspired other studios to expand into the teen market and was tangentially responsible for the return of a spate of other teen-identified genres, including the teen romance—*Can't Hardly Wait, She's All That* (1999), *10 Things I Hate About You* (1999), *Drive Me Crazy, Save the Last Dance* (2001), the teen sex-farce—*American Pie* (1999) and its sequel (2001), the teenpic parody—*Scary Movie 1* (2000) and *2* (2001), *Not Another Teen Movie* (2001) and other high-school-based comedies—*Bring It On* (2000), *Sugar and Spice* (2001), as well as teen dramas—*Cruel Intentions, Varsity Blues*, and *O* (2001). All of these films displayed the postmodern qualities associated with *Scream* and engaged in the same marketing strategies described in the cross-media marketing matrix section.

Many of these later teen films adopted the qualities first embraced by *Scream*. Like the *Scream* trilogy, many teen films featured teen television stars that would work on these films when their television shows were on hiatus. *I Know What You Did Last Summer*, for instance, starred Jennifer Love Hewitt from FOX's teen-oriented television show *Party of Five*, and Sarah Michelle Gellar from the WB's *Buffy*. *Disturbing Behavior* (1998) starred Katie Holmes from the WB's *Dawson's Creek*. In the millennial era, the film and television industries and their teen stars ignored the boundaries between the different media and crossed these platforms with ease. Teen audiences in turn willingly embraced and supported the cross-media mobility of a group of teen-focused creative personnel and stars as they shifted back and forth between film and television projects.

The collapsing boundaries between different media were not limited to talent, and included an increasing aesthetic and stylistic convergence. Many millennial teen films embraced the visual styles that resembled the aesthetic characteristics of the smaller screen. *10 Things I Hate About You* adopted the visuals, format and aesthetic style most directly associated with MTV, offering musical scenes that were easily translated for broadcast on MTV (as both trailer and/or music video). In many cases, these teen films even took the film–MTV connection a step further. Miramax's teen romantic comedy, *She's All That*, featured extended homages/parodies of MTV programs. These included sequences in which the film's characters refer to and "appear" in popular MTV series such as the docu-drama *The Real World* and *Spring Break* that featured older teenagers and young adults "partying" at MTV events celebrating that particular student rite. During these sequences, the film self-consciously appropriated the MTV visual style associated with these actual television shows. The film also incorporated a musical-dance sequence moments before the film's climactic showdown which possesses all the earmarks of an MTV music video, with its emphasis upon a mixture of lip-synching, synchronized dancing, stylized visuals, kinetic editing, and music. In each instance, these films consisted of highly fragmented sequences displaying the excessive stylistic and aesthetic elements that signaled the increasing convergence of diverse media styles and formats (for instance film and music video). These conditions were driven by media structures committed to publicizing and marketing the product to better maximize profits.

These cross-media intersections was not restricted to the film, television and music industries but included the publishing and fashion industries as well. These practices resembled the activities I previously discussed with reference to MTV's commitment to fashion tie-ups, most overtly in its *Fashionably Loud* cable series. In 1998, Dimension's teen/sci-fi/horror film *The Faculty* committed to a tie-in with clothing brand Tommy Hilfiger.[68] Under the terms of the deal, Hilfiger, whose youthful brand of clothes had garnered a distinct following among younger hip-hop celebrities and actual teenagers, outfitted the stars in the film and contributed an estimated $9 million toward the movie's $30 million marketing budget.[69] The additional marketing took the form of an extensive print and television campaign that linked Hilfiger's Tommy Jeans line to Dimension's *The Faculty*.[70] As Dimension head, Bob Weinstein points out, "The Dimension film audience matches the Tommy Jeans demographic."[71]

Hilfiger's ads starred the young, mostly little known actors from the Robert Rodriguez–directed, Kevin Williamson–scripted movie. Many of the print ads directly targeted the teen demographic, running in youth-oriented magazines such as *Seventeen*, *Rolling Stone* and *Interview*. In the fashion designer's back-to-school commercials, the movie's teenage actors were seen relaxing between filming, sometimes talking about their clothes, while the movie's credits appear on screen: "Written by Kevin Williamson," "Directed by Robert Rodriguez," followed by "Starring Tommy Jeans." The Dimension-Hilfiger arrangement thus took the practice of product placement a step further. More than simply featuring a product on screen, the deal instead fostered a distinct association between the Dimension and Hilfiger brands, a link reinforced by the cross-promotional advertising they shared. As Paul Speaker, director of marketing for The Shooting Gallery, an independent production company, notes, "It's not one product placement, but instead a true film association. A marketing partner would be taking [a film's] imagery and using it as regular, everyday image-brand advertising."[72]

The Dimension-Hilfiger deal established the precedent for future merchandizing tie-ins, one that would eventually characterize a range of teen-oriented film and television texts. American Eagle's products were featured in Dimension's teen-oriented romantic comedy, *Boys and Girls* (2000). On July 21, 2000, Dimension Films and the teen-branded clothing line, American Eagle Outfitters, announced that they had reached an arrangement in which the clothing retailer's merchandise would appear in future Dimension films.[73] In exchange for the exposure, the retailer promoted the Dimension movie releases through its website, magazines and stores nation-wide. Subsequent teen films also participated in retailer tie-ins. *The Mod Squad* (1999), for instance, had a cross-promotion deal with youth brand, Levi's that clothed the characters in the film. Levi's ads then featured the film's stars in scenes that appeared to be from the film, and included freeze-frame shots that identified the specific clothing items worn by the characters.

Clearly, the intensification of postmodern intertextual elements within late-twentieth century popular teen culture was inextricably tied to issues of marketing, promotion, commodification, and consumption. Millennial teen films were increasingly emerging as multi-texts that were consistently linked in mutual cross promotions focused on encouraging media consumption and enhancing profit. The *Scream* trilogy emerged as the representative texts of both the '90s slasher film, and the '90s teen film and went on to have a significant impact on the entertainment industry. More significantly, the trilogy helped legitimize the slasher/horror/exploitation genre, as it enjoyed great public popularity while also earning critical acclaim and kudos.

The millennial teen films' propensity for ignoring film-specific boundaries in actively referencing, "borrowing," as well as influencing, the styles and formats of *other* media forms, including television and music videos is another quality associated with this later stage in postmodernism's evolution. These developments in teen media's style, content and aesthetics are invariably tied to macro-industrial forces, such as the industry's marketing and promotional strategies, as well as to the rise of a new teen demographic. In updating the genre to reflect a more adolescent female sensibility, featuring empowered central female characters that refuse to be victims and fight back against their attackers, the films have made the genre relevant and appealing to its traditional core male audience while also cultivating a new generation of avid female fans.

No longer neglected by the entertainment industries, teenagers returned to the multiplex in droves. By 1998, *Variety* was reporting that 92 percent of teens surveyed by the Artist Rights Foundation in Los Angeles and the Boston-based Institute for Civil Society said they regard watching films as their number-one pastime. The survey also revealed that 68 percent had seen a movie within the previous week — a statistic considerably higher than in the spring of 1993, when only 55 percent said that they had watched a film in a theatre in the preceding seven days. According to the survey, 82 percent of teenagers watched at least one movie in a theatre each month, while 87 percent caught one video at home in the same period; 30 percent watched at least three theatrical releases a month, while 65 percent rented at least the same number of videos; just 8 percent bought tickets to five movies a month, although as many as 49 percent rented that many films on tape.[74] These statistics suggest that Hollywood's conscious efforts to target and service the millennial teen's entertainment demands were paying off. As teen films returned to the cineplex, so too did their target audience.

SIX

From Teen Television Network to Teen Culture Nexus

At the turn of the millennium, during the 1999–2000 television season, the WB television network marked its fifth anniversary on the air as the acknowledged teen-oriented broadcast network, a media site actively engaged in creating, mediating and (re-)shaping teen entertainment culture. The network's success at attracting and servicing the entertainment demands of the teen demographic made it popular with advertisers and consumer corporations who were targeting that demographic. This chapter examines the emergence of a millennial teen television site that intently pursued activities to target teens while simultaneously extending its reach and influence beyond its own medium-specific boundaries. In particular, attention is paid to studying the millennial teen television program as a cultural and commercial product that has been shaped by the need to serve simultaneous inclinations towards both art and commerce. These shows joined the larger body of circulating teen media texts, including those generated by MTV and Dimension that I have already discussed, in redefining the nature, form and content of commercial teen entertainment in the millennium. The ways in which the specific industrial, economic, and creative contexts of the period influenced the distinctive characteristics of the millennial teen television text are this chapter's primary interest.

This investigation is inextricably tied to the launch and subsequent activities of the WB network, when its decision to target the teen demographic resulted in the creation of programs and a format that collectively constituted the WB as a teen-oriented cultural artifact in itself. From 1995–2005, the WB's development into a recognized and successful teen network allowed it to succeed in what was dubbed the post-network, post-broadcast era, before industrial and marketplace changes motivated a merger with its rival UPN network to create a new teen-focused CW network in January 2006.

In this chapter, I examine how teen broadcast television evolved into a significant component of a larger teen-focused multi-media entertainment matrix in the millennium, linking these developments to the strategies the WB utilized in marshaling the increasingly vital teen market for the network's initial survival and success and tracing how these strategies evolved with the launch of the CW. The WB emerged as the network of choice for the youth/teen audience by cultivating a teen brand shaped by a range of distinctive teen shows (including *Buffy the Vampire Slayer* [WB, 1997–2001], *Dawson's Creek*, and *Roswell* [WB, 1999–2001]) that consciously borrowed from the tradition of quality television texts. The following pages consider how the conventional characteristics of quality television were adapted to effectively target a teen audience while simultaneously servicing advertiser interests. The final section traces the evolving social, industrial and marketplace conditions that led to the WB–UPN merger resulting in the rise of the CW, and discusses the new marketing strategies and programming changes that resulted from these contextual events.

Television in the 1990s: From Network Broadcasting to a Post-Network, Post-Broadcast Era

The rise of the WB must be examined against the contemporary television landscape and the numerous industrial changes that have taken place since the 1970s. During the heyday of network broadcasting, from the 1940s to the 1960s, "television" consisted of a three-channel universe ruled by the established broadcast networks, NBC, CBS, and ABC. "Television" then, meant broadcasting to the widest, most general audience and delivering that mass audience to advertisers. The 1970s, however, marked the beginning of numerous changes within the television industry. The advent of cable technology led to the launch of cable networks/channels that rejected the broadcast mandate, predicated on servicing an undifferentiated mass audience, in preference of narrowcasting to a select, niche market. As cable penetration increased, television viewers began turning their attention from the three broadcast networks towards these cable alternatives. Highlighting the network broadcaster's diminishing supremacy over the medium, network broadcast audience numbers declined from 95 percent of the nation-wide television audience in the 1960s to under 50 percent of the audience in the 1990s. The subsequent developments of alternative entertainment delivery platforms in the 1980s and '90s, including video and digital formats, and, more recently, web-based television, have resulted in a much more complex, fragmented, and highly competitive television market. In the late 1980s and early 1990s, these events prompted the mainstream and trade press to herald the demise of traditional broadcasting and of network television, and forecast the birth of a post-network, post-broadcast era. By the 1990s it was clear that television could no longer be defined by or restricted to the conventional broadcasting and network model.

Yet, amidst these shifts, both Warner Bros. and Paramount Studios announced the creation of their own television broadcast networks in 1995.[1] Undoubtedly, both studios aspired to replicate the success of FOX, the television network launched by Rupert Murdoch and 20th Century Fox Films in 1986.[2] FOX demonstrated the tremendous synergistic and economic benefits that could accrue from such a venture.[3] With FOX, Murdoch and 20th Century Fox profited greatly from controlling the entire process of production, distribution and exhibition in television. As a supplier of programming for the networks, 20th Century Fox Studios had long been committed to program production. Owning their own network gave the studio control over the distribution of these programs, liberating the studio from its dependence upon the other networks for distributing 20th Century Fox programming. Furthermore, FOX's exhibition arm, its owned and operated television stations, profited greatly from advertising revenues. As then Fox vice-president of marketing David Johnson points out, "If you can link together production and distribution in the television business, you can face enormous growth...."[4] FOX therefore served as both an inspiration and model for both the WB and Paramount's UPN network.

Having control of a television distribution platform became even more vital with the lifting of the FCC's Financial Interest and Syndication Rules (Fin/Syn) in 1995.[5] This regulation had prohibited broadcast networks from owning and producing their own entertainment programming. In 1991, however, media watchers began predicting that the Fin/Syn rules would be phased out — an event that would allow the four major broadcast networks to produce their own prime-time entertainment programs in-house, leaving the studios without a guaranteed means of distribution for their products. As the number one supplier of prime-time programming, animated programming, and first-run, syndicated programs, the stakes were especially high for Warner Bros. Acting in anticipation of this potentially significant upheaval in the studio-network relationship, both Warner Bros. and Paramount launched the WB and UPN respectively, to ensure themselves a distribution platform for their own programs.[6]

Launching the WB Network

In the summer of 1992, Warner Bros. named Jamie Kellner, the man responsible for launching the FOX television network in 1986, the managing general partner of the WB network.[7] According to Kellner, conventional network practices were no longer viable routes to success for a newly launched television network. He maintained that the WB needed to deviate from the traditional network commitment to mass marketing and broadcasting, arguing that the future of a network, particularly a fledgling one, lay in the cable-inspired strategies of niche marketing and narrowcasting.[8] Theorizing that a new television network could never successfully compete with the established big three networks by broadcasting to a broad, general audience, Kellner steered the WB towards narrowcasting to a select, niche audience. Unlike the three established network powerhouses' long-held commitment to the broadest range of television audiences (the general 18 to 49 adult viewer of both sexes), the WB targeted a younger, more narrowly defined demographic: 12- to 34-year-olds of both sexes.[9] Kellner strategically marketed the network to a specific segment of viewers and advertisers by committing to shows that would appeal to this core audience.

The WB's decision to target the niche teen demographic coincided serendipitously with the renaissance of the teen market and teen popular culture, a development that effectively reversed the entertainment industries' earlier belief that the teen demographic did not have a large enough presence to support strictly "teenaged" entertainment products.[10] Consequently, the youth/teen demographic market encompassed by the 12- to 34-year-old category, that had traditionally taken a back seat to the more valuable 18- to 49-year-old "quality" demographic, began to attract significant advertiser attention.

Revising Notions of "Quality": Riding the Wave of the Millennial Teen Market

The notion of "quality television" has always been associated with two related issues: the quality of the television audience, and the quality of the television show. With regard to the former, "quality" is traditionally equated with "up-scale urbanites whose status as active consumers rendered them a desirable 'target market' for TV advertisers," a demographic the television industry defines as "18- to 49-year-old adults."[11] This interest in a quality audience in turn motivated the rise of the quality television show — in essence the type of show that could effectively attract the quality audience valued by advertisers. Until the mid–1990s, considerations of quality television programs were largely restricted to adult-oriented dramas popular with the valuable 18- to 49-year-old adult demographic. But in the mid–1990s, the surging teen demographic numbers and the realization that teens possessed the disposable income, the propensity for active consumerism, and the access to advertised products traditionally associated with an adult quality audience, caused networks and advertisers to focus their attention on the long neglected teen demographic and to view teenagers and youth as a new subset of the traditional "quality" demographic. The television industry, marketers and advertisers' response to this emerging demographic was quick and focused.

The WB strategy centered on attracting the increasingly valuable teen audience, so as to profit from servicing the advertisers eager to reach this niche market. Significantly, the teen component of the 12 to 34 audience segment is generally regarded as the most elusive. As Kellner notes, "From an advertising standpoint, teens are the hardest-to-reach audience on TV. People make their brand decisions at an early life, and follow them for the rest of their life. It's an extremely valuable audience for advertisers and thus a business...."[12] At the time, however, the established "Big Three" networks, ABC, CBS and NBC, remained primarily focused on the traditional adult audience. None were directly targeting the teen audience in prime time. Furthermore, the initially youth-oriented FOX had been steadily "aging up" into the general broadcast demographic since the early 1990s.[13] As a result, advertisers were often willing to overpay to reach the increasingly attractive youth segment. Kellner further justified the WB's decision to court this niche audience claiming, "our audience ... replenishes itself. Kids move into teens, teens move into 18–34's. We're focused on 12–34's, but with a big spillover both up and down."[14]

Establishing the WB Teen Brand: Constructing the WB Teen

The WB began consolidating its teen-identified brand by launching a number of distinctly teen-targeted television series. In January 1997 the WB premiered *Buffy the Vampire Slayer* (henceforth *Buffy*), a fantasy-horror-drama series which revolved around a teenage girl who, as the world's one designated "vampire slayer," is forced to battle all manner of evil monsters with the aid of her high-school friends.[15] In the middle of the 1997-98 season, the WB debuted *Dawson's Creek*. Revolving around four teenage friends in a Cape Cod–like town, the series explored the angst, relationship crises, and the coming-of-age dilemmas faced by a group of introspective, intelligent, self-aware high-schoolers. The show's teen-identity and credibility was further reinforced by its pedigree: it was the creation of Kevin Williamson, the writer of highly successful teen films including the *Scream* trilogy, and *I Know What You Did Last Summer*. In 1998–99, the network increased its teen programming and further expanded its schedule with *Roswell*, a series about a group of teenage aliens growing up in the alien-obsessed town of Roswell, New Mexico[16]; *Charmed* (1998–2006), a fantasy drama about three sisters who discover they are witches; and *Felicity*, a series that followed a group of teenage friends as they embarked on their college years.

All these shows shared several distinct characteristics: they featured a young and highly attractive ensemble cast and they explored a range of youth-oriented, coming-of-age experiences with an appealing blend of intelligence, sensitivity, and knowing sarcasm. In addition, the shows addressed many sensitive and potentially controversial teen and youth issues, such as self-destructive teenage behavior, alcoholism, teenage sex, and sexual identity. Furthermore, these shows' central focus revolved around the relationships and friendships of the key teenage protagonists. These characteristic qualities may be traced to the WB's attempt to distinguish itself from its primary competition for the teen audience, MTV. If the WB hoped to attract a teen audience, it needed to offer programming that would provide an alternative to what was available on the teen-oriented cable network. The WB, therefore, needed to construct a brand identity via programming, publicity, and format that was distinctly different from its more established competitor.

An examination of the WB's teen identity/brand indicates a distinct deviation from MTV's. Unlike MTV's more irreverent, hedonistic, and anti-establishment teens, the WB's teenagers were significantly more morally idealistic.[17] The WB teens struggled to do the right thing; they loved and supported their siblings and friends; and, they respected their parents. The main teenage protagonists in the shows mentioned tended to be thoughtful and introspective, serious and responsible, mature and self-aware, while also attractive, intelligent, fun-loving, and young. Although the WB's teen characters often made mistakes, they learned from them. They faced numerous social, personal, emotional, and sexual crises but continually struggled to do the right and responsible thing. They suffered teenage angst but also knew how to enjoy their youth. These teen constructions lay distinctly outside the often risqué, urban edginess of MTV. It is also noteworthy that the "WB teen" tended to exist in a white, affluent, and suburban context that was in distinct contrast to the multi-racial, urban "MTV teen."[18]

Of course, adopting a more conservative, idealistic, teen identity was more appropriate for a mainstream "broadcast" network rather than a cable network.[19] Unlike MTV, the WB did not enjoy the leeway accorded to cable networks that remain, in many ways, less vulnerable to public, political and industry criticism. As a result, the WB consciously tried to avoid the more serious controversies that would alienate its advertisers or attract negative governmental and regulatory attention. Adopting a more conservative ethos in its programming allowed the network to side-step a significant degree of social and institutional criticism that would adhere to any "alternative" teen broadcast network.[20]

The WB and Quality Teen Television

In addition to constructing the WB's teen identity, the various WB teen series also consciously adopted a range of characteristics borrowed from mainstream "quality" television, albeit adapting them to the target teen demographic. The WB's interest in teen niche audiences had a distinct impact on the style and format of the quality television text. In the late 1990s, advertisers and networks needed to create a television text with the distinct content, style and form that would appeal to a new generation of teenagers. As Caldwell notes, "[t]his industrial reconfiguration of the audience ... helped spawn the need for cultural — ... specific styles and looks."[21] This ultimately involved the creation of a carefully targeted format, which involved "arranging materials—songs, articles, programs—into a package that people in a target audience would see as reflecting their identity,"[22] as a successful format would make "the community more pure and thereby more efficient for advertisers" and consumers.[23]

One of the notable qualities of the WB's teen-oriented schedule is the overwhelming popularity of the ensemble cast, hour-long, dramatic series format, characteristics linked to the quality television tradition. A "quality" television show, as various scholars have noted, was characterized by the use of an ensemble cast in an hour-long dramatic format, narratives that replaced the familial milieu with a focus on the familial relationships that existed between friends and colleagues, a tendency towards liberal humanism, a propensity for self-reflexivity, and the adoption of cinematic techniques and aesthetics.[24] Of course the WB shows were not themselves the pioneers of quality teen television. Rather, the WB's teen-oriented, hour-long dramas were the direct descendents of two earlier teen series: the short-lived, critically acclaimed, quality teen drama *My So-Called Life* (1994–1995) which treated teen experiences and angst with respect and sensitivity, and the long-running *Beverly Hills, 90210* which, in its early seasons, dealt with typical teenage experiences of close friendships, complicated romantic relationships, and the quest for identity, all presented in a glamorous and attractive package. Like these antecedents, *Buffy, Dawson's Creek, Roswell, Charmed,* and *Felicity* were all hour-long dramas that effectively blended *Beverly Hills, 90210*'s glossy visual style and physically attractive ensemble cast with *My So-Called Life*'s honest exploration of the teenage experience.

Quality Teen TV: Tackling Teen Issues

During the WB's decade as a broadcast network, its schedule was dominated by shows that actively cultivated the niche teen audience by intentionally acknowledging and addressing the coming-of-age concerns that would particularly resonate with teenagers. For instance, many WB shows explored the complicated, conflicted relationships teenagers have with family and friends. The teenage Buffy's relationship with her mother, Joyce, is marked by a series of misunderstandings and conflicts, despite the obvious affection they have for each other. In the first two seasons of *Buffy*, Joyce is unaware of Buffy's identity as the Vampire Slayer. Joyce sees her daughter as a typical teenager obsessed with clothes and boys and prone to irresponsible behavior when in fact, Buffy must shoulder the responsibilities of saving the world from myriad monsters and potential apocalypses. In *Roswell*, a group of human and alien teenagers struggle to protect each other from a threatening adult world determined to uncover and exploit their secret. In this series, the parents are ignorant of the teenagers' situation and ineffectual in providing any help. In *Dawson's Creek*, three of the teenage characters, Joey, Jen and Pacey, have either lost their parents, or suffer parental neglect and abandonment. The sense of alienation and isolation that these teenage characters experience as they try to negotiate their way in the world, as well as the strong friendship, support, and camaraderie they derive only from each other, may be read as fictional and metaphorical representations of an actual teenager's perception of lived reality.

Like earlier quality television shows, the WB's teen series also adopted an attitude of liberal humanism in its narratives, addressing difficult, often significant issues particularly relevant to a teen and youth audience. One *Buffy* episode, "Beauty and the Beasts," dealt with abusive relationships, highlighting the thin line that exists between love and abusive obsession, and providing an unflinching portrayal of the deadly consequences that can ensue. Another episode, "Earshot," addressed suicide, high-school violence, teenage alienation and loneliness. In the episode, Buffy confronts an awkward misfit intent on suicide, and reminds him that all teenagers encounter loneliness, isolation and insecurity and that violence of any form is no solution.[25] *Buffy* and *Dawson's Creek* also explored the issue of sexual identity — in particular, the struggles and prejudices faced by central characters who realize that they are gay. Over the course of several seasons, these series dealt with the confusion that these characters experience about their sexual identity, the implications it has for their friendships, and their fear of their friends' reactions. The series' deliberate decision not to portray these characters' sexuality as "alternative" or aberrant, as well as the attempts to represent their romantic relationships as largely functional, healthy, supportive and loving, highlights the series' liberal and humanist stance.

The quality markers of the WB's teen shows were not restricted to narrative elements or characterization but extended to aesthetic and stylistic elements as well. Stylistically, these shows embraced distinct cinematic qualities by adopting certain "film style" visuals. As Todd Gitlin notes, traditional television visuals emphasize a mechanical, standardized set of techniques based on clarity and efficiency, such as the three-camera method in sitcoms.[26] "Quality" television shows in the 1970s and after, such as *MASH* (1972–1983) and *Hill Street Blues* (1981–1987), adopted a single-camera shoot and advocated the use of more cinematic techniques and styles that rejected the clean and flat television image in preference of "messy" clutter, texture, and momentum.[27] While the WB's teen shows did not share the same cinematic style associated with these earlier quality series, they did embrace the single-camera format and were shot on film, offering the rich, organic visuals lacking in video. The film-trained creative personnel who worked on the WB's shows helped contribute a heightened cinematic touch. Notably, the creators of *Buffy* and *Dawson's Creek*, Joss Whedon and Kevin Williamson respectively, had both previously worked on teen-identified feature film projects.[28] Following the WB's success with Williamson and Whedon, the network actively sought out arrangements with filmmakers rather than established television personnel. *Felicity* creators J.J.

Abrams and Matt Reeves began in films, the former as a scriptwriter with films such as *Regarding Henry* (1991) and *Armageddon* (1998) to his credit, the latter as the director of *The Pallbearer* (1996). The producers and creative personnel on the WB's *Young Americans* (2000) include production designer Vince Peranio, who collaborated with John Waters on all his films, and camera operator Aaron Pazanti, who worked on the Oscar-winning *American Beauty* (1999).[29] The propensity for cinematic visuals and techniques linked these later shows to the precedent setting strategies associated with quality television shows such as *Hill Street Blues, Northern Exposure* (1990–1995) and *Twin Peaks* (1990–1991).

While the WB's teen shows obviously owed a significant debt to their quality television predecessors, these shows were not merely copies of quality series reconfigured for a teen audience. In a variety of ways, the WB texts represented the next step in the evolution of the quality series' characteristics, an evolution that consciously responded to the changing needs and perceptions of their target audiences. For instance, while earlier adult quality television shows were characterized by self-reflexivity and genre hybridity,[30] the WB shows indulged in a degree of postmodern intertextuality, pastiche, genre hybridity, media mixing and hyperconscious self-reflexivity, excessive enough to constitute a categorical distinction, a shift predicated on the distinct characteristics of the millennial teen's relationship with the media and entertainment.[31]

Quality Teen TV: Postmodernism and Multi-Media Hyper-Intertextuality

According to Feuer, "self conscious strategies" such as intertextuality and self-reflexivity "operate ... as a way of distinguishing the 'quality' from the everyday product."[32] As scholars like Collins, Caldwell, Feuer and Doherty point out, the shift towards excessive intertextual references is due in part to the audiences' increasing access to past entertainment media.[33] David Thorburn notes:

> Television's capacity to make its history and evolution continuously available (even to younger members in its ... audience) is surely without precedent, for the system of reruns has now reached the point of transforming television into a continuous, living museum which displays for daily or weekly consumption texts from every stage of the medium's past.[34]

By the 1990s, television's "archival" activities were no longer limited to reruns of the medium's own historical texts, but included the exhibition of a wider range of popular media content, including film and other visual media. The unprecedented degree to which the WB's shows reference, quote, and on occasion spoof, both past and current popular media culture made the practice one of the identifying traits of millennial teen television. Millennial teenagers had surpassed previous generations in their awareness of, and exposure to, both past and contemporary media texts. The teenager's familiarity with film history was founded on easy access to classic films and television shows on cable and video. Cable television, videotape and recorders, digital recording and computers, the forms of technology that have been associated with the rise of the information age, had all contributed to the aesthetic shift towards visual excess in media texts. These technologies also had a significant impact upon the era's teenagers, a generation steeped in a broad range of pop culture, and thus in possession of a heightened media-oriented hyperconsciousness. As a result, many of the WB shows consistently engaged in intertextual pop-culture references in an attempt to harness this target audience's interests.

For instance, *Dawson's Creek* habitually paid homage to popular films. *Dawson's Creek*'s homage to *Scream* and classic popular teen slasher films has already been discussed in earlier chapters. In another episode, the four main characters spend the night on a deserted, reportedly haunted island. The episode is rife with stylistic, verbal and narrative allusions to the phenomenally successful film *The Blair Witch Project* (1999). On another occasion, the teen characters are sent to detention, resulting in an episode that deliberately borrows narratives, situations and plot-points from the cult 1980s John Hughes teenpic *The Breakfast Club* (1985).[35] Like the film, the episode revolves around the teenage characters' experiences with a group of misfits during a day in detention. Yet another episode directly references the hit Warner Bros. film *The Perfect Storm* (2000)—while out sailing, two of the show's teenagers are caught in a vicious storm, leading to numerous instances of dialogue that cite the film and its plot points while they wait for their friends to rescue them. Each of these episodes portray the characters engaged in a significant amount of hyperconscious dialogue revolving around discussions of the films, with numerous self-aware quips regarding the similarities between the films and their experiences.

Buffy also consistently cites diverse popular culture texts such as *Jaws* (1975), *The Usual Suspects* (1995), *Dracula* (1931, et al), and *Star Trek: First Contact* (1996) among others. While *Buffy* tends to restrict these to dialogue references, the series, like *Dawson's Creek*, assumes a high level of media and popular culture awareness in its teen audience, since many of the references tend to be almost glib and sometimes even obscure, with throwaway lines of dialogue comparing the show's characters with characters from other television shows or popular films, or replicating famous movie dialogue.[36] Another teen-oriented WB series, *Popular* (1999–2001), was particularly prone to intertextual citations. In fact, every episode in the series employed film or pop-culture quotations. Entire scenes referenced films as diverse as *Psycho* and *Dangerous Liaisons* (1988). While shows on other more adult-oriented networks occasionally indulged in cinematic allusions, they did not approach the intensity and extreme degree that marked the WB shows.

In the above cases, the intertextual elements highlight some noteworthy qualities about late twentieth century/millennial teen culture, qualities also evident in teen films and other teen entertainment texts of the period. First and foremost, they illustrate the highly intertwined nature of the film and television industries' focus on attracting and harnessing the teen market. The ties that bind the *Scream* film series to the *Dawson's Creek* episode, for instance, allowed the film franchise to benefit from the promotional exposure on a hit television show, even as the television show itself actively set out to attract the very teenagers who were responsible for the success and popularity of the film franchise.[37] The fact that almost all of the WB's teen-oriented shows engaged in this practice, and did so repeatedly, suggested that the network used the technique to attract the pop-culture-obsessed teenager who visited the movie theaters regularly and who was, therefore, well equipped to recognize and appreciate the references.

Interestingly, the intertextual references found in the WB's teen shows were not only restricted to current pop cultural events or primarily teen-oriented trends. *Jaws, Dracula, Psycho*, and *Dangerous Liaisons* are more commonly associated with the adult, boomer generation. However, these references subtly ensured the currency of these texts, all of which are accessible on video, cable and the internet, and may, in fact, extend their "shelf-life" and profitability by introducing them to a new market by encouraging teens to acquaint themselves with these potentially unfamiliar older products.[38] This strategy is particularly self-serving since many of the entertainment texts mentioned on *Buffy* are owned and distributed by 20th Century Fox, the same studio that produces *Buffy*, and Warner Bros., the studio that owns the WB network.

Clearly, this increasing degree of narrative and stylistic/aesthetic intertextuality and excess cannot be viewed solely in terms of artistic expression or a quality aesthetic. Rather, marketing exigencies and advertisers' interests remained powerful considerations and in fact contributed to the textual complexity characteristic of millennial teen television. In these instances, it must be acknowledged that the show engaged in a range of practices that, while clearly inspired by a commitment to established notions of quality and tailored to its target teen demographic, were also largely guided by equally important commercial, advertising, and promotional concerns. This intersection of artistic and commercial inclinations is especially clear in the incorporation of music and music video stylistics into the television text.

From an artistic standpoint, many of the WB's teen series consistently relied upon music to establish a specific mood, enhance a particular emotion, or provide background commentary on the scene at a visceral level. Integrating music into the series affected the show's narrative and setting in specific ways. On *Buffy*, the teenage characters' regular haunts include The Bronze, a club for the high-school crowd. Over *Buffy*'s five seasons on the WB, alternative musicians, including Japanese cult group Cibo Matto, and Bif Naked, appeared at The Bronze. *Dawson's Creek, Roswell* and others also used music as commentary to reflect the mood and feelings of the teen characters. The musical performances were often opportunities to introduce an additional mood or emotional element to the narrative events in the episode, accompanied by visual montages that incorporate the aesthetic style of music videos. In addition, the choice of less mainstream musical acts helped the show maintain a hip, edgy credibility that appealed directly to teenagers. In adopting and melding together the many diverse forms of visual and aural media aesthetics to create a distinct teen-oriented television experience, the quality teen television text is perhaps one of the more richly layered and aesthetically complex forms of the medium.

Narrative and aesthetic complexity is not the sole function served by the inclusion of music, however. These strategies must also be recognized as a conscious attempt to create a supportive textual environment that could best serve the larger media industries' and advertisers' interests. As a segment, teens often played a significant role in embracing and popularizing undiscovered, less established musical acts. Since the WB was actively targeting the teen market that purchased CDs, the inclusion of contemporary alternative pop in various musical montages within the teen shows enabled the network to translate these musical segments into a deliberate marketing and promotional strategy via its pioneering use of promotional "end cards" to help the music industry promote its product.[39] Displayed at the end of each episode, these end cards identified songs featured on that week's episode, promoting both the musical artist and the CD while a snippet of the song is played.

Multi-Media Synergy and Cross-Media Promotion

The WB was able to further exploit this marketing innovation to serve its own synergistic interests, actively associating its shows with music by Time Warner musical artists, such as Madonna. While promoting the first season of *Felicity*, the WB acquired the rights to use Madonna's "Power of Goodbye," off her *Ray of Light* CD (1998), in movie trailers and television promotional spots for the series. This arrangement benefited both the television series as well as Madonna's single, which had been released mere weeks before. The single gained significant exposure, particularly with the teen market, while *Felicity* established an identity and audience recall via its association with the popular hit song.

Madonna's next album, *Music* (2000), also enjoyed similar cross-promotional benefits when her single "(Don't) Tell Me" was used in the promotional trailers for the fourth season of *Dawson's Creek*. The trailers, launched a little before Madonna's *Music* album was released, helped raise teen consumers' awareness and anticipation for the album, while also serving as an effective identifying tune for the series. Madonna was not the only Time Warner artist to benefit from such synergistic promotional support. Music coordinators, who made the song selections, claimed that they are not forced, merely "encouraged," to use material belonging to the corporate family. However, the fact remained that the bulk of the songs featured in the WB's promotional campaigns were by artists on the Warner Music Group label.[40] This arrangement allowed one branch of the corporation to synergistically promote and support the other.

The WB's most successful synergistic activities centered on the Warner Bros. produced prime-time series, *Smallville* (2001–), a retelling of the popular *Superman* myth as a young, often conflicted, vulnerable teenager, battling his sense of alienation while seeking his place in the world. AOL Time Warner's interests in *Superman* began in 1971, when Warner Communications acquired DC Comics and its stable of superheroes, which included both Superman and Batman.[41] Warner Bros. has since repackaged *Superman* as a highly successful movie franchise,[42] live-action and animated television series,[43] and several feature-length animated films.[44] Like previous *Superman* texts, *Smallville* was a pre-sold product with a distinct and committed fan base. As the series was created, produced and owned by Warner Bros., and broadcast on the WB network, Warner Bros. was able to profit from multiple revenue streams, from the show's licensing fees to the network, the returns on advertising rates, and subsequent earnings from ancillary media releases and tie-ins. Warner Bros. also profited from the show's eventual syndication in the national and global television market. In addition, as one of a series of multimedia products based on the Superman characters, the show could be used to cross-promote and market the other Superman-related commodity texts. With *Smallville*, the WB exploited its parent company's vertically and horizontally integrated structure and fully benefit from its synergistic potential.

Teen TV: Cross-Corporate Promotional Tie-Ins

In addition to synergistic exploitation, the WB actively worked to meld its entertainment mandate with a promotional one. In the 1990s, there appeared to be a return to sponsorship strategies reflective of the late 1940s and early 1950s, when "highly visible sponsors dramatized both their shows and themselves on television."[45] This made it increasingly difficult to distinguish between the entertainment text and the commercial advertisement, a trend that was also adopted by Dimension Films and MTV. The WB's teen texts were shaped by the network's commitment to cultivating a range of product placements and commercial tie-ins with teen-oriented consumer companies. In addition to reaping advertising profits, the practice allowed the network and its series to brand itself by associating with a range of established teen-oriented consumer brands.

One of the first instances of a series tie-in with a consumer company revolved around a mutually beneficial marketing venture between youth-oriented retailer J.Crew and the WB's *Dawson's Creek*. Reminiscent of the Dimension-Hilfiger arrangement for *The Faculty*, J.Crew dressed the main characters on *Dawson's Creek*. The show's final credit sequence identified and promoted the retailer for supplying the show's wardrobe.[46] In exchange, the retailer's Fall/Winter 1998 catalogue, which was nationally distributed to a youthful, affluent, suburban consumer, publicized the series with photo spreads that prominently featured the show's young, attractive cast modeling the J.Crew collection. Thus, the network and the show enjoyed increased exposure to the very audience it was targeting, while the retailer had the opportunity to align itself with a popular and successful teen television series.

In later seasons, *Dawson's Creek* went on to affiliate with another clothing retailer, American Eagle Outfitters, which was arguably even more teen-oriented than J.Crew. After *Dawson's*, other WB teen oriented shows also followed a similar strategy, aligning themselves with distinctly teen-oriented products. *Roswell* had a highly publicized cross-promotional campaign with Levi's. As part of the commercial tie-in, the stars from the show did in-store appearances cross-promoting the show and Levi's products. These were accompanied by nation-wide print and Internet advertising campaigns that promoted the show, its stars and their Levi's-sponsored wardrobe. The exercise provided the same promotional benefits as the *Dawson's Creek*–J.Crew/American Eagle campaigns. *Dawson's Creek* and *Roswell* were able to displace their production costs via the wardrobe sponsorship, while J.Crew, American Eagle Outfitters and Levi's enjoyed increased promotional and advertising exposure, particularly with the teen market.

As touched on in Chapter Three in my discussion of MTV's commitment to fashion label tie-ins, and in Chapter Four, with Dimension's various arrangements with clothing retailers including Tommy Hilfiger and American Eagle Outfitters, such marketing arrangements directly affected the style and look of the shows involved. Clothing was a vital element of a television series; it contributed to the show's overall identity and personality, indicating a specific lifestyle, and with it, specific values, interests and concerns. Associating with nation-wide retailers that had a distinct teen identity made the show and its characters more accessible to its teen viewers. *Dawson's Creek* and *Roswell* fans could easily dress like their favorite characters/actors by shopping in the stores. This opportunity to "connect" with the show, to enjoy something in common with the cast effectively creates a bond between the characters on the show and its viewers. The product tie-ins also further enhanced the shows' online profile when the American Eagle and Levi's retail websites featured information on the shows, their casts, and their wardrobe and also provided a link to the show's official website.

In fact, the Internet was yet another way for the WB to appeal to teen consumers. The network's popular teen shows, *Dawson's Creek*, *Buffy*, *Roswell*, *Charmed* and *Felicity* all had official websites— a significant trans-media phenomenon specific to late 1990s/millennial teen culture. The shows' teen fans could log on to these websites to discover information on upcoming episodes, read exclusive interviews with the shows' stars, and chat with other fans about various show-related topics. These official websites served an additional, and perhaps more important purpose — they were another conduit for the promotion and marketing of products and merchandise associated with the shows. Visitors to the websites could purchase a whole range of merchandise, including soundtracks, CDs from featured artists, books, and even clothing that had been featured on the shows.

Perhaps the most integrated cross-promotional campaign on the WB involved Coca-Cola's sponsorship of the network's short-lived summer 2000 series, *Young Americans*.[47] Revolving around a group of teenagers attending a boarding school in New England, the series possesses all the attributes of a WB teen hour-long serial drama: an attractive ensemble cast of teenage characters forced to confront the struggles of growing up. Narrative plot-points include neglectful or potentially abusive parents, star-crossed romantic entanglements, questions of sexual identity, issues of social class and alienation, and the suggestion of potential sexual scandal. Like *Buffy*, *Dawson's Creek*, *Roswell* and *Felicity* before it, *Young Americans* revolves around the romances and friendships that develop between the teenage characters, relationships that are tested by inherently melodramatic incidents.

The series was initially slated for the 1999–2000 television season, when the WB decided against acquiring it. The show was saved, however, when Coca-Cola approached the network with an offer to sponsor the series during a summer broadcast run.[48] Consequently, the WB premiered *Young Americans* in July 2000, after an intense promotional campaign publicizing the series as part of "The WB/Coca-Cola Summer Theatre." Trailers promoting the series offered wholesome, warm images of the attractive young characters "hanging out" and frolicking in a bucolic, small-town, suburban setting drinking Coke while an upbeat pop song played in the background. The trailers abounded with suggestions of youth, romance, energy, vitality, promise, and prominent displays and mentions of Coca-Cola. Ultimately, the show's trailers became almost indistinguishable from actual Coke ads.

Like the trailers, the series' content, visuals and style were also tailored to accommodate the sponsorship deal. Additional scenes were shot including an initial, opening-scene encounter between rich preppie student Scout Calhoun and local small-town girl Bella that takes place over the purchase and sharing of bottles of Coke. In subsequent episodes, the teenagers meet at the neighborhood diner and hold discussions over pitchers of the soft drink. With numerous scenes shot in warm colors and soft-focus, featuring images of young Americans celebrating their youth amidst sun-dappled, small-town, lake-side surroundings, the series, like the trailers, had numerous sequences that played out as little more than long-form Coke ads, with their familiar nostalgic palettes. The Coke–*Young Americans* case is further proof of television's increased adoption of the advertising industry's style and aesthetics. Significantly, the show was cancelled when Coke's sponsorship deal expired.

Branding the WB Teen Star

In addition to the WB's commercial arrangements, the network also practiced a unique form of talent management. The WB further reinforced its distinct teen brand by consistently associating itself with the increasingly popular stars of its teen shows. The network established the careers of stars such as Sarah Michelle Gellar (Buffy in *Buffy*), James Van Der Beek, Katie Holmes, Joshua Jackson and Michelle Williams (Dawson, Joey, Pacey and Jen, respectively, on *Dawson's Creek*).

The media attention that the WB's shows attracted played a significant role in publicizing the WB network, establishing its teen brand and drawing the network's target demographics. The WB network and its stars from *Buffy*, *Dawson's Creek*, *Roswell*, *Charmed* and *Felicity* increased their public profile by appearing on the covers and between the pages of high-profile, popular, youth-oriented publications (some of them owned by WB parent Time Warner) that ranged from the teen targeted, wholesome magazines such as *Teen People*, *Seventeen*, *Teen Vogue* and *YM* to the edgier, sexier ones including *Rolling Stone*, *Nylon*, and *Maxim*. The young stars also enjoyed exposure on more mainstream publications including *Entertainment Weekly*, *TIME*, *TV Guide* and *Premiere*. In addition to garnering positive reviews and publicity for their shows and, by extension, the WB, these promotional appearances played a significant role in targeting specific demographics while also influencing the public perception of these stars and their series in particular ways.

Appearances in teen-oriented magazines targeted at the 12 to 20 years olds helped to keep the WB, its shows and stars at the forefront of the teen audience's awareness and interest. These teen magazines presented the stars as valid role models, emphasizing their wholesome, hardworking, mature character traits and emphasizing the teen-focused nature of their WB shows. *Rolling Stone*, *Nylon*, *Detour* and *Maxim*, on the other hand, cater to a more adult, more male-oriented readership. These publications tended to accentuate the stars' and the shows' sexier, more risqué aspects.[49] In combination, these different collections of magazines effectively reinforced the WB's teen identity as simultaneously edgy/sexy *and* wholesome/youthful. Appearances in the more mainstream, entertainment publications reached a broader, more general audience and garnered the shows and the network itself greater publicity and exposure, as well as a degree of credibility and validity via the critical praise and recognition earned.

By 1998, after the WB had developed into a teen-branded network, almost every star of the network's the teen-focused series had successfully crossed-over to features, appearing in a range of teen-oriented films while still maintaining their television careers. James Van Der Beek of *Dawson's Creek* appeared in the box-office success *Varsity Blues*. Another successful teen film, *Cruel Intentions*, starred *Buffy*'s Sarah Michelle Gellar, Selma Blair from the WB's sit-com

Zoe, Duncan, Jack and Jane (1999–2000), and featured a cameo appearance by *Dawson's Creek*'s Joshua Jackson. Katie Holmes, also from *Dawson's Creek*, had roles in the teen-horror film *Disturbing Behavior* and the teen-oriented *Go* (1999), and she co-starred with Barry Watson, from the WB's *7th Heaven*, in Kevin Williamson's high-school teenpic, *Teaching Mrs. Tingle* (1999). Another *Dawson's Creek* star, Michelle Williams had a lead role in the teen slasher, *Halloween: H2O* (1998). As these stars began to garner media attention, media discourses revolving around these stars consistently associated them with the WB. When all of these actors went on to consolidate their teen-icon status by starring in a series of highly popular teen films, the WB initiated a new mode of synergistic cross-corporate marketing by engaging in a series of aggressive publicity efforts that ultimately mutually benefited the network, its stars, and their films, even when the films are made by rival studios.

When Columbia's *Cruel Intention* was released, the WB paid for a satellite press tour for actresses Selma Blair and Sarah Michelle Gellar in the belief that the publicity would benefit their WB television shows. When Joshua Jackson starred in *The Skulls* (2000), the WB inserted a promotional segment publicizing the film's opening during a broadcast of *Dawson's Creek*, the WB series in which Jackson stars. As Suzanne Daniels, the WB's president of programming notes, each movie featuring a WB television star, "is like an ad for WB."[50] In each instance, the WB was quick to capitalize on the publicity and exposure offered when its television stars appeared in teen-oriented features, recognizing that as these stars acquired their status as teen icons, they also reinforced the WB network's teen profile and brand identity. Furthermore, the WB was in a prime position to profit from its rival film studios' needs to purchase advertising time to promote these teen-oriented films to the WB's teen audience. By accommodating and supporting its network stars' film careers, the WB was able to benefit from yet another promotional opportunity, even as it enjoyed an exclusive advertising revenue stream. These activities added to the increasing degree of integration between the entertainment media that characterized the final years of the twentieth century.

In addition to launching and capitalizing on the careers of these young actors, the WB also engaged in a strategy to identify, test and groom other young actors. This involved the network's tendency to feature young actors in guest roles on popular, established shows, before casting them as main characters in new WB series. *Buffy* and *Dawson's Creek* launched a number of its teen guest-stars into their own series. For example, *Roswell* star Jason Behr guest starred on both *Buffy* and *Dawson's Creek* before landing the lead in the WB's alien-high-school series, *Roswell*. Scott Foley appeared on *Dawson's Creek* before winning a starring role in *Felicity*. Dylan Neal had a recurring role on *Dawson's Creek* before landing the lead in *Safe Harbor* (1999). Interestingly, this practice was not the traditional one of spinning-off characters from one series into another since Jason Behr, Scott Foley and Dylan Neal played different characters in each of the series. Nor was it a case of having stars from one show crossover to guest appear on another series as part of an attempt to raise ratings. Rather, the WB seemed to be borrowing from its classical studio personnel practices of the past, when it kept a stable of stars under contract who consistently appeared in Warner Bros. films. The WB was actively nurturing a select group of actors, testing and training them via guest appearances on the network's shows before rewarding a lucky, select few with starring roles in new WB series.

These cross-media appearances effectively exploited the growing wave of media and cultural interest in the teen market and all things youth-oriented during the period and kept the shows, its starts and the WB network at the center of the high-profile circulating discourses on popular culture, the media and entertainment. This deluge of media material effectively generated a complex web of intertextual cross-references that stretched between diverse media, all of which worked to promote the teen shows, the network and its particular "teen" identity and brand, raising them to broad public awareness and generating public interest and curiosity. These activities certainly contributed to the increased media-oriented hyperconsciousness characteristic of the postmodern perspective. As was true of Dimension's numerous cross-promotional activities, the WB's attempts to link its programming with a variety of other media texts, including film cross-promotions, music, teen-oriented product tie-ins, and magazine features, were part of a strategy to maximize the teen audiences' "points of contact" with the network and its shows.[51]

The WB's commitment to maximizing its teen audiences' "points of contact" was even applied across the range of its own teen-oriented series, a strategy aimed at helping the network further define and consolidate its teen brand. As Lew Goldstein, a co-executive vice-president of marketing at the WB notes, "the great thing about these shows is that they are a set. You'll notice in our print ads and other areas-tonally — they take on the same impression. Even though they are different shows, they belong together."[52] To reinforce the network's teen brand and enhance the teen audiences' awareness of the WB shows, many of the WB series engaged in a distinctive, hyperconscious, self-reflexive tendency to reference each other, particularly through sly, overtly self-aware, dialogue. For instance, on a *Dawson's Creek* episode, Pacey explicitly referenced key *Buffy* plot-points during a conversation. *Buffy* reciprocated in a scene in which the vampire, Spike, watches television and addresses the screen with comments and romantic advice for the *Dawson's Creek* characters. On yet another *Dawson's Creek* episode, a character declines a social invitation by pointing out that "*Roswell* is on in five minutes," referring to the impending start of *Roswell*, which followed *Dawson's Creek* on the WB's prime-time schedule at the time.

While it may be tempting to dismiss these occurrences as trivial in-jokes, the cross-series citations bring the WB's varied and various teen-oriented series in contact, uniting them into a distinct corpus of teen texts. Each reference constructs a connection or suggests shared qualities between these texts by building unique links between the network's teenage viewers.[53] The fact that each citation implies that the teenage characters on each show "watched" or were "fans" of the other WB shows worked to encode these shows as teen-oriented products across what teenagers might consider different cliques, thus consolidating the shows' and the WB network's teen brand. These references also functioned to raise different teen audiences' awareness and interests in the other shows, thereby encouraging them to watch the network's other programs.

These "in-house" cross-series references, coupled with the wider range of cross-media intersections and commercial tie-ins were invaluable because (1) they gave the network and its shows much needed publicity and promotion while attracting both a teenage as well as a broader youth-oriented audience; and, (2) the multimedia publicity avenues extended beyond the television-watching audience and helped to introduce and identify the WB's teen brand to the larger public. Each of the cross-promotional activities mentioned here helped the WB consolidate its teen brand identity and raise its profile with the target teen audience. In addition, they contributed to the ever-expanding, yet increasingly integrated matrix of circulating teen-oriented texts. Due to the numerous links that existed between these media texts, it became more and more difficult to identify the boundaries between them.

The WB shows' intentional verbal and visual borrowings from film texts, the adoption of music video aesthetics, the inclusion of advertising's visual style, helped to erase the medium and format boundaries separating these traditionally distinct texts, effectively blurring the textual and aesthetic differences that conventionally served to distinguish the different media formats. This practice acknowledges the specific ways in which millennial teens consume and experience their media in the era of multi-media convergence, when films, television shows, music videos, video gaming, and the Internet are all available on a single digital device. With the shift towards media convergence, teens no longer seem to make any traditional distinctions between the filmic, the televisual, or digital/online experience and formats, a point discussed in greater detail in Chapter Eight.

Kellner's conviction that niche marketing, narrowcasting, programming, and branding would carry the day proved accurate. Indeed, in the 1997-98 television season, the fledgling WB was the only network that saw its audience grow from year to year, increasing their audience share by 25 percent. In the 1998-99 season, the WB successfully attracted more viewers, increasing their viewing households by 24 percent in general. In addition, the network had begun attracting more than just teenagers, seeing its audience share of adults in the key 18 to 49 demographic rise by 35 percent.[54] It is worth noting that the WB saw increases in each of these categories at a time when every other broadcast network had seen audience numbers decline from the previous year.[55]

Network television is a business, and advertising revenues define the success of a network and its shows. With the WB's teen series successfully attracting the valuable teen audience, advertisers became the biggest fans of the WB. By 1998, the WB was on its way to becoming the number one network among the crucial teen demographic; it was also particularly popular with the teenage girls and young women that advertisers were specifically courting at the time. By 1998, five of the WB's dramas, *Buffy the Vampire Slayer*, *Dawson's Creek*, *7th Heaven* (WB, 1996–2002; CW 2002–2007), *Charmed*, and *Felicity* all placed in the Top 20 most watched shows among teenagers age 12 to 17.[56] The success of the WB's programming and scheduling decisions enabled the network to double its advertising revenue in a single season. Advance bookings of advertising time on the WB rose from $150 million in 1998 to $300 million for the 1999 fall season. More than two-thirds of that revenue came from advertisers seeking the 12- to 34-year-old audience.[57] These advertising numbers are particularly significant if we consider the fact that none of the WB's shows thus far have ever risen above the 5 to 8 share range and tended to rank at the bottom of the Nielsen ratings.

From the WB to the CW

Despite the WB's success in targeting a teen-audience, the network continued to struggle for profitability.[58] In the WB's early years, its primary competition for the teen market was MTV. By 2002, other network and cable outlets, including UPN,[59] FOX, The N, and ABC Family, had also begun to target a teen/youth audience. The fact that these broadcast and cable networks were adopting the WB's programming strategies and targeting teens highlight the on-going and growing value of the demographic, as well as the success of the WB's teen-focused content. Unfortunately, this validation of the WB's strategic commitments to narrowcasting and niche programming ultimately undermined the network's long-term success and viability. In the early 2000s, the increased competition from these other television outlets began to erode the WB's valuable teen audience.[60] While the teen market was undeniably a significant one, the proportion of the demographic's numbers that were watching broadcast television proved insufficient to support the growing number of competing television networks targeting the same niche 12- to 34-year-old demographic, particularly in an environment where teens had access to multiple other forms of entertainment in a variety of (new) media.

By the mid–2000s, new technologies and delivery platforms presented the technologically-savvy teen with access to multiple forms of media and entertainment. The growing popularity of new digital media platforms offered teens alternative ways to acquire entertainment. Unlike the established networks that catered to adult audiences who were less inclined to break with familiar and established media consumption patterns and adopt these new digital technologies, the decade-old WB and UPN struggled to turn a profit amidst the growing challenges posed by the increased competition from these alternative media platforms.

On January 24th, 2006, CBS, UPN's parent company, and Warner Bros. Entertainment, which controlled the WB, announced that the two networks would merge into the CW, a new youth-oriented network that would pool the resources and programming from both the WB and UPN. This decision was born of the realization that rather than competing against each other, it made better business sense to combine their efforts against their competition.[61] Like the WB did ten years before, the CW announced its decision to target teens and young adults, with a minor revision. Where the WB focused on the 12 to 34 demographic, the CW narrowed its objective to the 18 to 34 demographic. In 2006, the CW faced challenges that the WB experienced a decade ago— the need to attract the millennial teen audiences by addressing their specific interests, exploit the synergistic opportunities of their corporate parents' holdings, and enhance profits by fulfilling advertiser's needs. But this time, the situation was exacerbated by an increasingly cluttered and fragmented cultural, technological and media landscape.

The CW's first season on air began in Fall 2006, barely eight months after the creation of the network was announced. This initial season's ratings were mediocre as the network struggled to attract wider public awareness, even as it tried to retain the audiences from both the WB and UPN. Although the CW consisted of various popular shows culled from the WB and UPN,[62] the new network faced the challenge of retaining audiences from the old networks that may not have realized that the shows had moved to a new network/channel.[63] Its schedule also failed to give the CW a distinct identity as the shows were largely linked to the now defunct WB and UPN. These problems were addressed in the CW's second season when it began to focus on building its brand identity.

In the 2007-2008 season, the CW launched a range of original shows aimed at branding the network as a popular site for older teens and young adults, thereby connecting advertisers with the CW's target 18 to 34 audience. Acknowledging this target demographic's commitment to the Internet, online streaming websites such as YouTube, and blogs, several CW shows directly incorporated these elements into its content. *Online Nation* (2007) combined the concept of *America's Funniest Videos* with a digital perspective, bringing online video content to television by showcasing the funniest or oddest video clips available on the Internet. The digital revolution was even incorporated into the networks' scripted series. *Gossip Girl* (2007–) revolved around several wealthy Manhattan teens whose activities are described in a blog by a mysterious character known only as "Gossip Girl." In addition, the show had a parallel online existence on the network's official website (www.cwtv.com).

The CW's website, where episodes of the network's shows are streamed for viewers who missed the on-air broadcast, allows viewers a heightened interactive experience. In addition to offering information, previews and additional content on the network's shows, fans watching the network's shows online could simultaneously Instant Message each other. The CW Lounge link hosts forum pages, blogs and interactive links via which communities of viewers can share their thoughts, upload photographs or engage in other program-specific activities. Another link, CW Mobile, offers images from the network's shows that can be downloaded to mobile devices. Access to CW–specific sites on social networking sites like Facebook further allowed fans of the network's series to publicize their interests and introduce others to the CW's content. The online platform also enhanced fan's access to CW–associated products and advertisers; a "music" link let viewers purchase and download songs featured on the CW shows. The *Gossip Girl* online site also serves as a promotional and retail portal, allowing viewers to buy the various products that appear on the series, including music featured on the show, and clothing worn by the shows characters. These arrangements highlight the CW's commitment to servicing their advertisers, a dedication that extended beyond the CW's online portal to include decisions on their programming content as well.

In addition to creating content that directly appealed to the perceived interests of the millennial teen, the CW's programming actively focused on integrating advertising into its content, a necessary strategy arising from the proliferation of alternative delivery platforms such as DVRs, iTunes, and online video streaming websites in the millennium. These platforms, particularly popular with younger audiences, have allowed viewers to avoid traditional advertising content. Consequently, the CW launched *CW Now* (2007–2008), an "ad-free" weekly magazine show that essentially functions as advertising. Sponsored by three or four advertisers, *CW Now* primarily consists of product placements and lifestyle segments. The limited number of advertisers and the integration of these advertisers' products into the show's content are all directed at ensuring that viewers are exposed to the consumer messages. Information on retailers and their products pop up onscreen during the various segments. The CW's commitment to product placements and corporate tie-ins is also apparent on *Gossip Girl*, which has an exclusive arrangement with Verizon Wireless — *Gossip Girls'* teenage characters spend a significant amount of time communicating on their Verizon Wireless cell phones.

The CW has also introduced several advertising innovations to further accommodate advertisers and retain audience interest in advertising. "CWickies" are short five to ten second ads that are scattered thought the CW's shows. The assumption is that younger viewers are less likely to "channel surf" during these short ad breaks. For longer advertising segments, the CW pioneered "content wraps," a series of long-form ads distributed over the course of an evening's programming. Specially created by the CW and the advertiser, content

wraps offer mini-narratives in which an advertised product is prominently featured. In some instances, stars from the CW's shows appear in these content
wraps to promote the product.[64] Further acknowledging the trend towards
multi-media, multi-platform convergence, the CW introduced "CWingers,"
multi-part, linked ads that appear both on television and online, to better appeal
to the teen and young adult viewers that no longer viewed the television and
computer as separate entertainment platforms.

The CW's programming and advertising decisions point to the further
erosion of media and platform boundaries. With online videos appearing on
television, television content adopting pop-up "windows" traditionally associated with the web, multi-part advertising and entertainment content bridging the television and online platforms, the hyper-intertextuality of the earlier
millennial teen texts has advanced further. The technological, aesthetic, expe-
riential, and content-specific lines differentiating one media platform from
another had largely ceased to exist by the mid–2000s.

Millennial teen television, like millennial teen films and music, was no
longer confined to the specific boundaries of a single medium. Instead, teen-
oriented entertainment texts had evolved and expanded into complex, multi-
media, multi-platform interconnected texts. This transformation can be traced
to the increasingly sophisticated synergistic activities of multi-media conglomerates, evolving technologies, and the changing attitudes and behaviors of teen/
youth media consumers.

In this chapter, I tracked the events that motivated the launch of a broadcast network that rejected the traditional broadcast model to embrace narrowcasting and focus on an increasingly significant niche teen demographic in the
final years of the twentieth century. The WB's teen focus allowed it to make
the most of a key demographic shift taking place in America at the time, when
the number of American teenagers began to rise to significant proportions,
even as society at large embraced a more teen-oriented lifestyle. Coinciding
with a booming American economy, these combined events made the network's
target audience particularly vital and valuable. Realizing the opportunities, the
WB network consciously began developing programming with a distinct teen-
focus. Programming teen-oriented series that consistently borrowed from and
adapted a range of quality television characteristics for a teen audience, allowed
the network to cultivate a recognizable brand image that gave it a specific identity and helped distinguish WB from other existing and established networks.

The WB restructured the teen television text, even as it redefined and
extended the textual boundaries of this teen entertainment product. The network's subsequent strategies have had a notable impact on the nature, form
and content of the millennial teen entertainment text. The WB's teen-oriented
programming was so successful that the network's creative decisions have transcended the network's boundaries and became markers for teen-oriented television in general. The key qualities associated initially with the WB's teen

shows began appearing in teen television shows on other networks in later television seasons. Subsequent teen shows, including FOX's *The O.C.* (2003–2007) and UPN's *Veronica Mars* (2004–2007), display the characteristics of teen quality television (including self-referentiality, intertextuality, and the adoption of a liberal, humanist perspective) that I have examined above.

In addition, many of the tactics first adopted by the WB, including its focused commitment towards advertisers, demonstrated in the varied and numerous commercial tie-ins and cross-promotional arrangements between the network and its advertisers, its introduction of innovative commercial practices such as promotional end cards, and its intentional adoption of alternative media aesthetics and (visual) styles, have directly influenced the promotional, creative, and aesthetic developments at the CW. Many of the practices and strategies launched by the CW have their roots in the WB's earlier activities.

The millennial teen entertainment text has evolved in response to distinct industrial, cultural and social forces. Many of the characteristic qualities identified in this chapter have filtered into subsequent teen and tween texts. In the next chapter, I detail how Disney, yet another major multi-media conglomerate, has adapted these strategies to better target the younger 8- to 14-year-old tween market, which represents the next wave of the millennial youth demographic.

SEVEN

Disney and the Youth Market —
It's a T(w)een World After All

Before the 1990s, the term "tween" was not part of the popular vocabulary of an American public that still tended to refer to those under the age of 14 as "children." First coined by the clothing industry to describe adolescents aged between 8 and 14 "who [had] outgrown children's styles, but could not yet wear teenage looks,"[1] the term began appearing with increasing regularity in mainstream newspapers such as *The New York Times* and the *Los Angeles Times*, and in media and marketing trade journals including *Variety*, *Broadcasting and Cable*, *MediaWeek* and *Advertising Age* in the millennium. These publications, that had trumpeted the resurgence of the teen market just a few years earlier, had turned their attention to identifying and cultivating a new youth demographic.

According to the 2000 census, there were 24.8 million tweens in the United States.[2] Growing numbers of media reports and circulating discourses began to transform these "tweens" into a new, commercially significant, consumer market. By 2002, tweens had replaced teens as "the hottest demo in Hollywood," at least according to *Variety*.[3] In 2003, Youth Intelligence, a marketing research firm, numbered the U.S. tween market at an estimated 30 million consumers.[4] According to Michael Wood, vice president of Teenage Research Unlimited, "[t]he fastest growing power is the younger [teen] market, 12 to 15, [with the cohort] accounting for 50 percent of the overall teen market" in 2008.[5] Market researchers further augmented the significance of these sizable figures with claims of the demographic's heightened economic power and consumer influence. Reports of tween purchasing power in 2002 included declarations that they were a "$50 billion a year" market, and speculations that they also influenced an extra "$250 billion" of parental spending.[6] Many of the reports extolling the characteristics of the tween market and consumer recall the breathless fervor last witnessed in the late 1990s, when the teen market was first being hailed as an emerging phenomenon. Clearly, Hollywood's evolving interest in the youth market had shifted to a new demographic group of 8- to 14-year-olds who began to replace the late 1990s teenagers as the next significant cohort to target. While Hollywood continued to maintain its ties with the millennial teen, in the years after 2000, it was the younger tweens who received more of the media attention and dominated most of the media discourses.

Media producers and marketers focused on targeting teens are perpetually conscious of the short shelf life of the teen demographic. One of the distinct challenges of targeting this niche market is that even though the cohort is inherently self-replenishing — one group ages into the demographic even as another ages out of it — this constant cyclical change introduces the difficulty of tracking the (sometimes subtle) differences between each cohort. Since the received wisdom regarding the youth market assumes that teens as a group tend to chase the new and are constantly on the quest for the latest trends, each new cohort is unlikely to embrace the entertainment and commodities popular with the previous group. This feature of the teen market has compelled marketers and media producers to temper their predilection for replicating previously successful entertainment products with the recognition that innovation, differentiation and evolution are equally vital strategies in their continuing attempts to harness the full potential of each new segment within this demographic group. One company particularly successful at these activities was Disney.

By 2006, the earlier media discourses predicting the importance of the tween demographic had given way to media reports describing Disney's emerging, and eventually overriding, dominance over the millennial tween market, that younger segment of Generation Y still in their tweens or about to enter their teen years after 2000. This chapter examines several of Disney's most successful t(w)een entertainment franchises with the intention of identifying the qualities and characteristics of some of the most popular tween texts of the period. I also highlight how the activities discussed in the earlier case studies (in chapters four to six), including the heightened commitment to multi-media synergy, the exploitation of new media delivery platforms and technologies, and the blurring boundaries between disparate media formats, gained further momentum and intensified within a few short years. I pay particular attention to understanding how the strategies adopted in the late 1990s to target the first wave of Generation Y have evolved to influence and shape the media activities directed at this later cohort of emerging teens. The discussion of these developments acknowledges how Disney's industrial structure and holdings have been harnessed and deployed in its increasingly complex, multi-media tween-oriented activities. Although this chapter will focus primarily on Disney and the various strategies it adopted to target the tween market, Disney was not the sole media institution interested in the 8- to 14-year-old demographic. In fact, after the turn of the millennium, tweens were enjoying the kind of focused Hollywood attention that was previously bestowed on their older teen predecessors.

Hollywood and Tweens in the Millennium

Hollywood responded quickly and efficiently to cater to the entertainment needs of this emerging tween cohort. In the first decade of the twenty-first century, millennial tweens established their value to the media industries at the movie box-office, on television, in music, and across a range of other entertainment platforms. Initial signs of tween consumer power emerged in 2001 after a series of tween films earned significant amounts at the box-office. Warner Bros. released the first installment of the *Harry Potter* film franchise, *Harry Potter and the Sorcerer's Stone*, in 2001. The film, tracing the adventures of a group of twelve-year-old wizards battling evil, was the highest grossing film of the year, earning in excess of $317 million domestically. *Spy Kids*, another tween film released in 2001, earned $113 million, further confirming the power of the tween audience.[7] By then, interest in the tween viewer was not restricted to the film industry.

That same year, *Variety* declared "kid eyeballs ... some of the most coveted in the [television] business. Cablers and networks are bringing out a record 33 new shows this season trying to woo young viewers.... Teens and tweens are the most targeted demo this season...."[8] The television industry's surging interest in tween programming was a response to Madison Avenue's growing interest in reaching the millions of tween consumers who reportedly spend billions on fast food, clothing and entertainment. This motivated the scheduling of numerous tween-oriented television series on both network and cable television including *Mary-Kate and Ashley in Action* (2001) on ABC, *Braceface* (2001–2005) on FOX Family, and *Lizzie Maguire* (2001–2004) on Disney.

By 2005, the value of the tween market was further confirmed in a study by the Recording Industry Association of America that stated that tweens aged 10 to 14 purchased 8.6 percent of all recorded music, accounting for over $1 billion of the recorded music market valued at over $12 billion.[9] These figures gain greater significance if we consider that sales of recorded music, in particular CD sales, had been steadily declining in the age of music downloads and online retailers such as iTunes, that offer consumers the option of buying single tracks rather than paying for an entire CD.[10] As CD sales continued to shrink, reports that tweens were still actively purchasing CDs made the demographic increasingly vital to the survival of those still engaged in the traditional business activities in the music industry.

Hollywood's efforts in identifying and targeting the tween market points to the increasing degree of market fragmentation and the media industry's intensifying commitment to identifying narrower niche markets to exploit. Not content with carving out a teen market, marketers and the media had begun actively identifying smaller segments within the cohort to target. Having done so, the various media channels intent on reaching this specific demographic began to engage in specific branding activities that would help them attract their preferred viewers. Just as MTV, Dimension, the WB and the CW branded themselves in distinct ways in bids to more efficiently identify and lure their preferred teen customer, the tween-focused entertainment platforms were careful to build their brand identities via a range of texts, stars, genres and aesthetic choices. This was certainly the case with Disney.

In 2000, Disney was already an established name equated with child and family-friendly entertainment across a broad range of media. This particular identity had been carefully nurtured and protected through the decades, even as The Walt Disney Company evolved into a global, multi-media conglomerate with extensive media and lifestyle holdings that extended beyond the child and family-niche. Any attempt to understand Disney's emergence as a top tween multi-media site in the millennium, must first consider how the corporation guided the Disney brand through its decades of growth and expansion.

The Walt Disney Company and the Disney Brand

The Walt Disney Company's history is one characterized by focused attempts at diversification and corporate expansions that allowed the company to grow into a globally powerful multi-media entertainment entity. In 2005, The Walt Disney Company was a "diversified worldwide entertainment company with operations in four business segments: Media Networks, Parks and Resorts, Studio Entertainment and Consumer Products."[11]

Its media network holdings comprised "[a] domestic broadcast television network, domestic television stations, cable/satellite networks and international broadcast operations, television production and distribution, domestic broadcast radio networks and stations and internet operations."[12] These included the ABC Television Network, The Disney Channel, and the ABC Family channel in the United States. In addition, international Disney Channels were available in territories including Europe, South America, and most of Asia. Disney's television production and distribution arm included the Walt Disney Television label, Buena Vista Television, Buena Vista Productions, and Touchstone Television. The ABC Radio Networks division oversaw the ESPN network and the Radio Disney Network. Disney.com functioned as the central website that integrates all of the Disney-branded internet sites including sites for the Disney Channel, Walt Disney Parks and Resorts and Walt Disney Pictures. In 2005, plans were also being developed for Disney Mobile, a mobile phone service targeted at families.

These holdings were separate from Disney's "Studio Entertainment" holdings, which involved feature film and television production and distribution activities under the Walt Disney Pictures and Television subsidiary that included Walt Disney Pictures, Touchstone Pictures, Hollywood Pictures, and Miramax Film Corporation. In addition, The Walt Disney Records group produced and distributed music under several labels including Hollywood Records, Buena Vista Records and Lyle Street Records. The Buena Vista Theatrical Group included Disney Theatrical Productions and Disney Live Family. Where the former developed, produced and licensed Disney-branded stage musicals worldwide, the latter licensed live entertainment touring productions of Disney on Ice and Disney Live!

Under Parks and Resorts, the company owned and operated the Disney World and Disneyland resorts and Disney Cruise Line in several states nationwide, and held ownership interests in Disneyland resorts in France, Hong Kong and Japan. The Disney "Consumer Products" segment in turn "partners with licensees, manufacturers, publishers, and retailers throughout the world to design, promote and sell a wide variety of products based on existing and new Disney characters and other intellectual property."[13] Many of these licensed products are marketed and sold by Disney's retail holdings that include The Disney Store, by direct mail in the Disney Catalogue, and over online retail sites such as DisneyDirect.com. Disney's further attempts to exploit the developing digital technologies involve Buena Vista Games, which "creates, develops, markets and distributes multi-platform video games worldwide" that are "derived from the Company's creative content."[14]

The Walt Disney Company's wide-ranging vertically and horizontally integrated multi-media holdings are characteristic of the dominant global entertainment conglomerates in the millennium. In Disney's case, it's approach to its various holdings involved carefully structuring and differentiating the different brands under its control to ensure that each label had a distinct identity that would not interfere with, or dilute the others within the group. In considering Disney's tween-oriented identity in the millennium, it is helpful to distinguish between its Disney-branded holdings, and the corporation's more adult-focused media labels and activities. The Disney label has long been associated with wholesome family entertainment, beginning with the release of Snow White and the Seven Dwarfs in 1937, and continuing through the 1950s, with the decision to build the family theme park Disneyland, and into its deal to supply the then-youth and kid-focused ABC television network with the hour-long, weekly, Disneyland television series. In the years since, concerted efforts were made to reinforce and refine this distinct brand identity. As such, the specifically Disney-branded entities within each business segment that were focused on kid and family friendly entertainment activities, were generally kept distinct from its other holdings such as the ESPN networks, Hollywood Pictures, or Touchstone Television, all of which referenced their "Disney" connection in relatively discrete terms.

In the millennium, the Disney brand, with its well-established, decades-long commitment towards family-oriented entertainment, was particularly suited to the company's focused interest in the younger tween market. In refining the Disney brand for the millennial tween, Disney's activities were directed by a set of distinct parameters. Like the multi-media corporations that turned their attention to the teen audience several years earlier, Disney needed a strategy that would allow it to effectively attract its target 8- to 14-year-old demographic. Focusing on such a young demographic, however, entailed several unique constraints.

Any attempt to create entertainment directed at the tween demographic, carried certain challenges. Disney needed to ensure that in targeting chi its content and its brand stayed clear of any controversial content or acti that could taint or undermine its public credibility. The relative youth o. its target demographic meant that the conglomerate needed to be conscious of, and carefully manage, the social, moral and ethical concerns shared by parents, legislators, and other groups who remain suspicious of the media industries' on-going attempts to pursue a relationship with children and young audiences. The long-established Disney brand of quality family entertainment would help significantly in this area. Families headed by baby-boomer parents who had grown up with the Mouseketeers, *Disneyland*, and Disney's animated films, would be secure introducing their children to the trusted brand's content.

These concerns aside, any content that Disney produced to target tweens had to contend with two commonly held perceptions about children and teenagers. The first revolved around the notion of "age compression," a phrase referring to the contemporary phenomenon in which children's tastes and habits mature at an accelerated pace that outstripped their actual ages. Age compression is linked to the second tween-related phenomenon of aspirational viewing and consumption, a situation in which younger audiences prefer entertainment featuring characters and situations associated with a (slightly) older age group. The notion is based on the assumption that younger audiences aspire to the lifestyles, behaviors, values and habits of those a few years older than they are. The popular belief is that tweens are drawn to media that offers them access to these realities. In targeting tweens, Disney needed to toe the line between offering its young audiences a window into the older lifestyles and experiences they aspired to, while ensuring that such content did not feature elements that might be deemed inappropriate for these young viewers.

While guarding against such developments, the Disney Corporation's activities were also directed by its active commitment to pursuing the full synergistic and economic potential of its corporate holdings. Even as it remained mindful of the necessity of retaining parental and societal trust and goodwill, its primary focus centered on profit. In addition to creating content that directly addressed the interests of the niche market, the company was committed to pursuing a series of cross-media practices that would best exploit the synergistic potential of its highly diversified multi-media organization. All of these considerations came into play in shaping the nature, content and form of the Disney tween text.

The Disney Tween Media Empire

Between 2006 and 2009, a number of Disney releases established the company's dominance over the tween entertainment landscape. On January 20th 2006, the cable premiere of Disney's made-for-television movie *High School*

Musical attracted 7.7 million, primarily tween, viewers. It then proceeded to draw another 6.1 million viewers for the show's second telecast the night after, placing *High School Musical* in the number one and two spots for the top cable shows that week regardless of target demographic, even as the show's soundtrack CD topped Billboard's album charts.[15] *High School Musical 2* debuted on the Disney Channel in August 2007, and drew an estimated 17.2 million (presumably tween) viewers, making it not only the most watched program on both cable and network television that week,[16] it has also remained the most watched program in cable history.[17] That same year, the soundtrack to another Disney cable series, *Hannah Montana,* the number one cable show for 6- to 14-year-olds,[18] debuted at the top of the Billboard album charts.[19] In February 2008, *Hannah Montana/Miley Cyrus: Best of Both Worlds,* a Disney 3-D concert film starring Miley Cyrus, the star of Disney's *Hannah Montana* series, topped the box-office grossing $31 million in its first week.[20] Eight months later, in October 2008, Disney's *High School Musical 3: Senior Year* grossed $42 million in its opening weekend at the top of the American box-office, and earned an additional $40 million from 22 overseas markets.[21]

Clearly, Disney's highly successful and profitable relationship with the tween consumer extended across the company's multi-media platforms, ranging from films, to television, to music. In addition, the events above hint at Disney's success in repurposing its various entertainment concepts across its entire range of media holdings. Disney's commitment to nurturing its tween stars across the conglomerate's multiple platforms, including television, film, and music, while simultaneously branding them as Disney stars, is yet another indication of its highly efficient, tween-focused, corporate activities.

Disney's attempts to target tweens in the millennium began with the Disney Channel. By 2007, the Disney Channel would become the most prominent and powerful component of the Disney Company's tween-oriented media empire. First launched in 1983, the Disney Channel's early years were marked by limited reach and seemingly random programming. In its early incarnation, between 1983 and 1997, the Disney Channel's premium channel status meant that subscribers to the channel had to pay a separate fee above and beyond the basic cable subscription to receive the channel, a condition that restricted the channel's subscriber base. In addition, the channel's programming, consisting of a mix of Disney and foreign animated series, live-action children's variety series *Kids Incorporated* (1986–1994) and *The All-New Mickey Mouse Club* (1989–1994), and syndicated reruns of *The Adventures of Ozzie and Harriet* (1952–1966), lacked a specific niche-focused format. These were problems that Disney tried to solve in the late 1990s. Disney attempted to refine the channel's focus by dividing the schedule into separate programming blocks aimed at more defined audience segments.[22] The channel's limited reach was finally resolved in 2000 when it became part of the extended basic cable line-up, making the channel available to the much larger market that had access to basic cable. However, it wasn't until the cable network's evolution into a distinct tween-oriented media site in the early 2000s, that the channel's profile began to rise.

By 2006, the Disney Channel had become "the highest-rated basic cable channel among children 6 to 11 and 9 to 14," a position it held again in 2007 and 2008.[23] Furthermore, the cable channel was at the center of a multi-media Disney tween empire where several of Disney's popular tween entertainment properties that first debuted on the channel was efficiently repurposed and translated across a wide range of related media products. These entertainment properties include *High School Musical, Hannah Montana,* and *Camp Rock* as well as the tween stars of these projects, Ashley Tisdale, Miley Cyrus, and the Jonas Brothers. Disney transformed each of these entities into Disney-related brands that helped attract the increasingly desirable tween viewers. In every instance, these brands and personalities all originated on the cable channel but quickly expanded beyond the limits of this single media platform to become tween-focused multi-media popular culture phenomena.

How did Disney build this multi-media tween entertainment empire in the millennium? What are the characteristics of the Disney millennial tween text? How does the Disney tween text lend itself to the conglomerate's synergistic activities? How have Disney's multi-media holdings shaped the nature, form and content of the Disney tween entertainment product? Disney's quest for the tween demographic involved a similar range of strategies employed by the other multi-media conglomerates to target the teen audience. Disney's tween content share the distinct characteristics of the millennial teen text that I identify in Chapter Three. In order to target the tween viewer, Disney created content that was specifically directed at, and that reflect the dominant concerns of, tweens and younger teens. Also, these tween media products are characterized by the same cross-media, cross-genre intersections that I have identified in millennial teen texts, a development reflected in the intensification of stylistic and aesthetic convergence across the range of multi-media formats. In addition, each entertainment concept was repurposed to synergistically exploit the parent company's multi-media holdings. And even as each text developed into a brand amidst a range of promotional activities, the stars in these texts also emerged as tween-branded personalities who easily shifted between a diverse range of media platforms. In fact, every aspect of Disney's franchises was carefully organized to exploit the company's multi-media holdings while effectively targeting its preferred demographic.

Targeting Tweens: Reworking Teen Content for Tween Viewers

Like the media companies discussed in previous chapters, Disney attracted its target demographic by addressing the experiences and primary concerns of tweens, albeit with the addition of a small measure of built in fantasy and wish fulfillment. According to Gary Marsh, Disney Channel Worldwide president, the Disney tween shows concentrated on exploring "the universal themes of tweendom," specifically "school, friends, ethical choices" and, "how to navigate the pitfalls of adolescence," which include peer pressures and rivalries, and struggling with commitments and loyalties to friends and parents.[24] Despite the commitment to the "universal themes of tweendom," however, Disney clearly kept the notion of aspirational viewing firmly in mind. Though directed at tweens aged 6 to 14, many Disney's productions featured the lifestyles and experiences associated with teenage characters that were in the 14 to 18 age range. Though Marsh claims that the shows on the Disney Channel are committed to recreating "real life ... the world reflected back in the clothes, the music, the food they eat," the fact remains that the lifestyles on display are not that of typical tweens, but of those aged a little older.[25] *High School Musical*, *Hannah Montana*, and *Camp Rock* all feature protagonists who are in high school. While having slightly older protagonists provided the opportunity to hint at some issues more commonly associated with the slightly older life phase, Disney was careful to offer highly innocent and "sanitized" representations of teendom. Disney's strategy was to borrow the plots and settings of familiar teen genres, but carefully tailor them for a younger tween audience. The resulting texts tended to offer wholesome, positive messages to its tween audience while offering a G, or at worst a PG, version of the teenage high school experience.

The *High School Musical* franchise, with its focus on the budding romance between a popular jock and an academic-achiever, ostensibly follows in the established teen tradition of the High School Romance film. *High School Musical* introduces Gabriella, a straight-A student, and Troy, a high-school jock, who first meet when they are both on family holidays at a ski resort. When Gabriella transfers to Troy's high school after she moves to Albuquerque, a close friendship develops. Their friendship deepens as they challenge and encourage each other to embrace new ideas and experiences, including trying out for the school musical. In the process, they bond with their classmates and discover common goals and ideals. While the first film traces the couple's budding relationship, the sequel, *High School Musical 2* follows the characters' experiences during their vacation at a summer resort where Troy and Gabriella's romance and the group's friendships are tested by misunderstandings and confused loyalties. Following the original group of characters into their final year and graduation, *High School Musical 3: Senior Year* bids farewell to Troy, Gabriella and the rest of their senior class with their final appearance in their high school graduation musical. As the characters anticipate their entry into the next phase of their lives, they are faced with difficult choices about which colleges to attend and what dreams to follow.

Each installment of *High School Musical* borrows familiar elements from the typical High School/Teen Romance film. From the unlikely romance between opposites, the angst and anxieties of growing up, the challenges of trying to fit in, the unhealthy lure of the clique identity, to the importance of discovering one's own interests and identity, and of being true to oneself amidst potential conflicts with group loyalties, these issues and conflicts are the cornerstones of typical High School films and have been explored in various installments of the genre ranging from 1950s classics such as *Rebel Without a Cause* to '80s classics such as *Sixteen Candles* (1984), *The Breakfast Club*, *Pretty in Pink* (1986), and '90s releases including *Drive Me Crazy* and *10 Things I Hate About You*.

However, because the film is directed at the younger tween set, there is a decidedly "softer," more innocent, and wholesome, treatment of these issues. Unlike the teen films that served as inspiration and blue-print, where tensions tend to culminate in violence and ugly behavior, the conflicts in the *High School Musical* series are often quickly dealt with in cheerfully energetic song and dance numbers that almost always end with the problems resolved. Where the romance in teen films invariable raises issues of sex, the romance in *High School Musical* is entirely chaste and stripped of any sexual element. Instead, the relationships are expressed in longing glances shared while singing romantic ballads. In adopting such an approach, *High School Musical* displays a sensibility associated with the tradition of the classic 1930s Hollywood backstage musical.[26] *High School Musical*, whose narrative centers on a teenage boy and girl who discover common interests and goals when they try-out and rehearse for the school musical, trades on the values, beliefs and aesthetics of the classic backstage musical in which social integration, a sense of community, and shared values dominate the narrative and the dominant ideologies of the text. In classic backstage musical tradition, many of the musical performances in *High School Musical* emphasize innocent romance and the pursuit of personal dreams amidst a loyal commitment to community and shared interests. These traditions and perspectives are particularly suited to a conglomerate interested in targeting a young audience, and retaining the trust and good will of their concerned parents.

Another popular Disney property, *Hannah Montana*, began as a series on the Disney Channel. Starring the teenage Miley Cyrus, the series traces the adventures of high-schooler, Miley Stewart, a seemingly ordinary tween who harbors a secret identity. Unbeknownst to her friends, Miley Stewart is also Hannah Montana, a famous tween rock star. Again, the secret identity narrative in which the main character must hide her true persona from her closest friends is not a stereotypical tween narrative. In Disney's hands, the scenario is an opportunity to explore the common tween anxieties of split responsibilities and loyalties in a lighthearted way. The alter ego narrative element allows the show to switch between the familiar, ordinary school and family-oriented realities that teenage Miley experiences, which would be familiar to the show's ordinary tween fans, and the more escapist pleasures associated with the fantasy lifestyle associated with her rock star Hannah Montana alter ego, a lifestyle evoking issues and encounters that may be fascinatingly unfamiliar.

Similarly, *Camp Rock*, another Disney Channel movie, borrows the setting of the teen summer camp film and blends realism and fantasy in a plot where Mitchie Torres, a talented but ordinary girl-next-door type attends a music camp and befriends a popular pop star, Shane Grey. In *High School Musical*-tradition, they develop a close friendship/wholesome romance on their journey toward self-discovery and maturity while struggling with typical tween anxieties, including peer pressure, the quest for self-identity, and independence. Cognizant of sending the "right message" to its impressionable tween audience, every one of these Disney texts underlines the need to be true to oneself, to looking beyond surface attributes and behaviors, to accept and understand others, to appreciate the importance of friendship, loyalty and honesty, and most of all, to follow one's dreams.

Multi-Media, Cross-Platform Content Convergence

In addition to tailoring and adapting many of the conventional teen film genres for a distinct tween audience, Disney also adopted and adjusted many of the stylistic and aesthetic elements characteristic of millennial teen entertainment for its niche audience. In particular, teen entertainment's increasing propensity to incorporate and blend together a wide range of cross-media stylistics and aesthetics, resulting in texts that are a complex amalgamation of diverse media elements, found heightened and intense expression in the Disney millennial tween text. Like its teen predecessors, many of the Disney tween texts were a blend of music video elements, teen drama, live concert event, and in some cases, even a Broadway stage production.

High School Musical, for instance, incorporates a wide range of music including innocently romantic ballads, more kinetic and energetic hip-hop numbers, perky pop songs, and even music in the tradition of the Broadway musical, with each musical performance adhering to its own music video conventions. The influence and adoption of music video aesthetics are apparent in several sequences. In the romantic pop duets and solo ballads performed by Troy and Gabriella, the scenes conform to the familiar music video visuals associated with the genre. These sequences are often filmed in a combination of medium shots and close-ups to better showcase the performer and foreground the song's emotional aspects. As these performances emphasize the emotive, the larger environment and setting are largely irrelevant, with long and wide shots kept to a minimum. Though these songs are largely performed in a realistic environment, most often in the corridors of the high school, there is little interest in maintaining visual or spatial continuity in the shots, a characteristic typical of music video aesthetics. Instead, the primary focus lies with maintaining an atmospheric and emotional coherence within the musical sequence. While carefully adopting these stylistic conventions, the images and message of the songs themselves are decidedly structured to the innocent young tween sensibility.

In the harder-driving hip-hop performance involving the school's basketball team, the conventions of that particular music video genre come to the fore. Incorporating an energetic dance within a basketball practice session featuring a group of young men, the synchronized funk/hip-hop dance moves involving basketballs as props are captured in wide shots with numerous edits that help to heighten the kinetic beat of the music itself. Aimed at 8- to 14-year-olds whose musical tastes and repertoires are potentially more limited by parental control and restrictions, all these songs, though patterned in the style and conventions of the rock ballad, funk, or hip-hop, offer messages and lyrics that are safely free of the more risqué and potentially controversial ideas and content commonly found in the more adult versions of such music genres.

Disney's attempts to introduce its young tween audience to a wide range of musical genres continued to shape *High School Musical 2*. *High School Musical*'s success allowed for an increased budget and more sophisticated musical productions in the sequel. As a result, the musical set pieces were relatively more complex and on a grander scale than what was seen in the original, with many of them displaying the visual and stylistic influences of earlier film musicals. Like its predecessor, the sequel offered a range of songs marked by the distinctive aesthetic and stylistic influences of specific visual and musical genres. One song sequence featuring the show's stereotypical spoiled, rich, "princess," takes place in a poolside setting, allowing for Busby Berkeley style dance sequences, elaborate, stylized costumes, and underwater swimming scenes that recall the visuals from classic Esther Williams musicals. In contrast, the pop-rock solo sung by Troy Bolton, "Bet On It," has a harder beat, and is styled in the tradition of a rock video, featuring the type of limited visual continuity between shots, stylized camera angles, and the overt visual styling in which Troy channels the attitude of an angst-ridden, frustrated rock star. The musical finale, in which Troy, Gabriella and their close friends take the stage, which is set up beside a pool, to perform for their high school classmates who are frolicking in and around the pool, draws its inspiration from various sources including the 1960s teen beach party movies, the "school's out, summer's here" finale in *Grease 2* (1982), and the musical performances from MTV's *Spring Break* series, in which music stars often performed poolside for a swimsuit-clad audience of (college) students.

Taking place in a summer music camp attended by teenagers dedicated to music and dance, *Camp Rock*, like *High School Musical* and *Hannah Montana*, employs a set up specifically organized to include various music and dance sequences, many of which take place in numerous "Jam" sessions that occur throughout the duration of the camp. These are opportunities for the Camp Rock attendees/characters to engage in an array of performances that include

a wide range of music from the sentimental ballad, to pop, rock and hip-hop.
In addition to the various musical styles, the narrative also incorporates opportunities for several extended dance routines. In the tradition of the *High School
Musical* franchise, these sequences allowed for the inclusion of different aesthetic conventions from various media formats and platforms. While at camp,
pop star/camp counselor Shane invites his fellow band mates to join him in a
performance for the camp participants. Their subsequent stage performance is
characterized by the visual conventions typical of music concert footage, including hand-held camera work, tilted camera angles, and familiar editing techniques including the cross-cutting between shots of the performers, and the
frenzied response of their audience. In contrast, when the mean-spirited,
blonde, Tess Tyler performs her pop song, the visuals are styled in the tradition of a glossy pop video in the tradition of once-teen pop starlets Britney
Spears and Christina Aguilera, with its (albeit toned down) sexy dance moves,
stylized sets and costumes, along with a significant use of soft-focus cinematog-
raphy and visual dissolves accompanying the over-processed, manipulated
soundtrack. *Camp Rock*'s final song competition, in which all the camp attendees participate, includes a highly energetic and raucous hip-hop performance
that includes the synchronized dance moves, costumes, and kinetic camera
work associated with the genre.

It is also important to recognize that Disney's texts overtly depicted
t(w)eens whose lives and lived experiences are dominated by entertainment and
media-related activities. *High School Musical, Hannah Montana* and *Camp Rock*
are peopled by characters whose everyday existences revolve around creating
and consuming entertainment. Gabriella, Troy and their friends are committed to performing in their High School musical, Hannah Montana is a rock star,
Camp Rock's Mitchie Torres and the other camp attendees all sing, dance, com-
pose and perform music. Even as Disney is focused on targeting tweens, its
activities are also centered on shaping the behaviors, attitudes, values and perspectives of this impressionable group. Couched within the positive messages
of following your dreams, believing in yourself and accepting others, are other
messages focused on encouraging tweens to embrace the kinds of media products that Disney and its fellow media conglomerates are engaged in creating
and marketing. In targeting tweens, Disney was in a position to influence the
entertainment tastes and evolving preferences of an entire new generation of
youth. In targeting such a young audience, whose exposure to entertainment
texts was still relatively limited and whose tastes were clearly still being formed,
Disney was in a powerful position to direct these developments. In loading its
tween texts with a broad and diverse range of aesthetic conventions, entertainment genres, and musical styles, Disney is clearly engaging in deliberately self-
serving moves that would have long term benefits. If Disney could effectively
shape the entertainment interests of this next generation of teens, then it would
be in a strong position to guide this generation's entertainment interests in

ways that aligned with its own corporate activities, ensuring that it would be best poised to cater to this group as it aged up into their subsequent teen and adult years.

The Postmodern Tween Text and Its Industrial Motivations

In addition to exposing its tween audience to a wide range of entertainment styles and genres, these Disney productions also feature the intertextual references and citations of other popular culture texts, another feature typical of postmodern millennial youth culture. *High School Musical 3*, for instance, pays homage to both Fred Astaire and Quentin Tarantino's *Kill Bill, Vol. 1* (2003). Mid-way through Troy's musical solo in which he expresses his anxieties about his future, Troy's frustration and confusion is visually expressed when his world literally tilts off its axis so that he finds himself singing and dancing on the walls and ceiling of his high school. This sequence is an overt reference to the iconic Fred Astaire cinematic moment in which Astaire walks and tap dances on the walls and ceiling of his hotel room.[27] Although the film's tween audience may not fully appreciate the significance of the sequence, this homage hints at the significant debt that *High School Musical* owes to its classic musical predecessor. Other musical sequences also engage in the intertextual citations that have come to characterize contemporary, postmodern youth culture. In "The Boys are Back," in which Troy and his best friend sing and dance in a salvage yard, there are numerous visual references to Tarantino's *Kill Bill, Vol. 1* by way of the stylized backdrops that feature simulated "sword" fights shown in silhouette, a direct visual copy of a climactic sword battle between two of *Kill Bill*'s protagonists.

Certainly, these references to Fred Astaire musicals and the R-rated *Kill Bill* are likely to fall outside the cultural awareness of most 8- to 14-year-olds. Yet, if we consider the intensely postmodern nature of contemporary culture, it is possible that these tweens may have encountered other intertextual citations of these original texts even if they are unfamiliar with the original texts themselves. Considering the numerous pop culture references circulating, and the availability of both Astaire's and Tarantino's films on cable, DVD, and online, these same audiences may eventually encounter these original images when they get older. Furthermore, these postmodern citations in *High School Musical* may function as early introductions to the much broader range of intertextual citations that tweens will eventually encounter as they age. The point here has less to do with whether these tween audiences comprehend or recognize these references. Rather, these references exist as part of the larger entertainment culture's trend towards the circulation and recirculation of popular entertainment images and reference. These early exposures to (initially) unfamiliar citations still work to induct these young viewers into the contemporary popular culture experience.

Where some of these intertextual references are particularly postmodern in their seeming irrelevance and playfulness, *High School Musical 3* also offers other intertextual references that are recognizable and significant to the franchise's tween fans: the film traces Troy and Gabriella's graduating class' efforts to put on their graduation musical, a show that recreates the characters' most important high school experiences. Consequently, several of the key narrative moments depicted in the first two installments are re-envisioned and restaged in the third, as part of the senior class' musical show. This strategy echoes *Scream 3*'s focused attempts at mining its two earlier films for narrative and visual content. At various points in *High School Musical 3*, an odd sense of déjà vu is experienced as Troy, Gabriella and their friends, play themselves in their graduation musical and replicate several scenes/musical sequences from the previous films. Along the way, a further, heightened playfulness is added when some of the characters, including Gabriella and Troy, are unable to play themselves and their roles are taken over by their understudies who attempt to play "Gabriella" and "Troy" in the final senior musical. These postmodern practices effectively remind its tween audience of their earlier experiences with the previous texts, offering them a nostalgic opportunity to revisit some of the franchises' most significant moments.

These instances of self-reflexivity and intertextuality extend across a range of Disney texts. In fact, many of Disney's texts explicitly and consistently blur the lines between disparate Disney texts, between distinct media platforms, and between "reel" and "real." In every instance, these self-reflexive elements and multi-platform blendings serve more than a creative or aesthetic purpose. They allow Disney to pursue synergistic, cross-media promotional activities is more efficient and effective ways.

On *Hannah Montana*, teenage Miley Cyrus plays Miley Stewart/Hannah Montana. There are numerous similarities between the star and her character that heighten the show's self-reflexivity. Like the character she plays, Miley Cyrus hails from the mid-west. Both Mileys also share the same father, as Miley Cyrus' own father Billy Ray Cyrus plays Miley Stewart's father. Like Hannah Montana, Miley Cyrus has a music career with a significant tween/teen fan base. Furthermore, *Hannah Montana*, which explores the struggles and challenges that Miley Stewart encounters in balancing her "ordinary" life with her life as a "rock star" derives some perceived authenticity from its link to star Miley Cyrus' own experiences with the process. These numerous points of intersection allow for a significant degree of perceived convergence between the fantasy world of Miley Stewart/Hannah Montana, and the "real" world inhabited by Miley Cyrus. All of these issues result in a heightened intertextuality across the various Miley-related texts that are circulating within popular tween culture.[28] Disney has carefully nurtured this self-reflexivity, combined with a heightened intertextuality. The Disney Company has continued to manage the expansion and repurposing of the Miley Cyrus/Miley Stewart phenomenon across multiple, interrelated media in complex and sophisticated ways.

Disney was quick to exploit the multi-media profitability of the hit series, extending the *Hannah Montana* experience across a wide range of entertainment platforms and interfaces. In October 2006, Miley Cyrus' TV series-linked CD, the first *Hannah Montana* soundtrack featuring the show's theme song, "Best of Both Worlds," was produced and released by the Walt Disney Company's Hollywood Records. This was followed, nine months later, with the release of a follow-up CD, *Hannah Montana 2/Meet Miley Cyrus* in July 2007. In late 2007, Cyrus embarked on a 70-date live concert tour. Disney again saw an opportunity to extend the profit potential of the tour itself by filming it and repurposing it into a 3-D film that could be marketed to Cyrus' fans, particularly those who did not have an opportunity to attend her live performances. In February 2008, the day after Cyrus' tour ended, Disney released the film *Hannah Montana/Miley Cyrus: Best of Both Worlds Concert Tour*. As Disney president of Distribution, Chuck Viane notes, "Here's a concert that ended Thursday night and everybody could see it on Friday. The beauty of 3-D is that when you are in a theatre, every seat is like you are in the front row. It's a better seat than what you'd have in most concert venues...."[29] Produced by Disney at a cost of under $7 million, the film appeared in limited release on only 682 screens nationwide, yet it grossed $31 million at the box office in its first week.[30] Cyrus' concert tour and its linked concert film, continued to blur the boundaries between the actual Miley Cyrus and her television alter-ego, Hannah Montana, and between the live concert experience, the 3-D cinematic one, and the television show itself. Tween fans of Hannah Montana are thus more likely to transfer their allegiance to other Miley Cyrus texts, regardless of whether they are directly linked to her Hannah Montana persona as there appears to be so little difference between these various identities.

Disney adopted a similar strategy of blending and blurring the lines between its tween stars' actual personas, the characters they play, and the multiple texts they appear in with *Camp Rock*. In the television movie, the self-reflexivity is enhanced by the many live and staged performances throughout the telefilm. The popular pop-rock boy band central to *Camp Rock*'s narrative, although ostensibly named Connect-3, is virtually indistinguishable from the Jonas Brothers who play them. Significantly, the original script for *Camp Rock* featured a solo pop star whose negative behavior alienates his fans and draws public criticism. To salvage the situation, he is sent to serve as a counselor at Camp Rock, the summer camp that first launched his career.[31] However, Disney subsequently revised the film's narrative when it decided to offer the role to Joe Jonas, accommodating a request from the Jonas Brothers' co-manager/father to include roles for all three brothers. This was achieved by re-envisioning the pop singer, Shane Gray (Joe Jonas), as a member of a popular three-member boy band, Connect-3, who is forced to work at the camp by his fellow band-mates (Nick and Kevin Jonas).[32]

Viewers watching Connect-3's performance at Camp Rock are essentially watching the Jonas Brothers' performance. In the show, members of Connect-3 mention a summer concert. Notably, several weeks after *Camp Rock*'s multi-platform broadcast in June 2008, the Jonas Brothers began a 46-date North American tour on July 4th, in part to promote *A Little Bit Longer*, the Jonas Brothers' CD, which was released on August 21, 2008, under the Disney-owned Hollywood Records. Disney had already embarked on promotion for the CD, arranging for the Jonas Brothers' music video for their new single, "Burnin' Up," to follow immediately after the debut broadcasts of *Camp Rock*. By showcasing the Jonas Brothers as Connect-3 on *Camp Rock*, Disney was effectively publicizing the Jonas Brothers' summer tour, and the group's new CD release. Having cross-promoted the band's CD release and summer tour, Disney then leveraged on the band's growing popularity by filming segments of their tour performances for a planned 3-D theatrical release, yet another part of Disney's strategy to repeat the success it previously enjoyed with the *Hannah Montana/Miley Cyrus Best of Both Worlds* tour and movie tie-in.[33] *Jonas Brothers: The 3D Concert Experience* was released in 2009, and featured a cameo appearance by Demi Lovato, who co-starred with the brothers on *Camp Rock*.

Cultivating the Disney Multi-Media Tween Star

In addition to the carefully controlled and directed creation, promotion, and release of each tween-focused entertainment property, Disney further consolidated its position within tween media by actively nurturing and developing the careers of a stable of Disney tween stars. Just as the WB previously established a coterie of WB teen stars by casting them in several of its signature teen drama series, Disney also adopted similar practices in signing on young talent that the conglomerate then proceeded to train, promote and repurpose across its various media holdings. Several of Disney's most popular stars from its *High School Musical*, *Hannah Montana* and *Camp Rock* franchises had all appeared in other Disney productions. Ashley Tisdale, who starred in *High School Musical*, first appeared on Disney's *The Suite Life of Zack and Cody* (2005–). The Jonas Brothers made their mark as a singing trio that first appeared on Disney's *Hannah Montana* television show, and then served as the opening act in Cyrus' *Best of Both Worlds* concert tour and concert film, before being cast in *Camp Rock*. *Camp Rock* star Demi Lovato's appearance in *Jonas Brothers: The 3D Concert Experience* continues in the Disney tradition of cultivating and launching the careers of young performers that would eventually become Disney-branded tween stars.

Disney's attempts to direct and leverage on its stars' growing popularity found other forms of expression. Recognizing the importance of developing Cyrus' post–*Hannah Montana* career, Disney's Hollywood Records released Miley Cyrus' album *Breakout*, in July 2008. Independent of any overt links to the *Hannah Montana* franchise, *Breakout* debuted at number 1 on the album chart and sold more copies in the first week than the combined first-week sales figures of the two earlier *Hannah Montana* CDs, suggesting that her tween fans were willing to support Cyrus even without the lure of the *Hannah Montana* brand.[34] In September 2008, Disney announced that it was in negotiations with author Nicholas Sparks who was invited to write an untitled novel and related screenplay adaptation that would be produced by Disney and serve as a star-vehicle for the teenage Cyrus.[35] Disney's continuing interest in the Jonas brothers, meanwhile, led to the development of a television series *Jonas*. In the half-hour situation comedy, the brothers essentially play themselves, three brothers who are part of a pop group. The show's set up provides ample opportunities for the brothers to perform their music, which serves as highly efficient promotional stage for the brothers' celebrity personas, as well as the show's related spin-off merchandise.

Exploiting the Power of Synergy

These activities provide a good illustration of Disney's highly complex, integrated, cross-media, cross-promotional strategies. In fact, many textual elements in the Disney tween texts were primarily motivated by Disney's corporate structure, which was ideally organized to encourage cross-media, cross-promotional synergies. Recognizing that success depended on ensuring that the target tween audience was fully aware of these entertainment events, Disney engaged its highly diversified, multi-media holdings to aid in its promotional activities. As many of the activities described earlier suggest, a typical Disney release was accompanied by an active collaboration between the company's television, radio, online, retail and where possible and relevant, the film studio, branches, all engaged in publicizing and promoting the corporate product.

At the center of Disney's tween-oriented publicity and marketing endeavors lies the Disney Channel. Although the Disney Channel does not sell commercial time, it is actively committed to self-promotional "advertising" activities that take the form of in-house trailers publicizing and marketing a wide range of Disney products including Disney movies, music, its theme parks, and an immense selection of ancillary products. Disney's music videos are heavily featured on the cable channel and many of them are linked to the corporation's latest entertainment releases. The ways in which Disney structured and organized its textual content directly served a promotional purpose. For instance, as I have already shown, many of the Disney texts included musical sequences. When these sequences occur, the narrative largely comes to a halt while the musical performance is highlighted, effectively allowing these sequences to be separated from their narrative contexts and transformed into related music video promotional material. In their adoption of recognizable music video visuals and conventions, each of these sequences functions as a distinct and complete music video in itself and can be simply and easily "lifted" from the telefilm and played as a music video without much additional modification.

The Disney channel shows and its myriad list of related content and products are further promoted on the DisneyChannel.com website. The online entertainment hub offers program information, updates, photos, games, videos, music and other downloadable entertainment related to the many tween shows on the cable channel. On the parent company's Disney.com, streaming videos play on the website, promoting the company's merchandise, including DVDs, music releases, and new feature films. Links direct online visitors to Disney live events, to the Disney theme parks, and to the online Disney store where shoppers can purchase a wide range of products linked to specific shows, characters, or the larger Disney brand itself. Of course, many of the same products are also available at the over 300 brick-and-mortar Disney Stores in North America, or the over 100 overseas Disney Stores that are primarily in Europe. "What we're really trying to do," admits Disney's Gary Marsh, "is be all places that kids are. Kids are media snackers. They will consume media in many, many different places. We want to make sure that when they are hungry, we are available."[36]

In addition to promotional power, Disney's multi-media interests allowed it to repurpose its entertainment content across multiple media platforms for further profit. Disney's concerted efforts to fully leverage its various media holdings led to an active commitment to multi-platforming and repurposing strategies. These involved intensely synergistic practices in which every text is repackaged into a wide range of products. In a telling statement on the strategies needed to target the tween consumer audience, Ron Fair, the chairman of Geffen Records, notes, "All the platforms have to be open for business or it doesn't work anymore.... It's radio, it's Internet, it's TV, it's cellphones...."[37] In embracing a multi-platform distribution and release strategy, Disney's goal was to extend each show's reach across the wide range of media platforms that appealed to the increasingly tech-savvy tween audience, including online, DVD, and other new media services such as video podcasting. To that end, each of Disney's entertainment properties benefited from highly choreographed multi-platform releases, with each one helping to promote and publicize the other related components in the linked product chain. Consequently, the textual boundaries of a Disney commodity are never restricted to a solitary text in a lone media format. Instead, Disney's entertainment properties, including *High School Musical, Hannah Montana*, and *Camp Rock* all encompass a television component, DVDs, soundtracks, music videos, novelizations, catalogues worth of merchandise and possible tie-ins with Disney on Ice, and live stage tours.

The original *High School Musical* contains the various elements that essentially allowed the Disney channel to fully exploit the parent company's multimedia synergies in promoting and profiting from the property. The show's carefully structured hybrid of family-oriented coming-of-age drama, and song and dance musical contained numerous textual elements that could be repurposed and transferred across all the media platforms mentioned. In the weeks leading up to the telefilm's premier, Disney carefully orchestrated a series of promotional and marketing strategies to attract and interest its target tween audience. Disney's publicity plan before the TV movie's debut involved leveraging on its wide multi-media network. Weeks before the show premiered, the Disney Channel aggressively promoted the show and its soundtrack, including having the show's cast appear on a Disney New Year's Eve show and ensuring that the music videos for the show were heavily broadcast on the channel. These video broadcasts primed the target tween audience to anticipate Walt Disney Records' release of the film's soundtrack on January 10th 2006.[38] In addition, significant airplay over Radio Disney also helped to promote the soundtrack. To further stoke interest in the show's premiere broadcast, Disney offered a free song that could be downloaded through DisneyChannel.com. Evidence of the show's potential popularity emerged when the song was reportedly downloaded half-million times.[39]

At every level and platform of distribution, Disney also opportunistically planned for multiple releases of a single product, often introducing minor variations to each item, to further lure fans to purchase more. For instance, Disney's strategy with DVD releases involved scheduling several staggered release dates for a single popular title. In these cases, each DVD release offered "new, additional" material, such as deleted scenes or additional features such as cast interviews that were unavailable in previous DVD versions, thereby allowing the Disney Company to wring further profits from every single entertainment commodity. Other narrative elements in the film also paved the way for Disney's subsequent plans for further exploiting the *High School Musical* phenomenon. In February 2006, a month after the show premiered, Disney began to promote the broadcast of a karaoke version of the film on The Disney Channel. It cannot be an accident that Troy and Gabriella first meet when both reluctantly participate in a karaoke duet at a party. Prior to the broadcast of the karaoke version on The Disney Channel, an estimated 1.2 million viewers downloaded the lyrics online. In the case of *High School Musical*, the original DVD release of the cable movie was followed by subsequent releases of the karaoke versions of the film that contained addition material. The karaoke DVD was released at the same time the tie-in novelization was published.[40]

Disney's on-going promotion and marketing of the franchise continued to expand to ensure that tween audiences remained focused on the series. Not content with leveraging on its own extensive multimedia platforms, and recognizing the significant role that its website played in attracting the target audiences' interest in all things *High School Musical*–related, a strategy that acknowledged the tween market's adoption of the internet and digital technologies as ways to experience and access their entertainment, Disney reached beyond its own online resources and joined with online entertainment companies to further attract this target audience. Two months before the theatrical release of *High School Musical 3: Senior Year*, Disney teamed up with JibJab, an online entertainment company, to offer its tween audience the ability to create and customize their own *High School Musical*–linked entertainment creations by "starring" in their own *High School Musical* music video.[41] The Disney-JibJab arrangement allowed the franchise's burgeoning tween fans to cast themselves in the show's "Now or Never" music video by inserting their own faces in place of the show's stars.

Further embracing and exploiting the power of the internet, Disney collaborated with MySpace, one of the world's largest online social networking sites, to promote the feature film release of *High School Musical 3: Senior Year*.[42] The promotion involved a month-long event that would allow high-school graduating classes nation-wide to compete for a trip to a Walt Disney Resort. Contestants had to log on to the film's official MySpace profile and complete various online tasks and vote via text message to earn points for their schools' graduating class.

Disney embraced similar multi-platform linked releases with *Hannah Montana*. In addition to the two series soundtrack releases, the live-concert tour, and the Disney produced 3-D concert film *Hannah Montana/Miley Cyrus: Best of Both Worlds* that I have already mentioned, Disney Interactive also released a series of Hannah Montana video games, including *Hannah Montana: Spotlight World Tour* (2007), and *Hannah Montana: Music Jam* (2007). Accessed on a variety of platforms including Playstations, Nintendo DS and the Wii, these interactive games allowed the series' tween fans to adopt the Miley Stewart/Hannah Montana persona and "appear" as the pop star during her tour performances, or follow the pop star on her adventures by serving as a photo-journalist accompanying the singer on tour. Disney also began refashioning the star/series into a consumer product lifestyle brand with tie-ins to cosmetics, accessories and clothing lines.[43]

Despite the already vast range of multi-media products associated with the *Hannah Montana* franchise, the brand still held significant profit potential, as evidenced by Disney's decision to follow the strategy it first embraced with *High School Musical* and release a movie based on the popular *Hannah Montana* series. Unlike the *Best of Both Worlds Concert Tour* film, *Hannah Montana: The Movie* (2009) translates the television character's adventures to the large screen. The film traces Miley Stewart's experiences on her grandmother's farm where she is sent to rediscover her roots after her rock star success goes to her head and she begins to indulge in selfish, arrogant behavior. While staying on the farm, Stewart decides to stage a fund raising concert to help some of the neighbors, a narrative development that provides the opportunity for several musical performances, which could then be repackaged as soundtracks and serve as promotional videos that could be aired on The Disney Channel.

Disney's attempts to repurpose its tween entertainment properties did not stop with their translation into films, CDs, and television shows. In fact, Disney was also able to further translate some of its tween franchises into an even greater range of products. Not content to limit *High School Musical* to its niche oriented cable channel or to feature films, Disney chose to extend the show's cultural reach to a broader public to ensure that the *High School Musical* experience was available over multiple platforms. In the winter of 2006, most of *High School Musical*'s principle cast went on a 40-city concert tour that featured songs from the telefilm, alongside original recordings from the stars own individual albums.[44] In January 2007, Disney expanded the *High School Musical* franchise further, launching a stage version that involved a 60-city national tour that replicated the *High School Musical* narrative, with the addition of two new songs.[45] Whether originally intended to facilitate the cable film's transformation into a live stage performance or not, certain key elements in the original telefilm seemed perfectly suited to the translation.

As mentioned earlier, several sequences reveal the influence of the classical backstage film musical, an influence that incorporates the adoption of Broadway/theatrical staging techniques. While these filmic and aesthetic traditions may be less familiar to the young tween audience, the inclusion of the backstage musical's conventions within the film's narrative and visual aesthetics ultimately helped serve Disney's larger synergistic interests. *High School Musical*'s narrative, in which the two leads encourage their friends to participate in their school's end of the year musical production, centers on activities associated with the staging of a live musical. In addition to allowing for the inclusion of traditionally humorous moments involving disastrously funny auditions, the introduction of the theatrical element primed the content for its eventual transformation to the live stage. Following in the wake of the stage version, *Disney's High School Musical: The Ice Tour* debuted at Madison Square Garden on September 29, 2007, before embarking on a 100-city international tour.[46]

Further extending the franchise's cultural influence, Disney also offered performance licenses for the original *High School Musical* to U.S. schools and amateur theatrical groups; by 2008, 2, 500 licenses had been granted. According to Disney Theatrical Group, *High School Musical* enjoyed more than ten thousand performances by amateur and community groups.[47] Interestingly, *High School Musical 3: Senior Year*, which was released as a feature film, contained textual elements that may have helped encourage the popularity of these amateur performances. As previously mentioned, a significant segment of the film revolves around the characters restaging a number of key scenes from the franchises' first two installments as part of their senior's graduation show, these sequences, which translate the previously realistic scenes into stylized stage sequences function as clear intertextual links to the touring stage versions of the shows. Fans watching the film are reminded that they too can play Troy and Gabriella, as the opportunity is available to any school or group willing to acquire a performance license for the original *High School Musical* from Disney Theatrical Group.[48]

Sensing another opportunity for extending the *High School Musical* franchise, Disney also developed a multi-episode, summer 2008 reality series, *High School Musical: Get in the Picture* (2008). The show featured a nationwide contest, in which a group of competitors attempt to develop their talent at a music conservatory, for broadcast over its mainstream, more adult-oriented broadcast network, ABC. The show featured numerous *High School Musical*–themed performances and had a promotional tie-in with K-Mart stores across the nation carrying *High School Musical* promotional merchandise in the weeks leading up the show's premier.[49]

Over the almost three years between *High School Musical*'s first installment's premiere on cable and the third part's feature film release, Disney also participated in various advertising tie-ins and promotional partnerships with various brands to ensure that the *High School Musical* brand remained at the forefront of tween awareness. Between the premieres of the first two films on cable, Disney had cross-promotional advertising deals with Major League baseball, Wal-Mart and Dannon yogurt.[50] Teen and tween magazines, including *CosmoGirl*, and mainstream publications such as *People*, featured "behind the scenes" gossip and updates on the *High School Musical* sequel. The Internet was also harnessed to publicize the franchise, with the show's stars having an official presence on popular digital media platforms including YouTube and MySpace. A year later, before the release of the *High School Musical* feature film and premiere of the summer reality series, *High School Musical: Get in the Picture*, *High School Musical* star Vanessa Hudgens appeared in a Sears "back to school" advertising campaign on national television to heightening public awareness of both productions.[51]

Disney's release of *Camp Rock* revealed a significant escalation of its multi-platform launch strategy. Where the first installment of *High School Musical* rolled out across a broad range of platforms over several months, *Camp Rock* was aired across Disney's multiple media channels within a matter of days. The show's soundtrack, released June 17th, 2008, just days before the show's debut, received significant airplay on Radio Disney even as the movie was first made available in limited release on Disney Channel on Demand, a service available to some Time Warner Cable, Cablevision and Verizon customers.[52] The TV-movie was then first broadcast over the Disney cable channel on Friday, June 20th, 2008. During this initial broadcast, the show could also be heard simultaneously over Radio Disney. A day later, *Camp Rock* was aired on ABC, Disney's broadcast network, and then on ABC Family, its other youth-focused cable channel, a day after that, on Sunday, June 22nd, 2008. The show was then made available to viewers online, on Disney.com.[53]

Finally, Disney's interest in dominating the tween market must also be understood within a larger, long-term context of audience engagement and consumption. There is an enduring industry belief that upholds the importance of establishing a relationship with viewers/consumers early in life, the assumption being that once audiences/consumers have bonded with a particular brand, especially if they do so in their youth, they are less likely to switch loyalties as they age. Considering Disney's highly efficient practices of brand-extension across a range of multiple media platforms, cementing the Disney brand awareness and allegiance in children makes for good corporate strategy. The Disney Corporation has become particularly skilled at attracting children to its core Disney brand, and then ushering this audience across the conglomerate's various cable holdings as the audience ages. Tweens attracted to the Disney channel would then feed into the conglomerate's teen-oriented ABC Family outlet. In subsequent years, these same viewers would eventually age up into Disney's mainstream ABC broadcast network.

Far from leaving such developments to chance, Disney initiated a series of programming and scheduling tactics to ensure the greatest likelihood of such an evolution. Disney's attempts at increasing its tween audiences' awareness of its broader media holdings was in part responsible for the week-long multi-channel, multi-platform release of *Camp Rock*, as well as its attempts at expanding the *High School Musical* phenomenon beyond the cable channel to the ABC network with the launch of the *High School Musical*–linked reality series, *High School-Musical: Get in the Picture*, that featured actually teenagers trying out for a stage version of the TV movie.

The Value of the Disney Tween Brand

In *High School Musical 1*'s first eight airings on the Disney channel, it reportedly drew an aggregate 30.6 million unduplicated viewers.[54] As previously noted, *High School Musical 2* remains the highest rated program in cable history.

The tween market's economic and purchasing power was confirmed in February 2008 when media reports announced that the first two *High School Musical* television movies had sold 15 million DVDs and an equal number of CDs.[55] In the 18 months after *High School Musical* debuted on The Disney Channel, the show which had cost Disney an estimated $5 million to produce,[56] had "generated $100 million in profits from the DVD and soundtrack sales, touring concerts and ice shows, and numerous other brand extensions...."[57]

Hannah Montana's two series soundtracks debuted at the top of the Billboard album charts.[58] By 2008, on the strength of her tween fan base alone, Miley Cyrus had sold 8 million CDs, with her album sales and digital music downloads earning in excess of $50 million.[59] Her 70-date concert tour generated $36 million,[60] while her *Hannah Montana/Miley Cyrus: Best of Both Worlds 3-D* concert film grossed $65.3 million in 2008.[61] The Jonas Brothers star vehicle *Camp Rock* was the top rated cable show for 2008 and their albums *Jonas Brothers* (2007) and *A Little Bit Longer* (2008), released under Disney's Hollywood Records label, have sold in excess of 3 million copies, while Jonas Brothers albums have sold 8.1 million CDs worldwide.[62]

Based on their success with the tween market, Disney's various media holdings were able to raise profits when their competitors were experiencing the opposite.[63] For instance, The Disney Music Group, particularly via their Hollywood Records label that released their tween-oriented products, was able to gain market share, even as the larger music business witnessed a persistent drop in global CD sales.[64] Disney's success in promoting and marketing its media offerings online and over digital platforms including iTunes, highlights the extent to which teens and tweens have been able to harness new technologies and delivery platforms to enhance their influence over the media marketplace. Disney's tween-focused media also had a significant impact on the Disney Corporation's revenues via Disney's licensing agreements with other marketers. The Disney Channel's tween programming was responsible for generating licensed consumer product sales amounting to $23 billion in 2006.[65]

The success of Disney's tween franchises is due in large part to Disney's ability to synergistically repurpose a single concept across an increasingly broad range of media platforms even as it taps into the (stereo)typical concerns and anxieties of the tween mindset, while earning the trust of parents and larger concerned social institutions. These activities originated with the careful manipulation of the nature and form of the textual content. The Disney "formula" for success involved featuring teen characters in narrative scenarios that offered opportunities for a multi-media format organized around a mixture of pop music, dance and drama. This resulted in the creation of entertainment texts that comprised of a complex hybrid of multiple media features and effects, while also combining a range of entertainment genres including the teen coming-of-age text, the high school teen romance, the (movie) musical, music videos, the concert/live performance genre, and even aspects of the traditional stage musical. These characteristics allowed Disney to repurpose a single text into a wide range of circulating consumer products.

The show's narrative and aesthetic content was carefully organized to effectively and efficiently fulfill the conglomerate's synergistic and financial interests by offering a framework founded on the inclusion of numerous elements that could then be repurposed into a wide range of ancillary products. In addition to fully optimizing the profit potential of a single media product, the release of such a wide range of related merchandise allowed the Disney Company to more effectively leverage its advertising and marketing activities, since a single campaign essentially promoted every item in the assemblage. These advertising activities also directly benefited from Disney's complex corporate structure.

In targeting the millennial tween, the strategies Disney adopted strongly resembled the ones used to target the teen market through the late 1990s and into the new millennium. These include the exploitation of synergistic potential across a widening range of related texts, an approach that led to a heightened shift to multi-media, multi-textual repurposing in which a single entertainment concept was spun into an ever increasing assortment of linked (commercially available) products. As a related development, media texts became increasingly postmodern, distinguished by the intensification of intertextual elements and heightened mixed-media aesthetics within each text. The only difference appears to be a discernable intensification of the techniques.

The Disney approach, which involves offering its tween demographic a wide range of interlinked, multi-media, cross-platform entertainment may have significant repercussions for what this particular youth generation will expect from their media entertainment as they age. If they carry these experiences and expectations into adulthood with them, we are likely to see these media trends translated into mainstream media. Disney itself is not content to restrict its activities to those discussed in this chapter. In 2009, Disney announced its decision to launch a new cable network specifically targeted at tween boys, acknowledging the fact that its success so far was primarily relegated to the tween girl market.[66] This announcement provides further indication of the extent to which Hollywood appears to be committed to further market fragmentation in its quest for the youth demographic and consumer dollar.

EIGHT

Bridging the Digital Divide —
Media in Transition

In April 2009, MTV pitched a new series to advertisers. To be launched in the coming summer, *What You're Watching with Alexa Chung*, would be a daily one-hour talk/variety show in the tradition of *TRL* that would bring together and integrate the existing range of traditional and new media platforms. Like *TRL*, host Alexa Chung would be joined by celebrity guests focused on publicizing their latest movie, CD or television series, with the innovative addition of allowing viewers to interact with both the host and her guests via various online social networking sites, including Facebook and Twitter, and RockYou, a video-sharing application. Presumably, the show would continue MTV's commitment to blurring the boundaries between promotion and entertainment long practiced since MTV first broadcast music videos. *What You're Watching* would be a "joint venture" between MTV, Facebook and Twitter, all of which would share advertising revenue from the show, indicating the extent to which new media platforms were integrating with traditional entertainment media.[1]

That same month, the CW debuted its first "cwinger" advertising campaign on its flagship teen/young adult series *Gossip Girl*, where the adventures of the main characters are the subject of an online blog written by "Gossip Girl." In a tie-in between CW and Unilever's Dove, Dove sponsored a series of video vignettes, labeled *Gossip Girl: Real New York Stories Revealed*. Featuring the real-life stories of women whose lifestyles mirrored the characters on the CW series, the first half of these vignettes aired in 90-second advertisements on *Gossip Girl*, before viewers were directed to catch the remainder of the videos online by logging on to cwtv.com/dovegofresh on either their computers or mobile devices. Further blending the line between the television series and this online promotional content, *Gossip Girl* cast member Jessica Szohr served as the host for these vignettes. The television series-advertisement tie-in was reinforced via the online content, which further promoted the CW series, the Dove-sponsored videos, and Dove products by offering behind-the-scenes, "making of" videos of the *Real New York Stories* series, interviews with Szohr and the women profiled in the videos, alongside information on Dove's product line.[2]

These two events are indicative of several noteworthy developments within the media industry and teen culture. MTV's *What You're Watching* and the CW's "cwinger" advertising campaigns highlight the traditional media industry's acceptance that their target audiences, specifically teens and tweens, are no longer consuming their entertainment via the established, traditional media formats and platforms or engaging with traditional media in the same way as their parents. The events also point to the increasing collaboration between traditional and digital or "new" media, highlighting the complex relationship between the two. These latest cross-media collaborations also represent the extent to which medium specificities, stylistic distinctions, platform differences, and textual boundaries have collapsed, heralding the further intensification of the postmodern, hyperintertextual tendencies discussed in the earlier chapters of this book. Even as the emergence of Generation Y forced Hollywood to develop new strategies to cope with this new audience demographic, the rise of the digital era has encouraged another form of multi-media transition. The changes motivated by these social and demographic shifts are linked to the technological developments in various ways.

Although the rise of new media technologies is discussed in preceding chapters, a number of key developments, many of them dating from 2000, deserve attention, particularly in terms of their (potentially) significant, and still actively debated, impact on the media industries. As highlighted in Chapter Two, the rise of digital media technologies has had significant consequences and implications for Hollywood in the twenty-first century, particularly in how these developments have significantly affected the evolving corporate structures, traditional practices and activities of the multi-media conglomerates. The nature of new media platforms and technologies offer interesting opportunities and challenges to the entertainment conglomerates that have established their power and influence on the foundations of traditional media. In the new digital age, however, many of the conventional strategies, business models, and standardized practices in Hollywood have been undermined, destabilized, or no longer function adequately. In addition, the development of new media technologies and devices has prompted changes in how people access, use, and consume media content and information. As a consequence, Hollywood has been forced to evolve and adapt to the emergence and tremendous growth of a wide range of new digital media technologies if it is to thrive in the new millennium.

How has Hollywood responded to the emergence of new media technologies? What is at stake for traditional media companies in the age of new media, particularly in their continuing efforts to target and attract the youth and teen markets? What strategies has Hollywood adopted to exploit the marketing, distribution and profit potential of these diverse new media? How has Hollywood adapted and refined its traditional content to accommodate these new media platforms? These are some of the questions addressed here. While my primary interest in this chapter lies in investigating how new media technologies will

shape the evolving relationship between the youth market and the media industries, the evaluations, observations and speculations offered in the following
pages are no less relevant to more general debates on the impact of new media
on popular media culture in general.

In the first decade of the twenty-first century, what constitutes new/digi-
tal media is fairly broad, with experimentation the dominant feature of the terrain. It would be impossible to fully document the full scope of the
developments within this period. So, this chapter limits its inquiry to two
specific new media platforms that are popular with the youth and teen demographics, and that are directly changing traditional media activities and practices: the Internet and mobile technologies. These two platforms are of
particular interest as they offer the potential for new consumer/entertainment
experiences and interfaces, and they are linked to heightened viewer/consumer
agency and interactivity. Unlike older viewers/consumers who came of age in
the era of traditional media, which are built on controlled schedules and relatively passive media consumption, the emerging digital technologies allow audiences—particularly technologically-savvy, teen, early adopters—to access
entertainment as, when, and to an increasing extent, where, they want it. Generation Y and millennial t(w)eens reject the established constraints associated
with traditional media systems, preferring and demanding increasing independence and control over their entertainment options.

Youth and New Media Technologies

According to a 2003 Yahoo! survey of teenagers aged between 13 and 18,
82 percent of the respondents had computers, 62 percent owned videogame consoles, and 49 percent possessed cell phones.[3] Anecdotal evidence also suggests
that teens and tweens are spending considerable amounts of time on these
devices, often at the expense of more traditional media consumption, suggesting the extent to which teens and tweens were transferring their entertainment
activities towards the web, shifting to video-streaming sites, and using their
mobile devices to remain updated on news and entertainment developments.
Advertising Age quotes a study of media consumption habits that revealed that
younger consumers tended to spend more time on the Internet, and preferred
to watch television shows recorded on digital video recorders.[4] In addition, the
study showed that consumers between the ages of 18 and 34 access an average
of eight-and-a-half hours of media overall, with approximately three-and-a-
half hours devoted to television. These figures fall below the media consumption patterns of more mature viewers (aged between 45 and 54), who tended
to spend more time on media, averaging nine-and-a-half hours of media consumption, of which more than five-and-a-half hours a day was devoted to the
television.[5] Another report by *Advertising Age* notes that television viewing is

slowly being replaced by online Web-viewing. The report states that half of the people who admitted to viewing television shows online were using the internet as a replacement for more traditional television viewing practices, while the other 50 percent access online shows to catch programs they had previously missed, or to re-access segments of episodes they had already seen.[6] These statistics, coupled with the revelation that younger viewers preferred online video-on demand or DVR viewing options, have significant implications for teen and tween oriented entertainment platforms. Taken together, the information highlights a potentially significant trend in which younger viewers were likely to continue shifting away from television towards new delivery platforms while simultaneously reducing the amount of time spent watching television.

These statistics and studies have resulted in a commonly held perception about teen media consumption habits and behaviors within the media industries. Samantha Skey, Senior vice-president of strategic marketing at Alloy Media and Marketing asserts a popular view of the relationship between teens and new media, "Other audiences may not view the desktop as an audio platform or wireless devices as a video platform, but teens do."[7] John Shea, executive vice president for integrated marketing at MTVN Music and Logo group concurs, maintaining that while audiences in general are beginning to access and consume media via computers, mobile devices, and video-on-demand, these behavioral shifts are particularly true of younger viewers in the 12 to 24 age group.[8] These perspectives encouraged the media industries in the belief that any attempt to retain the attention of younger, particularly millennial audiences/consumers (the generation that has come of age in a digital world), would require the development of entertainment content that would effectively transcend specific mediums and instead exist across the entire range of media.

Traditional/Analog vs. New/Digital Media

The emergence of digital new media technologies, devices and interfaces occurred amidst a fairly volatile period for the media industries in general. Even without the new media developments, Hollywood was already witnessing several significant developments industrially and aesthetically within a period marked by an increasing degree of media convergence across the various forms of what was quickly becoming termed "traditional" or "old" media. As highlighted in Chapter Two and other earlier chapters, once separate media specific industries had merged into global multi-media conglomerates, and as a symptom of conglomeration and the commitment to synergy, media content was shifting across media platforms in increasingly fluidly ways, aided by, and in turn reflecting a wide range of stylistic and aesthetic blendings and heightened shifts towards cross-media hybridity.

It is within this larger environment of industrial consolidation and textual evolutions that new media developments emerged, introducing greater changes (and instabilities) for the traditional media industries due to the significant differences between the two media approaches. These developments have had interesting consequences for multi-media conglomerates, both in terms of their industrial practices and modes of production, distribution and exhibition, and also in terms of how their products are accessed, experienced, and consumed.

Early discourses comparing traditional and new media tended to emphasize differences and characterize the relationship in binary terms. Where traditional media was shaped by high barriers to entry, and often tied to complex and very costly infrastructures, most of which required significant financial commitments to operate and maintain,[9] new media was touted as an "open" technology, with low barriers to entry, and offering easy access to both content users/consumers, and content producers and distributors. As a consequence of these distinctions, traditional media has been characterized as a highly controlled, oligopolistic system, in contrast to the depictions of new media platforms such as the Internet as an uncharted "wilderness" of seemingly unlimited and largely unregulated content and information.

While traditional media continues to evolve in response to changes within its internal structures, the industries' efforts at consolidation, commitment to growth and expansion into related media, and their on-going commitments to broaden market share, take place within a context of established and standardized business and operational practices. Where traditional media industries, such as film and television (both network and cable), have stabilized business models with clearly structured standards and protocols, discourses and descriptions of new media tend to emphasize instability, volatility and experimentation. Mainstream press, trade journals, and academic perspectives still struggle to define just what the new media platform(s) is/are, what it/they can do, what it/they should do, and how it/they should do it.

These differences have significant implications for the contemporary, evolving media landscape. As media scholars have noted, the rise of new media, and the need to accommodate its varying possibilities, raise a range of interesting issues. While the structures and practices of traditional media are built on a notion of mass communication, where content and information tends to flow from a single source to many recipients, new media's open, largely unregulated structure and low barriers to entry offer the opportunity for content and information to flow from many sources to many recipients. This has resulted in the prediction that the distinction between interpersonal and mass communications, between public and private communications, will weaken significantly.[10]

New media developments also affect how information is accessed and experienced. Where traditional media were once encountered and consumed in specific venues, via distinct devices and technologies, and offered identifiably different experiences, new media with their digital networks and the promise of "convergence" helped negate these previous boundaries.[11] In the millennium, film, television, music, and various other forms of content and information, could and were becoming increasingly available over a range of multi-media devices, most commonly on personal computers, mobile phones, and other mobile entertainment devices such as portable Playstations and iPods. This has resulted in the emergence of a new range of delivery outlets and platforms, including Internet video-distribution sites, of which YouTube is the dominant example, mobile delivery systems controlled by wireless carriers such as Verizon, and online entertainment retailers such as Apple's iTunes, a dominant distributor/retailer of commercial-free downloadable content, and Xbox Live Video Marketplace, another retailer that allows consumers to download movies and television shows onto their Xbox consoles. These online entertainment retailers are like brick and mortar retailers in offering consumers the option to directly purchase entertainment content. The distinction lies in the ease and speed at which such entertainment is available. Media consumers with access to a computer and broadband Internet connection can purchase these products with several clicks of the mouse without ever leaving their homes.

These developments have been accompanied by significant changes in the behaviors and attitudes of consumers who are enjoying a greater degree of agency and selective power in how and when they access Hollywood content. In the age of traditional media, the media conglomerates determined how, when and where viewers/consumers accessed media products by controlling release dates or broadcast schedules, owning exhibition outlets, and instituting a profitable business model. Digital systems have undermined this situation by giving users/consumers greater independence and agency in making their entertainment decisions. Digital convergence allows viewers to access entertainment content over a wide range of new platforms including personal computers and mobile phones, devices that are arguable more viewer-friendly by giving users greater control over their viewing experience by freeing them from content provider/distributor imposed broadcast or release schedules, allowing viewers to avoid advertising, and determine their own schedules and preferences by accessing content when and where they prefer.

One such device was the Digital Video Recorder that, like the videocassette recorder before it, allowed viewers to record shows and avoid the advertising, only in more efficient ways. In 2005, ten million homes had digital video recorders (DVRs), with the figure projected to increase to 42 million in 2010.[12] The proliferation and penetration of DVRs have significant implications for the traditional broadcast-advertising model. According to Davina Kent, vice-president of TiVo, a dominant digital video recording system, its customers skip 70 percent of the commercials when they watch recorded programs.[13] DVR penetration and adoption was accompanied by a rise in online Internet viewing of Hollywood content, another interface that allowed viewers to avoid advertising content. Similarly, the growing dominance of iTunes, which allowed viewers to purchase and download advertisement-free content to the computers or mobile devices such as iPods, considerably weakened and threatened the traditional advertising model. Even without iTunes, access to a personal computer and broadband connections allowed viewers/consumers/users to retrieve and watch entertainment content at their convenience.

The shift to digital also encouraged content users/consumers to develop increasing expectations of interactivity and (fan) input. Interactivity is yet another feature of new media that is transforming the nature of media entertainment. Digital formats give users and viewers the ability to rework and redistribute the content and information they encounter, with few constraints or restrictions. While viewers, users, and fans have historically "poached" professional media content, using and transforming it to serve the users' own purposes and interests, these activities have often been personal and contained to small communities.[14] Going digital allowed viewers to more easily and efficiently "customize" and generate their own content from existing material. Digital platforms and systems offer t(w)eens the opportunity to create, generate, and distribute content, much of which is cannibalized from existing, professional, commercial, popular entertainment material. The advent of the Internet has significantly changed the ways in which these activities have been conducted, allowing "poachers" to distribute and publicize their "hijacked" and revised content to a global audience. This has had the effect of reducing the degree of control and ownership that media conglomerates have over the content they produce, which in turn has led to a complex, conflicted relationship between (teen) audiences and the media conglomerates. While the media industries need the teen consumer/viewer, and acknowledge the potential profits that can accrue by targeting this segment and encouraging them to promote the media company's content and products, there is a simultaneous concern with copyright/intellectual property considerations, an issue I discuss in greater detail later in this chapter. The question of who controls the content and information being distributed online is becoming increasingly contentious, as are related issues of copyright, authenticity and reliability.

The media conglomerates are not the only industries contending with challenges posed by these shifts in the digital age. As viewers/consumers find newer, more efficient ways to dodge advertisements, both Madison Avenue and the media industries that rely on advertisers for their revenues must discover new ways to target consumers and deliver marketing messages that cannot be easily and efficiently avoided and ignored by consumers. As new media technologies and devices allow audiences to actively avoid advertisements, the new media interfaces themselves function in ways that are distinct from traditional media's ability to generate, engage and manage consumer demands and desires.

The popular view is that while traditional media is particularly effective in "demand generation," i.e. the process of enticing viewers/consumers to desire and "want" the products created by the media companies and the advertisers and marketers they serve, new media is more commonly engaged in the practice of "demand fulfillment." Where new media such as the Internet is concerned, consumer/user activities are motivated by preexisting individual, and often personal, needs and desires. As a consequence of the seemingly infinite availability of content and product on the Internet, audiences are required to actively seek out and pursue their particular interests and desires, behavior that requires prior audience awareness of and interest in the content or product to motivate them to hunt down the material. This awareness and interest is often difficult to incite and control due to the immense clutter and vastness of the Internet landscape.

The features of new media, and the convergences and divergences with traditional media have forced the multi-media conglomerates to adopt and adapt a series of strategies to cope with the impending brave new media world. In doing so, Hollywood has had to evaluate and negotiate the perceived possibilities and obstacles contained within the prospect and realities of digital new media. The activities explored in the following pages highlight the media conglomerates' intense interest in online distribution, and offer some idea of the degree of experimentation that they are willing to engage in. They also provide insight into the challenges and obstacles that accompany the new technologies and their potential. The online medium is still in its early experimental stages with a variety of structures and organizing frameworks being explored and tested.

(New) New Hollywood in the Digital Age

The digital era is marked by changes in the nature, form, and structure of the existing media landscape, changes that affect all parties involved within the complex entertainment media matrix. In the millennium, the various stakeholders, including the media and communications industries, consumers, and advertisers, were all engaged in active struggles to shape and determine what a digital media system would (eventually) be, how digital media would function, and what roles and behaviors the different parties would (be allowed to) play. Certainly, this is a process that has taken place with every new media technology that has historically come into existence.

In the contemporary environment, the Internet and mobile technologies are all un(der)-exploited windows of commercial opportunity for Hollywood. Each platform exists as another means for branding, content promotion, distribution, and exhibition that could benefit the existing multi-media conglomerates. Recognizing the vast potential available, Hollywood has engaged in a diverse range of activities as part of its committed efforts to assert a presence, and perhaps discover a means of dominating these new media platforms. Hollywood's varied and experimental responses to new media signals both the untested, unfamiliar terrain of these emerging platforms, as well as a lack of awareness of what would and would not work, what viewers/users/consumers would want and accept, or reject and ignore.

Hollywood's primary response to digital involved the adoption of a familiar and largely effective tactic, the extension of the multi-platform. As younger viewers shifted from traditional to new media, the media brands most reliant on the youth demographic were also the most motivated to fully exploit the potential of the Internet and the various "third screens" related to the emerging technologies. Media brands began experimenting with the new platforms and innovative technological opportunities. Hollywood's responses to digital developments were broadly divided into attempts to use new media for promoting and marketing their content and related products, and developing new distribution and exhibition avenues for these properties. All these efforts were motivated by Hollywood's unchanging commitment to increasing profits by extending the commercial windows for its content. Despite the specific nature of this goal, the activities and strategies that Hollywood adopted were complex and varied.

Branded Entertainment Websites

The establishment of an online multi-media platform for teen-branded media content represents one of Hollywood's earliest responses to the potential of the Internet. These tended to involve repurposing existing content for distribution over the Internet, and often included the offer of "new" or "additional" material, for example, behind the scenes content, related music videos, cast interviews and "making of" videos, as additional "bait" to lure viewers/users. In some other cases, media companies also engaged in the creation of entirely original content to be distributed over the Internet.

These cross-media, cross-platform experimentations and activities have inevitably affected the nature, form and content of the entertainment text itself. Writing in 2004, John Caldwell discusses textual "resistance" as a possible obstacle to such repurposing, arguing that hour-long narrative prime-time series and (tele)films tend to "resist" the attempts at repurposing and hybridization that characterize transferring such content to digital platforms.[15] However, as I have argued in the preceding chapters, contemporary film and television texts have evolved stylistically and aesthetically in ways that specifically reduce these obstacles and resistances, often via the integration of different media aesthetics, including music video visuals, online aesthetic conventions, and narrative structures that allow specific sequences to be easily repurposed or transferred to alternative delivery (and promotional) platforms.

Many of the teen and tween-focused media brands were at the forefront of these activities to "colonize" the new media frontier. Though I have examined some of these new media innovations in earlier chapters, a more detailed exploration of one such representative venture is useful in illustrating just how the Internet was used to leverage and further promote an interlinked range of teen entertainment content to its target audience. As discussed in earlier chapters, the teen-oriented *Dawson's Creek* had a tendency to exceed its television boundaries in its many complex attempts to target its teen audience and leverage the promotional opportunities at its disposal. Just as the show mined its links to the *Scream* trilogy via its creator, Kevin Williamson, referenced other teen-oriented series on its WB network, and engaged in various commercial tie-ins with teen-focused retailers, the show's creators also recognized the need to engage its viewers over the Internet, which would also offer further marketing and advertising activities. To that end, Dawsonscreek.com was created to offer users/viewers further opportunities to engage with the characters and the world of *Dawson's Creek*. This online portal/platform further extended the teen entertainment experience beyond the limits of traditional media. By accessing Dawsonscreek.com, the show's fans could explore and gain insight into the "personal lives" of the show's key characters as the site offered fans regularly updated computer desktops and homepages belonging to each character. On the desktop pages, fans could voyeuristically enjoy the instant messages and e-mails that the characters sent each other, read the essays they were writing for class, and even look over the characters' Christmas gift lists. In offering fans this additional level of access to the *Dawson's Creek* world, the show's creators had an additional means of enhancing the fan's commitment to the series.

The site's producers also actively sought out and even collaborated with the show's fans in an attempt to reinforce the fans' relationship with the show. *Dawson's Creek* fans were encouraged to take on the personas of students at the show's fictional high school. On the site, fans that take on the guise of the characters' classmates could "interact" with the characters via e-mail. According to Andrew Schneider, who led the Dawsonscreek.com project, "We're in touch with [the shows fans] all the time. We wanted to make sure the fans were getting what they wanted. They helped us design the interface and they told us what they liked and did not like."[16] In this way, fans could contribute their own content to the show's site, allowing the producers to better tailor the site's and the show's content to the preferences and demands of their target audience.

Creatively, the website also allowed the show's creators to further explore narrative developments that would not have been feasible within the constraints of an hour-long television drama. In fact, various plot developments that could not be depicted within the show were pursued and elaborated on via the website. When the third season closed with two of the characters embarking on a summer sailing trip together, Dawsonscreek.com extended that narrative element online by allowing the show's viewers to track the characters' journey and adventures by reading their summer diary entries. The information in these dairy entries was also used to clear up minor plot points raised in the third season finale and to hint at events in the upcoming season. Similarly, when one of the main characters leaves to travel through Europe in another season, the website allowed viewers to share her travels via the many online messages and communications she continued to have with the show's characters, including the postcards she sent them. In doing so, the website afforded fans the opportunity to further engage with their favorite characters, ensuring that the fans were more likely to tune in to each new episode. By further developing the various narrative arcs over the Internet, the creators were constructing a much more complex, intricately evolved story world, one that clearly transcended the medium-specific limitations of the original text. According to Henry Jenkins, one consequence of the increasing attempts to explore and exploit cross-media convergences is "the emergence of new story structures, which create complexity by expanding the range of narrative possibilities rather than pursuing a single path with a beginning, middle, and end."[17] These attempts at expanding the series' narrative possibilities are focused on heightening the fans' interest in and commitment to the *Dawson's Creek* world.

The cross-media matrix that formed the *Dawson's Creek* experience, stretching from the television show, to numerous overt film references, into the online realm via Dawsonscreek.com, represents the trend towards what Henry Jenkins has labeled "transmedia storytelling," a development that has gained momentum with the advent of the digital age and the media industries' growing commitment to exploring and exploiting the possibilities of multimedia convergence. As Jenkins notes,

> a transmedia story unfolds across multiple media platforms, with each new text making a distinctive and valuable contribution to the whole. In the ideal form of transmedia storytelling, each medium does what it does best — so that a story might be introduced in a film, expanded through television, novels, and comics; its world might be explored through game play or experienced as an amusement park attraction.[18]

In addition to the postmodern, highly intertextual, multi-media-oriented cross-referencing characteristic of this enterprise, the website also explored a range of commercial opportunities. Scattered amidst the editorial material of the show, Dawsonscreek.com also allowed users to listen to music featured on the show, which they could then purchase online. In fact, the Dawsonscreek.com store stocked DVDs of the show, alongside various back-to-school items such as notebooks, locker magnets, and class planners. The site also hosted links to retailers' and merchandisers' websites that had tie-ins with the series.

Though Dawsonscreek.com represents one of the more committed, complex, and sustained attempts to extend a teen entertainment brand and the teen viewing experience into the online realm, it was by no means alone in such Internet activities. In fact, almost every teen-oriented media product discussed in this book had an official, corporate-controlled website to target the technologically-oriented teen viewer. Teen-focused media websites tended to leverage on the power and recognition of established teen media brands. MTV's various early forays into the digital realm were explored in Chapter Four, and I discussed the significant success that Disney enjoyed by exploiting its broad range of tween-focused content on Disney.com in Chapter Seven. In these cases, rather than running individual websites for each entertainment property, these corporate entities established an umbrella site that served as a gateway to the various shows under its aegis. In the case of MTV.com and Disney.com, such a strategy further enhanced their corporate brand's youth-focused identity by linking it to other established teen and tween-branded content. It also brought the corporate parent's various media properties into contact online, which would more efficiently expose online visitors to alternative shows while prolonging the duration of each visit. Such strategies are vital in view of the highly cluttered nature of the Internet, and the demand fulfillment aspect of its interface.

These specific qualities of the World Wide Web have further motivated a range of other online strategies to better lure the distinct demographic segments targeted by particular websites. Tween-focused Nickelodeon, for instance, attempted to establish its online presence and explore the potential of a multi-platform distribution strategy by leveraging on its extremely popular event, the *Kids Choice Awards,* by streaming the show live over its broadband platform TurboNick. To further attract its target tween demographic, Nickelodeon also distributed promotional clips from its shows on iTunes.[19] Nickelodeon, MTV and Disney's expansion into new digital platforms represents the media industries' concern that younger audiences were shifting attention away from traditional television towards a range of new media platforms.

This concern was not restricted to niche-oriented cable networks. In fact, even broader-focused broadcast networks were exploring ways to better target, attract, and forge relationships with younger audiences. This was particularly important for FOX and the CW, both of which were targeting younger, more technologically-inclined viewers. One particular strategy that FOX adopted involved debuting the network's new television shows online to attract younger audiences. At the start of the 2008-2009 television season, FOX simultaneously — and exclusively — streamed the premieres of two of the network's series, *Fringe* (2008–) and *Terminator: The Sarah Connor Chronicles* (2008–2009) to computers in college campuses on the same night the shows premiered on television in an attempt to access the teen/young-adult college audience who were more likely to have access to computers than television sets in their dorm rooms. FOX content strategy senior VP Bill Bradford explained the decision, highlighting that a significant number of visitors to FOX.com's website originated from college-based ".edu" domains, "We talked about what we could do with colleges given the fact that we have so much traffic coming from them ... by simulstreaming *Fringe* and *Sarah Connor,* (the college students) get to see the show, and we get the increased fanbase and buzz."[20] In addition, these online college viewers also gained additional access to behind-the-scenes footage and interviews with the shows' cast, and related music videos, content not available to television viewers.

Internet Video Distribution

The potential of online webcasting and video streaming that encouraged the migration of video content to the Internet was further exploited by the launch of numerous online media delivery platforms. In the first decade of the twenty-first century, various video distribution/video-sharing portals emerged on the Internet. As these video-sharing portals have evolved, they appear to develop along two distinct trajectories. The first adheres to the distinct characteristics associated with new media — emerging as "democratic" sites hosting primarily user-generated content and embracing interactivity via a system that supports the exchange of material between many senders and recipients. The other is shaped by the characteristics and demands of traditional media — where established practices, existing business models, and familiar structures are mapped onto the new webcasting platform.

The dominant player in the video-sharing field, and one that best represents the qualities and potential of new media, is undoubtedly Google-owned YouTube. In March 2009, YouTube was the top video-clip sharing website, logging in excess of 5.2 billion views a month.[21] Launched in November 2005, YouTube represents both the potential for online video distribution as well as the intense challenges that mark the new technology. YouTube's conflicted relationship with Hollywood highlights the differences between old/analog and new/digital media, and the possibilities and problems of attempting to integrate the two traditions.

Hollywood studios and television networks initially viewed the video-sharing website as an efficient tool for promoting and branding their content. As media discussions began predicting the migration of younger viewers away from traditional media towards new media platforms, Hollywood began to view YouTube as a potentially effective ally in targeting teens and youth online. Trailers, movie clips, music videos and other related promotional and ancillary products could be made available on YouTube, ensuring that younger audiences remained aware of their entertainment options. However, this initial enthusiastic response was quickly supplanted by conflicts, many of which arose from the differing tendencies of traditional vs. new media.

Where YouTube is characterized by qualities and values aligned with new media, Hollywood remains committed to the established practices of traditional media. While YouTube is a site dominated by user-generated content, where the user's interests and needs take precedence, where viewers actively interact with the available content, and where questions of financing and profitability remain largely elusive, Hollywood's interests are founded on the creation of copyright protected content, where corporate interests dominate, and where activities are organized around controlling content for profit. Interestingly, despite YouTube's immense presence on the Internet, its global reach, and its phenomenal popularity with users, the website struggled with profitability throughout the first decade of the twenty-first century. According to unconfirmed estimates by researcher Screen Digest, YouTube generated $114 million in U.S. revenue, but earned no gross profits in 2008.[22] While viewers worldwide flocked to YouTube, uploading and watching billions of video clips a month, YouTube continued to encounter difficulties in monetizing these views. Part of the problem lay in the content available on the site. Visitors to YouTube were unlikely to pay for access to a site dominated by user-created content that included a wide assortment of home videos, filmed pranks and gimmicky clips. Advertisers were also leery of joining the site as there was little control over the kind of video content they might be associated with. YouTube faced additional challenges with another category of fan-created content that involved the rampant uploading of copyrighted material by fans "poaching" Hollywood-owned intellectual property. Hollywood responded to such infringements with a series of lawsuits, souring the nascent relationship between both parties.[23] These developments have made YouTube a potentially problematic site for both Hollywood and advertisers.

While YouTube's evolution highlights the challenges and potential of Internet video-sharing, another video-streaming platform has emerged that may hint at how Hollywood can more effectively stake a claim on the Internet. Unlike sites that host user-generated content, this alternative model offers studio-produced material only. Hulu.com, initially co-owned by media conglomerates News Corp. and NBC Universal, is one of the most successful sites engaging in such activities. Launched in April 2008, Hulu.com, a digital distribution platform, recorded 63 million total content streams in its first month of operation, placing it in tenth position on the list of top online video-streaming sites.[24] Hulu.com is distinct from YouTube in several ways. While the latter is available to a global audience, Hulu.com restricts access to most of its content to users within the United States; where YouTube is dominated by user-generated content, Hulu.com offers only professional, studio-created content. YouTube embraces the new media tradition of heightened user interactivity, bringing together multiple content producers with multiple recipients, whereas Hulu.com functions more like traditional media, where content still tends to flow in one direction from a single source towards multiple users/consumers. Hulu.com's success offers some insight into how a corporate-dominated Internet domain could evolve.

Hulu.com embraces a "department-store model" for premium entertainment and offers a case in point of how a TV-Web convergence might develop. Based on its initial success, it may also indicate what audiences may prefer, or at least accept, with Web-based video distribution. The site offers a fairly wide inventory of music videos, films and recently released broadcast television content that viewers can access on demand. In addition to the appealing independence from network or movie screening schedules, several other features make Hulu.com appealing for both viewers and advertisers. For one thing, Hulu.com offers online viewers convenient and easy access to professional content without the need for additional equipment, downloads or registrations to view its content online. To further enhance the user-experience, the site offers a search function that will direct users to alternative sites offering shows unavailable on Hulu.com. Thirdly, while content on the site is free, as it continues the television model of being advertiser-supported, viewers can watch full episodes of recently broadcast television shows in high resolution while encountering fewer and shorter advertisements than they would on television.

This latter feature also makes the site attractive to advertisers as they can still access these viewers/consumers online. Since the Hulu.com system requires users to watch the advertisements, which cannot be skipped, unlike on TiVo or other DVRs, advertisers are guaranteed exposure to the audience they have paid for. In addition, the shows on Hulu.com often rely on a single sponsor and the number of advertisements amount to approximately a quarter of what would be traditionally appear in a television broadcast. Consequently, these advertisements may have a greater impact and retention rate as there is less advertising "clutter" in the online program to dilute viewer attention, factors that advertisers are often willing to pay premium rates for. Having users register and join Hulu's social community also allows the portal to track audience demographics according to location, viewing history, and preferences while offering these registered users customized recommendations.[25] This in turn allows Hulu greater insight into its audience that can then be tailored to advertiser needs and preferences. In addition, due to the relatively new, experimental nature of the online streaming enterprise, online advertising rates, which can run to $40 to $50 per thousand viewers online,[26] are still relatively low compared to traditional television advertising rates, particularly for hit shows.

In 2008, Hulu.com earned as estimated $65 million in U.S. ad revenue and generated $12 million in gross profit, a significant figure in comparison to YouTube.[27] Hulu.com's success is due in large part to its access to valuable, professional, advertiser-friendly content. In marrying many of the key aspects of the traditional media system with new media's ability to accommodate a heightened degree of user independence, Hulu.com bodes well for the shift of professional media content to the Web, indicating both the potential popularity of such content, and its drawing power on a new platform.[28]

Other media companies have also joined the News Corp. and NBC Universal–owned Hulu.com in establishing an Internet video site. The Internet's potential was even exploited by television networks that were no longer broadcasting. In September 2008, two years after the WB network folded and its original website had been abandoned, Warner Bros. Television Group re-launched TheWB.com. In this newly resurrected form, TheWB.com, like Hulu.com, was an ad supported, video-on-demand online network.[29] Unlike Hulu.com, however, TheWB.com did not stream recently broadcast television episodes. Instead, it featured full-length episodes of classic WB signature shows including *Buffy the Vampire Slayer*. TheWB.com also streamed several short form web series targeted at the same teen demographic that the WB Network previously pursued.[30] One web series, *Sorority Forever*, consisted of two-minute episodes sponsored by clothing retailer H&M.[31]

TheWB.com's decision to stream older series alongside original web series offers yet another means by which established media companies could stake a claim on the web, while raising some other content-related issues. One main challenge lies with determining what types of content would work best with the medium. While YouTube suggests that the one-off (often gimmicky) videos have managed to generate significant audience interest with some of the most successful and popular hits gaining in excess of ten or twenty million online viewings,[32] and Hulu.com has shown that professional content remains a powerful lure, experiments with online web series have had comparatively less success, where an audience in excess of one hundred thousand viewers is considered "healthy."[33]

Attempts to create original, professional entertainment content for the web remain at the experimental stage through 2010, with a fair amount of uncertainty circulating about the nature, form and content of what constitutes a web-episode. Questions remain on various issues including episode length — the current perception is that online viewers prefer web-episodes (dubbed "webisodes") to be relatively short, lasting three to five minutes; the number of episodes that would constitute a single "season" or series; the schedule for new content — online viewers appear more impatient for updates and new material, expecting fresh content within days rather than on a weekly basis. Furthermore, while the cheap cost of producing online content may be appealing, there remain significant difficulties in finding ways to profit from such content as problems with monetization continue to be a challenge, with advertisers still reluctant to pay for seemingly paltry viewership numbers.[34]

Another issue lay in building and retaining an audience for serialized online shows. While traditional broadcast media had effectively trained its audience to commit to an established program schedule, the nature of the online platform had evolved in a different direction (demand fulfillment) with users viewing the platform as a means of accessing programming if, as, and when, they wish to watch. This has led to an on-going struggle for dominance and control between the different stakeholders, specifically the content producers, the advertisers, and the viewers/consumers/users. Problematically for the media industry and its advertisers, the traditional broadcasting model built on accessing content at regularly appointed times has not (yet) been successfully translated to the new medium.

At this point, it is impossible to predict if the YouTube or Hulu model will dominate the Internet. It is possible that there may even be enough room on the World Wide Web to accommodate both options. It is, however, worth noting that amidst YouTube and Hollywood's legal disagreements over intellectual property rights, both parties continued to recognize the potential benefits that could result if they could find a means of collaboration. In that quest, YouTube and Hollywood have actively explored ways to cultivate an effective partnership. In October 2008, YouTube announced a partnership with CBS to air a number of the network's full-length TV shows on the popular web video portal. Under the arrangement, the shows would be ad-supported with CBS selling the advertising and YouTube receiving a portion of the revenue.[35] In another attempt to represent itself as a viable and potentially profitable distribution outlet, YouTube also partnered with online content retailers iTunes and Amazon.com to allow YouTube viewers to click on links to the retailers to purchase products related to the content they were watching.[36] In YouTube's continuing evolution, it remains unclear if the site will remain primarily focused on user-generated content or whether it will tip towards adopting more professional, Hollywood produced material. These recent arrangements hint at YouTube's commitment to exploring both options.

Social Networking

Hollywood's forays into the digital realm were not restricted to creating branded websites or exploring video-distribution options. It also actively sought out alternative means of interacting with potential viewers/consumers. This interest motivated several experiments with social networking, with various tie-ins with Facebook, MySpace, and other social networking sites representing yet another way that multi-media conglomerates were attempting to access and target audiences.

Social networking sites or services first emerged on the Internet as online communities of people brought together by particular shared interests. These communities evolved into vast, global networks that users could join to interact with others. By 2005, the online social network landscape was dominated by Facebook and MySpace, two sites that allowed users to upload personal profiles, invite others to join them as friends on the site, update their profiles to inform these friends of particular developments, and track the lives of other linked friends online. Though ostensibly sites for maintaining social relationships, these systems also included features that made it particularly attractive to media companies and advertisers by allowing users to link media content to their profile, make entertainment recommendations and build communities based on specific entertainment interests. These features, coupled with its global reach, access to (occasionally detailed) user profiles, and a highly networked system, made social networking sites an ideal means of servicing Hollywood's own interests.

In July 2005, Hollywood's interest in social networking sites was confirmed when News Corp. acquired MySpace. By then, musicians had already been establishing their profiles on MySpace Music, which allowed them to make their entire discographies available to visitors in playable MP3 format. In addition to providing publicity, such profiles also allowed fans/users to directly promote these artists to their friends within the network. These features were also available for other media. In 2008, MySpace emerged as the top online destination for 15- to 24-year-olds looking for movie information.[37]

Media conglomerates targeting teens and youth could not afford to ignore the potential posed by MySpace or Facebook. Consequently, media brands with already established presences online began to link with dominant social networking sites as part of on-going attempts to attract heightened web traffic to their media sites. Hulu.com, for example, announced the launch of a social-networking/community feature, "Hulu Friends," in March 2009. The new addition "allows users to import profile information and contacts from Facebook and MySpace, as well as e-mail clients Gmail, Yahoo Mail and Hotmail," allowing users to make recommendations and view what their friends are watching.[38] This feature represented part of Hulu's efforts to encourage users to spend more time on Hulu rather than on third-party distributors. This is because Hulu receives a higher proportion of the gross advertising sold for viewers on Hulu (30 percent), as compared to viewers watching Hulu on its partner sites that are then entitled to a 10 percent cut of the advertising.[39] The longer Hulu can retain its users/viewers, the greater the amount of advertising these consumers can be exposed to.

To further access their target youth audience, The WB.com partnered with Facebook, allowing users to access their Facebook accounts to share videos and photographs via their profile pages while still on the WB site.[40] MTV's *What You're Watching* is yet another example of the media conglomerates attempts to actively and directly engage with and integrate social network activities into their evolving media content.

The Internet is not the only device gaining significance as a new means of delivering and accessing entertainment. The mobile phone is slowly emerging as a new platform for accessing entertainment content with significant projected growth rates.

Mobile Technologies

The concept of mobile entertainment is largely predicated on the growing popularity of new generation smart phone devices that allow users to surf the Internet and download data/content at enhanced speeds. Mobile phone companies have actively promoted their smart phones as devices that allow users to enjoy entertainment on the go. However, discussions exploring the intersection of entertainment access and mobile technologies remain primarily focused on potential rather than actual practice. A number of obstacles remain in the quest for "entertainment on the go."

The one area in which Hollywood has successfully made inroads into the mobile phone market lies in the music industry, with ringtones enjoying distinctive popularity. Leveraging on the pervasive integration of music onto mobile devices, music companies are joining with cell phone companies with arrangements to offer music downloads to mobile phones. Nokia, for instance, has deals with Warner Music Group, Universal Music Group International, and Sony BMG Music, allowing customers who buy select Nokia phone models to have unlimited music downloads for a year.[41] Such licensing deals have helped music companies offset significant declines in CD sales.

While music has experienced some success in the mobile phone arena, the same cannot be said for Hollywood's attempts to repurpose its visual content. As of 2006, market size, technology and cost remain significant obstacles to mobile video distribution. According to estimates, only five million people in the United States own a third-generation (3G) smart phone equipped to play video and audio of a decent quality, and of this group, only about two million users have subscribed to receive data and video packages that can cost between $10 and $25 a month.[42] Indeed, subscriber costs are a distinct impediment to mobile entertainment growth as they involve incurring additional and potentially substantial costs in addition to the monthly cell-phone bills for strictly voice communications. According to researcher eMarketer, even though the numbers of consumers accessing and watching videos on their phones are rising, the projection is that by 2009, less than 10 million subscribers will be willing to pay for premium services.[43] Finally, user behaviors and perceptions need to evolve as the extent to which consumers have embraced the mobile phone as a new entertainment platform remains unclear in 2008. According to estimates, "pure mobile entertainment — games, music and video — accounted for about $500 million last year, less than 5 percent the wireless carriers' data revenue. And the data revenue represented a small fraction of voice revenue."[44]

Despite these uncertainties, media and communications analysts remain optimistic in their predictions. According to research firm SNL Kagan, the use of mobile phones to watch video and television is projected to increase at a compound annual growth rate of nearly 23 percent, while downloads of games will increase by 13 percent, with a similar figure for music downloads between 2007 and 2017.[45] Also, as phones compatible with the ATSC-MH mobile broadcast TV standard are launched between 2010 and 2012, the use of mobile phones to download video and other forms of entertainment content are also predicted to increase significantly. Furthermore, the stakes will rise as the youth generation, specifically the generation that has never known a world without digital and mobile devices, come of age. The prediction is that this cohort "for whom a cell phone is not just a phone but an entertainment center, a dating service, a scrapbook, a virtual hangout and a fashion statement," will intensify the demand for cellular entertainment, a shift that will signify considerable profits for the corporations who can best predict and direct the evolution of this particular development.[46] In light of these possibilities, Hollywood has been actively experimenting with mobile content.

Like their response to the Internet, traditional media companies are viewing mobile technologies as yet another distribution window and promotional opportunity. This has encouraged Hollywood to focus on adapting and repurposing their existing content for the mobile phone or gadget, even as they simultaneously experiment with new content creation. FOX, for instance, has been exploring the marketing and promotional potential offered by mobile phones by assembling a small team of marketers dedicated to developing original clips and content that could be used to promote FOX's feature films over mobile phones.[47] In another strategy, FOX television's *American Idol* (2002–) allows viewers/users to download the competitors' auditions onto their mobile phones. Warner Bros. have taken more concerted steps to embrace multi-platform distribution, including creating the *Smallville Legends* mobile series, a six-episode series of short videos for mobile devices linked to the studio's television hit, *Smallville*, featuring the young adult experiences of Superman. Tracing the history of another DC Comic superhero, the Green Arrow, the series was aimed a providing a back-story for the character that appeared on *Smallville*. Yet another teen-focused brand, MTV Networks, offers original mobile shows, including *Dances from the Hood*, a ten episode hip-hop series.

ABC's *LOST* (2004–) has shown the greatest interest in the potential and challenges of mobile content creation and distribution. Where other media producers appear content with treating the mobile platform as a second-tier window, and creating content that falls below the production standards of its television relative, the creators of *LOST* insisted on direct involvement in the creation of wireless content related to the cult television show. This commitment resulted in the use of the show's actors in the mobile episodes. *The Lost Diaries* features two-to three-minute video diaries of the show's various characters offering viewers a deeper insight into these characters. In each of these instances, Hollywood remains focused on repurposing its content across yet another media platform, with the intention of deriving and profiting from yet another revenue stream. In doing so, Hollywood also benefits from further solidifying its relationship with fans and viewers.

Although these mobile episodes have yet to achieve notable exposure or reach a critical mass of viewers, these initial attempts at transferring existing content into yet another delivery platform is likely to pave the way for further cross-platform aesthetic merging. Considering the very distinctive formats of existing mobile phone technologies and devices, it may also lead to new stylistic/aesthetic developments. If Hollywood remains committed to embracing mobile technologies as yet another way of distributing and connecting with possible audiences, this is likely to impact the way visual entertainment looks, feels and sounds.

Most mobile screens are tiny, with some screens measuring no more than two inches by two inches. This places significant constraints on the aesthetic organization of the image, specifically precluding the use of long shots and demanding the adoption of tight close-up shots if the viewer is to be able to identify the image. Furthermore, the (slow) streaming rates of the existing technology, and the fact that mobile phones can only offer 15 frames of video per second in comparison to television's 30 frames per second, mean that images are prone to deterioration and blurring. This rules out the use of quick camera movements, pans or zooms. Program lengths are also severely constrained, with the average mobile episode limited to less than five minutes. These limitations place significant restrictions on the visual and narrative potential of the mobile content, most of which tend to feature highly static images, often shot in close-up to enhance visual clarity. While these aesthetic features have not filtered into mainstream media due to the very limited adoption of such content, if mobile episodes gain enough exposure to become another component of the steadily expanding multi-platform Hollywood entertainment text, there may come a time when the distinct features of this medium are integrated into mainstream content, in the tradition of music video aesthetics or online visual elements.

While some in Hollywood have focused on repurposing film and television content for the mobile platform, others have decided to approach the mobile device as a gaming platform. This has resulted in the development of alternative material that may be better suited to the technological dimensions of the devices.

Some content creators have attempted to translate branded content into games for mobile phones. Universal Studios Consumer Products Group developed a *Battlestar Galactica* single-shooter mobile game.[48] Hollywood is not alone in experimenting with such activities. Start-ups companies and businesses have begun focusing on developing games and applications for mobile phones.

Ongoing debates rage about what kinds of applications will work best with the available mobile technologies, and that will appeal most to users. Some advocate social interactivity above fancy graphics and glitzy gaming experiences. Trip Hawkins, an ex-employee of Apple who went on to establish Electronic Arts, one of the most prominent video game makers in the millennium, argues for the primacy of social interaction, claiming "content is just a means to an end, so there's something to talk about."[49] Hawkins, who then launched Digital Chocolate, a mobile phone games and applications developer, created mobile applications that tend towards the low-tech, lacking the complex graphics and involved narratives that typify online digital games. Instead, the company is committed to developing content that fosters social interaction and conversation.[50]

Interestingly, while the various experimental activities highlighted above indicate Hollywood and other media companies' interest in pursuing these alternative formats and distribution platforms, advertisers seem reluctant to migrate to the miniature screens associated with mobile technologies. In 2006, a study by research film eMarketer noted that $421 million was spent on mobile phone advertising compared to an estimated $48 billion spent on broadcast television advertising.[51] However, various Hollywood individuals remain optimistic. Leslie Moonves, chief executive of CBS Corporation revealed that the company's arrangement with mobile phone operator Verizon Wireless to distribute CBS content over its VCast network, resulted in approximately $3 million in subscription revenue in 2006, while News Corp. president and chief operating officer Peter Chernin announced that a short-form mobile series, *24: Conspiracy*, based on FOX's television show *24* (2001–), was profitable based on payments from global wireless carriers.[52] In addition to profiting from carrier payments, FOX's attempts at repurposing existing television content for the mobile platform also drew sponsorship and product integration revenues from interested advertisers.[53] To further leverage on existing content, FOX has also repurposed its regular television content for the tiny third screen, even editing down full-length regular episodes into two-minute "mobisodes" for mobile access.

Despite the potential for growth, monetization problems remain. Part of the difficulty lies in the absence of a proven, effective business model. Due to the novelty of the technology, most of the activities remain in the experimental stage, with multiple possibilities being tried and tested. This is true with business models. In one existing arrangement, wireless carriers function like cable providers, charging customers a premium on top of their existing cell phone bills for a package of video clips that can be accessed at any time. In turn, the carriers pay content providers either a flat fee for shows or a portion of the revenues. For instance, in 2006, Verizon charged $15 per month for approximately 30 "channels" offering a range of shows including weather information, and short cartoons.[54] Subscribers who pay $4.95 a month to Cingular Wireless for HBO Mobile, could access five-minute versions of episodes from several HBO original series the day after the full-length episodes are broadcast.[55] Yet another possible business model follows in the tradition of Apple's iTunes store, allowing customers greater flexibility and freedom by offering individual clips for a flat fee. This primarily benefits the carriers, however, with content providers earning limited profits.

Certainly, advertising would be one way to overcome these limitations. Unfortunately, Hollywood's attempts to exploit cell-phone/mobile delivery platforms have been undermined by a lack of advertiser interest. Advertising revenue is vital if mobile entertainment is to enjoy the kind of growth and fulfill the financial promise predicted by media scholars and researches. However, advertisers remain wary about the new medium as there is little awareness, let alone agreement, on what a mobile commercial would be. How long would a mobile commercial last when the duration of mobile entertainment content averages three minutes?

In 2009, mobile content providers remain hampered by an unclear (yet to be established) business model in this highly unstable, experimental stage of mobile technology development. Subscriptions, ad-supported free models, and a la carte content purchases are just some of the practices vying for dominance. In addition, an industry-wide standardized technical specification remains absent, resulting in the random adoption of different technical systems jockeying for position.

Hollywood's interest in digital platforms such as the Internet and mobile technologies have tended to center on its own vested interests in promoting the entertainment content it owns, and engaging viewers. Its focus has tended to center on shaping these new media into new distribution outlets for existing premium content, thereby expanding the shelf life and potential profitability of existing media products. I have examined some of the dominant ways in which Hollywood has attempted to extend its reach and influence into both arenas. Despite some success in the activities discussed above, there remain several key challenges that Hollywood will need to grapple with.

Perhaps the greatest obstacle involves finding an effective and efficient means of monetizing digital platforms. The on-going question remains how to generate profits from digital platforms, whether on the Internet or on mobile devices. Is the pay-per-download system the solution? Or would subscription services, where users pay a flat fee to access content in media libraries a more viable option? While sites such as Hulu.com suggest that the familiar advertiser-supported system may be an effective option, problems remain, including the lack of a reliable third-part arbiter of audience analytics to verify the number or demographics of viewers accessing the content/advertising. The absence of an agreed-upon standard of audience measurement is yet another gap in the system that must be plugged. Until then, it will remain difficult to determine online or mobile advertising rates.

Digital developments have resulted in a "video-on-demand" world in which viewers access content when, where and how they want it, essentially threatening the existing broadcasting-advertising model. In the traditional system, advertising rates are measured according to the number of viewers exposed to the advertisement within a scheduled broadcast, however, audience measurements have been increasingly compromised as a result of time-shifted viewing on digital video recorders, media-shifted viewing on online video websites, and the direct purchase of advertising-free content from delivery platforms such as iTunes. As Jim Kite, president-connections, research and analytics at Publicis Groupe's MediaVest notes, in the contemporary digital age, "Not everything that is counted counts, and not everything that counts can be counted."[56]

The Hulu.com model is also weakened by several other factors. While

Hulu.com and other online portals like it, attracted viewer interest by distributing television content coupled with limited or minimal advertising, this strategy may not remain sustainable in the long run as the costs of streaming a single television episode may far exceed the relatively paltry earnings from the online advertising rates. Consequently, numerous pressures are emerging to increase the amount of advertising for streamed content, a development that would make the online experience closely resemble the televisual one.[57]

Even as Hollywood attempts to transfer its entertainment content onto the Internet, these activities have provoked considerable unhappiness on the part of traditional media distributers (in particular, network affiliates and cable providers) who argue that redistributing newly broadcast content over the internet has led to a sharp drop in traditional audience numbers. Since the traditional television system is founded on profits from advertising, and the cost of advertising is measured by the audience ratings for the television shows on the traditional television platform,[58] viewers that abandon television and shift to the internet viewing platform reduce the advertising revenues for the network and affiliates broadcasting these shows and eventually affect the bottom lines of these media companies. Cable providers, who profit from monthly subscriptions from households, are also concerned that if television content is readily (and in many cases, freely) available on the Internet, households are likely to drop their cable subscriptions and migrate to the Internet. These concerns, while not yet dire, are likely to intensify as younger viewers, many of whom have come of age treating their computers as "all-in-one" entertainment devices, age into adulthood and retain these specific behaviors and attitudes.

Yet another challenge lies in the vast, uncharted nature of the Internet and mobile landscape. These qualities make it difficult for users, advertisers and the media conglomerates to navigate the web. Consequently, new content can, and often does, go unnoticed. Just as many new television shows or blockbuster movies enjoy tremendous promotional support in the form of multimedia marketing campaigns, web content will similarly need significant promotional support if they are to cut through the vast amounts of "clutter" on the Internet. Interestingly, these very features of the digital landscape may in fact reinforce the very importance of "offline," traditional media. Hollywood, with its access to established brands and reliable products, with its ability to generate "buzz" across its multiple media platforms, may be best positioned to attract the interest of media audiences and consumers and direct them online. Perhaps the ideal relationship between old and new media should be a collaborative one. Certainly, the range of mergers and acquisitions between multi-media conglomerates and new media entities that I have already mentioned, could be paving the way for such activities.

Finally, the mutual benefits that could potentially accrue from cross-media, cross-platform collaborations within a single multi-media conglomerate remain under explored (despite the preceding instances). The relationship between different media branches of a multi-media conglomerate remains largely competitive, undermining the potential for synergy. Often, the full potential of multi-textual expansion and true synergy remains reliant on a single visionary who can oversee the complex cross-media activities, and there are very few people committed enough and adequately familiar with the varied and wide-ranging media practices, who are able to do so.[59]

Developments in digital technologies have resulted in the proliferation of (new) media platforms. This, in turn, has motivated changes within the structures of continually evolving multi-media conglomerates, as well as the complex relationships and organizations across these multiple media platforms. As multi-media conglomerates remain committed to synergy and repurposing, the common practice of transferring or redistributing entertainment content across different media has expanded to include experimental forays into the Internet and mobile phones platforms.

This has led to the rise of a related range of multi-media texts that are linked in an intricately branched network. Artistically, this offers an opportunity for heightened narrative and aesthetic complexity. Commercially, there is significant potential for profit maximization, cross-promotional advertising, and repurposing. As a consequence, linear developments (whether textually in terms of narrative, or contextually, in terms of product development) are no longer the most ideal nor efficient strategies. Instead, in the digital, multi-media age, any text is only a single component of a greater range of interrelated products. This requires highly collaborative relationships across texts and between content creators and fans.

Even as the shift from analog to digital has accelerated the convergence between once separate and distinct media platforms, and media producers are actively seeking ways to expand the textual iterations of a single entertainment concept across an increasing range of interfaces and formats, these activities have also been accompanied by developments in audience and fan behavior. In the digital age, fan (inter)activity is becoming the norm, nowhere more so than with younger/teen audiences who are often viewed as the group most likely to be early adopters of technology, who are often characterized as the digital generation, and who tend to have the most amount of free time to spend on developing and pursuing their entertainment interests. As Jenkins asserts, "convergence represents a cultural shift as consumers are encouraged to seek out new information and make connections among dispersed media content."[60] Although Jenkins is referencing a larger cultural development rather than discussing teens in particular, his comment is no less relevant to the events and demographic I have focused on in this chapter, and this book as a whole.

In addition to instigating the development of increasingly complex and interconnected creative and industrial activities, the rise of new media technologies and devices has also affected viewership patterns, changing the ways in which audiences/consumers access, experience, and interact with entertainment media. Digital video recorders, online streaming, the ability to purchase content from online media "stores" have given audiences a greater sense of independence and agency. Viewers engaging in deferred viewing have motivated the need for new ratings measurements, forcing the development of Nielsen's commercial ratings systems, which measure the number of viewers watching an advertisement rather than the television show, and C3 ratings, a measure that counts viewers who watch a show they recorded on their DVRs within three days of its broadcast.

These developments are inextricably linked to younger audiences' low tolerance for advertising. While still fairly avid consumers of entertainment content, teen and tween viewers have increasing access to technologies that allow them to efficiently avoid commercial messages. This has prompted youth-focused advertiser-supported entertainment platforms to adopt a range of advertising strategies to counter these challenges. These include heightened network and advertiser collaborations in the development of advertisements, such as the CW's "content wraps" that involve mini-narratives featuring stars from the network's television series promoting featured products across several ad segments, and "cwingers" that, as described at the beginning of this chapter, feature advertising that bridges both the television and online platforms. Writing in 2001, a media analyst noted in *Broadcasting and Cable*, "We've already seen a blurring of the lines between providing information and advertising.... Advertisers and programmers are going to have to blur those lines even further in the future."[61] By 2009, content creators were increasingly accommodating the demands of advertisers, integrating commercial messages/tie-ins into the editorial content. Even as evolving technological devices such as the DVR, iTunes, and online web-casters such as Hulu.com have given viewers increasing means of avoiding advertising, the growing collaboration between the media and Madison Avenue have resulted in activities that hint at the ever increasing commercialization of everyday life in the media. Where the latter is concerned, many of the activities hold an "ironic echo of earlier broadcast advertising practices in the new world of digital television, including the return of single sponsorship, the integration of commercial and program, and the reprise of the celebrity pitch man."[62]

The fact remains that these newly emerging media platforms pose a challenge for Hollywood because the potential of, and the means of profiting from, these technologies, still remain unclear and unresolved at this point. While Hollywood has become extremely efficient in exploiting the established and familiar forms of traditional media, the practices and structures that the media industries have adopted in response to new media, have met with varying degrees of success. The digital terrain is still being fought over. In this unstable, volatile, experimental period, it remains to be seen if the Internet will be able to accommodate both the amateur, grainy, personally created video clips alongside the premium, commercially-oriented studio produced content, or whether one form will dominate the other. Will the rise of media-conglomerate-backed online video streaming sites ultimately relegate amateur video clips to the margins of the World Wide Web? Can low-cost, "webisodes" find and maintain an audience on the Internet? Or will commercial interests encroach on and ultimately colonize the new digital frontier? Is the Internet an "open system" in which anyone can participate and contribute, or will it eventually morph into a "closed system" controlled, or at least dominated, by powerful gatekeepers? These questions remain unresolved.

Conclusion

When the teen demographic reemerged as a valuable audience and consumer market in the late 1990s, Hollywood's evolution into a vertically and horizontally integrated, multi-media–oriented entertainment industry dominated by conglomerates with an increasingly global focus allowed it to embrace a range of industrial, economic and textual practices to target and profit from the demographic in significantly more efficient ways. Leading into the new millennium, the rising dominance of digital technologies and an evolving youth audience further provoked the dominant corporate Hollywood players to experiment with alternative strategies to ensure their continued cultural and commercial supremacy.

This book has focused primarily on examining how larger, macro forces, including industrial structures, technological changes, and social and cultural shifts, have shaped and transformed the nature, form, and content of the millennial teen and tween entertainment text. In these concluding pages, I summarize the main issues and comment on how this study redefines our understanding of the relationship between popular culture and economics; between text and industrial structure; and between industrial structure and market(place). The primary interest here lies in highlighting how this study offers an alternative, or evolving, framework through which teen texts and teen culture in general can be understood, and considering what this implies for our greater understanding of popular and commercial culture, in particular, teen entertainment media's role with regard to the development of larger cultural trends, the modification of consumer and social identity, and the changing structure and nature of the entertainment industries.

As explored in the preceding chapters, millennial youth-focused entertainment content is characterized by a number of distinct and notable characteristics. They include

- the intensive exploitation of multimedia synergies in the wake of the heightened media conglomeration of the 1990s;
- the increasing importance of branding as a promotional activity, resulting in the emergence of the branded teen text;
- the evolution of the multi-media teen-branded personality who easily and consistently "crossed-over" between different media;
- the intensification of stylistic and aesthetic convergence across the

219

range of multi-media, marked by the collapsing boundaries between film, television, music and music-video texts, and new media; and,
- the turn towards postmodern "hyper-"intertextuality, indicated by a notable degree of interaction and cross-referencing across an expanding range of related teen media content.

Multimedia Synergies in the Wake of Multi-Media Conglomeration

The case studies in this book have focused on several specific teen/tween-oriented (multi-)media sites: MTV Networks, the WB, the CW, Dimension Films and the Disney Channel. Every one of these media entities is a component of a larger multi-media corporation. Viacom owns MTV Networks; the WB television network was part of AOL Time Warner; the CW that emerged out of the WB and UPN television merger belonged to two media behemoths, Time Warner and Viacom-linked CBS Television. Both Dimension Films and the Disney Channel share the same corporate parent, The Disney Company.

Leading into the millennium, these corporations have been actively engaged in exploiting their multi-media holdings in the quest for enhanced synergy, nowhere more so than in the arena of teen-focused media entertainment. In every instance, teen media, whether they originated on MTV's or Disney's cable network, or the WB's television network, or from Dimension's studios, have consistently pursued a highly complex, extended, shelf life across a range of media platforms. Millennial teen and tween culture almost never exists in a single medium. Rather, each entertainment concept evolves as a network of interconnected texts, existing often simultaneously in music, film, television, and online formats. This type of networking can take two slightly different forms. Some t(w)een media matrixes emerge out of cross-corporate, mutually beneficial interactions, as occurred in the heightened intertextual exchanges between the Kevin Williamson–created television series *Dawson's Creek* on AOL Time Warner's WB network and Disney-owned Dimension Film's *Scream* trilogy, written by Kevin Williamson, or the cross-industry tie-ups between Dimension's teen–sci-fi film *The Faculty* and youth-clothing brand Tommy Hilfiger. Others are directed by strictly organized interactions between the multi-media arms of the corporate parent. Disney's carefully choreographed repurposing of its *High School Musical* franchise across music, television, film, online, and live theatre, among other platforms, is a perfect example of the latter instance. While multi-media corporations have long been focused on enhancing synergy, it is in the realm of teen and tween entertainment that these activities appear most intense.

The Branded T(w)een Text

These synergistic, multi-media activities have evolved alongside the rise of the branded t(w)een text. In a complicated, increasingly multi-media entertainment reality, where the term "clutter" is constantly evoked to describe the state of the contemporary popular culture world, establishing a brand that can effectively represent the specific qualities of a range of texts, attract the attention of the targeted demographic, and cut through the distractions offered by other products, has become particularly valuable.

In the world of millennial t(w)een commercial entertainment, the practice of branding has been applied to entertainment sites (the WB, MTV, the Disney Channel), to entertainment texts/franchises (*Buffy the Vampire Slayer*, *Hannah Montana*), and to individual stars or acts (*Buffy* star Sarah Michelle Gellar was a teen brand in the late 1990s, as are *Hannah Montana*'s Miley Cyrus and *High School Musical*'s Zac Efron in the 2000s). Each of these brands was clearly and directly associated with an array of teen- and/or tween-related texts and products. Each guaranteed a distinctive, carefully shaped and controlled range of values, experiences, and perspectives that were specifically relevant and appealing to its target demographic. Although all these brands targeted teens and tweens, each made specific efforts to distinguish itself from the others. For instance, MTV in the millennium, shaped itself as the arbiter of the urban, multi-racial, edgy and ultramodern youth, embracing programming and content that reflect these qualities and attract that demographic. In contrast, the WB targeted the suburban, idealistic, largely white, middle class teen, emphasizing teen-angst and the challenges of young adulthood through a sincere, sympathetic, and largely realist lens. The Disney Channel, in targeting a younger tween demographic explored the more innocent desires and anxieties of tween-hood.

In many instances, these corporate brands were built on associations with specific branded media texts. MTV's programming, including *Spring Break* and *Undressed*, reflected a hedonistic commitment to fun, freedom, independence and a heightened sexuality associated with the older teen/college lifestyle. The WB's white, idealistic, suburban teen brand was founded in part via the network's association with teen television shows including *Buffy the Vampire Slayer* and *Dawson's Creek* among others, which featured older teenage characters who largely conformed to the network's target teen audience. Buffy, Dawson and their friends all live in primarily white suburbs, and embrace liberal values in confronting difficult challenges ranging from issues of sexual identity, dysfunctional family dynamics, mental illness, to substance abuse, displaying an active commitment to doing the right thing along the way. In contrast, the Disney Channel's programming, such as *Hannah Montana* and *Camp Rock*, centered on younger teens and tweens whose adventures and exploits tended towards the more innocent and naïve, including disagreements between good friends, and the challenges of peer pressure.

These commitments to branding were extended to include the teen and tween stars and personalities of the period, many of whom established distinctive personas that were featured across a range of multi-media texts and content.

The Multi-Media Teen-Branded Star/Personality

Teen and tween stars in the millennium have carefully cultivated brands and identities that extend across a range of media. The simultaneity of such cross-media extensions in this particular period distinguish these activities from previous eras, where a star's shift across media platforms tended to take place across years, with no connections or intersections between their various media projects. Millennial teen culture, in contrast, has evolved a highly efficient strategy to leverage on the popularity and success of any teen star and text by repurposing them across every possible media platform. Such activities are particularly popular if they occur within a media conglomerate's horizontally diversified holdings.

To that end, in 2002, then-teen singer Britney Spears, almost a mainstay on MTV between 1998 and 2009, starred in *Crossroads*, a film co-produced by MTV Films and Filmco, a newly-launched arm of Spears' record label, Zomba. Spears, Zomba and MTV actively collaborated on publicizing and promoting the film, its soundtrack and music videos, and other Spears-related paraphernalia on MTV, ensuring that the Spears brand extended across music, television, and film. Seven years later, Disney leveraged its tween star Miley Cyrus across Disney's multi-media holdings. Between 2006 and 2009, Cyrus starred in the Disney Channel's *Hannah Montana* television series, the singer/actress also released two series soundtracks and several original albums, all of which Cyrus promoted in several live-performances at Disneyland which were then broadcast on the cable channel. Cyrus' 2007–2008 *Hannah Montana* live concert tour was filmed and released as a 3-D feature film in 2008, and *Hannah Montana: The Movie*, a feature film version of her television series was released in 2009, even while episodes of the TV series were being cablecast on the Disney Channel. While these two examples may represent some of the most intense and committed activities of the period, many of the millennial teen stars enjoyed such cross-media career opportunities.

Millennial, Postmodern, Multi-Media Teen Entertainment Content

The commitment to synergy motivated by the multi-media organization of the entertainment industry, coupled with the intent cross-media repurposing of teen entertainment stars and their content, have significantly reshaped the nature, form and content of the teen text. Prior to these developments, it was possible, and instructive to adopt a medium-specific focus when examining commercial teen culture. In previous teen cycles, the format and platform boundaries between distinct teen texts were fairly clear and identifiable. Even with popular teen franchises that evolved across formats, from novels, to television, to film (such as the *Gidget* franchise), there remained a hierarchy of evolution in which each text existed largely independently of the others. In the millennium, this is no longer the case. In the contemporary context, teen/tween franchises often consist of highly interlinked multi-media texts. In fact, the traditional notion of the term "text," with its connotations of singularity, of clear textual boundaries, and a contained medium and format, no longer accurately describes the contemporary teen entertainment experience. In the millennium, the teen "text" more often refers to a single concept that traverses different platforms and exists in multiple media formats across a range of interconnected products.

Furthermore, in addition to exploiting a media concept across the conglomerate's traditional media holdings, the cultivation of the youth market in the late 1990s and 2000s has evolved alongside Hollywood's attempts to lay the foundation for new entertainment platforms such as digital media and other innovative distribution technologies, including webcasting and mobile entertainment. These present even more opportunities for entertainment texts to expand into other media. As technologies have continued to evolve and change, the media industries have continued to experiment with and try to "colonize" the new digital media platforms, thereby extending the practices, values and protocols they have previously embraced within traditional media into the new emerging media. These new media technologies have given traditional media conglomerates potential new revenue windows and enhanced opportunities for creativity. In addition to (re)shaping the nature, form, and content of the multimedia texts themselves, many of the industrial, technological, and cultural developments have transformed how t(w)eens define and experience entertainment media in various ways.

When an entertainment concept or entity exists simultaneously as (or in) a film, a television show, soundtracks, a website, in episodes available on mobile devices, in novelizations, and in potentially other formats, it becomes increasingly difficult to accurately draw the media boundaries that contain such a text. Any attempts at medium-specific definitions are further undermined by the heightened degree of stylistic and aesthetic exchange and cross-adoptions that have also been taking place. Millennial teen culture is increasingly characterized by stylistic and narrative content that draws from and reflects a wide range of media forms. The teen slasher genre, with narrative and aesthetic conventions that were once primarily associated with the film medium, is now common on television, and in music videos, while the stylized camera work, disjointed narrative and frenetic editing techniques once typical of music videos are apparent in both film and television shows. The visual formats of online websites have infiltrated some television shows, even as behaviors and activities previously associated with online sites, such as social networks, are being actively integrated into the televisual experience. As such, any attempt to fully explore the range, impact, organization and function of the millennial teen text, must acknowledge the complexities of the contemporary intertext.

These practices and qualities have intensified through the first decade of the new millennium, with many of these activities shifting beyond the confines of teen/tween culture to characterize popular culture in general. This larger trend has already received some attention. In *Convergence Culture*, Henry Jenkins discusses the rise of "transmedia entertainment," a situation in which industrial evolutions, technological developments and changing viewer/consumer behavior have motivated the emergence of media texts that deliberately transcend the boundaries of any single medium to emerge as highly complex, multimedia–oriented, interlinked entities.[1] Where Jenkins has adopted a broader examination of popular culture in general, my focus has primarily addressed youth/teen millennial culture. Certainly, many of the events and case studies discussed in this book reflect the increasing trend towards transmedia entertainment. In fact, it is within millennial youth culture that the trends and characteristics of transmedia entertainment identified by Jenkins have intensified and gained increasing momentum. At the level of content, these transmedia texts are characterized by new storytelling techniques and structures that consciously and deliberately extend across a range of media. Industrially, the transmedia trend reflects the exigencies of corporations focused on fully benefiting from the synergistic opportunities of their multi-media configurations. Culturally, the transmedia movement has encouraged the emergence of media consumers/audiences who are developing increasingly sophisticated literacies across a wide range of intersecting media platforms.

T(w)een Media in the Digital Age

In the contemporary digital media age, when television shows, films, music videos, and online sites intersect and where all these texts can be accessed on a single screen, traditional definitions of different media platforms are becoming redundant. For instance, conventional definitions of the television universe used to distinguish between broadcast networks and cable channels. In the millennium, the distinction between the two is disappearing. The collapsing boundaries between network and cable has been motivated by the larger context of convergence and the evolving expectations and perspectives of audiences, particularly younger audiences who, having grown up with cable channels including Disney, Nickelodeon, and MTV, no longer make distinctions between broadcast and cable networks. Unlike older viewers who came of age in the era of broadcast television, for whom the familiar television season and schedule have become part of the ritualized television experience, the teen and tween viewing experience is no longer organized or constrained by traditional television schedules. This has encouraged the broadcast and cable networks to adopt programming activities, content, and schedules that are bringing them closer to each other. Where broadcast networks were once the sole outlets that premiered original television series, while cable outlets acquired the rights to these series for secondary runs, by the late 1990s, cable outlets were producing their own original series, and many were approaching the quality of broadcast series. Free of the scheduling traditions of the broadcast networks, cable channels experimented with programming schedules that included shorter series that rejected the network practices of reruns and repeats—a strategy that broadcast networks have begun to adopt in their attempt to halt the growing audience attrition they have been suffering. As a result, broadcast networks have begun to replicate cable scheduling strategies, including screening popular series without reruns, and acquiring more original series to fill slots originally filled by repeat screenings.

In 2009, new experiments may further erode the distinctions between television and online delivery platforms. Time Warner's TV Everywhere and Comcasts' Project Infinity are two initiatives that would make cable content available to broadband subscribers. Both TV Everywhere and Project Infinity offer the opportunity to stream entire networks online, a development that would further complicate and potentially change the traditional definition, experience and cultural significance of television in the future. If full networks can be streamed online, what then becomes of (any remaining) distinctions between television and the Internet, between network and cable, between broadcast and webcast? These distinctions are unlikely to be restricted to the television and Internet industries and are likely to ripple through the other media formats as well.

Another significant impact that the digital shift has had on audience behaviors and expectations lies in a growing rejection of corporate control over where, when and how entertainment is accessed and enjoyed. Since 2000, digital technologies have offered viewers a growing degree of independence from corporate controlled entertainment schedules and platform limitations, younger viewers have embraced the availability of, and access to, new entertainment delivery platforms that allow them to find and consume entertainment as and when they want it.

The Rise of a Global T(w)een Media Culture?

Even as we consider the convergence of once-distinct media formats, and acknowledge the challenges posed by new technologies to both the media industries and advertisers, we must also recognize new media's ability to transcend geographical space and national boundaries to lay the foundation for a possible global market and culture. Digital/New technologies have certainly accelerated the emergence of a global youth media culture. Accessible globally, and thus offering access to a global audience/market, online sites and delivery platforms including YouTube and social networks such as Facebook and MySpace can make media content available to anyone and everyone with broadband Internet access, regardless of where they are located in the world.[2] The Internet's networked system stretches across the globe, allowing people all over the world to experience cultural phenomena simultaneously. This development has significant consequences for an entire host of communications-related issues that deserve further exploration. For instance, the ease of transcending national or geographical boundaries essentially forces a reconsideration of any traditional notions of the "public sphere," of conventional notions and practices of distribution, whether spatial or temporal, and complicating issues of national or community cultures, among many other complex concerns.

In considering the emergence of a global t(w)een media culture, this book's focus on millennial Hollywood t(w)een entertainment is particularly important because it is American t(w)een media that is having a significant impact globally — a situation brought about by the American media conglomerates' continuing expansion internationally, amidst the rise of new media technologies that offer individuals, particularly teens, easy access to all forms of American media texts and culture. Historically, past cycles of teen culture were largely conceptualized and targeted to a national, "local" North American market. I am not suggesting that these earlier teen products did not reach an international audience, rather that they were not necessarily or consciously constructed with a global audience in mind. Previously, when American media products traveled to other parts of the world, they were imported by locally owned distributors and exhibitors.

Over the years, however, the American culture industries evolved into multi-national corporate entities that could efficiently distribute teen culture across national borders, expanding the global possibilities, profitabilities and influence of American teen culture. Through the 1990s and into the twenty-first century, a handful of American-based, American-owned multi-national multi-media corporations began amassing increased global power and influence. MTV's global expansion has enabled its emergence as the international arbiter of youth culture. Similarly, music corporations such as the internationally based Zomba Music Group are well positioned to launch their artists globally, so that teens worldwide can access the same products simultaneously. Disney's international influence, via its global cable network, and its popular theme parks allows the conglomerate to influence and shape the media and consumer habits of children the world over. The continual merging of media institutions, accompanied by the increasing turn towards global cultural exchange and international cultural flows—much of its aided by the rise of the borderless World Wide Web—has ushered in an era in which cultural texts and their representations of American teen culture have become available to international audiences.

These developments suggest that we are on our way to witnessing the rise of a global teen culture that embraces and shares a host of similar media products. The American culture industries' strategies with regard to teen culture raise some interesting implications regarding the politics of narrowcasting and niche targeting a global teen market. The hegemonic impact of these American media products is already unavoidable and will inevitably grow stronger. The distribution of these texts around the world places native cultures and non–U.S. values and interests at risk. As John Tomlinson notes, a global culture threatens "native" cultures because it involves "the simultaneous penetration of local worlds by distant forces, and the dislodging of everyday meanings from their 'anchors' in the local environment."[3] As American teen culture achieves global influence, Western, capitalist values and ideologies will gain ever-increasing influence over entire generations of youth, supplanting the native values of their national cultures. This may lead (and perhaps already has led) to the emergence of generations of teens world-wide that have more in common, culturally, with their North American peers, in terms of the media they consume, the technology they use, and the ideas/ideologies they are exposed to, regardless of geographical location, than they might have in common with other generational segments in their own cultures. Such a development is likely to have significant implications for the evolving nature of local and global cultures in the future.

When we consider the impact of commercial American t(w)een culture on its (global) audience, we must recognize that the multi-media conglomerates producing most of this media culture are driven by, and respond to, primarily commercial and marketplace imperatives. The media industries are targeting teens in response to industry and advertiser interests and demands rather than out of any altruistic motivation to service the global teen audiences' entertainment needs. Consequently, these entertainment conglomerates largely offer very specific inscriptions of teen/youth oriented programming that overwhelmingly emphasize Western, capitalist, middle-class values and ideologies. These American t(w)een texts also reflect industry-oriented values that emphasize capitalism and consumerism. As these texts will inevitably exercise some influence on their audiences, we need to pay considerably more attention than we have so far on how dominant industrial and advertisers' interests shape textual content. The observations and arguments expressed in this project provide a preliminary overview of the key developments that will impact teen culture in the twenty-first century.

This project began as an attempt to look beyond the more traditional approaches to studying youth culture that emphasize issues of representation, effects and reception concerns, and media-specific perspectives. While these other approaches remain relevant and continue to reveal valuable and interesting insights into teen and tween media culture, a series of industrial, technological, social and cultural developments emerged in the late 1990s and into the millennium prompted the need for a broader multi-media view of how the specific exigencies of the contemporary era have shaped and revised the nature, form, and content of the millennial youth entertainment text.

It may be argued that the activities and textual qualities characteristic of millennial teen media may not, in fact, be distinctly teen-oriented but could be applied to almost all media experiences/texts/audiences within the stipulated period. Far from being a flaw, this is an indication of the wider relevance of this study. Even as I emphasize the need to adopt a narrower, more detailed focus that privileges specificity and in-depth analysis over broader media generalizations, the contributions of this study ultimately extend beyond the boundaries of teen culture. The studies offered here stand as preliminary investigations into a phase of Hollywood's youth entertainment history, and indeed in the history of Hollywood itself, that is likely to continue changing and evolving in significant ways. While youth culture remains only a small segment of Hollywood's media activities, the practices and developments in this area are likely to have significant consequences, for as each generation of teenagers has aged out of the demographic category, they take with them the kinds of cross-media entertainment demands, expectations, behaviors and perspectives that they developed in their youth. This has distinct implications for how the media industries will have to evolve and accommodate these new consumption activities.

The Road Ahead...

In the third quarter of 2008, the United States experienced a series of financial crises that plunged the country into a recession that continued well into 2009 and sparked off predictions of a potentially long-term global economic slowdown. National and international discourses described the situation in sometimes alarmist terms, making references to "another Great Depression."[4] Certainly, this event had significant impact on the media industries. By the first quarter of 2009, dire predictions were followed by announcements that the media conglomerates were suffering notable losses.[5] Amidst these developments, the commonly held belief was that the youth/teen market would be the silver lining, as teens and tweens have been viewed historically as a recession-proof demographic since they were the one consumer segment that could and often did spend almost all their disposable income. While this view was undermined by an *Advertising Age* report that suggested that even teens were becoming increasingly aware of, and concerned by the financial crisis, and were shifting their consumer activities accordingly, the report did have positive news for Hollywood, for even as t(w)eens were restricting their spending on retail products and merchandise, they remained dominant and committed consumers of Hollywood entertainment content.[6] Despite claims that teens were "cutting back on ... excursions to movies" among other activities,[7] reports from the box-office offer a different view. In November 2008, *Twilight*, a teen vampire romance that cost approximately $37 million to produce, topped the box-office earning close to $70 million its opening weekend, and had a total domestic gross in excess of $190 million at the end of its theatrical run.[8] In April 2009, *17 Again*, starring teen star Zac Efron, with a $20 million production budget, debuted at number 1 with an opening gross of $23 million, and more than doubled the figure in its first two weeks of release.[9] A week later, *Hannah Montana: The Movie*, Disney's film spin-off of its Disney Channel hit cable series that cost an estimated $35 million, had a $32 million opening weekend and grossed over $70 million in its first three weeks of release.[10] In addition, the percentage of teen spending on video games in April 2009 increased to 8 percent from 7 percent a year ago. While music and DVD spending increased to 11 percent of teens budgets from 8 percent the year before.[11] In the light of the economic situation, where spending on entertainment was being reduced in most other market demographics, the teen demographic's continuing consumption of entertainment media, and their willingness to spend, continue to make them a vital market for Hollywood.

Chapter Notes

Preface

1. Existing studies focused on teen media representations include David Considine, *The Cinema of Adolescence* (North Carolina: McFarland, 1985); Timothy Shary, *Generation Multiplex: The Image of Youth in Contemporary American Cinema* (Austin: University of Texas Press, 2002). Ethnographic or anthropological considerations of teenagers and the media include E. Graham McKinley, *Beverly Hills, 90210: Television, Gender, and Identity* (Philadelphia: University of Pennsylvania Press, 1997).

2. See Ben Bagdikian, *The Media Monopoly*, 5d ed. (Boston: Beacon Press, 1997); David Croteau and William Hoynes, *The Business of the Media: Corporate Media and the Public Interest* (Thousand Oaks, California: Pine Forge Press, 2001).

3. Thomas Doherty, *Teenagers and Teenpics: The Juvenilization of American Movies in the 1950s* (Boston: Unwin Hyman, 1988).

4. Jack Banks, *Monopoly Television: MTV's Quest to Control the Music* (Colorado: Westview Press, 1997).

5. Glyn Davis and Kay Dickinson, ed., *Teen TV: Genre, Consumption and Identity* (London: British Film Institute, 2004).

Introduction

1. When *Camp Rock* was released, the three members of the Jonas Brothers were between 15 and 20 years of age.

2. Rick Kissell, "Kids Line Up for *Camp Rock*," *Variety*, 22 June 2008. <http://www.variety.com/article/VR1117987906.html?categoryid=14&cs=1> (Accessed 27 June 2008); Edward Wyatt, "Summer Advisory: A Jonas Front Looms," *The New York Times*, 17 June 2008. <http://www.nytimes.com/2008/06/17/arts/television/17jona.html?scp=1&sq=%22Summer%20advisory:%20A%20jonas%20front%20looms%22&st=cse> (Accessed 23 June 2008).

3. Douglas Gomery and Robert C. Allen, *Film History: Theory and Practice* (New York: McGraw-Hill, 1985), 16.

4. Jon Lewis, *The Road to Romance and Ruin: Teen Films and Youth Culture* (New York: Routledge, 1992), 77.

5. William Healy, *The Individual Delinquent* (Boston: Little, Brown, 1915); William H. Short, *A Generation of Motion Pictures* (New York: The National Committee for the Study of Social Values in Motion Pictures, 1928. Reprint New York: Garland Publishing, 1978); William M. Seabury, *The Public and the Motion Picture Industry* (New York: Macmillan, 1926); William M. Seabury, *Motion Picture Problems* (New York: Arondale Press, 1929. Reprint New York: Arno Press, 1978).

6. Susan J. Douglas, *Where the Girls Are: Growing Up Female with the Mass Media* (New York: Times Books, 1994).

7. E. Graham, McKinley, *Beverly Hills, 90210: Television, Gender, and Identity* (Philadelphia: University of Pennsylvania Press, 1997).

8. Stuart Hall and Paddy Whannel, "The Young Audience," in *On Record: Rock, Pop and the Written Word*, ed. Simon Frith and Andrew Goodwin (New York: Pantheon, 1990), 27–37; Dick Hebdidge, *Subculture: The Meaning of Style* (London: Methuen, 1979); Simon Frith, *Sound Effects: Youth Leisure and the Politics of Rock n' Roll* (New York: Pantheon, 1981); Sarah Thornton, *Club Cultures. Music, Media and Subcultural Capital* (Hanover and London: Wesleyan University Press, 1996).

9. Lewis, *The Road to Romance and Ruin*, 77.

10. Hall and Whannel, "The Young Audience," 29.

11. Considine, *The Cinema of Adolescence*; Lewis, *The Road to Romance and Ruin*; Shary, *Generation Multiplex*.

12. Lewis, *The Road to Romance and Ruin*, 2.

13. Thomas Doherty, *Teenagers and Teenpics: The Juvenilization of American Movies in the 1950s* (Boston: Unwin Hyman, 1988).

14. Justin Wyatt, *High Concept: Movies & Marketing in Hollywood* (Austin: University of Texas Press, 1994).

15. See Thomas Schatz, "The Return of the Hollywood Studio System," in *Conglomerates and the Media*, ed. Erik Barnouw, et al. (New York: The New Press, 1997), 73–106; Bagdikian,

The Media Monopoly; Robert McChesney, "The Political Economy of Global Communication," in *Capitalism and the Information Age: The Political Economy of the Global Communication Revolution*, ed. Robert McChesney, Ellen Wood and John Foster (New York: Monthly Review Press, 1998), 1–26.

16. See Bagdikian, *The Media Monopoly*; McChesney, "The Political Economy of Global Communication"; Edward S. Herman and Noam Chomsky, *Manufacturing Consent: The Political Economy of the Mass Media* (New York: Pantheon, 1988).

17. Bagdikian, *The Media Monopoly*; McChesney, "The Political Economy of Global Communication"; Herman, and Chomsky, *Manufacturing Consent: The Political Economy of the Mass Media*.

Chapter One

1. Bruce Orwall, "Teen Tidal Wave Hits Hollywood in the Head," *The Toronto Star*, 19 December 1997, sec. D.

2. *Billboard*'s 25 January 1997 issue featured a number of articles tracing how teenagers have been marginalized and ignored by the major music labels and discussing the contemporary challenges of targeting the current cohort. See "Pop Music's Teen Market: The Jilted Generation?" *Billboard*, 25 January 1997, 1+; Jimi LaLumia, "Music Biz Is Ignoring Vital Teen Mkt," *Billboard*, 25 January 1997, 2.

3. Tom Bierbaum, "The WB's Getting the Girls," *Variety*, 2–8 November 1998, 30+.

4. Valerie Burgher, "The Fifth Network's Second Coming," *AdWeek: TV UPFRONT*, 2 June 1997, 42–44. The WB network had primarily targeted the younger 18–34 demographic since its launch in 1995, but in 1997, the network revised its target audience by deliberately and overtly targeting a younger range of viewers within the 12–34 demographic. The specific details of this shift are discussed in Chapter Six.

5. Jim Farber, "Young, Rich and Hanson: Bubblegum Set Is Popping with Teen Idol Wanna-bes," *New York Daily News*, 28 August 1997, 59.

6. Melinda Newman, "The Beat: In an Anything-Goes Year, Girl Power Sticks, Vets Score, Teens Are Triumphant," *Billboard*, 27 December 1997, 20.

7. Noreen O'Leary, "The Boom Tube," *Adweek*, 18 May 1998, 44–52.

8. Valerie Block, "The WB Gets Set to Leapfrog Rivals," *Crain's New York Business*, 31 August 1998, 4; Jefferson Graham, "WB and Teen-agers Make a Most Felicitous Combination," *USA Today*, 29 September 1998, sec. D.

9. Leonard Klady, "Studios Focus on Teen Stream," *Variety*, 13–19 January 1997, 11–12.; Orwall, "Teen Tidal Wave Hits Hollywood in the Head," sec. D.; Annette Cardwell, "Generation Next: Recent Hits Have Studios Screaming for More Teen Flicks," *The Boston Herald*, 23 September 1998, 55.

10. Peter Zollo, *Wise Up to Teens. Insights into Marketing and Advertising to Teenagers*, 2d ed. (New York: New Strategist Publications, Inc., 1999), 6.

11. Lawrie Mifflin, "Where Young Viewers Go (and Ads Follow)," *The New York Times*, 8 September 1998, sec. E.

12. Marilyn Beck and Stacey Jenel Smith, "Movies for Teen-agers Dwindle with Market," *The Times-Picayune* (New Orleans, LA), 2 July 1995, sec. A.

13. Quoted in Jill Brooke, "Forth Estate: Girl Power," *Adweek*, 2 February 1998, 19.

14. It is worth remembering that the late '80s and early '90s was the era of Generation X. At the time, advertisers, the media and the culture industries were primarily focused upon this narrow demographic of college-age (as opposed to teenage) young adults who were also labeled the "Slacker" generation.

15. See Beck and Smith, "Movies for Teen-Agers Dwindle with Market," sec. A; Paul Verna, "Retailers See Signs of Hope for Teen Music," *Billboard*, 22 March 1997, 1+; Peter Watrous, "Pop View: White Singers + Black Style = Pop Bonanza," *The New York Times*, 11 March 1990, sec. 2.

16. Teenagers reportedly returned to theatres to watch the film multiple times. See Brooke, "Forth Estate: Girl Power," 18.

17. Brooke, "Fourth Estate: Girl Power," 22.

18. See Doherty, *Teenagers and Teenpics*; Douglas, *Where the Girls Are*; Kelly Schrum, "'Teena Means Business': Teenage Girls' Culture and Seventeen Magazine, 1944–1950," *Delinquents and Debutantes: Twentieth Century American Girls' Cultures*, ed. Sherrie Innes (New York and London: New York University Press, 1998), 134–163. Doherty argues that the first group of teenagers to become self aware of their status and market significance emerged in the 1950s, a claim that Douglas agrees with, while Schrum maintains that teenagers were viewed as a distinct and separate consumer market as early as the 1940s.

19. David K. Foot with Daniel Stoffman, *Boom Bust & Echo 2000. Profiting from the Demographic Shift in the New Millennium* (Toronto: MacFarlane Walter & Ross, 1998), 2.

20. Douglas, *Where the Girls Are*, 22.

21. Doherty, *Teenagers and Teenpics*, 45.

22. Foot, *Boom Bust & Echo*, 3.

23. Zollo, *Wise Up to Teens*, 19.

24. Douglas, *Where the Girls Are*, 23.

25. Between 1939 and 1945, federal expenditures as a result of wartime production rose from

$8.8 billion to $100 billion. During the same period, increased employment opportunities and rising wages meant that men, women and children enjoyed enhanced consumer purchasing power. Schrum, "'Teena Means Business,'" 135. See also, George Thomas Kurian, *Datapedia of the United States, 1790–2000* (Lanham, MD: Bernan, 1994), 13–14; John Blum, *V Was for Victory: Politics and American Culture During World War II* (New York: Harcourt Brace Jovanovich, 1976), 91–92; Susan Hartmann, *The Home Front and Beyond: American Women in the 1940s* (Boston: Twayne, 1982), 4; Maureen Honey, *Creating Rosie the Riveter: Class, Gender, and Propaganda During World War II* (Amhurst: University of Massachusetts Press, 1984), 54–59.

26. Schrum, "Teena Means Business," 135.

27. Robin Pogrebin, "The Media Business: Time, Inc.'s Take on Teen-agers," *The New York Times,* 8 January 1998. <http://www.nytimes.com/1998/01/08/business/media-business-times-take-teen-agers-yes-house-that-luce-built-girls-magazine.html?scp=1&sq=%93The%20Media%20Business:%20Time,%20Inc.%92s%20Take%20on%20Teen-agers%94%20&st=cse>. (Accessed 25 January 2008).

28. Doherty, *Teenagers and Teenpics,* 46.

29. Schrum, "Teena Means Business," 136.

30. Lucy Rollin, *Twentieth Century Teen Culture By the Decades* (Connecticut: Greenwood Press, 1999), 103–146.

31. Leslie Johnson, *The Modern Girl: Girlhood and Growing Up* (Philadelphia: Open University Press, 1993), 39–40.

32. Johnson, *The Modern Girl,* 44.

33. Doherty, *Teenagers and Teenpics,* 46.

34. Lewis, *The Road to Romance and Ruin,* 3.

35. Andrew Goodwin, *Dancing in the Distraction Factory: Music Television and Popular Culture* (Minneapolis: University of Minnesota Press, 1992), 169.

36. Julie D'Acci, *Defining Women: Television & the Case of Cagney & Lacey* (Chapel Hill: University of North Carolina Press, 1994), 65.

37. See for example, Leonard Klady, "Taken Unawares, H'w'd Refocuses on Youth," *Daily Variety,* 15 January 1997, 10; Lynn Hirshberg, "Desperate to Seem 16," *The New York Times Magazine,* 5 September 1999, 42+; Shelley Reese, "The Quality Of Cool," *Marketing Tools,* July 1997, 34.

38. Zollo, *Wise Up to Teens,* 6.

39. Elissa Moses, *The $100 Billion Allowance: Accessing the Global Teen Market* (New York: John Wiley & Sons, Inc., 2000), 3.

40. O'Leary, "The Boom Tube," 46.

41. Pogrebin, "The Media Business: Time Inc.'s Take on Teen-Agers."

42. Kenneth Hein and Mae Anderson, "The Age of Reason," *MEDIAWEEK,* 27 October 2003, 22.

43. Klady, "Taken Unawares, H'w'd Refocuses on Youth," 10.

44. "Reality Check — What's Up with All the Hot Teen Movies?" *The Seattle Times,* 4 April 1999, sec. M. The subsequent statistics and references to MPAA findings are all derived from this article, unless otherwise indicated.

45. "Reality Check," sec. M.

46. "Reality Check," sec. M.

47. Zollo, *Wise Up to Teens,* 50–51.

48. Brooke, "Fourth Estate: Girl Power," 18.

49. Doherty, *Teenagers and Teenpics,*52.

50. O'Leary, "The Boom Tube," 46.

51. Brooke, "Fourth Estate: Girl Power," 19.

52. O'Leary, "The Boom Tube," 46.

53. O'Leary, "The Boom Tube," 46.

54. O'Leary, "The Boom Tube," 48.

55. O'Leary, "The Boom Tube," 48.

56. O'Leary, "The Boom Tube," 50.

57. As a result, a May 1997 issue of *Seventeen* featured advertising from Sears and Mazola oil.

58. O'Leary, "The Boom Tube," 48.

59. Quoted in O'Leary, "The Boom Tube," 46.

60. Quoted in Brook, "Fourth Estate: Girl Power," 18.

61. Quoted in O'Leary, "The Boom Tube," 48.

62. O'Leary, "The Boom Tube," 49.

63. Mifflin, "Where Young Viewers Go (and Ads Follow)," sec. E.

64. Andrea Adelson, "The Media Business: Advertising; A Growing Number of Media Companies Are Trying to Shake MTV's Grip on the Teen-age Market," *The New York Times,* 15 March 1994. <http://www.nytimes.com/1994/03/15/business/media-business-advertising-growing-number-media-companies-are-trying-shake-mtv-s.html?scp=1&sq="The%20Media%20Business:%20Advertising;%20A%20growing%20number%20of%20media%20companies%20are%20trying%20to%20shake%20MTV's%20grip%20on%20the%20teen-age%20market%22&st=cse > (Accessed 25 January 2008).

65. Verna, "Retailers See Sign of Hope for Teen Music," 1.

66. Quoted in Craig Rosen, "Wide Appeal Is Key to New Crop of Teen Acts," *Billboard,* 22 March 1997, 1.

67. Becky Ebenkamp, "Tipping the Balance," *Upfront Markets,* 10 May 1999, 4.

68. When FOX was launched in 1986, it faced direct competition with the three existing television broadcast networks ABC, CBS, and NBC, all of which had decades to successfully attract the coveted 19–49 adult demographic. As the newest entry to an established market, FOX adopted the strategy of focusing on a younger television audience rather than competing with the established networks for adults, a strategy first formulated in the 1950s and employed by ABC, the newest (and consequently least successful) network in the nascent television industry in its quest for viewers while competing

against the more established NBC and CBS. A number of scholars have argued that ABC's initial success could be attributed to the youth-oriented *Disneyland* television show. FOX's success at targeting youth further proved the effectiveness of the practice. See Christopher Anderson, *HollywoodTV: The Studio System in the Fifties* (Austin: University of Texas Press, 1994), in particular, Chapter Six.

69. I am not suggesting that networks or advertisers began to ignore the adult demographic in preference of the teen cohort. The adult demographic remained the most important segment, however, the teenage demographic had become sufficiently significant that some advertisers and networks were beginning to view them as almost as important as the adult consumer.

70. A point raised by Justin Wyatt in *High Concept*. Also, Lauren Chattman highlights how *Beverly Hills, 90210* actively participated in the "selling…[of] youth." She notes, "while teenage girls are the series' target audience, *90210* does not limit its address to the biologically young and female. Rather, by beckoning all viewers to make themselves young consumers, it partakes of the larger cultural practice of constructing the public as a mass of desirable and desiring young women." Lauren Chattman, "Smells Like Teen Spirit: Gender, Adolescence, and the Culture of Consumption in *Beverly Hills, 90210*," *Spectator* 13, no. 2 (1993): 14.

71. Chattman, "Smells Like Teen Spirit," 14.

72. For more in-depth discussions of the relationship between teenagers and popular commercial media, see Douglas, *Where the Girls Are*, 1994; Lewis, *The Road to Romance and Ruin*, 1992; Mark Crispin Miller, "North American Youth and the Entertainment State: A Talk," in *Pictures of a Generation on Hold; Selected Papers*, ed. Murray Pomerance and John Sakeris (Media Studies Working Group: Toronto, 1996), 131–146.

Chapter Two

1. See Bagdikian, *The Media Monopoly*; Barnouw, et al., *Conglomerates and the Media* (New York: The New Press, 1997); David Croteau and William Hoynes, *The Business of the Media: Corporate Media and the Public Interest* (Thousand Oaks, California: Pine Forge Press, 2001); Edward S. Herman and Robert W. McChesney, *The Global Media: The New Missionaries of Global Capitalism* (Washington: Cassell, 1997); William M. Kunz, *Culture Conglomerates: Consolidation in the Motion Picture and Television Industries* (New York: Rowman & Littlefield Publishers, Inc., 2007); McChesney, "The Political Economy of Global Communication," 1–26.

2. George Lipsitz, "We Know What Time It Is: Race, Class and Youth Culture in the Nineties," *Microphone Fiends: Youth Music and Youth Culture*, ed. Andrew Ross and Tricia Rose (New York and London: Routledge, 1994), 17.

3. Grace Palladino, *Teenagers, An American History* (HarperCollins Publishers: New York, 1996), 5.

4. Clearly, radio and publishing have played significant roles in the development and evolution of teen culture. However, these industries will not receive much detailed attention here because my primary sites of study for millennial teen culture are film, television, the television-music link, and the impact and potential of new media/digital technologies. As such, I am restricting my historical overviews of previous teen cultures to these specific aspects. Consequently, I will not be addressing the nature of the radio or publishing industry, or the content and textual aspects of radio programming and teen publications, despite their established and continuing importance to teen culture as a whole.

5. Georganne Scheiner, "The Deanna Durbin Devotees: Fan Clubs and Spectatorship," in *Generations of Youth: Youth Cultures and Histories in Twentieth Century America*, ed. Joe Austin and Michael N. Willard (New York and London: New York University Press, 1998), 81.

6. Though *The Aldrich Family* did, as its title suggests, focus on the antics and experiences of the middle class Aldrich family, one of the show's more popular characters was the teenaged Henry Aldrich, a bit character who first appeared in Clifford Goldsmith's Broadway play, *What a Life* (first staged in 1938). Henry Aldrich then became a central character in a series of skits for a radio show sponsored by Jell-O. *The Aldrich Family* was broadcast on NBC radio stations from 1939 to 1944. In 1949, NBC also broadcast a television series of *The Aldrich Family* sponsored by General Foods.

7. Paramount Pictures released *What a Life* in 1939. Subsequently, eleven more films featuring the teenage Henry Aldrich were produced and released by Paramount. They were *Life with Henry* (1941), *Henry Aldrich for President* (1941), *Henry and Dizzy* (1942), *Henry Aldrich, Editor* (1942), *Henry Aldrich Gets Glamour* (1943), *Henry Aldrich Swings It* (1943), *Henry Aldrich Haunts a House* (1943), *Henry Aldrich, Boy Scout* (1944), *Henry Aldrich Plays Cupid* (1944), and *Henry Aldrich's Little Secret* (1944). See <www.imdb.com>

8. Anderson, *HollywoodTV*, 26–27. See also Jonathon Buchsbaum, "Zukor Buys Protection: The Paramount Stock Purchase of 1929," *Cine-Tracts* 2 (1979): 49–62; Douglas Gomery, *The Hollywood Studio System* (New York: St Martin's Press, 1986), 124–132; Michelle Hilmes, *Hollywood and Broadcasting: From Radio to Cable*

(Champaign: University of Illinois Press, 1990), 36–46.

9. Anderson, *HollywoodTV*, 28. According to Anderson, the Great Depression also placed a damper on these initial cross-media ventures. Ultimately, however, the Great Depression and the legislative decisions would only delay the rise of the multi-media conglomerates by several decades.

10. The sale of their movie theatres was in accordance with the court's ruling that they "divorce and divest" their vertically integrated holdings.

11. Media scholars and historians have argued that this license freeze effectively gave CBS and NBC the opportunity to dominate the television industry and allowing them to consolidate their hold over local markets amidst conducive conditions in which competition was nonexistent. See William Boddy, *Fifties Television: The Industry and Its Critics* (Champaign: University of Illinois Press, 1990); Douglas Gomery, "Failed Opportunities: The Integration of the Motion Picture and Television Industries," *Quarterly Review of Film Studies* 9 (1984): 219–228.

12. For more detailed discussions of the studios' attempts to enter the television industry, see Anderson, *HollywoodTV*; Boddy, *Fifties Television*; Gomery, "Failed Opportunities," 219–228; Timothy R. White, "Hollywood's Attempt at Appropriating Television: The Case of Paramount Pictures," in *Hollywood in the Age of Television*, ed. Tino Balio (Boston: Unwin Hyman, 1990), 145–163.

13. According to Anderson, "Since the movie studios began producing television, the diversification of media corporations into related fields and the consolidation of capital through corporate mergers have produced an environment in which the media industries are increasingly interwoven." Anderson, *HollywoodTV*, 5.

14. See Anderson, *HollywoodTV*; Boddy, *Fifties Television*; Gomery, "Failed Opportunities"; Hilmes, *Hollywood and Broadcasting*; White, "Hollywood's Attempt at Appropriating Television."

15. The studio's decision to become the television industry's key supplier of programming led to significant changes in both the studios' production practices, as well as the studio product itself. See Anderson, *HollywoodTV*; Gomery, "Failed Opportunities"; Hilmes, *Hollywood and Broadcasting*.

16. Nina C. Leibman, *Living Room Lectures: The 50s Family in Film and Television* (Austin: University of Texas Press, 1995), 5.

17. For a more detailed discussion of ABC's relationship with Disney and Warner Bros., see James L. Baughman, "The Weakest Chain and the Strongest Link: The American Broadcasting Company and the Motion Picture Industry, 1952–60," in *Hollywood in the Age of Television*, ed. Tino Balio (Boston: Unwin Hyman, 1990), 91–114; Anderson, *HollywoodTV*, particularly Chapters Six and Seven.

18. See Anderson, *HollywoodTV*, Chapter Six.

19. A broadcast network consists of a nationwide linked system of largely independent television or radio stations that sign on with the network as affiliates and agree to carry the network's programming. In addition, network owners are also allowed to "own and operate" a limited number of these stations, often referred to as O & Os, themselves. The bulk of the network's profits come from these O & Os. Legislation limiting the number of O & Os a network would own nationally was aimed at containing the network's dominance over the national broadcast market.

20. See Mara Einstein, *Media Diversity: Economics, Ownership and the FCC* (New York: Routledge, 2004), 21–22. This rule represented another attempt at limiting the power and influence of the growing broadcast networks in individual markets. The duopoly rule was rescinded in 1999, paving the way for Viacom, which owned the television network UPN under its Paramount holdings, to purchase CBS, thereby owning two television stations in the same local market.

21. For detailed discussions of the growing alliance between the film and music industries, see Doherty, *Teenagers and Teenpics*; Alexander Doty, "Music Sells Movies: (Re)New(ed) Conservatism in Film Marketing," *Wide Angle* 10, no. 2 (1988): 70–79; Jeff Smith, *The Sounds of Commerce: Marketing Popular Film Music* (New York: Columbia University Press, 1988).

22. Janet Wasko, *Movies and Money: Financing the American Film Industry* (Norwood, NJ: Ablex Publishing Corporation, 1982), 184–185. Gulf & Western also purchased Desilu, the production company responsible for the *I Love Lucy* television series, thus giving Gulf & Western ownership of both a film and television studio, however, since the majors had the FCC and legislators' tacit approval to serve as producers and suppliers of television series, and Gulf & Western did not own a television network at the time, monopolistic and anti-trust concerns were not an issue.

23. See Tino Balio, *The American Film Industry*, revised ed. (Madison: The University of Wisconsin Press, 1985), 439; Wasko, *Movies and Money*, 182–183.

24. Balio, *The American Film Industry*, 576; Kunz, *Culture Conglomerates*, 28–29.

25. Kunz, *Culture Conglomerates*, 29. In an interesting synergistic strategy, Kerkorian leveraged on the MGM brand by opening the MGM Grand hotel and casino in Las Vegas in 1973,

bringing a taste of Hollywood glamour to the Strip.

26. For insight into the rise of video technology and Hollywood's attempts to exploit the discovery, see Bruce Austin, "Home Video: The Second Run 'Theater' of the 1990s," in *Hollywood in the Age of Television*, ed. Tino Balio (Massachusetts: Unwin Hyman, 1990), 319–349.

27. For an in-depth examination of cable technology's emergence as well as the entertainment industries' response, see Michelle Hilmes, "Pay Television: Breaking the Broadcast Bottleneck," in *Hollywood in the Age of Television*, ed. Tino Balio (Massachusetts: Unwin Hyman, 1990), 297–318,

28. It is worth noting that cable began as a rural phenomenon, growing out of a need to provide basic television services and programming to areas outside major cities that were not able to receive over-the-air network broadcasts due to weak or non-existing television stations in the region. In the early 1960s, the FCC established its jurisdiction over cable and began establishing regulations to direct and control the technology's development. Until the early 1970s, broadcasters successfully lobbied the FCC to restrict cable's growth and protect broadcasters' interests. With the launch of SATCOM I in 1975, commercial pay cable was established, paving the way for the growth of cable programming in the late 1970s and early 80s. See Hilmes, "Pay Television," and Hilmes, *Hollywood & Broadcasting*, Chapter Seven.

29. Hilmes, "Pay Television," 297–318; Thomas Streeter, "Blue Skies and Strange Bedfellows: The Discourse of Cable Television," in *The Revolution Wasn't Televised: Sixties Television and Social Conflict*, ed. Lynn Spiegel and Michael Curtin (New York: Routledge, 1997), 221–242.

30. Spectrum scarcity is one of the key reasons for the oligopolistic nature of the broadcast network television system. In the first half of the twentieth century, Congress and the FCC often justified their regulatory interventions into broadcasting on the basis that because broadcasting must serve the public interest, the medium cannot be allowed to develop free of governmental guidelines. Many FCC regulations, including the national station ownership cap (which stipulated the number of stations a company could own nationally), the duopoly rule, Fin/Syn, and others, were motivated by concerns for the public interest. This view would shift dramatically in the second half of the twentieth century, when Republicans who increasingly favored deregulation dominated both Congress and the FCC. See Kunz, *Culture Conglomerates*, 8–9, and 64–65.

31. That the technology delivered programming through cable networks, rather than over the public airwaves, further freed the system from the standards and regulations imposed on broadcast networks.

32. In the cable universe, networks such as Turner Classic Movies and American Movie Classics served the interests of classical film fans, golf enthusiasts could turn to The Golf Channel for their entertainment needs, and history buffs could tune in to The History Channel.

33. R. Serge Denisoff and William D. Romanowski, *Risky Business: Rock in Film* (New Jersey: Transaction Publishers, 1991), 347–357.

34. See Kunz, *Culture Conglomerates*, 32; Laurie Thomas and Barry R. Litman, "Fox Broadcasting Company, Why Now? An Economic Study of the Rise of the Forth Broadcast 'Network,'" *Journal of Broadcasting & Electronic Media*, 35 (1990): 139–157.

35. Kunz, *Culture Conglomerates*, 77.

36. The FCC initially only allowed a single company to own three television stations within the national market, a rule instituted in 1941. In 1944, the number was raised to five stations. Ten years later, in 1954, the FCC instituted the "Seven Station Rule," raising nation-wide ownership to seven broadcast stations. In 1984, national ownership was again raised; this time to 12 AM and 12 FM radio stations, and 12 television stations nationally. See Kunz, *Culture Conglomerates*, 66–67.

37. Although television broadcast networks control prime-time programming for their nation-wide web of affiliates, they make the bulk of their profits from selling advertising time on their owned and operated television stations (termed "O & Os").

38. Roger Cohen, "Rupert Murdoch's Biggest Gamble," *The New York Times*, 21 October 1990, 31.

39. Cited in McKinley, *Beverly Hills, 90210*, 16.

40. See Thomas Schatz, "The New Hollywood," in *Film Theory Goes To The Movies*, ed. Jim Collins, Hilary Radner and Ava Preacher Collins (New York, London: Routledge, 1993), 8–36; Wyatt, *High Concept*. For more information on Warner Communications' vertical and horizontal diversification, see also Tino Balio, "Adjusting to the New Global Economy: Hollywood in the 1990s," in *Film Policy: International, National and Regional Perspectives*, ed. Albert Moran (New York: Routledge, 1996), 23–38; Eileen Meehan, "'Holy Commodity Fetish, Batman!': The Political Economy of a Commercial Intertext," in *The Many Lives of the Batman: Cultural Approaches to a Superhero and His Media*, ed. Roberta E. Pearson and William Uricchio (New York: Routledge, 1991), 66–89.

41. Schatz, "The New Hollywood"; Wyatt, *High Concept*.

42. Foot, *Boom Bust & Echo 2000*, 28–30.

43. Fin/Syn was rescinded in 1995; see Dennis Wharton, "FCC Seals Fin-Syn's Death," *Va-*

riety, 11–17 September 1995, 36. The Duopoly Rule was lifted in 1999; see Einstein, *Media Diversity*, 21–22. The Newspaper/Television Cross-Ownership Prohibition Rule was revised in 2003; see Kunz, *Culture Conglomerates*, 73.

44. *Forbes'* list of the largest corporations in the world cited these six global media conglomerates: General Electric (at number two); Time Warner (at number 42); Viacom (number 61); Sony (number 82); Walt Disney (number 85) and News Corp (number 110). See Kunz, *Culture Conglomerates*, 35.

45. Bagdikian, *The Media Monopoly*; Meehan, "'Holy Commodity Fetish, Batman!,'" 66–89; Schatz, "The Return of the Hollywood Studio System," 73–106.

46. As many political economists point out, one negative consequence of this media consolidation and heightened synergistic practices lies in the severe reduction in the variety of entertainment texts available. As a result, audiences find that the available entertainment options are substantially reduced, as is competition. See Bagdikian, *The Media Monopoly*; Kunz, *Culture Conglomerates*; Croteau and Hoynes, *The Business of Media*; Robert McChesney, Ellen Wood and John Foster, ed., *Capitalism and The Information Age: The Political Economy of the Global Communication Revolution* (New York: Monthly Review Press, 1998).

47. Steve Neale and Murray Smith, "Introduction," in *Contemporary Hollywood Cinema*, ed. Steve Neale and Murray Smith (New York: Routledge, 1998), xvii.

48. Schatz, "The Return of the Hollywood Studio System," 74.

49. Schatz, "The Return of the Hollywood Studio System," 75.

50. Some might argue that these activities are not distinctly teen-oriented, and can be applied to almost all media experiences/texts/audiences in this period. While I acknowledge that media in general do engage in synergistic practices, I contend that the degree and range with which teen-oriented media texts access and exploit each other for promotional and marketing purposes are extreme enough to distinguish them from the more general media cultures.

51. Daniel Okrent, "Happily Ever After?" *TIME*, 24 January 2000, 41.

52. Croteau and Hoynes, *The Business of Media*, 2–3. See also Eileen Meehan, *Why TV Is Not Our Fault: Television Programming, Viewers and Who's Really in Control* (New York: Rowman & Littlefield Publishers, Inc., 2005), 69–74.

53. Okrent, "Happily Ever After?" 41.

54. See Shelly Palmer, "Internet," in *Television Disrupted: The Transition from Network to Networked TV* (Boston: Focal Press, 2006), 37–51.

55. In the first quarter of 2008, *Advertising Age* reported "91 million Americans, or 36 per-cent of all U.S. mobile-phone subscribers, owned what Nielsen called a 'video capable' phone." Brian Steinberg, "Viewers Spend More Time Watching, but Not All on TV," *Advertising Age*, 8 July 2008. <http://adage.com/print?article_id=128220> (Accessed 9 July 2008).

56. Mike Vorhaus, "Younger Demos Shift Focus from TV Screens to YouTube," *Advertising Age*, 8 October 8 2007. <http://adage.com> (Accessed 11 October 2007).

57. Brian Steinberg, "Web Surfers Spending More Time with Content," *Advertising Age*, 14 August 2007. <http://adage.com> (Accessed 16 August 2007).

58. Michelle Quinn and Andrea Chang, "More Teenagers Ignoring CDs, Report Says," *Los Angeles Times*, 27 February 2008. <http://www.latimes.com/entertainment/news/music...> (Accessed 28 February 2008).

59. See Kunz, *Culture Conglomerates*, chapter 6.

60. McChesney, "The Political Economy of Global Communication," 12, italics his.

61. Other American media brands that have a significant global presence include Time Warner's CNN, and HBO, and Disney owned, ESPN.

62. Robert McChesney, "The Global Media Giants," in *Critical Studies in Media Commercialism*, ed. Robin Andersen and Lance Strate (Oxford: Oxford University Press. 2000), 59–70.

63. Kunz, *Culture Conglomerates*, 5.

64. Upfront costs involve expenditure incurred during the production of media content, including the cost of pre- and post-production activities.

65. See Croteau and Hoynes, *The Business of Media*, 95–99; Kunz, *Culture Conglomerates*, 5–6, for a more detailed discussion of how globalization is affecting the American media conglomerates.

66. Douglas Kellner, *Media Culture* (London: Routledge, 1995), 235.

Chapter Three

1. See Chris Barker, *Television, Globalization and Cultural Identities* (Buckingham and Philadelphia: Open University Press, 1999); McChesney, "The Political Economy of Global Communication," 1–26; Georgette Wang and Jan Servaes, "Introduction," *The New Communication Landscape: Demystifying Global Media*, ed. Georgette Wang, Jan Servaes and Anura Goonesekera (New York: Routledge, 2000), 1–18.

2. Joseph Turow, *Breaking Up America: Advertisers & The New Media World* (Chicago: University of Chicago Press, 1997).

3. The factors motivating America's turn from notions a mass market towards smaller,

more focused, niche markets, are discussed in greater detail in Turow, *Breaking Up America*, see especially Chapter Three, "The Roots of Division."

4. Turow, *Breaking Up America*, 43–49.

5. Discussions on the rise of the quality television audience can be found in Jane Feuer, Paul Kerr and Tise Vahimagi, ed., *MTM: 'Quality Television'* (London: BFI Publishing, 1984); Mark Alvey, "'Too Many Kids and Old Ladies': Quality Demographics and 1960s US television," *Screen* 45, no. 1, (2004): 40–62; Sally Bedell, *Up the Tube* (New York: Viking, 1981); Muriel Cantor, *Prime-Time Television: Content and Control* (Beverly Hills, CA: Sage, 1980).

6. Turow, *Breaking Up America*, 5. Italics his.

7. Turow, *Breaking Up America*, 5.

8. Turow, *Breaking Up America*, 11.

9. Turow, *Breaking Up America*, 6.

10. By the 1990s, the television series itself had joined the expanding entertainment line as a consumer product in itself, a result of technological advances and industry practices that effectively reconfigured the television text to place it on a more equal footing with the other media as revenue sources. Historically, films and music were always conceptualized as commodities for sale. In contrast, television series were not since they are broadcast into the viewer's home without charge. Conventionally, television programs were considered the "filler" that surrounded the commodities for sale, specifically, the products featured in the advertisements. In the past, television shows were little more than "bait" to attract viewers to the advertisements promoting a range of products including sodas, cars and computers. Prior to the 1990s, the profitability of television programs was largely restricted to syndication. By the 1990s, new delivery systems, including videocassettes and digital videodiscs, transformed the television show into a product for public purchase and it became common practice to market previously broadcast television shows on video and DVD.

11. Cited in Doherty, *Teenagers and Teenpics*, 91.

12. While there were musical performances and reviews on television prior to *American Bandstand*, Dick Clark's series was one of the pioneering shows that were produced specifically for teenagers, featuring (musical) content tailored primarily for that audience segment.

13. Denisoff and Romanowski, *Risky Business*, 82.

14. Wyatt, *High Concept*, 44.

15. Some might argue that these activities are not distinctly teen-oriented, and can be applied to almost all media experiences/texts/audiences in this period. While I acknowledge that media in general do engage in synergistic practices, I argue that the degree and range with which teen-oriented media texts access and exploit each other for promotional and marketing purposes are extreme enough to distinguish them from the more general media cultures.

16. Schatz, "The Return of the Hollywood Studio System," 86.

17. Turow, *Breaking Up America*, 91–92.

18. In stating that MTV, the WB and Dimension's signature texts all adopted a teenage perspective, I am not suggesting that the texts all espoused the same interests and attitudes. As I highlight in the chapters that follow, there are distinct differences between an MTV program and a WB teen series. Each network has a vested interest in distinguishing itself from the other, the better to differentiate its identity, its product and its implied target audience. At this point, however, I am merely emphasizing the *teenage* nature of the shows in question.

19. The early definition of cross-over centered upon issues of race and was used to describe incidents in which non-white, usually African-American, entertainers' abilities to transcend their racial "identities" and "cross-over" into the mainstream. I am not using the term in this particular definition. Rather, I use "cross-over" to describe the practice of transcending the boundaries separating the different entertainment media and "crossing-over" (or crossing-between) them. Therefore, an entertainer "crosses-over" when s/he moves between working in the film, television and music industries, rather than being restricted to a single one.

20. The "teen" label is not meant to suggest that these stars and personalities are teenagers, rather, it is used to mark the fact that they are associated primarily with teen-oriented entertainment and are most popular with teenagers.

21. Cardwell, "Generation Next," 55.

22. Cardwell, "Generation Next," 55.

23. Patrick Goldstein, "Screamwriter; Kevin Williamson, The Pied Piper of the Video Generation, Has Breathed New Life into the Teen Horror Genre," *Los Angeles Times*, 27 October 1997, sec. F.

24. Quoted in Jenny Hontz, "Pic Scribes Flocking to Web Deals," *Daily Variety*, 31 August 1998, 1.

25. Hontz, "Pic Scribes Flocking to Web Deals," 1.

26. Timothy Corrigan, *A Cinema Without Walls: Movies and Culture after Vietnam* (New Brunswick, N.J.: Rutgers University Press, 1991), 23.

27. Bagdikian, *The Media Monopoly*, 236.

28. The figure simply meant that the width of the screen image was 1.33 times broader than the height of the image.

29. In television, this aspect ratio tended to be referred to by the equivalent measure, 4:3.

30. The film industry not only adopted the

16:9 widescreen format, but also experimented with Cinemascope, which stretched the film image even more, to 2.66:1, twice the width of the Academy Standard/traditional television screen.

31. For discussions of differences between television and film narratives and aesthetics in the 1950s and 1980s, see Anderson, *HollywoodTV* and Todd Gitlin, *Inside Prime Time* (New York: Pantheon, 1985), respectively.

32. Wyatt, *High Concept*, 188.

33. Wyatt, *High Concept*, 7.

34. Wyatt, *High Concept*, 9–13.

35. As Wyatt points out, "all mainstream Hollywood filmmaking is economically oriented, through the minimization of production cost and maximization of potential box office. However, the connection between economics and high-concept is particularly strong, since high-concept appears to be the most market-driven type of film being produced." Wyatt, *High Concept*, 15.

36. Wyatt, *High Concept*, 26.

37. Wyatt, *High Concept*, 36.

38. John Thornton Caldwell, *Televisuality: Style, Crisis, and Authority in American Television* (New Brunswick, New Jersey: Rutgers University Press, 1995), 9.

39. Thomas Doherty, "Genre, Gender and the *Aliens* Trilogy," *The Dread of Difference*, ed. Barry Keith Grant (Austin: University of Texas Press, 1996), 189.

40. Doherty, "Genre, Gender and the *Aliens* Trilogy," 189.

41. Doherty, "Genre, Gender and the *Aliens* Trilogy," 189.

42. Serial films tended to feature an on-going narrative shown in short weekly installments. Screened before the main full-length feature film, each episode had a 15–20 minute run time that would pick up the narrative from the previous week, before ending on a cliff-hanger to entice audiences back for the following installment. *The Perils of Pauline* was perhaps the most popular series in the genre.

43. Leibman, *Living Room Lectures*, 44.

44. The *Jaws, Superman, Batman,* and *Indiana Jones* film series are examples. As are the slasher films of the 1980s. While '80s slasher films have sustained numerous sequels, there is seldom any narrative continuity from film to film. Instead, continuity generally takes the form of the killer's return or resurrection. Perhaps the only notable serialized film series of the period is George Lucas' *Star Wars* Trilogy, which traced a single narrative across three films and even incorporated the generic tradition of the cliff-hanger ending. Lucas has often asserted that the *Star Wars* franchise was an homage to the serialized films that he loved as a child.

45. Discussions of postmodernism, particularly as they intersect with the teen media text, have tended to center on MTV and the music video format's characteristics. See Fredric Jameson, *Postmodernism, or the Cultural Logic of Late Capitalism* (Durham, North Carolina: Duke University Press, 1991); Pat Aufderheide, "Music Videos: The Look of the Sound," in *Watching Television*, ed. Todd Gitlin (New York: Pantheon, 1986), 111–135; E. Ann Kaplan, *Rocking Around the Clock: Music Television, Postmodernism and Consumer Culture* (London: Methuen, 1987); David Tetzlaff, "MTV and the Politics of Postmodern Pop," *Journal of Communication Inquiry* 10, no. 1 (1986): 80–91; Peter Wollen, "Ways of Thinking About Music Video (and Postmodernism)," *Critical Quarterly* 28 (1986): 167–170. In these discussions, Jameson discusses music videos as examples of pastiche or "blank parody," while scholars including Aufderheide, Kaplan, Tetzlaff, and Wollen examine music videos and comment on how the interplay of images and the domination of the visual result in the loss of critical distance.

46. Wyatt, *High Concept*, 58.

47. Jim Collins, "Television and Postmodernism" in *Channels of Discourse, Reassembled*, ed. Robert C. Allen. 2d ed. Chapel Hill: University of North Carolina Press, 1992, 331.

48. Quoted in Collins, "Television and Postmodernism," 333.

49. Caldwell, *Televisuality*, 206.

50. Collins, "Television and Postmodernism," 333.

51. Collins, "Television and Postmodernism," 333.

52. Collins, "Television and Postmodernism," 331.

53. Collins, "Television and Postmodernism," 335.

54. Caldwell, *Televisuality*.

55. Caldwell, *Televisuality*, 4.

56. Caldwell, *Televisuality*, 6.

57. Jean Baudrillard, "Consumer Society," in *Selected Writings*, ed. Mark Poster (Cambridge: Polity Press, 1988), 29–56. See also Peter Corrigan, *The Sociology of Consumption* (London: Sage Publications, 1998), 20.

58. Jean Baudrillard, *For a Critique of the Political Economy of the Sign* (St. Louis: Telos Press, 1972/1981), 38.

59. Steven Miles, *Consumerism As a Way of Life* (London: Sage Publications, 1998), 147–153.

60. Todd Gitlin, "Prime Time Ideology: The Hegemonic Process in Television Entertainment," in *Television: The Critical View*, 4d ed., ed. Horace Newcomb (Oxford: Oxford University Press, 1987), 513.

Chapter Four

1. Numerous comprehensive studies of MTV's early years exist including Banks, *Mo-*

nopoly Television; R. Serge Denisoff, *Inside MTV* (New Jersey: Transaction Publishers, 1988); Goodwin, *Dancing in the Distraction Factory*; Tom McGrath, *MTV: The Making of a Revolution* (Philadelphia: Running Press, 1996).

2. See Denisoff, *Inside MTV*; Banks, *Monopoly Television*; McGrath, *MTV*.

3. American Express' interest in MTV represented the credit card company's attempt to diversify into the communication/media business.

4. It is worth noting that cable began as a rural phenomenon, growing out of a need to provide basic television services and programming to areas outside major cities that were not able to receive over-the-air network broadcasts due to weak or non-existing television stations in the region. With the launch of Satcom I in 1975, commercial pay cable was established, paving the way for the growth of cable programming in the late 1970s and early 80s. At the time, the earliest adopters of cable technology and paid programming were middle- or upper-class, white, affluent suburban households who could afford, and were willing to pay for entertainment to be delivered directly to the home. Hence MTV's decision to cater to the white, suburban, youth demographic.

5. Quoted in Banks, *Monopoly Television*, 34.

6. According to Banks, MTV executives made certain initial assumptions regarding the demographic's musical interests and entertainment preferences. Robert Pittman, the director of the network, decided that MTV's programming would embrace a rock format while eschewing most other non-white oriented musical formats such as rhythm and blues, and soul. Pittman reasoned that suburban, white males would harbor "a strong commitment to rock music and an equally strong aversion to contemporary soul." As a result of the perceived "ethnocentric nature of [MTV's] core audience," its playlist would be restricted "almost exclusively [to] white rock artists." Banks, *Monopoly Television*, 34.

7. Denisoff and Romanowski, *Risky Business*, 44.

8. Aufderheide, "Music Videos: The Look of the Sound," 111–135; John Fiske, "MTV: Post Structural Post Modern," *Journal of Communication Inquiry* 10, no. 1 (1986): 74–79; Kaplan, *Rocking Around the Clock*; Tetzlaff, "MTV and the Politics of Postmodern Pop," 80–91; Wollen, "Ways of Thinking About Music Video (and Postmodernism)," 167–170.

9. Tetzlaff, "MTV and the Politics of Postmodern Pop," 80.

10. Marsha Kinder, "Music Video and the Spectator: Television, Ideology and the Dream," *Film Quarterly* 38, no. 1 (1984): 2–15.

11. Banks, *Monopoly Television*, 7.

12. Collins, "Television and Postmodernism," 327–349; Mike Featherstone, *Consumer Culture & Postmodernism* (California: Sage Publications, 1991); Aufderheide, "Music Videos: The Look of the Sound," 111–135; Margeret Morse, "Postsynchronizing Rock Music and

Television," *Journal of Communication Inquiry* 10, no.1 (1986): 15–28.

13. Pat Aufderheide comments upon how music videos "dissolve the traditional boundary between programs and commercials since music clips constitute both types of content." Quoted in Banks, *Monopoly Television*, 4.

14. Morse, "Postsynchronizing Rock Music and Television," 16–17.

15. Virginia Fry and Donald Fry, "MTV: The 24 Hour Commercial," *Journal of Communication Inquiry* 10, no. 1 (1986): 29–33.

16. Wyatt, *High Concept*.

17. Doty, "Music Sells Movies," 72.

18. Rob Owen, *Gen X TV: The Brady Bunch to Melrose Place* (New York: Syracuse University Press, 1997), 51–52. Denisoff and Romanowski, and Andrew Goodwin all comment upon the economic and marketplace considerations that shaped MTV's development and its media mixing tendencies. See Denisoff and Romanowski, *Risky Business*; Goodwin, *Dancing in the Distraction Factory*.

19. Wyatt, *High Concept*, 58.

20. McGrath, *MTV*, 135.

21. Banks, *Monopoly Television*, 117; McGrath, *MTV*, 139, 141.

22. Banks, *Monopoly Television*, 117; McGrath, *MTV*, 141.

23. Banks, *Monopoly Television*, 118.

24. Banks, *Monopoly Television*, 119.

25. Banks, *Monopoly Television*, 119.

26. Banks, *Monopoly Television*, 120.

27. Meehan, "'Holy Commodity Fetish, Batman!,'" 56.

28. Banks, *Monopoly Television*, 120.

29. *Joe's Apartment* cost $13 million to make, and only grossed $4.5 million at the box-office. In contrast, *Beavis and Butt-head Do America* cost $12 million and grossed in excess of $63 million. Rebecca Asher-Walsh, "Behind the Music," *Entertainment Weekly*, 12 March 1999. <http://www.ew.com/ew/article/0,,274745,00.html> Accessed January 25, 2008.

30. These characteristics of the 1908s high concept films are discussed in Wyatt, *High Concept*.

31. Andrew Hindes, "Par Likes MTV's Tune," *Variety*, 19–25 July 1999, 8.

32. McGrath, *MTV*, 178.

33. Barker, *Television, Globalization and Cultural Identities*, 49–51. Certainly, cable penetration across the globe has not kept pace with the U.S. According to Barker, as of 1995, only 23 percent of television households in the European Union had access to cable, Asia enjoyed 20 percent access and in South America, only 7 percent. Satellite penetration differs in different geographical locations but is generally less than cable. In India, commercial satellite television had begun threatening state-owned television's dominance by the late 1990s. As of 1999, Britain's BSkyB satellite system achieved only an 8 percent audience share, in contrast to the Netherlands, where satellite had a more significant presence. While these cable and satellite figures generally paled in contrast to the U.S. market, the likelihood was that these figures would rise.

There was, therefore, significant future growth for these international markets compared to the almost saturated U.S. one. Thus, if MTV could gain early entry into these emerging markets, it would be well placed to profit from the coming expansion.

34. Banks, *Monopoly Television*, 115.

35. Ray Richmond, "MTV Opens Dance Card to More Musicvideos," *Variety*, 24–30 March 1997, 26.

36. Moses, *The $100 Billion Allowance*, 6.

37. Moses, *The $100 Billion Allowance*, 2.

38. Eric Boehlert, "Rap's Grip on Suburbs Loosens as Teens Turn to Modern Rock," *Billboard*, 3 June 1995, 1+; Havelock Nelson, "Hip-Hop, Rap Wrestle with Predictability as Demand Dips," *Billboard*, 3 June 1995, 1+.

39. Michael Paoletta, "Jive Rides Teen-Pop Wave," *Billboard*, 30 October 1999, 1+; Dominic Pride, "The Secret of Jive's Int'l Success," *Billboard*, 30 October 1999, 72; Andrew Essex and Dave Karger, "Bubble Gum Blows Up!" *Entertainment Weekly*, 5 March 1999, 20–26.

40. David Thigpen, "Jive Records Presents: Teen Idols," *TIME — Music Goes Global*, Special Issue, Fall 2001, 26.

41. Pride, "The Secret of Jive's Int'l Success," 72.

42. Paoletta, "Jive Rides Teen-Pop Wave," 73.

43. Thigpen, "Jive Records Presents: Teen Idols," 26; Dominic Pride and Michael Paoletta, "'N Sync's Indirect Path to the Top," *Billboard*, 20 March 1999, 84; Paoletta, "Jive Rides Teen-Pop Wave," 72; Larry Flick, "After Quiet Build, Jive's Teen Star Spears Breaks Out," *Billboard*, 12 December 1998, 25.

44. Paoletta, "Jive Ride Teen-Pop Wave," 73.

45. Jive participated in promotional tie-ins with publisher Bantam Doubleday Dell to distribute free samples of Backstreet Boys cassettes to readers of Bantam's teen romance book series. See Doug Reece, "Backstreet Boys Move Onto Main," *Billboard*, 19 July 1997, 21. Spears' publicity campaign involved a 28-date performance tour of shopping malls co-sponsored by several of the nation's most established teen magazines including *Seventeen*, *YM*, *Teen* and *Teen People*, several months before the album's release. See Flick, "After Quiet Build, Jive's Teen Star Breaks Out," 1+. While launching Backstreet Boys' second American release, *Millenium*, Jive targeted the teen market with television advertising spots that played on MTV, the WB and Nickelodeon, all networks that catered primarily to a teen network. See Ed Christman, "Backstreet Could Hit 1 Mil. In First Week," *Billboard*, 29 May 1999, 3+.

46. By the late 1990s, MTV declared an intention to increase the proportion of music-oriented programming on its schedule and reorient "its primary emphasis back on the videos that made it an international phenomenon in the first place." See Richmond, "MTV Opens Dance Card to More Musicvideos," 23+. In 1998, *Billboard* reported on MTV's decision to increase its music video programming and to "embark on a new image campaign that [would] include a tighter playlist, new music programs, and a re-vised marketing strategy aimed at the music industry and consumers." See Carla Hay, "MTV Aims for Tighter Music Focus," *Billboard*, 9 May 1998, 6+. MTV's new musical direction was a timely shift towards a much more teen-oriented direction.

47. It must be pointed out, however, that the process is not as democratic as it might initially appear. While requests are sought, the fact remains that *TRL* has a relatively select video playlist from which their teenage viewers can make their selections. The playlist is largely restricted to videos from established, mainstream musicians and artists. MTV, therefore, retains control over the videos broadcast by using its position as a media gatekeeper to promote and introduce those videos already pre-selected by the network.

48. Caldwell, *Televisuality*, 93–94.

49. Asher-Walsh, "Behind the Music."

50. Hindes, "Par Likes MTV's Tune," 8.

51. Richard Katz, "Graden Grows MTV Off-Kilter — and Up," *Variety*, 3–9 May 1999, 71–72.

52. During the early '80s, when British pop and new wave music was a mainstay of the network's programming, MTV adopted the rebellious, anti-authority, irreverent attitude and image of the musical genre and its musicians. Punk-rocker Billy Idol was one "poster boy" of the era whose appearances on MTV helped popularize the punk look with American youth. In the mid 1980s, pop stars such as Madonna, Prince and Michael Jackson emerged as celebrity fashion icons and influenced fashion via their numerous appearances on MTV. By the late '80s and early '90s, recessionary times and the increasing cynicism, alienation and jaundiced indifference ascribed to Generation X ushered in a change in musical trends, fashions, values and attitudes. MTV evolved accordingly, embracing both the grunge perspective best represented by Kurt Cobain and Nirvana, that eschewed glamour and high style for a pared-down, slacker-inspired grittiness, and hip-hop style associated with Kriss Kross and LL Cool J, who combined an urban inner-city way of dressing with the Southern California surfer look.

53. Certainly, I am not suggesting that this interest in fashion, style and image in music videos is new or unique, there have been numerous precedents. However, I argue that it is only in the late 1990s that we witnessed an unprecedented obsession in showcasing designer fashions, when the glamorous, high fashion image became the *raison d'être* of the music video form.

54. Caldwell, *Televisuality*, 149.

55. Katz, "Graden Grows MTV Off-Kilter — and Up," 71.

56. Steve Pond, "She's Here, She's Spears, Get Used to It," *Premiere*, October 2001, 38–41.

57. McChesney, "The Political Economy of Global Communication," 14.

58. Wyatt, *High Concept*, 60.

59. Pond, "She's Here, She's Spears, Get Used to It," 41.

60. Wyatt, *High Concept*, 129.

61. Wyatt, *High Concept*, 131.

62. Wyatt, *High Concept*, 45–46.

63. Scholars including Barker, McChesney and Goonasekera have all highlighted the significant role that digital technology, particularly the rise of the Internet, played in supporting the rise of globalization in the 1990s. See Barker, *Television, Globalization and Cultural Identities*; Anura Goonesekera, "Media in the Information Highway: Representing Different Cultures in the Age of Global Communication," in *The New Communication Landscape: Demystifying Global Media*, ed. Georgette Wang, Jan Servaes and Anura Goonesekera (New York: Routledge, 2000), 265–287; McChesney, "The Political Economy of Global Communication," 1–26.

64. Brett Attwood, "MTV Expands Its Online Programming," *Billboard*, 29 July 1995, 8.

65. MTV2 was launched in the mid-'90s and offered much more music-related programming. In significant ways, MTV2's programming harks back to the 24-hour music video strategy used by MTV in its early years, and represents an attempt to cater to that particular audience demographic that had been alienated by MTV's shift towards more conventional, non-music, programming series.

66. Richard Siklos, "Not in the Real World Anymore," *The New York Times*, 18 September 2006. <http://www.nytimes.com/2006/09/18/business/media/18avatar.html?scp=1&sq="Not%20in%20the%20Real%20World%20Anymore"%20&st=cse> (Accessed 19 September 2006).

67. Glenn Gamboa, "Forever Young: MTV," *Newsday (New York)*, 29 July 2001, sec. D.

Chapter Five

1. Chris Nashawaty, "Teen Steam," *Entertainment Weekly*, 14 November 1997, 26.

2. See Susan Wloszczyna, "Something to 'Scream' About," *USA Today*, 22 August 1997, sec. D; Susan Wloszczyna, "'Scream 2' Takes a Stab at Sophistication," *USA Today*, 12 December 1997, sec. D; James Cummings, "Cut! Dimension Films brings back the slasher movies," *Star Tribune (Minneapolis, MN)*, 13 November 1997 sec. E.

3. Doherty, *Teenagers and Teenpics*, 61–66.

4. Doherty, *Teenagers and Teenpics* for a detailed examination of the rise of the teenpic in the 1950s.

5. See Carol Clover, *Man, Women and Chainsaws: Gender in the Modern Horror Film* (Princeton: Princeton University Press, 1992), 14.

6. See Clover, *Man, Women and Chainsaws*, 24; Michael Ryan and Douglas Kellner, *Camera Politica: The Politics and Ideology of Contemporary Hollywood Film* (Bloomington Indiana: University of Indiana Press, 1988), 191; Andrew Tudor, *Monsters and Mad Scientists: A Cultural History of the Horror Movie* (Oxford: Basil Blackwell, 1989), 68–72.

7. See Clover, *Man, Women and Chainsaws*, 24; Tudor, *Monsters and Mad Scientists*, 198.

8. See Ryan and Kellner, *Camera Politica*, 191; Tudor, *Monsters and Mad Scientists*, 68, 70, and 199; Clover, *Man, Women and Chainsaws*, 30, for discussions these key teen slasher conventions.

9. A study of the box-office gross of key slasher franchises highlights the popularity and profitability of these movie franchises. The first *Halloween* film (1978) cost $325, 000 and grossed $47 million. The first *Friday the 13th* (1980) cost $700,000 and grossed $37.5 million, while *Nightmare on Elm Street* (1984) cost $1.8 million and grossed $25.5 million. With the release of each installment in these film series, the conventions of the genre were repeated and consolidated in the late '70s and early '80s.

10. Quoted in Clover, *Men, Women and Chainsaws*, 9.

11. Clover, *Men, Women and Chainsaws*, 23. By the early 1990s, the number of slasher film releases had fallen sharply.

12. Klady, "Studios Focus on Teen Stream," 11–12.

13. Orwall, "Teen Tidal Wave Hits Hollywood in the Head," sec. D.

14. Harry Berkowitz, "Now at Disney: Sex, Lies and *Aladdin*," *Newsday*, 1 May 1993, 14.

15. For instance, Miramax's *sex, lies and videotape* (1989) won the coveted *Palme d'Or* and the film's star, James Spader, won best actor at the Cannes Film Festival. The film, which cost $1.2 million to make, grossed $24.7 million and won Steven Soderbergh an Academy Award nomination for Best Screenplay. Another Miramax distributed film, *My Left Foot* (1989), earned Oscar nominations in four categories, including Best Picture and Best Actor for star Daniel Day-Lewis. Miramax's *The Crying Game* (1992) grossed an unexpected $62.6 million at the U.S. box-office and earned several Oscar nominations including Best Actor, Best Supporting Actor, Best Director and Best Picture. See Terry Pristin and James Bates, "The Climbing Game; Miramax Film Corp. Is Atop the Hollywood Heap," *Los Angeles Times*, 29 March 1993, sec. A.

16. I want to thank Alisa Perren for sharing her conclusions regarding Miramax's tremendous impact on both the film industry in general, and on the independent film arena in particular.

17. Bernard Weinraub, "Business Match Made in Hollywood," *The New York Times*, 1 May 1993, 39.

18. Disney's substantial multi-media assets included the Disney Channel, Disney Home Video and the Disneyland/Disney World theme parks.

19. Weinraub, "Business Match Made in Hollywood," 39.

20. Berkowitz, "Now at Disney: Sex, Lies and *Aladdin*," 14; Claudia Eller, "On-Screen Chemistry," *Los Angeles Times*, 1 December 1995, sec. D.

21. Eller, "On-Screen Chemistry," sec. D

22. Orwall, "Teen Tidal Wave Hits Hollywood in the Head," sec. D.

23. Orwall, "Teen Tidal Wave Hits Hollywood in the Head," sec. D.

24. Pinedo argues that "the horror film is an exquisite exercise in coping with the terrors of everyday life ... the pain of loss, the enigma of death, the unpredictability of events, the inadequacy of intentions," while Williams notes, "Although most commentators dismiss these films as worthless trash, they are symptomatic of their particular era and deserve attention." See Isabel Christina Pinedo, "Postmodern Elements of the Contemporary Horror Film," in *The Horror Film*, ed. Steven Prince (New Jersey: Rutgers University Press, 2004), 39; Tony Williams, *Hearths of Darkness: The Family in the American Horror Film* (London: Associated University Press, 1996), 183.

25. Jim Collins, "Genericity in the Nineties: Eclectic Irony and the New Sincerity," in *Film Theory Goes to the Movies*, ed. Jim Collins et al. (New York: Routledge, 1993), 262. The films Collins examined include *Batman* (1989), *Back to the Future III* (1990) and *Thelma and Louise* (1991)

26. Pinedo, "Postmodern Elements of the Contemporary Horror Film," 86.

27. See Kim Newman, *Nightmare Movies: A Critical Guide to Contemporary Horror Films* (New York: Harmony Books, 1988), 211–215; and Pinedo, "Postmodern Elements of the Contemporary Horror Film."

28. Tania Modleski, "The Terror of Pleasure: The Contemporary Horror Film and Postmodern Theory," in *Studies in Entertainment: Critical Approaches to Mass Culture*, ed. Tania Modleski (Bloomington: Indiana University Press, 1986), 155–166.

29. See Pinedo, "Postmodern Elements of the Contemporary Horror Film," 85–117; and Todd F. Tietchen, "Samplers and Copycats: The Cultural Implications of the Postmodern Slasher in Contemporary American Film," *Journal of Popular Film and Television* 26, no. 3 (1998): 98–107.

30. This is primarily to suggest the shift to a heightened, more postmodern phase than we have previously encountered in the tradition of the slasher film.

31. The fact that *Halloween* stars Jamie Lee Curtis, the daughter of Janet Leigh, the star of *Psycho*, suggests that the Loomis reference is unlikely to be coincidental.

32. *Scream* begins when teenager Sidney Prescott (Neve Campbell) and her friends at Woodsboro High School become the targets of a serial killer. The killings attract ambitious television journalist Gale Weathers (Courtney Cox), who arrives in town determined to solve the crimes. Amidst a rising body count, Sidney and her friends engage in numerous debates, comparing their circumstances with those of the protagonists in famous slasher films such as *Halloween* and *Friday the 13th*. The film concludes with Sidney and Gale Weathers cooperating to save each other and defeat the killers.

33. *Scream 2* is set two years after the Woodsboro murders. Sidney is enrolled in Windsor College, and Gale's book about the Woodsboro killings has been turned into a movie called *Stab*. *Stab*'s release leads to a new round of copycat killings, and discussions about slasher film sequels and their conventions. Sidney and her friends again become targets. Once again, Sidney and Gale help each other defeat a new set of villains.

34. In *Scream 3*, set three-and-a-half years after the events of *Scream 2*, another series of murders occur on the set of *Stab 3: Return to Woodsboro*, luring Sidney Prescott out of a life of seclusion. Targeting the original Woodsboro survivors as well as those associated with *Stab 3*, a murderer has again adopted the original killer's costume and strategy of chatting with his victims on the phone before killing them, motivating conversations about the relationship between *Stab 3* and the events in *Scream*, as well as the conventions surrounding the final installment of a horror franchise.

35. It is worth noting that while *Scream 2* referenced the original film by recreating scenes from the first film, these were clearly "marked" as reenactments, and a measure of distance was maintained by having different actors performing the scenes. In *Scream 3*, this distance is erased as we see the original Sidney going through the same motions in the same familiar space.

36. Collins, "Television and Postmodernism," 226.

37. *Buffy* creator Joss Whedon has often maintained that the character was his feminist-inflected response to horror films in which the young, female, blonde victim is the first to die.

38. See Wyatt, *High Concept.*

39. Wyatt, *High Concept*, 17 and 36.

40. Caldwell, *Televisuality*, 77.

41. Catherine A. Olson, "Soundtracks: It's a *Scream*," *Billboard*, 6 December 1997, 16.

42. "The Scare" does not restrict its homages to Williamson's *Scream*. The episode opens with the show's characters watching and discussing another Kevin Williamson scripted slasher film, *I Know What You Did Last Summer*.

43. The WB television network was particularly aggressive in crossing media-specific boundaries and actively sought out arrangements with filmmakers rather than established television personnel. Recognizing the teen viewer's love of movies, the WB network actively tried to fortify the television-film connection, injecting film-like visual styles and techniques in its teen-oriented shows. All of the WB's teen shows adopt the single-camera format and are shot on film, offering the rich, organic visuals lacking in video. See Chapter Six for a detailed discussion of the WB's cross-media strategies.

44. Betty Goodwin, "Screen Style; Fashion; A New 'Scream' and a New Look," *Los Angeles Times*, 22 January 1998, sec. E.

45. Michael Kleinschrodt, "Secrecy About This Movie Is Enough to Make You Scream," *The Times Picayune* (New Orleans, LA), 4 February 2000, sec. L.

46. Fredric Jameson, "Postmodernism and Consumer Society," *The Cultural Turn: Selected Writings on the Postmodern 1983–1998* (London: Verso, 1998), 1–20; Featherstone, *Consumer Culture & Postmodernism.*

47. Clover, *Men, Women and Chainsaws*, 23.

48. Although both *Clueless* and *William*

Shakespeare's Romeo and Juliet, can be credited with indicating just how valuable and significant the teenage girl market could be, as well as hinting at the teen movie-going market's potential, these films did not motivate the resurgence of the teen film in the late 1990s. Unlike *Scream,* neither films inspired studios to begin churning out teen films in bulk, nor did they generate the intense amount of media discourses declaring the resurgence of the teen market.

49. Tudor, *Monsters and Mad Scientists,* 69.

50. Sarah Trencansky, "Final Girls and Terrible Youth: Transgression in 1980s Slasher Horror," *Journal of Popular Film and Television* 29, no. 2 (2001): 73. Despite recognizing the possible link between *Scream* and actual high-school violence, Trecansky does not go on to interrogate the connection in any detail as the focus of her paper lies elsewhere.

51. Clover, *Men, Women and Chainsaws,* 35.

52. Clover, *Men, Women and Chainsaws,* 6.

53. In the final moments of *The Texas Chainsaw Massacre,* the final girl escapes by flagging down a passing vehicle, while *Halloween's* final girl is saved by another character in the film.

54. Clover, *Men, Women and Chainsaws,* 39–40.

55. See Trencansky, "Final Girls and Terrible Youth," 68.

56. Clover, *Men, Women and Chainsaws,* 48.

57. Clover, *Men, Women and Chainsaws,* 30.

58. Williams, *Hearths of Darkness,* 214.

59. Janet Weeks, "'*Scream*' Movies Cultivate Special Audience: Girls," *USA Today,* 12 December 1997, sec. A. Williamson's other teen-oriented creations, including *Dawson's Creek,* with its presentation of female characters who are grounded, smart, brave and mature, were also very popularity with the female teen audience.

60. Weeks, "'*Scream*' Movies Cultivate Special Audience: Girls," sec. A.

61. Weeks, "'*Scream*' Movies Cultivate Special Audience: Girls," sec. A.

62. See Valerie Wee, "Resurrecting and Updating the Teen Slasher—The Case of *Scream,*" *Journal of Popular Film and Television* 34, no. 2 (2006): 50–61, for a more detailed discussion of how the *Scream* trilogy renegotiated the traditional gender politics and conservative ideologies associated with the slasher film genre.

63. Wloszczyna, "*Scream 2* Takes a Stab at Sophistication," sec. D.

64. Wloszczyna, "*Scream 2* Takes a Stab at Sophistication," sec. D.

65. Weeks, "'*Scream*' Movies Cultivate Special Audience: Girls," sec. A.

66. Josh Chetwynd and Andy Seiler, "Expectations Rise for 'Scary' Body Count," *USA Today,* 23 June 2000, sec. E.

67. This list includes information from Michael Kleinschrodt, "Audiences Enjoy Laughing Themselves to Death," *The Times-Picayune,* 4 February 2000, sec. L.

68. Lisa Lockwood, "Tommy Hilfiger Signs Pact With Dimension," *WWD,* 7 May 1998, 7.

69. Marla Matzer, "Marketing Budget for Disney Film Hits $30 Million," *Los Angeles Times,* 7 May 1998, sec. D.

70. It is worth noting that William Morris, who brokered the deal, also represents several actors in the movie.

71. Phyllis Furman, "Hilfiger's Taking It to the Miramax," *Daily News (New York),* 7 May 1998, 70.

72. Karen Hudes, "Holiday Movies; Independent Film, But with a Catch: A Corporate Logo," *The New York Times,* 15 November 1998, sec 2A.

73. "American Eagle to Star in 4 Upcoming Movies," *Pittsburgh Post-Gazette,* 21 July 2000, sec. D.

74. Nick Madigan, "For Teens, Movies Are a Big Deal, Really Big," *Variety,* 2–8 November 1998, 3–4.

Chapter Six

1. John Lippman, "Warner Bros. Unveils Plans for 5th Network Television," *Los Angeles Times,* 3 November 1993, sec. D.

2. Howard Rosenberg, "2 Networks Bow as Fox Dreams On," *Los Angeles Times,* 20 January 1995, sec. F.

3. Thomas and Litman, "Fox Broadcasting Company," 139–157, provides a concise examination of the Fox network launch, as well as the strategies that Fox used to circumvent FCC regulations.

4. Quoted in S. Farber, "Fox Chases the Ratings Rabbit," *American Film,* March 1987, 33.

5. See Elizabeth Kolbert, "Warner Bros. Enters Race for Network," *The New York Times,* 3 November 1993, sec. D; Bill Carter, "The Media Business; 2 Would-Be Networks Get Set for Prime Time," *The New York Times,* 9 January 1995, sec D. The easing of the FCC's "fin-syn" rules began in 1991 and underwent gradual deactivation until its complete suspension in 1995. See Steve Coe, "Fall Comes Early for Fin-Syn," *Broadcasting & Cable,* 11 September 1995, 9; Wharton, "FCC Seals Fin-Syn's Death," 36.

6. Ronald Grover, "Television: Are Paramount and Warner Looney Tunes?" *Business Week,* 8 January 1995, 46.

7. Joe Flint, "Exec Joins WB, Keeps 'Lake' Duties," *Daily Variety,* 13 May 1994, 1.

8. Lynette Rice and Steve McClellan, "Kellner's Latest Surprise: The WB Gets New Legs," *Broadcasting & Cable,* 11 August 1997, 20–24; Brian Lowry, "For Rivals WB & UPN, the Future is a Matter of Focus," *Los Angeles Times,* 27 July 1998, sec. F.

9. Mifflin, "Where Young Viewers Go (and Ads Follow)," sec. E; Josef Adalian, "WB Still Thinking Young," *Daily Variety,* 27 July 1998, 3; Josef Adalian, "Frog Net Sez It Won't Grow Up," *Variety,* 11–17 January 1999, 57+; Robert Bianco, "WB Sticks with Youth; UPN Seeks Middle Ground," *USA Today,* 28 July 1998, sec. 3D.

10. Klady notes that after the early 1980s, studios began ignoring the teen audience, as evidenced by the declining number of teen films produced between the mid-'80s and mid-'90s.

According to Beck and Smith, "the teen market [in the 1990s] has dwindled markedly since the '70s–'80s era when films like *Pretty in Pink* [1986] and *Ferris Bueller's Day Off* [1986] generated big box-office." See Klady, "Taken Unawares, H'w'd Refocuses on Youth," 10; Beck and Smith, "Movies for Teenagers Dwindle with Market," sec. A.

11. Thomas Schatz, "*St. Elsewhere* and the Evolution of the Ensemble Series," in *Television: The Critical View*, 4d ed., ed. Horace Newcomb (New York: Oxford University Press, 1987), 89.

12. Quoted in Graham, "WB and Teenagers make a felicitous combination," sec. D.

13. When FOX was first launched, the network pursued the urban youth audience by programming edgy, racy, and irreverent youth-oriented shows such as *21 Jump Street* (1987–1991), *The Simpsons* (1989–) and *Married with Children* (1987–1997). But by the late 1990s, FOX's schedule was becoming increasingly indistinguishable from its fellow mass audience broadcasters.

14. Quoted in Mifflin, "Where Young Viewers Go (and Ads Follow)," E1.

15. *Buffy the Vampire Slayer* debuted on the WB in 1997 and ran for five seasons on the network, until 2001. In its sixth season, the series moved to the UPN network, which was shifting its focus to younger audiences at the time.

16. UPN picked up *Roswell* for the 2001–2002 television season after it was cancelled by the WB, however poor ratings on UPN led to its cancellation in 2002.

17. Representations of the MTV teen can be found in a range of its programs, including *MTV's Spring Break*, a reality show documenting the college-break ritual in which teenagers descend on popular holiday destinations for parties, drinking, and concerts. *MTV Undressed* (1999–2002), a series centered on the sexual exploits of a group of teenagers, is another example of the envelope-pushing programming on the cable network that portrays teenagers as anti-authority, amoral individuals who casually pursue sexual and other pleasures with seeming impunity.

18. My thanks to John McMurria for pointing out the distinctive and different constructions of the WB and MTV "teen."

19. By "mainstream network" I mean the broadcast networks such as NBC, ABC, CBS, and FOX, which are distinct from cable networks that function by a different set of rules and are governed by different regulations.

20. The N is one example of a more "alternatively" inclined teen media site. Free of the greater constraints placed on broadcast networks to maintain standards of "decency," and less reliant on advertisers' goodwill, The N, a teen-oriented cable network, was launched in 2002. The N re-ran a range of American teen shows such as *Sabrina The Teenage Witch* (1996–2003) and *Dawson's Creek* (1998–2003), but also included in their schedule *Degrassi: The Next Generation* (2001–), a Canadian series that actively tackled a range of controversial teenage issues, featuring a pregnant teenager who considers abortion, and one teenager dealing with a gay father's decision to leave his family for his lover, issues that would not have been seen on a teen series appearing on an American mainstream, broadcast network. In fact, one *Degrassi* episode featuring a teenager having an abortion was banned and never aired on American television.

21. Caldwell, *Televisuality*, 9.

22. Turow, *Breaking Up America*, 92.

23. Turow, *Breaking Up America*, 5.

24. See Feuer, Kerr and Vahimagi, *MTM: "Quality Television"*; Betsy Williams, "'North to the Future': *Northern Exposure* and Quality Television," in *Television: The Critical View*, 5d ed., ed. Horace Newcomb (New York: Oxford University Press, 1994), 141–154; Schatz, "*St. Elsewhere* and the Evolution of the Ensemble Series," 85–100.

25. Ironically, the broadcast of this anti-violence, anti-suicide episode was postponed for several months. A week before the episode's originally scheduled March 1999 broadcast, the Columbine High School massacre occurred, prompting the network to postpone its telecast until September 1999.

26. Gitlin, *Inside Prime-Time*, 290.

27. Gitlin, *Inside Prime-Time*, 291.

28. Whedon wrote the script for the *Buffy the Vampire Slayer* movie, while Williamson worked on several teen slasher films, including the *Scream* trilogy.

29. Jill Brooke, "Star Struck: Well known people directing television programs," *AdWeek*. 27 April 1998, 18. Although film directors have previously worked on network television shows, these tended to involve highly publicized, high-profile, television "events." In contrast, the WB's collaborations with film personnel were part of the network's typical mode of production.

30. Feuer, Paul and Vahimagi, *MTM: "Quality Television,"* 44.

31. Certainly, hybridity, postmodern intertextual referencing, and self-reflexivity, are not unique or original to WB shows. FOX's *The Simpsons*, which was also targeted at youth and teens when it was launched, was an early predecessor who actively practiced many of the techniques and aesthetic strategies that came to characterize the WB shows.

32. Feuer, Paul and Vahimagi, *MTM: "Quality Television,"* 44.

33. See Caldwell, *Televisuality*; Collins, "Television and Postmodernism," 327–353; Doherty, "Genre, Gender and the *Aliens* Trilogy," 181–199; and Feuer, Kerr and Vahimagi, *MTM: "Quality Television."*

34. David Thorburn, "Television Melodrama," in *Television: The Critical View*, 5d ed., ed. Horace Newcomb (New York: Oxford University Press, 1994), 544.

35. The 1990s teenage audience may not have watched *The Breakfast Club* during its initial theatrical release; however, they would have accessed the film on video/DVD or during its numerous (re-)runs on cable.

36. Acknowledging the obscurity of some of the references, a series of books titled *The Watcher's Guide* have been published. These

books conscientiously identify and explain each pop cultural citation for the edification of its (teen)age (or otherwise) audience. See Christopher Golden and Nancy Holder, *The Watcher's Guide Buffy the Vampire Slayer* (New York: Pocket Books, 1998).

37. This tendency to overtly and self-consciously discuss other (teen) media texts was part of a larger trend in mainstream, commercial teen entertainment media, as evidenced in *Scream*'s heightened, inter-textual dialogue, which I examined in Chapter Five.

38. By employing a media/cultural literacy special (but not isolated) to its key demographic, the network also successfully avoided alienating viewers from a broader demographic. Instead, these intertextual references could be viewed as an attempt to target and "reward" older viewers who could best appreciate these references. The WB, as a mainstream, broadcast network, was primarily dependent on advertising for revenue and profits. As such, traditional measures such as high-ratings and a larger audience share, which would determine advertising rates, remained important. These intertextual references, therefore, represent the network's attempt to acknowledge and engage with its media-saturated, target teen audience, while simultaneously interpolating them into a more mainstream, adult culture.

39. See Josh Chetwynd, "Networks Promote Musicians for a Song," *USA Today*, 28 October 1998, sec. D; Joanne Ostrow, "WB shows an entree for unsung musicians," *The Denver Post*, 13 February 2000, sec. H; T. L. Stanley, "*Dawson's Creek*, The Record," *Adweek: Marketers of the Year*, 11 October 1999, M92.

40. Ostrow, "WB Shows an Entree for Unsung Musicians," H01.

41. Eileen Meehan provides valuable insight into how Warner Bros. (re-)packaged and profited from the *Batman* franchise. See Meehan, "Holy Commodity Fetish, Batman!" 66–89.

42. In 1978, Warner Bros. released the first *Superman* film directed by Richard Donner and released. Its success led to three more films in the franchise, released in 1980, 1983 and 1987. In 2006, the studio resurrected the cinematic franchise with *Superman Returns*, directed by Bryan Singer.

43. *Lois & Clark: The New Adventures of Superman* was produced by Warner Bros. and broadcast over ABC, running from 1993–1997. Warner Bros. also created *Superman: The Animated Series* and used it to anchor the WB's afternoon children's programming block launched in 1996. The series ran until 2000.

44. These were broadcast on the WB and subsequently marketing and distributed on video by Warner Bros.'s home video division.

45. Caldwell, *Televisuality*, 163.

46. T. L. Stanley, "Net Gains," *AdWeek: Marketers of the Year*, 11 October 1999, M88.

47. Tom Conroy, "Television: *Young Americans*," *US Weekly*, 17 July 2000, 43; David Zurawik, "Pretty as a Picture," *The Baltimore Sun*, 2 May 2000, sec. F.

48. Conroy, "Television: Young Americans," 43; Zurawik, "Pretty as a Picture," 1F.

49. *Rolling Stone*'s cover of Sarah Michelle Gellar featured her in a dominatrix-inspired costume, while *Nylon*'s January/February 2000 cover styled Gellar as a hard-edged "bad-girl" with darkly shadowed eyes and glossy, poutylips. Katie Holmes's *Rolling Stone* cover showed her in a damp white tank-top and cut-off denim shorts, she also appeared on the cover of *Detour* magazine's November 2000 issue wrapped only in a blanket. *Maxim*'s October 2000 issue offered a photo gallery of "The WB Girls" in which almost every one of the network's actresses posed seductively in lingerie.

50. Eric Schmuckler, "Honey, I Targeted the Kids," *US*, June 1999, 54–55.

51. Wyatt, *High Concept*, 46.

52. Quoted in Wayne Friedman, "Event-like Promos Build Loyal Young Core for WB," *Advertising Age*, 1 February 1999, sec. S.

53. This strategy is different from the traditional practice of having stars or guest stars cross-over to appear on different series (for example, as when NBC's *ER* stars, George Clooney and Anthony Edwards, made cameo appearances on NBC's *Friends*, or when *Friends* star Lisa Kudrow made appearances on NBC's *Mad About You*). In these instances, these practices tended to be isolated attempts aimed at increasing the network's ratings. These crossovers did little to enhance the NBC brand identity, nor are they part of a consistent network strategy to attract a specific target audience.

54. Bierbaum, "The WB's Getting the Girls," 30.

55. Bierbaum, "The WB's Getting the Girls," 30.

56. Brian Lowry, "Friday Night Fight Over Young Viewers," *Los Angeles Times*, 20 November 1998, sec. F.

57. Mifflin, "Where Young Viewers Go (and Ads Follow)," E1.

58. WB's problems began in the 1999–2000 television season when a number of the WB's most popular teen shows began slipping drastically in the ratings as they aged. *Dawson's Creek* and *Felicity*, two shows that had enjoyed great popularity with the 12 to 34 demographic just the season before, suffered a 15 percent drop in viewers. See Donna Petrozzello, "WB Woes Self-Inflicted," *Daily News* (New York), 17 May 2000, 81. Also, new shows, including the strongly hyped *Roswell*, launched strongly but failed to maintain their popularity. Another contributing factor posited for the network's decline involved the WB's over-reliance upon a very specific, narrowly defined and increasingly stagnant set of programs. Media journalists have suggested that the WB's downturn was linked to a burgeoning problem with the excessive similarities that existed across the WB's teen-oriented programming, speculating that what began as an inspired series of programming moves had become a liability. The WB had oversaturated its schedule with programs that were too similar. Without a sufficient degree of differentiation and distinction, the WB shows blended

together into an indistinguishable mass that stood and fell together. See Gary Levin, "Core Teen Viewership Tuning Out; WB creative woes, drama glut send ratings sliding," *USA TODAY*, 13 March 2000, 5D; Bill Goodykoontz, "WB network paying price for mistakes," *The Arizona Republic*, 20 January 2000, sec. E. Although the WB managed to correct some of these perceived problems, it continued to struggle for ratings in subsequent seasons, particularly in the face of increased competition for the teen/youth viewer.

59. UPN was launched in the same year as the WB, but unlike the latter, UPN initially committed to a broadcasting model in which it targeted the same broad demographic audience as the established networks, with little success. In 2001, UPN made a strategic decision to follow in the WB's footsteps and refocus on teenagers. Significantly, when the WB cancelled both *Buffy* and *Roswell* in 2001, UPN picked up both series, signaling the latter's growing interest in targeting the same teen audience that had contributed to the WB's success. See Josef Adalian, "UPN Sinks Teeth into WB's *Buffy*," *Variety*, 23 April 2001. <http://www.variety.com/article/VR111779 7571.html?categoryid=14&cs=1> (Accessed 24 April 2001); Lisa De Moraes, "The Real Deal behind the *Buffy* Network Switch," *The Washington Post*, 10 May 2001, sec. C.

60. At the same time, the WB's most popular shows were also beginning to lose their novelty and in some cases appeared to be experiencing creative slumps, further exacerbating the audience attrition.

61. The WB-UPN merger was also motivated by the expiration of both networks' contracts with their respective affiliates, which opened a window for negotiations between the two networks before they embarked on negotiations for new affiliate contracts. See Bill Carter, "UPN and WB to Combine," *The New York Times*, 24 January 2006. <http://www.nytimes.com/2006/01/24/business/media/24cnd-network.html?scp=1&sq=%93UPN%20and%20WB%20to%20Combine%94&st=cse> (Accessed, 25 January 2006). The histories of the WB and UPN, and the subsequent CW merger, are the subjects of Susanne Daniels and Cynthia Littleton, *Season Finale: The Unexpected Rise and Fall of the WB and UPN* (New York: HarperCollins, 2007).

62. The CW's 2006–2007 schedule consisted of *America's Next Top Model* (2003–), *Veronica Mars*, and *Everybody Hates Chris* (2005–2009) from UPN, and the WB's *Gilmore Girls* (2000–2007), *Smallville*, *Supernatural* (2005–) and *Beauty and the Geek* (2005–).

63. Michael Learmonth, "CW Plots Rookie Season," *Variety*, 18 May 2006. <http://www.variety.com/article/VR1117943543.html?categoryid=1614&cs=1> (Accessed 19 May 2006).

64. In one instance, Beverly Mitchell from the CW's *7th Heaven* appeared in a content wrap for a particular brand of mouthwash, extolling the product's role in enhancing her self-confidence. Learmonth, "CW Plots Rookie Season."

Chapter Seven

1. Lesley Jane Seymour, "Tweens 'R' Shoppers," *The New York Times*, 22 April 2007. <http://www.nytimes.com/2007/04/22/nyregion/nyregionspecial2/22RSHOP.html?scp=1&sq=%93Tweens%20%91R%92%20Shoppers%94%20&st=cse> (Accessed 25 January 2008).

2. Diane Werts, "Cashing In on Tween Viewers," *Newsday*, 19 March 2006. <www.newsday.com> (Accessed 9 January 2009).

3. David Bloom, "Targeting Those Tricky Teenagers," *Variety*, 28 April 2002. <http://www.variety.com/article/VR1117866102.html?categoryid=14&cs=1> (Accessed 10 April 2009).

4. Aimee Decken, "Tapping Into Tweens," *Mediaweek*, 3 November 2003, 30.

5. Quoted in Seymour, "Tweens 'R' Shoppers."

6. Bloom, "Targeting Those Tricky Teenagers."

7. Box-office grosses retrieved from <www.boxofficemojo.com>. *Harry Potter and the Sorcerer's Stone*, <www.boxofficemojo.com/yearly/chart/?yr=2001&p=.htm>; *Spy Kids*, <http://www.boxofficemojo.com/movies/?id=spykids.htm> (Accessed April 12, 2009).

8. Wendy Jackson Hall, "Children's Outlet Learn to Play the Sharing Game," *Variety*, 13 September 2001. <http://www.variety.com/article/VR1117852668.html?categoryid=1013&cs=1> (Accessed 10 April 2009).

9. Dave Itzkoff, "The Multimedia Synergistic Slumber Party," *The New York Times*, 24 September 2006. <http://query.nytimes.com/gst/fullpage.html?res=9A01E3D81031F937A1575AC0A9609C8B63> (Accessed 25 September 2006).

10. Quinn and Chang, "More Teenagers Ignoring CDs."

11. Form 10-K, The Walt Disney Company, 1 October 2005, 1.

12. Form 10-K, The Walt Disney Company, 1 October 2005, 1.

13. Form 10-K, The Walt Disney Company, 1 October 2005, 19.

14. Form 10-K, The Walt Disney Company, 1 October 2005, 20.

15. Werts, "Cashing In on Tween Viewers."

16. Dave Itzkoff, "Move Over Mickey: A New Franchise at Disney," *The New York Times*, 20 August 2007. <http://www.nytimes.com/2007/08/20/business/media/20disney.html?scp=1&sq="Move%20Over%20Mickey:%20A%20New%20Franchise%20at%20Disney"%20&st=cse> (Accessed 22 August 2007).

17. Andrew Hampp, "Tween Stars, and Marketing Tie-Ins in the Making," *Advertising Age*, 9 April 2008. <www.adage.com> (Accessed 10 April 2008).

18. Pamela McClintock, "'Montana' Mania Hits Theaters," *Variety*, 3 February 2008 <http://www.variety.com/article/VR1117980079.html?categoryid=13&cs=1> (Accessed 5 February 2008).

19. Dawn Chmielewski, "A Cinderella Story for Disney Music Group," *Los Angeles Times*, 9 July 2007. <www.latimes.com> (Accessed 9 January 2009).

20. McClintock, "'Montana' Mania Hits Theatres"; Marc Graser, "The Next Big Thing," *Variety*, 11–17 February 2008, 6.

21. Dade Hayes, "'HSM3' Makes Box Office Honor Roll," *Variety*, 26 October 2008. <http://www.variety.com/article/VR1117994680.html?categoryid=13&cs=1> (Accessed 29 October 2008).

22. Playhouse Disney was targeted at the youngest demographics—preschoolers, while Zoog Disney attempt to reach a preteen/teen audience with several original series including *The Famous Jett Jackson* (1998–2001), *So Weird* (1999–2001) and *Lizzie Maguire*. Finally, Vault Disney appeared to target baby boomer parents with classic Disney shows from earlier decades including *Zorro* (1957–1959), *The Love Bug* (1982), and original episodes of *The Mickey Mouse Club*.

23. Itzkoff, "Move Over Mickey."

24. Werts, "Cashing In on Tween Viewers."

25. Werts, "Cashing In on Tween Viewers."

26. Although the genre, which focused on a group of performers putting up a musical show, was popular in the 1930s, it had been replaced by the integrated musicals of 1940s and '50s. By the late 1960s, the musical had become a dormant genre, and remained largely neglected in the final decades of the twentieth century, in large part supplanted by the rise of the music video in the 1980s. It is worth noting that while popular music was increasingly featured on the soundtracks of popular Hollywood films and television series, the musical form itself largely disappeared from movie theatres and television in the 1990s and through the millennium, with a few exceptions. The few movie musicals released in the millennium were either adaptations of popular classic stage musicals (*Chicago* [2002], *The Phantom of the Opera* [2004], and *Rent* [2005]) or they were postmodern experiments that mixed popular contemporary songs with the stylized aesthetics of the classic movie musical (*Everyone Says I Love You* [1996], *Love's Labour's Lost* [2000], *Moulin Rouge!* [2001]).

27. Astaire's memorable dance sequence takes place in *Royal Wedding* (1951), when he sings and dances to "You're All the World to Me."

28. These Miley-related texts include those focused on the imaginary Miley Stewart, and the actual Miley Cyrus.

29. McClintock, "'Montana' Mania Hits Theatres."

30. McClintock, "'Montana' Mania Hits Theatres"; Graser, "The Next Big Thing," 6.

31. Wyatt, "Summer Advisory: A Jonas Front Looms."

32. Wyatt, "Summer Advisory: A Jonas Front Looms."

33. See Wyatt, "Summer Advisory: A Jonas Front Looms," for a discussion of Disney's multi-media repurposing of the Jonas Brothers' media releases.

34. Phil Gallo, "Miley Cyrus Tops the Charts," *Variety*, 30 July 2008. <http://www.variety.com/article/VR1117989765.html?categoryid=16&cs=1> (Accessed 31 July 2008).

35. Michael Fleming, "Miley Cyrus to Star in Disney Film," *Variety*, 16 September 2008. <http://www.variety.com/article/VR1117992306.html?categoryid=13&cs=1> (Accessed 22 September 2008).

36. Werts, "Cashing In on Tween Viewers."

37. Quoted in Itzkoff, "The Multimedia Synergistic Slumber Party."

38. Matea Gold, "Showy Success for Kids Musical," *Los Angeles Times*, 27 February 2006, sec E.

39. Gold, "Showy Success for Kids Musical," E1; Ben Sisario, "A Musical for Tweens Captures its Audience," *The New York Times*, 8 February 2006. <http://query.nytimes.com/gst/fullpage.html?res=9F04E4DF143EF93BA35751C0A9609C8B63&scp=1&sq="a%20musical%20for%20tweens%20captures%20its%20Audience"&st=cse> (Accessed 9 February 2006).

40. Werts, "Cashing In on Tween Viewers."

41. Beth Snyder Bulik, "JibJab Caters to New Crowd: 'High School Musical' Fans," *AdvertisingAge*, 18 September 2008. <www.adage.com> (Accessed 22 September 2008).

42. Claude Brodesser-akner, "MySpace Helps Promote 'High School Musical 3,'" *AdvertisingAge*, 2 September 2008. <www.adage.com> (Accessed 3 September 2008).

43. Jack Neff, "Sleeping Beauty: How Disney Bested Revlon's Sales," *Advertising Age*, 25 September 2006, 6.

44. Jacques Steinberg, "Back to School," *The New York Times*, 11 March 2007. < http://www.nytimes.com/2007/03/11/arts/television/11stei.html?scp=1&sq=Jacques%20Steinberg,%20march%2011,%202007&st=cse> (Accessed 14 March 2007).

45. Gordon Cox, "'Musical' Gets the Tour Treatment," *Variety*, 23 March 2007, 2+.

46. Cox, "'Musical' Gets the Tour Treatment," 27.

47. Information on *High School Musical* licenses and performances are detailed in Brodesser-akner, "MySpace Helps Promote 'High School Musical 3.'"

48. Brodesser-akner, "MySpace Helps Promote 'High School Musical 3.'"

49. Michael Schneider, "ABC Heads to 'High School,'" *Variety*, 2 March 2008. <http://www.variety.com/article/VR1117981732.html?categoryid=14&cs=1> (Accessed 4 March 2008); Brodesser-akner, "MySpace Helps Promote 'High School Musical 3.'"

50. See Itzkoff, "Move Over Mickey," for an overview of the *High School Musical 2* promotional activities.

51. Brodesser-akner, "MySpace Helps Promote 'High School Musical 3.'"

52. Wyatt, "Summer Advisory: A Jonas Front Looms."

53. Kissell, "Kids Line Up for 'Camp Rock.'"

54. The audience numbers for *High School Musical* is drawn from various news articles including Sisario, "A Musical for Tweens Captures Its Audience"; Itzkoff, "Move Over Mickey" and Graser, "The Next Big Thing," 6.

55. Graser, "The Next Big Thing," 6.

56. Gold, "Showy Success for Kids Musical."

57. Itzkoff, "Move Over Mickey."

58. Chmielewski, "A Cinderella Story for Disney Music Group."

59. Graser, "The Next Big Thing," 6

60. McClintock, "'Montana' Mania Hits Theatres."

61. Brooks Barnes, "Boy Band Is Starting to Feel the Heat," *The New York Times*, 25 May 2009. <http://www.nytimes.com/2009/05/25/arts/music/25jonas.html?_r=1&th&emc=th> (Accessed 29 May 2009).

62. Barnes, "Boy Band Is Starting to Feel the Heat."

63. Dade Hayes, "Disney Profits Up 21% in 2nd Quarter: 'Hannah Montana,' homevideo boost revenue," *Variety*, 6 May 2008. <http://www.variety.com/article/VR1117985168.html?categoryid=18&cs=1> (Accessed 9 May 2008).

64. Chmielewski, "A Cinderella Story for Disney Music Group."

65. Neff, "Sleeping Beauty: How Disney Bested Revlon's Sales," 6.

66. Brooks Barnes, "Disney Aims for the Boy Audience with a Cable Channel and a Web Site," *The New York Times*, 12 February 2009. <http://www.nytimes.com/2009/02/13/business/media/13disney.html?ref=television> (Accessed 15 February 2009).

Chapter Eight

1. Andrew Hampp, "'What You're Watching' to Use Twitter, Facebook," *Advertising Age*, 29 April 2009. <http://adage.com> (Accessed 4 May 2009).

2. Brian Steinberg, "CW's 'Cwinger' Ads Debut in 'Gossip Girl,'" *Advertising Age*, 20 April 2009. <http://adage.com> (Accessed 22 April 2009).

3. See Hein and Anderson, "The Age of Reason," 22.

4. Steinberg, "CW's 'Cwinger' Ads Debut in 'Gossip Girl.'"

5. Steinberg, "CW's 'Cwinger' Ads Debut in 'Gossip Girl.'"

6. Brian Steinberg, "Streamed TV Shows Attracting Their Own Audience," *Advertising Age*, 8 July 2008 <http://adage.com> (Accessed 9 July 2008).

7. See Larry Debrow, "Teen Angel? Kinda," *Advertising Age*, 2 January 2006, 14.

8. Thomas Mulligan, "No Breaking for Commercials," *Los Angeles Times*, 28 January 2008, sec. C.

9. The film and television industries, for instance, require huge financial commitments to sustain their production, distribution and exhibition activities. The cost of producing a typical Hollywood film or television series runs into tens of millions, as does the price of maintaining both a national and international distribution network to deliver the content to exhibitors. Similarly, operating budgets of exhibitors, whether that refers to a chain of multiplexes or television stations, are high.

10. David Croteau and William Hoynes, "Media Technology and Social Change," in *Media Society: Industries, Images and Audiences*, 3d ed. (California: Pine Forge Press, 2003), 303.

11. This is not to suggest that new media is entirely responsible for the collapse of media-specific distinctions. As I have explored throughout this work, the rise of cross-media/multimedia intersections and hybrids preceded the rise of new media, motivated by multi-media conglomeration and the synergistic practices. However, new media developments have functioned as a catalyst, intensifying and accelerating the process of media/content/aesthetic convergence.

12. Randall Stross, "Someone Has to Pay for TV. But Who? And How?" *The New York Times*, 7 May 2006. <http://www.nytimes.com/2006/05/07/business/yourmoney/07digi.html?scp=1&sq=%93Someone%20Has%20to%20Pay%20for%20TV.%20But%20Who?%20And%20How?%94%20&st=cse> (Accessed 8 May 2006).

13. Stross, "Someone Has to Pay for TV. But Who? And How?"

14. For a sustained discussion of such activities see Henry Jenkins, *Textual Poachers* (New York: Routledge, 1992).

15. John Caldwell, "Convergence Television: Aggregating Form and Repurposing Content in the Culture of Conglomeration," in *Television After TV: Essays on a Medium in Transition*, ed. Lynn Spiegel and Jan Olsson (Durham: Duke University Press, 2004), 49.

16. Darren Crosdale, *Dawson's Creek: The Official Companion* (London: Ebury, 1999), 145–147.

17. Henry Jenkins, "Searching for the Origami Unicorn. *The Matrix* and Transmedia Storytelling," in *Convergence Culture: Where Old and New Media Collide* (New York: New York University Press, 2006), 118–119.

18. Jenkins, "Searching for the Origami Unicorn," 96.

19. Mike Shields, "Short Order: Cable Nets Are Programming for Smaller Screens," *Media-Week*, 10 April 2006, 54–56.

20. Michael Schneider, "Fox to Stream Premieres for Dorms," *Variety*, 24 August 2008. <http://www.variety.com/article/VR1117991059.html?categoryid=14&cs=1> (Accessed 27 August 2008).

21. Michael Learmonth, "Hulu Now No. 2 Online-Video Site," *Advertising Age*, 12 March 2009. <http://adage.com> (Accessed March 13, 2009).

22. Daniel Lyons, "Old Media Strikes Back," *Newsweek*, 21 February 2009. <http://www.newsweek.com/id/185790> (Accessed 20 May 2009).

23. Ben Fritz and Michael Learmonth, "Showbiz's Site Fright," *Variety*, 12–18 March 2007, 1+; Larry Neumeister, "Viacom Alleges YouTube Copyright Infringement," *USA Today*, 27 May 2008. <http://www.usatoday.com/tech/news/techpolicy/2008-05-27-viacom-youtube-lawsuit_N.htm> (Accessed 18 May 2009).

24. Scott Collins, "Where TV and the Web Converge, There Is Hulu," *Los Angeles Times*, 16 June 2008. <www.latimes.com/entertainment/news/TV/la-et-channel16-2008jun16,0,2559613,print.story> Accessed 23 June 2008.

25. Learmonth, "Hulu Now No. 2 Online-Video Site."

26. Learmonth, "Hulu Now No. 2 Online-Video Site."

27. Lyons, "Old Media Strikes Back."

28. In a development that should reinforce Hulu.com's continuing success, Disney joined NBC Universal and News Corp. as an equity partner in the Hulu venture in April 2009. See Cynthia Littleton, "Disney Joins Hulu," *Variety*, 30 April 2009. <http://www.variety.com/article/VR1118003024.html?categoryid=13&cs=1> (Accessed 4 May 2009).

29. Max Lakin, "Buffy Returns to Life Online. WB Network Resurrected as a Website," *Advertising Age*, 29 August 2008. <http://adage.com> Accessed 3 September 2008.

30. Lakin, "Buffy Returns to Life Online."

31. Larry Debrow, "Quickie Nostalgia That's Easy to Skip," *Advertising Age*, 18 September 2008. <http://adage.com> (Accessed 22 September 2008).

32. One-off videos such as Sarah Silverman's "I'm (bleeping) Matt Damon," and Jimmy Kimmel's star-studded response, "I'm (bleeping) Ben Affleck," have been viewed in excess of 10 million times online. See Diane Garrett, "Skeins Swim in Web Stream," *Variety*, 1 March 2008, 16.

33. See Garrett, "Skeins Swim in Web Stream."

34. See Garrett, "Skeins Swim in Web Stream."

35. Abbey Klaassen, "YouTube Adds Full-Length CBS Content," *Advertising Age*, 10 October 2008. <http://adage.com> (Accessed 13 October 2008).

36. Diane Garrett, "YouTube Adds Retailer Links to Videos," *Variety*, 7 October 2008. <http://www.variety.com/article/VR1117993602.html?categoryid=1009&cs=1> (Accessed 13 October 2008).

37. Marc Graser, "MySpace Top Site for Young Moviegoers," *Variety*, 28 October 2008. <http://www.variety.com/article/VR1117994822.html?categoryid=13&cs=> (Accessed 29 October 2008).

38. Learmonth, "Hulu Now No. 2 Online-Video Site."

39. Learmonth, "Hulu Now No. 2 Online-Video Site."

40. Warner Bros. also targeted the child and tween demographic by launching KidsWB.com, which streams original cartoon shorts created by the WB Animation division. Signing on McDonald's and Mattel as early sponsors, the site also offered games and virtual worlds that allowed users to interact with the content. See Diane Garrett, "WB Revived as Online Platform," *Variety*, 28 April 2008. <http://www.variety.com/article/VR1117984772.html?categoryid=14&cs=1> (Accessed 30 April 2008).

41. Phil Gallo, "Warner Joins Nokia's Music Service," *Variety*, 1 July 2008. <http://www.variety.com/article/VR1117988366.html?categoryid=16&cs=1> (Accessed 8 July 2008).

42. Lorne Manly, "For Tiny Screens, Some Big Dreams," *The New York Times*, 21 May 2006.

<http://www.nytimes.com/2006/05/21/business/yourmoney/21mobile.html?scp=1&sq=%93For%20Tiny%20Screens,%20Some%20Big%20Dreams%94%20&st=cse> (Accessed 22 May 2006).

43. Manly, "For Tiny Screens, Some Big Dreams."

44. Manly, "For Tiny Screens, Some Big Dreams."

45. Justin Kroll, "Steady Rise for Mobile Revenues," *Variety*, 3 August 2008. <http://www.variety.com/article/VR1117990011.html?categoryid=1009&cs=1> (Accessed 14 August 2008).

46. Randy Kennedy, "The Shorter, Faster, Cruder, Tinier TV Show," *The New York Times*, 28 May 28 2006. <http://www.nytimes.com/2006/05/28/magazine/28mtv.html?scp=1&sq=%93The%20Shorter,%20Faster,%20Cruder,%20Tinier%20TV%20Show%94%20&st=cse> (Accessed May 29, 2006).

47. Laura M. Holson, "Hollywood Loves the Tiny Screen. Advertisers Don't." *The New York Times*, 7 May 2007. <http://www.nytimes.com/2007/05/07/business/media/07cell.html?scp=1&sq=%93Hollywood%20Loves%20the%20Tiny%20Screen.%20Advertisers%20Don%92t.%94%20&st=cse> (Accessed 11 May 2007).

48. Manly, "For Tiny Screens, Some Big Dreams."

49. Manly, "For Tiny Screens, Some Big Dreams."

50. Manly, "For Tiny Screens, Some Big Dreams."

51. Holson, "Hollywood Loves the Tiny Screen. Advertisers Don't."

52. Manly, "For Tiny Screens, Some Big Dreams."

53. For instance, Toyota sponsored and had product tie-ins with *Prison Break: Proof of Innocence*, a mobile series developed to accompany FOX's hit series *Prison Break* (2005–2009). Manly, "For Tiny Screens, Some Big Dreams."

54. Kennedy, "The Shorter, Faster, Cruder, Tinier TV Show."

55. Manly, "For Tiny Screens, Some Big Dreams."

56. Brian Steinberg, "The Broadcast Ad Model Is Broken. Now What?" *Advertising Age*, 27 October 2008. <http://adage.com> (Accessed 29 October 2008).

57. Michael Learmonth, "Distributors, Networks Push for More Ads in TV Shows Online," *Advertising Age*, 6 October 2008. <http://adage.com> (Accessed 13 October 2008).

58. As of 2009, there was no standardized measure for audiences watching specific programs across the different traditional and new media platforms.

59. See Jenkins, "Searching for the Origami Unicorn," 106–107.

60. Henry Jenkins, *Convergence Culture: Where Old and New Media Collide* (New York: New York University Press, 2006), 3.

61. Lee Hall, "Coming Soon to a PVR Near You; TiVo to Provide Uploadable Advertisements, While Giving Customers the Means to Skip Them," *Broadcasting and Cable*, 26 February 2001, 40.

62. William Boddy, "Interactive Television and Advertising Form in Contemporary U.S. Television," in *Television After TV: Essays on a Medium in Transition*, ed. Lynn Spiegel and Jan Olssen (Durham: Duke University Press, 2004), 127.

Conclusion

1. Henry Jenkins, *Convergence Culture: Where Old and New Media Collide* (New York: New York University Press, 2006).

2. Certainly, this notion of digital media offering global, universal access is currently more an idea than an actual reality. Nations and governments continue to find ways to block Internet access in various parts of the globe, hindering the emergence of a truly borderless, censorship-free, un-policed, communication network. Yet it remains true that these same, new, communications technologies also allow for a greater degree of exchange, interaction and debate on a global scale than has ever been available before.

3. John Tomlinson, *Globalization and Culture* (Chicago: University of Chicago Press, 1999), 29.

4. Robert J Shiller, "Depression Scares Are Hardly New," *New York Times*, 3 May 2009. <http://www.nytimes.com/2009/05/03/busine ss/economy/03view.html?scp=4&sq=2008%20fi nancial%20crisis,%20%22new%20depressi on%22&st=cse> (Accessed May 13, 2009). See also Larry Elliot, "A Financial Crisis Unmatched Since the Great Depression, Say Analysts," *The Guardian (UK)*, 18 March 2008. <http://www. guardian.co.uk/business/2008/mar/18/credit crunch.marketturmoil1> (Accessed May 13, 2009).

5. Cynthia Littleton, "News Corp.'s Profits Plunge," *Variety*, 6 May 2009. <http://www.vari ety.com/article/VR1118003258.html?category id=1056&cs=1> (Accessed 13 May 2009); Jill Goldsmith, "Viacom Profit Veers Down," *Variety*, 30 April 2009. <http://www.variety.com/arti cle/VR1118003020.html?categoryid=1009&cs=1> (Accessed 13 May 2009); Dade Hayes, "Time Warner Profits Fall 14% in Q1," *Variety*, 29 April 2009. <http://www.variety.com/article/VR11180 02977.html?categoryid=1237&cs=1> (Accessed 13 May 2009).

6. Natalie Zmuda, "Teens, Too, Are Tightening Budgets," *Advertising Age*, 27 April 2009. <http:adage.com> Accessed 28 April 2009.

7. Zmuda, "Teens, Too, Are Tightening Budgets."

8. Richard Verrier, "'Twilight' Leaves Its Box-Office Mark," Los Angeles Times, 24 November 2008. <http://www.latimes.com/busin ess/la-fi-boxoffice24-2008nov24,0,2796210.sto ry> (Accessed 19 June 2009); Twilight boxoffice, <http://www.boxofficemojo.com/movies /?id=twilight08.htm> (Accessed 19 June 2009).

9. Dave McNary and Pamela McClintock, "'17 Again' Tops Weekend Box Office," *Variety*, 19 April 2009. <http://www.variety.com/article/ VR1118002579.html?categoryid=13&cs=1> (Accessed 5 May 2009).

10. Dave McNary and Pamela McClintock, "'Hannah' Tops Easter Box Office," *Variety*, 12 April 2009. <http://www.variety.com/article/ VR1118002345.html?categoryid=&cs=1> (Accessed 5 May 2009).

11. Zmuda, "Teens, Too, Are Tightening Budgets."

Bibliography

Adalian, Josef. "Frog Net Sez It Won't Grow Up." *Variety*, 11–17 January 1999, 57+.

_____. "UPN Sinks Teeth into WB's *Buffy*." *Variety*, 23 April 2001. <www.variety.com> Accessed 24 April 2001.

_____. "WB Still Thinking Young." *Daily Variety*, 27 July 27 1998, 3.

Adelson, Andrea. "The Media Business: Advertising; A Growing Number of Media Companies Are Trying to Shake MTV's Grip on the Teen-age Market." *New York Times*, 15 March 1994. <http://www.nytimes.com/1994/03/15/business/media-business-advertising-growing-number-media-companies-are-trying-shake-mtv-s.html?scp=1&sq="The%20Media%20Business:%20Advertising;%20A%20growing%20number%20of%20media%20companies%20are%20trying%20to%20shake%20MTV's%20grip%20on%20the%20teen-age%20market%22&st=cse > (Accessed 25 January 2008).

Alvey, Mark. "'Too Many Kids and Old Ladies': Quality Demographics and 1960s US Television." *Screen*. 45.1 (2004): 40–62.

"American Eagle to Star in 4 Upcoming Movies." *Pittsburgh Post-Gazette*, 21 July 2000, sec. D1.

Anderson, Christopher. *HollywoodTV: The Studio System in the Fifties*. Austin: University of Texas Press, 1994.

Ascher-Walsh, Rebecca. "Behind the Music." *Entertainment Weekly*, 12 March 1999. <http://www.ew.com/ew/article/0,,274745,00.html> Accessed 25 January 2008.

Attwood, Brett. "MTV Expands Its Online Programming." *Billboard*, 29 July 1995, 8+.

Aufderheide, Pat. "Music Videos: The Look of the Sound." In *Watching Television*, edited by Todd Gitlin. New York: Pantheon, 1986.

Austin, Bruce. "Home Video: The Second Run 'Theater' of the 1990s." In *Hollywood in the Age of Television*, edited by Tino Balio. Massachusetts: Unwin Hyman, 1990.

Bagdikian, Ben. *The Media Monopoly*. 5th Edition. Boston: Beacon Press, 1997.

Balio, Tino. "Adjusting to the New Global Economy: Hollywood in the 1990s." In *Film Policy: International, National and Regional Perspectives*, edited by Albert Moran. New York: Routledge, 1996.

_____. *The American Film Industry*. Revised edition. Madison: The University of Wisconsin Press, 1985.

Banks, Jack. *Monopoly Television: MTV's Quest to Control the Music*. Colorado: Westview Press, 1997.

Barker, Chris. *Television, Globalization and Cultural Identities*. Buckingham and Philadelphia: Open University Press, 1999.

Barnes, Brooks. "Boy Band Is Starting to Feel the Heat." *New York Times*, 25 May 2009. <http://www.nytimes.com/2009/05/25/arts/music/25jonas.html?_r=1&th&emc=th> (Accessed 29 May 2009).

_____. "Disney Aims for the Boy Audience with a Cable Channel and a Web Site." *New York Times*, 12 February 2009. <http://www.nytimes.com/2009/02/13/business/media/13disney.html?ref=television> (Accessed 15 February 2009).

Barnouw, Erik et al. *Conglomerates and the Media*. New York: The New Press, 1997.

Baudrillard, Jean. "Consumer Society." In *Selected Writings*, edited by Mark Poster. Cambridge: Polity Press, 1970 [1988].

_____. *For a Critique of the Political Economy of the Sign*. St. Louis: Telos Press, 1972 [1981].

Baughman, James L. "The Weakest Chain and the Strongest Link: The American Broadcasting Company and the Motion Picture Industry, 1952–60." In *Hollywood in the Age of Television*, edited by Tino Balio. Boston: Unwin Hyman, 1990.

Beck, Marilyn and Stacey Jenel Smith. "Movies for Teen-Agers Dwindle with Market." *Times-Picayune*, 2 July 1995:, sec. A.

Bedell, Sally. *Up the Tube*. New York: Viking, 1981.

Berkowitz, Harry. "Now at Disney: Sex, Lies and Aladdin." *Newsday*, 1 May 1993, 14.

Bianco, Robert. "WB Sticks with Youth; UPN Seeks Middle Ground." *USA Today*, 28 July 1998, sec. D.

Bierbaum, Tom. "The WB's Getting the Girls." *Variety*, 2–8 November 1998, 30+.

Block, Valerie. "The WB Gets Set to Leapfrog Rivals." *Crain's New York Business*, 31 August 1998, 4.

Bloom, David. "Targeting Those Tricky Teenagers." *Variety*, 28 April 2002. <http://www.variety.com/article/VR1117866102.html?categoryid=14&cs=1> (Accessed 10 April 2009).

Blum, John. *V Was for Victory: Politics and American Culture During World War II*. New York: Harcourt Brace Jovanovich, 1976.

Boddy, William. *Fifties Television: The Industry and Its Critics*. Champaign: University of Illinois Press, 1990.

_____. "Interactive Television and Advertising Form in Contemporary U.S. Television." In *Television After TV: Essays on a Medium in Transition*, edited by Lynn Spiegel and Jan Olssen. Durham: Duke University Press, 2004.

Boehlert, Eric. "Rap's Grip on Suburbs Loosens as Teens Turn to Modern Rock." *Billboard*, 3 June 1995, 1+.

Brodesser-akner, Claude. "MySpace Helps Promote 'High School Musical 3.'" *AdvertisingAge*, 2 September 2008. <www.adage.com> (Accessed 3 September 2008).

Brooke, Jill. "Fourth Estate: Girl Power." *AdWeek*, 2 February 1998, 18–19.

_____. "Star Struck: Well Known People Directing Television Programs." *AdWeek*, 27 April 1998, 18.

Buchsbaum, Jonathon. "Zukor Buys Protection: The Paramount Stock Purchase of 1929." *Cine-Tracts*. 2 (1979): 49–62.

Bulik, Beth Snyder. "JibJab Caters to New Crowd: 'High School Musical' Fans." *AdvertisingAge*, 18 September 2008. <www.adage.com> (Accessed 22 September 2008).

Burgher, Valerie. "The Fifth Networks' Second Coming." *AdWeek-TV Upfront*, 2 June 1997, 42+.

Caldwell, John. "Convergence Television: Aggregating Form and Repurposing Content in the Culture of Conglomeration." In *Television After TV: Essays on a Medium in Transition*, edited by Lynn Spiegel and Jan Olsson. Durham: Duke University Press, 2004.

Caldwell, John Thornton. *Televisuality: Style, Crisis, and Authority in American Television*. New Jersey: Rutgers University Press, 1995.

Cantor, Muriel. *Prime-Time Television: Content and Control*. Beverly Hills, CA: Sage, 1980.

Cardwell, Annette. "Generation Next: Recent Hits Have Studios Screaming for More Teen Flicks." *Boston Herald*, 23 September 1998, 55.

Carter, Bill. "The Media Business; 2 Would-Be Networks Get Set for Prime Time." *New York Times*, 9 January 1995, sec. D.

_____. "UPN and WB to Combine." *New York Times*, 24 January 2006. <http://www.nytimes.com/2006/01/24/business/media/24cnd-network.html?scp=1&sq=%93UPN%20and%20WB%20to%20Combine%94&st=cse> (Accessed 25 January 2006).

Chattman, Lauren. "Smells Like Teen Spirit: Gender, Adolescence, and the Culture of Consumption in *Beverly Hills, 90210*." *Spectator*. 13.2 (1993): 13–19.

Chetwynd, Josh and Andy Seiler. "Expectations Rise for 'Scary' Body Count." *USA Today*, 23 June 2000, sec. E.

Chetwynd, Josh. "Networks Promote Musicians for a Song." *USA Today*, 28 October 1998, sec. D.

Chmielewski, Dawn. "A Cinderella Story for Disney Music Group." *Los Angeles Times*, 9 July 2007. <www.latimes.com> (Accessed 9 January 2009).

Christman, Ed. "Backstreet Could Hit 1 Mil. in First Week." *Billboard*, 29 May 1999, 3+.

Clover, Carol. *Man, Women and Chainsaws: Gender in the Modern Horror Film*. Princeton: Princeton University Press, 1992.

Coe, Steve. "Fall Comes Early for Fin-Syn." *Broadcasting & Cable*, 11 September 1995, 9.

Cohen, Roger. "Rupert Murdoch's Biggest Gamble." *New York Times*, 21 October 1990, 30.

Collins, Jim. "Genericity in the Nineties: Eclectic Irony and the New Sincerity." In *Film Theory Goes to the Movies*, edited by Jim Collins, et al. New York: Routledge, 1993.

_____. "Television and Postmodernism." In *Channels of Discourse, Reassembled*, edited by Robert C. Allen. 2d ed. Chapel Hill: University of North Carolina Press, 1992.

Collins, Scott. "Where TV and the Web Converge, There Is Hulu." *Los Angeles Times*, 16 June 2008. <www.latimes.com/entertainment/news/TV/la-et-channel16-2008jun16,0,2559613,print.story> (Accessed 23 June 2008).

Conroy, Tom. "Television: *Young Americans*." *US Weekly*, 17 July 2000, 43.

Considine, David. *The Cinema of Adolescence*. North Carolina: McFarland, 1985.

Corrigan, Peter. *The Sociology of Consumption*. London: Sage Publications, 1998.

Corrigan, Timothy. *A Cinema Without Walls: Movies and Culture After Vietnam.* New Brunswick, N.J.: Rutgers University Press, 1991.

Cox, Gordon. "'Musical' Gets the Tour Treatment." *Variety,* 23 March 2007, 2+.

Crosdale, Darren. *Dawson's Creek: The Official Companion.* London: Ebury, 1999.

Croteau, David and William Hoynes. *The Business of the Media: Corporate Media and the Public Interest.* Thousand Oaks, California: Pine Forge Press, 2001.

_____. "Media Technology and Social Change." In *Media Society: Industries, Images and Audiences.* 3d ed. California: Pine Forge Press, 2003.

Cummings, James. "Cut! Dimension Films Brings Back the Slasher Movies." *Star Tribune (Minneapolis, MN),* 13 November 1997, sec. E.

D'Acci, Julie. *Defining Women: Television & the Case of Cagney & Lacey.* Chapel Hill: University of North Carolina Press, 1994.

Daniels, Susanne and Cynthia Littleton. *Season Finale: The Unexpected Rise and Fall of the WB and UPN.* New York: HarperCollins, 2007.

Davis, Glyn and Kay Dickinson, ed. *Teen TV: Genre, Consumption and Identity.* London: British Film Institute, 2004.

Debrow, Larry. "Quickie Nostalgia That's Easy to Skip." *Advertising Age,* 18 September 2008. <http://adage.com> (Accessed 22 September 2008).

_____. "Teen Angel? Kinda." *Advertising Age,* 2 January 2006, 14.

Decken, Aimee. "Tapping Into Tweens." *Mediaweek,* 3 November 2003, 30.

De Moraes, Lisa. "The Real Deal Behind the *Buffy* Network Switch." *Washington Post,* 10 May 2001, sec. C.

Denisoff, R. Serge. *Inside MTV.* New Jersey: Transaction Publishers, 1988.

Denisoff, R. Serge and William D. Romanowski. *Risky Business: Rock in Film.* New Jersey: Transaction Publishers, 1991.

Doherty, Thomas. "Genre, Gender and the *Aliens* Trilogy." In *The Dread of Difference,* edited by Barry Keith Grant. Austin: University of Texas Press, 1996.

_____. *Teenagers and Teenpics: The Juvenilization of American Movies in the 1950s.* Boston: Unwin Hyman, 1988.

Doty, Alexander. "Music Sells Movies: (Re)New(ed) Conservatism in Film Marketing" *Wide Angle.* 10.2 (1988): 70–79.

Douglas, Susan J. *Where the Girls Are: Growing Up Female with the Mass Media.* New York: Times Books, 1994.

Ebenkamp, Becky. "Tipping the Balance." *AdWeek-Upfront Markets,* 10 May 1999, 4+.

Einstein, Mara. *Media Diversity: Economics, Ownership and the FCC.* New York: Routledge, 2004.

Eller, Claudia. "On-Screen Chemistry." *Los Angeles Times,* 1 December 1999, sec. D.

Elliot, Larry. "A Financial Crisis Unmatched Since the Great Depression, Say Analysts." *The Guardian (UK),* 18 March 2008. <http://www.guardian.co.uk/business/2008/mar/18/creditcrunch.marketturmoil1> (Accessed 13 May 2009).

Essex, Andrew and Dave Karger. "Bubble Gum Blows Up!" *Entertainment Weekly,* 5 March 1999, 20–26.

Farber, Jim. "Young, Rich and Hanson: Bubblegum Set Is Popping with Teen Idol Wanna-bes." *New York Daily News,* 28 August 1997, 59.

Farber, S. "Fox Chases the Ratings Rabbit." *American Film,* March 1987, 33.

Featherstone, Mike. *Consumer Culture & Postmodernism.* California: Sage Publications, 1991.

Feuer, Jane, Paul Kerr and Tise Vahimagi, ed. *MTM: "Quality Television."* London: BFI Publishing, 1984.

Fiske, John. "MTV: Post Structural Post Modern." *Journal of Communication Inquiry.* 10.1 (1986): 74–79.

Fleming, Michael. "Miley Cyrus to Star in Disney Film." *Variety,* 16 September 2008. <http://www.variety.com/article/VR1117992306.html?categoryid=13&cs=1> (Accessed 22 September 2008).

Flick, Larry. "After Quiet Build, Jive's Teen Star Spears Breaks Out." *Billboard,* 12 December 1998, 1+.

Flint, Joe. "Exec Joins WB, Keeps 'Lake' Duties." *Daily Variety,* 13 May 1994, 1.

Foot, David K. with Daniel Stoffman. *Boom Bust & Echo 2000: Profiting from the Demographic Shift in the New Millennium.* Revised edition. Toronto: Macfarlane, Walter & Ross, 1998.

Friedman, Wayne. "Event-like Promos Build Loyal Young Core for WB." *Advertising Age,* 1 February 1999, S1.

Frith, Simon. *Sound Effects: Youth Leisure and the Politics of Rock n' Roll.* New York: Pantheon, 1981.

Fritz, Ben and Michael Learmonth. "Showbiz's Site Fright." *Variety,* 12–18 March 2007, 1+.

Fry, Virginia and Donald Fry. "MTV: The 24

Hour Commercial." *Journal of Communication Inquiry*. 10.1 (1986): 29–33.

Furman, Phyllis. "Hilfiger's Taking It to the Miramax." *Daily News (New York)*, 7 May 1998, 70.

Gallo, Phil. "Miley Cyrus Tops the Charts." *Variety*, 30 July 2008. <http://www.variety.com/article/VR1117989765.html?categoryid=16&cs=1> (Accessed 31 July 2008).

_____. "Warner Joins Nokia's Music Service." *Variety*, 1 July 2008. <http://www.variety.com/article/VR1117988366.html?categoryid=16&cs=1> (Accessed 8 July 2008).

Gamboa, Glenn. "Forever Young: MTV." *Newsday (New York)*, 29 July 2001, sec. D.

Garrett, Diane. "Skeins Swim in Web Stream." *Variety*, 1 March 2008, 16.

_____. "WB Revived as Online Platform." *Variety*, 28 April 2008. <http://www.variety.com/article/VR1117984772.html?categoryid=14&cs=1> (Accessed 30 April 2008).

_____. "YouTube Adds Retailer Links to Videos." *Variety*, 7 October 2008. <http://www.variety.com/article/VR1117993602.html?categoryid=1009&cs=1> (Accessed 13 October 2008).

Gitlin, Todd. *Inside Prime Time*. New York: Pantheon, 1985.

_____. "Prime Time Ideology: The Hegemonic Process in Television Entertainment." In *Television: The Critical View*, edited by Horace Newcomb. 4th ed. Oxford: Oxford University Press, 1987.

Gold, Matea. "Showy Success for Kids Musical." *Los Angeles Times*, 27 February 2006, sec. E.

Golden, Christopher and Nancy Holder. *The Watcher's Guide: Buffy the Vampire Slayer*. New York: Pocket Books, 1998.

Goldsmith, Jill. "Viacom Profit Veers Down." *Variety*, 30 April 2009. <http://www.variety.com/article/VR1118003020.html?categoryid=1009&cs=1> (Accessed 13 May 2009).

Goldstein, Patrick. "Screamwriter; Kevin Williamson, The Pied Piper of the Video Generation, Has Breathed New Life into the Teen Horror Genre." *Los Angeles Times*, 27 October 1997, sec. F.

Gomery, Douglas. "Failed Opportunities: The Integration of the Motion Picture and Television Industries." *Quarterly Review of Film Studies*. 9.3 (1984): 219–228.

_____. *The Hollywood Studio System*. New York: St. Martin's Press, 1986.

Gomery, Douglas and Robert C. Allen. *Film History: Theory and Practice*. New York: Knopf, 1985.

Goodwin, Andrew. *Dancing in the Distraction Factory: Music Television and Popular Culture*. Minneapolis: University of Minnesota Press, 1992.

Goodwin, Betty. "Screen Style; Fashion; A New 'Scream' and a New Look." *Los Angeles Times*, 22 January 1998, sec. E.

Goodykoontz, Bill. "WB Network Paying Price for Mistakes." *The Arizona Republic*, 20 January 2000, sec. E.

Goonesekera, Anura. "Media in the Information Highway: Representing Different Cultures in the Age of Global Communication." In *The New Communication Landscape: Demystifying Global Media*, edited by Georgette Wang, Jan Servaes and Anura Goonesekera. New York: Routledge, 2000.

Graham, Jefferson. "WB and Teen-agers Make a Most Felicitous Combination." *USA Today*, 29 September 1998, sec. D.

Graser, Marc. "MySpace Top Site for Young Moviegoers." *Variety*, 28 October 2008. <http://www.variety.com/article/VR1117994822.html?categoryid=13&cs=> (Accessed 29 October 2008).

_____. "The Next Big Thing." *Variety*, 11–17 February 2008, 6.

Grover, Ronald. "Television: Are Paramount and Warner Looney Tunes?" *Business Week*, 8 January 1995, 46.

Hall, Lee. "Coming Soon to a PVR Near You; TiVo to Provide Uploadable Advertisements, While Giving Customers the Means to Skip Them." *Broadcasting and Cable*, 26 February 2001, 40.

Hall, Stuart and Paddy Whannel. "The Young Audience." In *On Record: Rock, Pop and the Written Word*, edited by Simon Frith and Andrew Goodwin. New York: Pantheon, 1990.

Hall, Wendy Jackson. "Children's Outlet Learn to Play the Sharing Game." *Variety*, 13 September 2001. <http://www.variety.com/article/VR1117852668.html?categoryid=1013&cs=1> (Accessed 10 April 2009).

Hampp, Andrew. "Tween Stars, and Marketing Tie-Ins in the Making." *Advertising Age*, 9 April 2008. <www.adage.com> (Accessed April 10, 2008).

_____. "'What You're Watching' to Use Twitter, Facebook." *Advertising Age* 29 April 2009. <http://adage.com> (Accessed May 4, 2009).

Hartmann, Susan. *The Home Front and Beyond: American Women in the 1940s*. Boston: Twayne, 1982.

Hay, Carla. "MTV Aims for Tighter Music Focus." *Billboard*, 9 May 1998, 6+.

Hayes, Dade. "Disney Profits Up 21% in 2nd Quarter: 'Hannah Montana,' Homevideo Boost Revenue." *Variety*, 6 May 2008. <http://www.variety.com/article/VR1117985168.html?categoryid=18&cs=1> (Accessed 9 May 2008).

_____. "'HSM3' Makes Box Office Honor Roll." *Variety*, 26 October 2008. <http://www.variety.com/article/VR1117994680.html?categoryid=13&cs=1> (Accessed 29 October 2008).

_____. "Time Warner Profits Fall 14% in Q1." *Variety*, 29 April 2009. <http://www.variety.com/article/VR1118002977.html?categoryid=1237&cs=1> (Accessed 13 May 2009).

Healy, William. *The Individual Delinquent.* Boston: Little, Brown, 1915.

Hebdige, Dick. *Subculture: The Meaning of Style.* London: Methuen, 1979.

Hein, Kenneth and Mae Anderson. "The Age of Reason." *MEDIAWEEK*, 27 October 2003, 22.

Herman, Edward S. and Noam Chomsky. *Manufacturing Consent: The Political Economy of the Mass Media.* New York: Pantheon, 1988.

Herman, Edward S. and Robert W. McChesney. *The Global Media: The New Missionaries of Global Capitalism.* Washington: Cassell, 1997.

Hilmes, Michelle. *Hollywood & Broadcasting: From Radio to Cable.* Chicago: University of Illinois Press, 1990.

_____. "Pay Television: Breaking the Broadcast Bottleneck." In *Hollywood in the Age of Television*, edited by Tino Balio. Massachusetts: Unwin Hyman, 1990.

Hindes, Andrew. "Par Likes MTV's Tune." *Variety*, 19–25 July 1999, 7–8.

Hirshberg, Lynn. "Desperate to Seem 16." *New York Times Magazine*, 5 September 1999, 42+.

Holson, Laura M. "Hollywood Loves the Tiny Screen. Advertisers Don't." *New York Times*, 7 May 2007. <http://www.nytimes.com/2007/05/07/business/media/07cell.html?scp=1&sq=%93Hollywood%20Loves%20the%20Tiny%20Screen.%20Advertisers%20Don%92t.%94%20&st=cse> (Accessed 11 May 2007).

Honey, Maureen. *Creating Rosie the Riveter: Class, Gender, and Propaganda During World War II.* Amhurst: University of Massachusetts Press, 1984.

Hontz, Jenny. "Pic Scribes Flocking to Web Deals." *Daily Variety*, 31 August 1998, 1.

Hudes, Karen. "Holiday Movies; Independent Film, But with a Catch: A Corporate Logo." *New York Times*, 15 November 1998, Sec 2A.

Itzkoff, Dave. "Move Over Mickey: A New Franchise at Disney." *New York Times*, 20 August 2007. <http://www.nytimes.com/2007/08/20/business/media/20disney.html?scp=1&sq="Move%20Over%20Mickey:%20A%20New%20Franchise%20at%20Disney"%20&st=cse> (Accessed 22 August 2007).

_____. "The Multimedia Synergistic Slumber Party." *New York Times*, 24 September 2006. <http://query.nytimes.com/gst/fullpage.html?res=9A01E3D81031F937A1575AC0A9609C8B63> (Accessed 25 September 2006).

Jameson, Fredric. "Postmodernism and Consumer Society." In *The Cultural Turn: Selected Writings on the Postmodern 1983–1998.* London: Verso, 1998.

_____. *Postmodernism, or the Cultural Logic of Late Capitalism.* Durham, North Carolina: Duke University Press, 1991.

Jenkins, Henry. *Convergence Culture: Where Old and New Media Collide.* New York: New York University Press, 2006.

_____. "Searching for the Origami Unicorn. *The Matrix* and Transmedia Storytelling." In *Convergence Culture: Where Old and New Media Collide.* New York: New York University Press, 2006.

_____. *Textual Poachers.* New York: Routledge, 1992.

Johnson, Leslie. *The Modern Girl: Girlhood and Growing Up.* Philadelphia: Open University Press, 1993.

Kaplan, E. Ann. *Rocking Around the Clock: Music Television, Postmodernism and Consumer Culture.* London: Methuen, 1987.

Katz, Richard. "Graden Grows MTV Off-Kilter-and Up." *Variety*, 3–9 May 1999, 71–72.

Kellner, Douglas. *Media Culture.* London: Routledge, 1995.

Kennedy, Randy. "The Shorter, Faster, Cruder, Tinier TV Show." *New York Times*, 28 May 2006. <http://www.nytimes.com/2006/05/28/magazine/28mtv.html?scp=1&sq=%93The%20Shorter,%20Faster,%20Cruder,%20Tinier%20TV%20Show%94%20&st=cse> (Accessed 29 May 2006).

Kinder, Marsha. "Music Video and the Spectator: Television, Ideology and the Dream." *Film Quarterly.* 38.1 (1984): 2–15.

Kissell, Rick. "Kids Line Up for *Camp Rock*." *Variety*, 22 June 2008. <http://www.varie

ty.com/article/VR1117987906.html?catego
ryid=14&cs=1> (Accessed 27 June 2008).

Klaassen, Abbey. "YouTube Adds Full-Length CBS Content." *Advertising Age*, 10 October 2008. <http://adage.com> (Accessed 13 October 2008).

Klady, Leonard. "Studios Focus on Teen Stream." *Variety*, 13–19 January 1997, 11–12.
_____. "Taken Unawares, H'w'd Refocuses on Youth." *Daily Variety*, 15 January 1997, 10.

Kleinschrodt, Michael. "Audiences Enjoy Laughing Themselves to Death." *Times-Picayune*, 4 February 2000, sec. L.
_____. "Secrecy About This Movie Is Enough to Make You 'Scream.'" *Times-Picayune*, 4 February 2000, sec. L.

Kolbert, Elizabeth. "Warner Bros. Enters Race for Network." *New York Times*, 3 November 1993, sec. D.

Kroll, Justin. "Steady Rise for Mobile Revenues." *Variety*, 3 August 2008. <http://www.variety.com/article/VR1117990011.html?categoryid=1009&cs=1> (Accessed 14 August 2008).

Kunz, William M. *Culture Conglomerates: Consolidation in the Motion Picture and Television Industries*. New York: Rowman & Littlefield Publishers, Inc., 2007.

Kurian, George Thomas. *Datapedia of the United States, 1790–2000*. Lanham, MD: Bernan, 1994.

Lakin, Max. "Buffy Returns to Life Online. WB Network Resurrected as a Website." *Advertising Age*, 29 August 2008. <http://adage.com> (Accessed 3 September 2008).

LaLumia, Jimi. "Music Biz Is Ignoring Vital Teen Mkt." *Billboard*, 25 January 1997, 2.

Learmonth, Michael. "CW Plots Rookie Season." *Variety*, 18 May 2006. <http://www.variety.com/article/VR1117943543.html?categoryid=1614&cs=1> (Accessed 19 May 2006).
_____. "Distributors, Networks Push for More Ads in TV Shows Online." *Advertising Age*, 6 October 2008. <http://adage.com> (Accessed 13 October 2008).
_____. "'Hulu Now No. 2 Online-Video Site." *Advertising Age*, 12 March 2009. <http://adage.com> (Accessed 13 March 2009).

Leibman, Nina C. *Living Room Lectures: The 50s Family in Film and Television*. Austin: University of Texas Press, 1995.

Levin, Gary. "Core Teen Viewership Tuning Out; WB Creative Woes, Drama Glut Send Ratings Sliding." *USA TODAY*, 13 March 2000, sec. D.

Lewis, Jon. *The Road to Romance and Ruin: Teen Films and Youth Culture*. New York: Routledge, 1992.

Lippman, John. "Warner Bros. Unveils Plan for 5th Network Television." *Los Angeles Times*, 3 November 1993, sec. D.

Lipsitz, George. "We Know What Time It Is: Race, Class and Youth Culture in the Nineties." In *Microphone Fiends: Youth Music and Youth Culture*, edited by Andrew Ross and Tricia Rose. New York and London: Routledge, 1994.

Littleton, Cynthia. "Disney Joins Hulu." *Variety*, 30 April 2009. <http://www.variety.com/article/VR1118003024.html?categoryid=13&cs=1> (Accessed 4 May 2009).
_____. "News Corp.'s Profits Plunge." *Variety*, 6 May 2009. <http://www.variety.com/article/VR1118003258.html?categoryid=1056&cs=1> (Accessed 13 May 2009).

Lockwood, Lisa. "Tommy Hilfiger Signs Pact with Dimension." *WWD*, 7 May 1998, 7.

Lowry, Brian. "For Rivals WB and UPN, the Future Is a Matter of Focus." *Los Angeles Times*, 27 July 1998, sec. F.
_____. "Friday Night Fight Over Young Viewers." *Los Angeles Times*, 20 November 1998, sec. F.

Lyons, Daniel. "Old Media Strikes Back." *Newsweek*, 21 February 2009. <http://www.newsweek.com/id/185790> (Accessed 20 May 2009).

Madigan, Nick. "For Teens, Movies Are a Big Deal, Really Big." *Variety*, 2–8 November 1998, 3–4.

Manly, Lorne. "For Tiny Screens, Some Big Dreams." *New York Times*, 21 May 2006. <http://www.nytimes.com/2006/05/21/business/yourmoney/21mobile.html?scp=1&sq=%93For%20Tiny%20Screens,%20Some%20Big%20Dreams%94%20&st=cse> (Accessed 22 May 2006).

Matzer, Marla. "Marketing Budget for Disney Film Hits $30 Million." *Los Angeles Times*, 7 May 1998, sec. D.

McChesney, Robert. "The Global Media Giants." In *Critical Studies in Media Commercialism*, edited by Robin Andersen and Lance Strate. Oxford: Oxford University Press, 2000.
_____. "The Political Economy of Global Communication." In *Capitalism and the Information Age: The Political Economy of the Global Communication Revolution*, edited by Robert McChesney, Ellen Wood and John Foster. New York: Monthly Review Press, 1998.

McChesney, Robert, Ellen Wood and John Foster, ed. *Capitalism and the Information Age: The Political Economy of the Global Communication Revolution.* New York: Monthly Review Press, 1998.

McClintock, Pamela. "Montana Mania Hits Theatres." *Variety,* 3 February 2008. <http://www.variety.com/article/VR1117980079.htm l?categoryid=13&cs=1> (Accessed 5 February 2008).

McGrath, Tom. *MTV: The Making of a Revolution.* Philadelphia: Running Press, 1996.

McKinley, E. Graham. *Beverly Hills, 90210: Television, Gender, and Identity.* Philadelphia: University of Pennsylvania Press, 1997.

McNary, Dave and Pamela McClintock. "'17 Again' Tops Weekend Box Office." *Variety,* 19 April 2009. <www.variety.com.index.asp ?layout=print_story&articleid=VR11180025 7&categoryid=1082> (Accessed 5 May 2009).

_____. "'Hannah' Tops Easter Box Office." *Variety,* 12 April 2009. <www.variety.com.in dex.asp?layout=print_story&articleid=VR11 18002345&categoryid=1082> (Accessed 5 May 2009).

Meehan, Eileen. "'Holy Commodity Fetish, Batman!': The Political Exonomy of a Commercial Intertext." In *The Many Lives of the Batman: Cultural Approaches to a Superhero and His Media,* edited by Roberta E. Pearson and William Uricchio. New York: Routledge, 1991.

_____. *Why TV Is Not Our Fault: Television Programming, Viewers and Who's Really in Control.* New York: Rowman & Littlefield Publishers, Inc., 2005.

Mifflin, Lawrie. "Where Young Viewers Go (and Ads Follow)." *New York Times,* 8 September 1998, sec. E.

Miles, Steven. *Consumerism as a Way of Life.* London: Sage Publications, 1998.

Miller, Mark Crispin. "North American Youth and the Entertainment State: A Talk." In *Pictures of a Generation on Hold; Selected Papers,* edited by Murray Pomerance and John Sakeris. Toronto: Media Studies Working Group, 1996.

Modleski, Tania. "The Terror of Pleasure: The Contemporary Horror Film and Postmodern Theory." In *Studies in Entertainment: Critical Approaches to Mass Culture,* edited by Tania Modleski. Bloomington: Indiana University Press, 1986.

Morse, Margaret. "Postsynchronizing Rock Music and Television." *Journal of Communication Inquiry.* 10.1 (1986): 15–28.

Moses, Elissa. *The $100 Billion Allowance: Accessing the Global Teen Market.* New York: John Wiley & Sons, Inc., 2000.

Mulligan, Thomas. "No Breaking for Commercials." *Los Angeles Times,* 28 January 2008, sec. C.

Nashawaty, Chris. "Teen Steam." *Entertainment Weekly,* 14 November 1997, 24–35.

Neale, Steve and Murray Smith. "Introduction." In *Contemporary Hollywood Cinema,* edited by Steve Neale and Murray Smith. New York: Routledge, 1998.

Neff, Jack. "Sleeping Beauty: How Disney Bested Revlon's Sales." *Advertising Age,* 25 September 2006, 6.

Nelson, Havelock. "Hip-Hop, Rap Wrestle with Predictability as Demand Dips." *Billboard,* 3 June 1995, 1+.

Neumeister, Larry. "Viacom Alleges YouTube Copyright Infringement." *USA Today,* 27 May 2008. <http://www.usatoday.com/ tech/news/techpolicy/2008-05-27-viacom-youtube-lawsuit_N.htm> (Accessed 18 May 2009).

Newman, Kim. *Nightmare Movies: A Critical Guide to Contemporary Horror Films.* New York: Harmony Books, 1988.

Newman, Melinda. "The Beat: In an Anything-Goes Year, Girl Power Sticks, Vets Score, Teens Are Triumphant." *Billboard,* 27 December 1997, 20+.

Okrent, Daniel. "Happily Ever After?" *TIME,* 24 January 2000, 38–43.

O'Leary, Noreen. "The Boom Tube." *AdWeek,* 18 May 1998, 44–52.

Olson, Catherine A. "Soundtracks: It's a Scream." *Billboard,* 6 December 1997, 16.

Orwall, Bruce. "Teen Tidal Wave Hits Hollywood in the Head." *Toronto Star,* 19 December 1997, sec. D.

Ostrow, Joanne. "WB Shows an Entree for Unsung Musicians." *Denver Post,* 13 February 2000, sec. H.

Owen, Rob. *Gen X TV: The Brady Bunch to Melrose Place.* New York: Syracuse University Press, 1997.

Palladino, Grace. *Teenagers, an American History.* HarperCollins Publishers: New York, 1996.

Palmer, Shelly. *Television Disrupted: The Transition from Network to Networked TV.* Boston: Focal Press, 2006.

Paoletta, Michael. "Jive Rides Teen-Pop Wave." *Billboard,* 30 October 1999, 1+.

Petrozzello, Donna. "WB Woes Self-Inflicted." *Daily News (New York),* 17 May 2000, 81.

Pinedo, Isabel Christina. "Postmodern Elements of the Contemporary Horror Film." In *The Horror Film*, edited by Steven Prince. New Jersey: Rutgers University Press, 2004.

Pogrebin, Robin. "The Media Business: Time, Inc.'s Take on Teen-agers." *New York Times*, 8 January 1998. <http://www.nytimes.com/1998/01/08/business/media-business-times-take-teen-agers-yes-house-that-luce-built-girls-magazine.html?scp=1&sq=%93The%20Media%20Business:%20Time,%20Inc.%92s%20Take%20on%20Teen-agers%94%20&st=cse>. (Accessed 25 January 2008).

Pond, Steve. "She's Here, She's Spears, Get Used to It." *Premiere*, October 2001, 38–41.

"Pop Music's Teen Market: The Jilted Generation?" *Billboard*, 25 January 1997, 1+.

Pride, Dominic. "The Secret of Jive's Int'l Success." *Billboard*, 30 October 1999, 72.

Pride, Dominic and Michael Paoletta. "'N Sync's Indirect Path to the Top." *Billboard*, 20 March 1999, 6+.

Pristin, Terry and James Bates. "The Climbing Game; Miramax Film Corp. Is Atop the Hollywood Heap." *Los Angeles Times,* 29 March 1993, sec. A.

Quinn, Michelle and Andrea Chang. "More Teenagers Ignoring CDs, Report Says." *Los Angeles Times*, 27 February 2008. <http://www.latimes.com/entertainment/news/music...> (Accessed February 28, 2008.)

"Reality Check — What's Up with All the Hot Teen Movies?" *Seattle Times*, 4 April 1999, sec. M.

Reece, Doug. "Backstreet Boys Move Onto Main." *Billboard*, 19 July 1997, 16+.

Reese, Shelley. "The Quality Of Cool." *Marketing Tools*, July 1997, 34.

Rice, Lynette and Stephen McClellan. "Kellner's Latest Surprise: The WB Gets New Legs." *Broadcasting & Cable*, 11 August 1997, 20.

Richmond, Ray. "MTV Opens Dance Card to More Musicvideos." *Variety*, 24–30 March 1997, 23+.

Rollin, Lucy. *Twentieth Century Teen Culture by the Decades*. Connecticut: Greenwood Press, 1999.

Rosen, Craig. "Wide Appeal Is Key to New Crop of Teen Acts." *Billboard*, 22 March 1997, 1+.

Rosenberg, Howard. "2 Networks Bow as Fox Dreams On." *Los Angeles Times*, 20 January 1995, sec. F.

Ryan, Michael and Douglas Kellner. *Camera Politica: The Politics and Ideology of Contemporary Hollywood Film*. Bloomington Indiana: University of Indiana Press, 1988.

Schatz, Thomas. "The New Hollywood." In *Films Theory Goes to the Movies*, edited by Jim Collins, Hilary Radner and Ava Preacher Collins. New York, London: Routledge, 1993.

_____. "The Return of the Hollywood Studio System." In *Conglomerates and the Media*, edited by Erik Barnouw, et al. New York: The New Press, 1997.

_____. "*St. Elsewhere* and the Evolution of the Ensemble Series." In *Television: The Critical View*, edited by Horace Newcomb. 4th ed. New York: Oxford University Press, 1987.

Scheiner, Georganne. "The Deanna Durbin Devotees: Fan Clubs and Spectatorship." In *Generations of Youth: Youth Cultures and Histories in Twentieth Century America*, edited by Joe Austin and Michael N. Willard. New York and London: New York University Press, 1998.

Schmuckler, Eric. "Honey, I Targeted the Kids." *US*, June 1999, 54–59.

Schneider, Michael. "ABC Heads to 'High School.'" *Variety*, 2 March 2008. <http://www.variety.com/article/VR1117981732.html?categoryid=14&cs=1> (Accessed 4 March 2008)

_____. "Fox to Stream Premieres for Dorms." *Variety*, 24 August 2008. <http://www.variety.com/article/VR1117991059.html?categoryid=14&cs=1> (Accessed 27 August 2008).

Schrum, Kelly. "'Teena Means Business': Teenage Girls' Culture and Seventeen Magazine, 1944–1950." In *Delinquents and Debutantes: Twentieth Century American Girls' Cultures*, edited by Sherrie Innes. New York and London: New York University Press, 1998.

Seabury, William M. *Motion Picture Problems*. New York: Arondale Press, 1929. Reprint New York: Arno Press, 1978.

_____. *The Public and the Motion Picture Industry*. New York: Macmillan, 1926.

Seymour, Lesley Jane. "Tweens 'R' Shoppers." *New York Times*, 22 April 2007. <http://www.nytimes.com/2007/04/22/nyregion/nyregionspecial2/22RSHOP.html?scp=1&sq=%93Tweens%20%91R%92%20Shoppers%94%20&st=cse> (Accessed 25 January 2008).

Shary, Timothy. *Generation Multiplex: The Image of Youth in Contemporary American Cinema*. Austin: University of Texas Press, 2002.

Shields, Mike. "Short Order: Cable Nets Are Programming for Smaller Screens." *Media-Week*, 10 April 2006, 54–56.

Shiller, Robert J. "Depression Scares Are Hardly New." *New York Times*, 2 May 2009. <http://www.nytimes.com/2009/05/03/business/economy/03view.html?scp=4&sq=2008%20financial%20crisis,%20%22new%20depression%22&st=cse> (Accessed 13 May 2009).

Short, William H. *A Generation of Motion Pictures*. New York: The National Committee for the Study of Social Values in Motion Pictures, 1928. Reprint New York: Garland Publishing, 1978.

Siklos, Richard. "Not in the Real World Anymore." *New York Times*, 18 September 2006. <http://www.nytimes.com/2006/09/18/business/media/18avatar.html?scp=1&sq="Not%20in%20the%20Real%20World%20Anymore"%20&st=cse> (Accessed 19 September 2006).

Sisario, Ben. "A Musical for Tweens Captures Its Audience." *New York Times*, 8 February 2006. <http://query.nytimes.com/gst/fullpage.html?res=9F04E4DF143EF93BA35751C0A9609C8B63&scp=1&sq="a%20musical%20for%20tweens%20captures%20its%20Audience"&st=cse> (Accessed 9 February 2006).

Smith, Jeff. *The Sounds of Commerce: Marketing Popular Film Music*. New York: Columbia University Press, 1988.

Stanley, T. L. "Dawson's Creek, The Record." *AdWeek: Marketers of the Year*, 11 October 1999, M92.

_____. "Net Gains." *ADWEEK: Marketers of the Year*, 11 October 1999, M86+.

Steinberg, Brian. "The Broadcast Ad Model Is Broken. Now What?" *Advertising Age*, 27 October 2008. <http://adage.com> (Accessed 29 October 2008).

_____. "CW's 'Cwinger' Ads Debut in 'Gossip Girl.'" *Advertising Age*, 20 April 2009. <http://adage.com> (Accessed 22 April 2009).

_____. "Streamed TV Shows Attracting Their Own Audience." *Advertising Age*, 8 July 2008. <http://adage.com> (Accessed 9 July 2008).

_____. "Viewers Spend More Time Watching, but Not All on TV." *Advertising Age*, 8 July 2008. <http://adage.com> (Accessed 9 July 2008).

_____. "Web Surfers Spending More Time with Content." *Advertising Age*, 14 August 2007. <http://adage.com> (Accessed 16 August 2007).

Steinberg, Jacques. "Back to School." *New York Times*, 11 March 2007. <http://www.nytimes.com/2007/03/11/arts/television/11stei.html?scp=1&sq=Jacques%20Steinberg,%20march%2011,%202007&st=cse> (Accessed 14 March 2007).

Streeter, Thomas. "Blue Skies and Strange Bedfellows: The Discourse of Cable Television." In *The Revolution Wasn't Televised: Sixties Television and Social Conflict*, edited by Lynn Spiegel and Michael Curtin. New York: Routledge, 1997.

Stross, Randall. "Someone Has to Pay for TV. But Who? And How?" *New York Times*, 7 May 2006. <http://www.nytimes.com/2006/05/07/business/yourmoney/07digi.html?scp=1&sq=%93Someone%20Has%20to%20Pay%20for%20TV.%20But%20Who?%20And%20How?%94%20&st=cse> (Accessed 8 May 2006).

Tetzlaff, David. "MTV and the Politics of Postmodern Pop." *Journal of Communication Inquiry*. 10.1 (1986): 80–91.

Thigpen, David. "Jive Records Presents: Teen Idols." *TIME — Music Goes Global* (Special Issue), Fall 2001, 26–28.

Thomas, Laurie and Barry R. Litman. "Fox Broadcasting Company, Why Now? An Economic Study of the Rise of the Forth Broadcast 'Network.'" *Journal of Broadcasting & Electronic Media*. 35.2 (1990): 139–157.

Thorburn, David. "Television Melodrama." In *Television: The Critical View*, edited by Horace Newcomb. 5th ed. New York: Oxford University Press, 1994.

Thornton, Sarah. *Club Cultures. Music, Media and Subcultural Capital*. Hanover and London: Wesleyan University Press, 1996.

Tietchen, Todd F. "Samplers and Copycats: The Cultural Implications of the Postmodern Slasher in Contemporary American Film." *Journal of Popular Film and Television*. 26.3 (1998): 98–107.

Tomlinson, John. *Globalization and Culture*. Chicago: University of Chicago Press, 1999.

Trencansky, Sarah. "Final Girls and Terrible Youth: Transgression in 1980s Slasher Horror." *Journal of Popular Film and Television*. 29.2 (2001): 63–73.

Tudor, Andrew. *Monsters and Mad Scientists: A Cultural History of the Horror Movie*. Oxford: Basil Blackwell, 1989.

Turow, Joseph. *Breaking Up America: Advertisers & the New Media World*. Chicago: University of Chicago Press, 1997.

Verna, Paul. "Retailers See Signs of Hope for Teen Music." *Billboard*, 22 March 1997, 1+.

Verrier, Richard. "'Twilight' Leaves Its Box-Office Mark." *Los Angeles Times*, 24 November 2008. <http://www.latimes.com/busin ess/la-fi-boxoffice24-2008nov24,0,27962 10.story> (Accessed 19 June 2009).

Vorhaus, Mike. "Younger Demos Shift Focus from TV Screens to YouTube." *Advertising Age*, 8 October 2007. <http://adage.com> (Accessed 11 October 2007.)

Walt Disney Company. Form 10-K, 1 October 2005.

Wang, Georgette and Jan Servaes. "Introduction." In *The New Communication Landscape: Demystifying Global Media*, edited by Georgette Wang, Jan Servaes and Anura Goonesekera. New York: Routledge, 2000.

Wasko, Janet. *Movies and Money: Financing the American Film Industry*. Noorwood, NJ: Ablex Publishing Corporation, 1982.

Watrous, Peter. "Pop View: White Singers + Black Style = Pop Bonanza." *New York Times*, 11 March 1990, sec. 2.

Wee, Valerie. "Resurrecting and Updating the Teen Slasher — The Case of *Scream*." *Journal of Popular Film and Television*. 34.2 (2006): 50–61.

Weeks, Janet. "'Scream' Movies Cultivate Special Audience: Girls." *USA Today*, 12 December 1997, sec. A.

Weinraub, Bernard. "Business Match Made in Hollywood." *New York Times*, 1 May 1993, 39.

Werts, Diane. "Cashing In on Tween Viewers." *Newsday*, 19 March 2006. <www.newsday.com> (Accessed 9 January 2009).

Wharton, Dennis. "FCC Seals Fin-Syn's Death." *Variety*, 11–17 September 1995, 36.

White, Timothy R. "Hollywood's Attempt at Appropriating Television: The Case of Paramount Pictures." In *Hollywood in the Age of Television*, edited by Tino Balio. Boston: Unwin Hyman, 1990.

Williams, Betsy. "'North to the Future': *Northern Exposure* and Quality Television." In *Television: The Critical View*, edited by Horace Newcomb. 5th ed. New York: Oxford University Press, 1994.

Williams, Tony. *Hearths of Darkness: The Family in the American Horror Film*. London: Associated University Press, 1996.

Wloszczyna, Susan. "*Scream 2* Takes a Stab at Sophistication." *USA Today*, 12 December 1997, sec. D.

_____. "Something to 'Scream' About." *USA Today*, 22 August 1997, sec. D.

Wollen, Peter. "Ways of Thinking About Music Video (and Postmodernism)." *Critical Quarterly*. 28.1–2 (1986): 167–170.

Wyatt, Edward. "Summer Advisory: A Jonas Front Looms." *New York Times*, 17 June 2008. <http://www.nytimes.com/2008/06/ 17/arts/television/17jona.html?scp=1&sq=% 22Summer%20advisory:%20A%20jonas%2 0front%20looms%22&st=cse> (Accessed 23 June 2008).

Wyatt, Justin. *High Concept: Movies & Marketing in Hollywood*. Austin: University of Texas Press, 1994.

Zmuda, Natalie. "Teens, Too, Are Tightening Budgets." *Advertising Age*, 27 April 2009. <http//:adage.com> (Accessed April 28, 2009).

Zollo, Peter. *Wise Up to Teens: Insights into Marketing & Advertising to Teenagers*. 2d ed. New York: New Strategist Publications Inc., 1999.

Zurawik, David. "Pretty as a Picture." *Baltimore Sun*, 2 May 2000, sec. F.

Index